2·22·78

The Yale Edition of the Works of St. Thomas More

SELECTED WORKS

*Published by the St. Thomas More Project,
Yale University, under the auspices of
Gerard L. Carroll and Joseph B. Murray,
Trustees of the Michael P. Grace, II, Trust,
and with the support of the National Endowment
for the Humanities*

Statue of St. Thomas More by L. Cubitt Bevis, Chelsea, London (1968).

ST. THOMAS MORE

A
Dialogue of
Comfort
against
Tribulation

edited with Introduction and Notes by
FRANK MANLEY

New Haven and London, Yale University Press, 1977

Designed by Crimilda Pontes and Sally Sullivan Harris
and set in VIP Baskerville type.
Printed in the United States of America by
Vail-Ballou Press, Binghamton, N.Y.

Published in Great Britain, Europe, Africa, and Asia (except Japan) by Yale
University Press, Ltd., London. Distributed in Latin America by Kaiman &
Polon, Inc., New York City; in Australia and New Zealand by Book & Film
Services, Artarmon, N.S.W., Australia; and in Japan by Harper & Row,
Publishers, Tokyo Office.

Library of Congress Cataloging in Publication Data

More, Thomas, Sir, Saint, 1478-1535.
    A dialogue of comfort against tribulation.

    (The Yale edition of the works of St. Thomas More: Selected works)
    "Published by the St. Thomas More Project, Yale University."
    Bibliography: p.
    Includes index.
    1. Consolation.   I. Manley, Frank.   II. Title.
BV 4904.M62 1977   242'.1   77-9938
ISBN 0-300-02082-1
ISBN 0-300-02185-2 pbk.

For Evelyn and Mary

ACKNOWLEDGMENTS

This book is based upon the full scholarly edition of *A Dialogue of Comfort* edited by myself and Louis Martz and published in 1976 as Volume 12 in The Yale Edition of the Complete Works of St. Thomas More. The present text represents a modernized version of the old-spelling text prepared by Louis Martz for the scholarly edition; the notes here are indebted to the Commentary and Glossary of that edition; and the present Introduction represents a reorganization and reduction of the Introduction to Volume 12. I am grateful to Louis Martz for preparing the second section of the present Introduction for inclusion in this book. The primary work of modernizing the text has been performed by the staff of the Thomas More Project at Yale. Professor Walter Gordon of the University of Georgia also worked on the text and glosses in the course of a year's leave of absence from the University of Loyola at Los Angeles. I am indebted to him for a number of valuable suggestions. I also wish to thank the Paul Mellon Centre for Studies in British Art (London) for providing the photograph of the statue of More by L. Cubitt Bevis.

The Emory University Research Fund assisted in the early stages of the typing, and Trudy Kretchman and the English Department arranged for it to be completed. My good friend Richard S. Sylvester, Executive Editor of the More Project, first introduced me to St. Thomas More in the years we spent together as fellows of Yale's Timothy Dwight College, and now that I have finished my work and put down my pen, I want to thank him for all that I have learned and all that More has come to mean to me. I also want to thank him for all that he has come to mean to me and to all of us on the More Project—something we all came to realize very strongly during the fearful summer and fall of 1975, when this book was nearing completion. This volume is dedicated to my children, in gratitude for all that they have given me. I leave them and all who read this book with the last words More wrote in his last letter to his favorite daughter, Margaret: "Fare well my dear child and pray for me, and I shall for you and all your friends that we may merrily meet in heaven."

Ellijay and Atlanta   Frank Manley
May 1976

CONTENTS

INTRODUCTION

The statue of St. Thomas More which appears as the frontispiece of this volume stands in a small park beside the Thames, on land he is said to have given in dowry to his favorite daughter, Margaret. Behind the statue is the rebuilt Chelsea Old Church, virtually destroyed in World War II, except for the More Chapel, which remains almost as it was when More was a parishioner and worshipped there. A few hundred yards away is the site of the Great House and the rural estate that More established for himself and his family on the edge of the city, the estate that once contained his gallery, his garden, his orchard—all the pleasant, comfortable things his wife itemized for him in prison when she tried to persuade him to violate his conscience and return home to her and his children and take up once again his position in the world.

All these marks of the great man are now gone. But the statue that commemorates More's refusal to exchange his soul for them stands, larger than life, heroic, and to some degree oversimplified, in the way that all heroic art is oversimplified when compared to the complications of life. The hands and face, the crucifix at More's neck and the collar of golden SS's on his knees are brightly gilded. The fur-trimmed robe and Tudor cap are dull bronze. The expression is that of a man who has come to a major decision in life, his thoughts turned inward. The golden chain, once a rich token of royal esteem, circling his neck in the great Holbein portrait, has been discarded and now lies on his knees, as though his hands were about to be manacled.[1] It is difficult to say whether this is a man

1. For the history of the golden chain of SS's, see Stanley Morison and Nicolas Barker, *The Likeness of Thomas More* (London and New York, 1963), Appendix B, pp. 86–88.

who has finally freed himself of the chains that bound him to this world or one who is about to be made a prisoner, though in this case they are probably both the same. For More, imprisonment was the consequence of becoming free. His hands are clasped in prayer or determination, or perhaps simply folded, ready to be bound when he is led away. The mood suggested by the statue is similar to the sense one has of More in reading *A Dialogue of Comfort*—the signs of worldly power broken on his lap like a child's toy, his back turned toward the people and places he loved, and his eyes looking out over the gray waters of the Thames, flowing like eternity, his head turned slightly downriver toward the Tower.

I

A Dialogue of Comfort was written during the fifteen months of More's imprisonment in the Tower of London before his execution on July 6, 1535, for refusing to bow to the will of Henry VIII. Considered biographically, the dialogue is one of the means by which More attempted to embody in some external form his fears for his family and himself during the last months of his life—the destitution of those he loved, the strong possibility of torture at the hands of Thomas Cromwell and other agents of the king, the fear that he would deny himself under the stress of hard handling and destroy his relationship with God, and finally the fear of death itself.

Yet the relationship of an author to his work is extremely complex. There is a sense in which every author both participates in his own creation and stands outside it as an observer, engaged in detachment in the very process of writing. But for a variety of reasons this seems to be particularly true of *A Dialogue of Comfort*. More creates different effects and different dimensions of meaning for different kinds of audience, depending on how much the individual reader knew about More himself and the circumstances of composition.

There are thus several kinds of audience addressed in the dialogue. The first is a hypothetical reader who might have existed if the work had been published anonymously, or who perhaps might have come upon a manuscript that did not identify the author. Such a reader would have had no reason to doubt the statement on the title page that the book had been written "by an Hungarian in Latin, and Translated out of Latin into French, and out of French into English." This general reader would tend to locate the work within the fictitious setting of the dialogue itself: the Christian bulwark of Hungary on the eve of Turkish invasion. For this audience the literary surface would be perfectly intelligible and sufficient within itself. More never departs from the fictional scene, and in Europe at the time, threatened for almost a century by the increasing military power of the Turks, it would have had great emotional reverberation. By 1526 the Turks were in firm control of all Asia Minor and North Africa. In Europe, they occupied the Greek peninsula and a good part of the Balkans. Only Hungary stood in the way of further expansion toward the West.

At this precise moment in history Europe was in no way prepared to meet the Turkish threat. The "common corps of Christendom," as More so fondly spoke of it, the *respublica Christiana*, was internally divided by what can only be described as a form of civil war. Beginning in March 1521, the decade was marked by a constant struggle for power and control among the rising national states. Savage wars of ambition and revenge broke out between the Holy Roman Emperor, Charles V, and Francis I of France, with Henry VIII and Wolsey attempting to affect the balance of power through adroit political maneuvering and direct military aid. And it was precisely at this low point of Christian discord and disunity that the new Ottoman Sultan, Suleiman the Magnificent, chose to make his move. On August 29, 1521, he took Belgrade, that "sure fortress and defense, not only of Hungary, but also of all Christianity," [2] which had successfully resisted both Amurath II in 1442 and Mahomet II in 1456. On December 21, 1522, after a five-month siege, Suleiman succeeded in capturing the island of Rhodes, the

2. Paulus Jovius, *A Shorte Treatise upon the Turkes Chronicles*, trans. P. Ashton (London, 1546), fol. 103^r. Quotations from contemporary sources are modernized throughout this Introduction.

key to the eastern Mediterranean, defended by the Christian Knights of St. John of Jerusalem. As the Papal Legate to England pointed out to Henry VIII, "Rhodes and Belgrade were the 'outworks of Christendom' and . . . , after their collapse, all Hungary or, alternately, Sicily and Italy lay open to conquest. Indeed he said that 'the rest of Christendom and England itself are in the greatest danger.'"[3] And in the summer of 1526, it would have seemed as though his prophecy were about to come true.

Invading Hungary, Suleiman defeated Louis II at the disastrous battle of Mohács on August 28, 1526, and occupied the capital. The bulwark of Hungary, which had successfully resisted the Turks for almost a century, had fallen. The wall had been breached, and Europe lay open to the infidel: "The Turk entered Buda on the 9th, and killed everyone over 13 or 14 years of age. He kept no prisoners, but sent those under age to Turkey. He has burnt many towns. The King, after his defeat, was drowned in a marsh, whither his horse had carried him. Those lords of Hungary who have escaped are not making any attempt to recruit the army, but are committing worse cruelties than the Turks, spoiling and burning their own domains."[4]

At the end of the campaign season, the Turk withdrew. "He had on the Danube 3,000 boats laden with Hungarian spoil. Among other things, bells of brass and all kinds of iron goods, 5,000 Hungarian prisoners, and 30 ships laden with Jews. . . . Of the 72 counties of Hungary, 12 have been plundered, and Buda and the other places visited by the Turk have been burnt."[5] "Next spring," the Lord Chancellor of Hungary prophesied, "the Turk intends to attack the rest of Hungary, which is without means of defence, and

---

3. Quoted by R. P. Adams, *The Better Part of Valor: More, Erasmus, Colet and Vives on Humanism, War, and Peace,* 1496–1535 (Seattle, 1962), p. 273.

4. *Letters and Papers, Foreign and Domestic, of the Reign of Henry VIII,* ed. J. S. Brewer, James Gairdner, and R. H. Brodie, 21 vols. (London, 1862–1932), *4,* part 2, 1114 (item 2496). Cited hereafter as *LP.*

5. *LP, 4,* part 2, 1146–47 (item 2588).

then Transylvania and the remainder of Europe. Can hardly hope for help, as Europe is in such discord."[6]

It is this same vision of Europe, threatened by the bloody conquests of the infidel, divided within by political and spiritual disharmony, that More evokes in *A Dialogue of Comfort*. "There falleth so continually before the eyen of our heart," Vincent says at the beginning of the book, "a fearful imagination of this terrible thing: his [the Turk's] mighty strength and power, his high malice and hatred, and his incomparable cruelty, with robbing, spoiling, burning, and laying waste all the way that his army cometh . . . so that such as are here and remain still shall either both leese [lose] all and be lost too, or forced to forsake the faith of our Savior Christ, and fall to the false sect of Mahomet" (pp. 6–7). "And therefore," Antony later concludes, "albeit I would advise every man pray still and call unto God to hold his gracious hand over us and keep away this wretchedness, if his pleasure be, yet would I further advise every good Christian body to remember and consider that it is very likely to come, and therefore make his reckoning, and cast his pennyworth's before, and every man and every woman both, appoint with God's help in their own mind beforehand what thing they intend to do if the very worst fall" (p. 200). This is the first, primary level of address.

But then the book turns inward and, without altering in any way the historical circumstances of the Turkish invasion of Hungary, something else appears. A second level of address is implied in the date More chose for the scene of the dialogue. The fictional conversation does not take place, as one might expect, in 1526, immediately after the battle of Mohács, when Hungary lay open to the Turks. This would have been the most logical and most dramatic moment to have chosen had More been interested only in exhibiting the Turkish threat to Europe. He chose instead the years 1527–28, the interval of relative calm between the first Turk-

---

6. *LP*, *4*, part 2, 1147 (item 2589).

ish invasion and the second. And the choice complicates considerably the impact and meaning of the book.

Since Louis II had died without issue, the surviving Hungarian nobility assembled in Diet at Alberegalis to elect a new king. They chose John Zapolya, Voivode of Transylvania. Another faction, however, supported the brother of Charles V, Ferdinand of Austria, who claimed the throne by right of inheritance. In 1527, the issue led to civil war. Ferdinand invaded Hungary and, after defeating Zapolya, occupied the capital. Zapolya fled to Poland and negotiated with Suleiman for the restoration of his throne, promising fealty as a vassal and annual tribute in return for Turkish assistance. Ferdinand attempted to ratify a truce, but in the spring of 1529, Suleiman once again invaded Hungary. By September, he was at the gates of Vienna. After only a three-week siege, he withdrew his forces on the coming of winter and bestowed the kingdom of Hungary as a fief upon John Zapolya.

By placing the scene of the dialogue sometime after Ferdinand's coronation in 1527 and before Suleiman's invasion on behalf of Zapolya in 1529, More is able to reach beyond the external threat of the Turks to include the internal threat of those false Christians who both literally and figuratively allied themselves with the Turks: Zapolya and his followers, the noblemen after the battle of Mohács who ravaged their own domains, the 20,000 Lutheran *Landsknechte* who were reported to have served in the Turkish army, the princes of Europe who sought out Turkish alliances to redress the balance of power, and by implication the growing Protestant sects, who in More's opinion had betrayed the faith. After describing fully the horrors of Turkish rule in *A Dialogue of Comfort*, More goes on to emphasize the dangers these false Christians present:

And yet, which we more fear than all the remnant, no small part of our own folk that dwell even here about us are (as we hear) fallen to him, or already confederate with him, which, if it so be, shall haply keep this quarter fro the Turk's incursion. But then shall they that turn to his law leave all their neighbors nothing, but shall have our goods given them and our bodies both, but if we turn as they do, and forsake our Savior too. And then (for there is no born Turk so cruel to Christian folk as is the false Christian that falleth fro the faith) we shall stand in peril if we persevere in the truth, to be more hardly handled and die more cruel death by our own countrymen at home than if we were taken hence and carried into Turkey. (p. 7)

The analogy seems perfectly natural, given the times and More's belief in a united Christendom founded on a universal church. Over and over, throughout his polemical works, More equates Protestant and Turk, heretic and infidel. But in *A Dialogue of Comfort* he is careful to keep the implications oblique and ambiguous—flexible, suggestive, and rich in possibility—so that they seem to rise spontaneously from the reader himself and not from any conscious intent on the part of the author. The metaphoric correspondence between persecution for the faith in Hungary and persecution for the faith in England, under the Great Turk, Henry VIII, is built into the very structure and meaning of the work, but it would be apprehended by a somewhat more intimate, more limited audience than the broader historical scene of the Turkish threat to Europe. It constitutes a second level of address, directed primarily to those who knew of More's authorship and were aware of the general circumstances of composition or, more broadly, those who, like More, regarded the Protestant sects as a threat to the universal church, and were thus able to apply the analogy themselves. For these readers the simultaneous disguise and revelation were part of the essential form and meaning of the work. As R. W. Chambers has pointed out, More chose "a really dangerous subject.... The *Dialogue* had to be kept very secret; it was a denial of the thesis that the head of the State might dictate the religious belief of his subjects."[7] Some protective covering was obviously necessary to attack the king from the king's own prison, but it is an oversimplification to dismiss the powerful,

7. *Thomas More* (London, 1935), p. 314.

historically affective scene of Turkish invasion in order to get at what one presumes to be the "real" meaning underneath the fiction. The book is not to be read simply as an allegory in which everything that is said really stands for something else. The Hungarian setting is important in its own right at the same time that it serves as an extended metaphor. The Turk burns, pillages, imprisons, tortures, and kills in order to destroy the faith. Ironically enough, Christians do the same to Christians.

Beneath this particular analogy lies the basic theme that appeals to all the persecuted in any generation: the overwhelming question of how to maintain one's integrity in the face of pain and death. On this level, the level of the individual conscience, More equates Protestant and Turk, heretic and infidel, in such a way as to make them more than mere metaphoric equivalents. The enemy within is identical with the enemy without, and both are to be seen as masks—forms or representatives—of a more ancient power of evil that uses men as agents of its will, whether they be Suleiman, Henry, Cromwell, Audley, Norfolk, or the more immediate manifestations in our own lives and time.

In addition to the levels of address described above, certain portions of the work would have had a more specific meaning for More's immediate family and circle of friends. For this more limited audience More deliberately dissolves at times the literary surface of the dialogue and speaks to them directly from behind the mask of his fiction. These brief flashes of intense personal recognition do not come together to form a consistent pattern; they are not part of the structure and architectonic design of the work. They do not alter in any way the surface of the text. They simply extend it momentarily, and the book becomes enriched by a plain, homely humanity.

Take, for example, the various anecdotes identified by More's sixteenth-century biographers with Dame Alice Middleton, More's second wife, or his adopted daughter, Margaret Giggs, or the anecdotes associated with Wolsey,[8] or better yet, the beast fable

8. For Dame Alice, see pp. 84-85, 172, 225, and 283-84; for Margaret Giggs, see the anecdote at pp. 91-93; for Wolsey, see pp. 218-23.

about the ass and the wolf who went to confession to Father Reynard, the fox. The fable occurs in Chapter 14 of Book II, a chapter dealing with the "night's fear" of scrupulosity. More attributes the fable to a childhood nurse, old Mother Maud, who "was wont when she sat by the fire with us, to tell us that were children many childish tales" (p. 118). The story is told with humor and gusto. It is probably More's most famous anecdote. But, as the members of More's family would have known, the origin of the story was a conversation between More's stepdaughter, Alice Alington, and Sir Thomas Audley, Lord Chancellor of England after More's resignation. In a letter to Margaret Roper of August 17, 1534, Alice explained that Audley had come to hunt deer in her park, and the next day, at a neighbor's house where he had spent the night, she asked him to use his influence to help her father, who was at that time a prisoner in the Tower. Like most politicians Audley was friendly but not of much help. "He marveled," Alice reports, "that my father is so obstinate in his own conceit, as that everybody went forth with all save only the blind Bishop [Fisher] and he. And in good faith, said my lord, I am very glad that I have no learning but in a few of Aesop's fables, of the which I shall tell you one." He then told her the story of a country of fools and a few wise men who thought with their superior wisdom they could take over and rule. But the fools would have none of it. They would rule themselves with their own cunning, and since there were so many of them, the wise men failed in their purpose. When the story was over, Audley laughed at his own joke "very merrily." Alice continued to press him. For all his merry tales, she said, she had no doubt but that he would befriend her father when the time came. But this was too strong, and Audley replied more bluntly, "I would not have your father so scrupulous of his conscience." He then tried to soften his point and laugh it off with another tale of "a lion, an ass, and a wolf and of their confession":

> First the lion confessed him that he had devoured all the beasts that he could come by. His confessor assoiled him because he was a king and also it was his nature so to do. Then came the poor ass and said that he took but one straw out of his master's

shoe for hunger, by the means whereof he thought his master did take cold. His confessor could not assoil this great trespass, but by and by sent him to the bishop. Then came the wolf and made his confession, and he was straightly commanded that he should not pass vi^d at a meal. But when this said wolf had used this diet a little while, he waxed very hungry, in so much that on a day when he saw a cow with her calf come by him he said to himself, I am very hungry and fain would I eat, but that I am bounden by my ghostly father. Notwithstanding that, my conscience shall judge me. And then if it be so, then shall my conscience be thus, that the cow doth seem to me now but worth a groat, and then if the cow be but worth a groat, then is the calf but worth ii^d. And so did the wolf eat both the cow and the calf.

Alice got nothing more from Audley than that. His "pretty fables" did not please her, but she did not know what to say, "for I was abashed of this answer."[9]

The next time Margaret visited her father in the Tower, she showed him the letter. More read it over twice, and in the reading, Margaret says, "he made no manner haste, but advised it leisurely and pointed every word." He then commented on Audley's fables. The first he had already heard from Cardinal Wolsey long ago when the Cardinal was Lord Chancellor. Wolsey used to repeat it in Council whenever he wanted England to form another alliance of war. The second fable he had never heard before, but observed that it was not by Aesop since it had to do with confession. The point of the fable, he said, was a little too subtle for him. He could not figure out who the lion and wolf with such flexible consciences were. But he identified himself correctly as the ass: "by the foolish, scrupulous ass that had so sore a conscience . . . my lord's other words of my scruple declare that his lordship merrily meant that by me: signifying (as it seemeth by that similitude) that of oversight and folly my scrupulous conscience taketh for a great, perilous

9. E. F. Rogers, ed., *The Correspondence of Sir Thomas More* (Princeton, 1947), pp. 512–13.

thing toward my soul if I should swear this oath, which thing, as his lordship thinketh, were indeed but a trifle."[10]

Audley was not the only one to accuse More of excessive scrupulosity. It was a common explanation of his obstinacy in refusing the Oath of Allegiance. The accusation was obviously one of great concern to More and considerable perplexity. If he had an overly scrupulous conscience, it was bound to cast him into further doubts; and even if he did not, the possibility was still something he could not afford to overlook. It was related to his fear of spiritual pride and demonic illusion, a subtle form of temptation in which a man's faith and his love of God are used against him. For what if he were led to take his position simply out of excessive scrupulosity, and what if it were to cost him his life? Would not that be a form of false martyrdom, perhaps even suicide, induced by the vain desire to prove himself better than other men?

For the family—and perhaps to some degree for More himself—the whole point of Mother Maud's tale would have been an answer to the accusation of excessive scrupulosity. More takes a story designed to illustrate the asininity of his own conscience, and turns it upside down. The moral of the fable as More tells it is that "a conscience somewhat scrupulous, though it be painful and troublous to him that hath it, like as this poor ass had here, is less harm yet than a conscience over large, or such as for his own fantasy the man list to frame himself, now drawing it narrow, now stretching it in breadth after the manner of a cheverel point, to serve on every side for his own commodity, as did here the wily wolf" (p. 124). For those who knew how Mother Maud's tale originated, this elaborate retelling of Audley's fable would have reverberated with a subtle and richly humorous inversion, and humor is not a characteristic of a man with a scrupulous conscience. If More is an ass, Audley and the others are wolves, just as in the original version, More perhaps remembered, the lion devoured all the beasts he came by, but was absolved because he was the king, and it was his nature to do so.

10. Rogers, pp. 514–20.

For those who knew More closely, this conscious play with the literary surface in which the author peers out from behind the mask of his own creation would have been only a part of the autobiographical dimension of the book. There were also the pervasive reminders of the man himself—habits, customs, likes and dislikes, turns of phrase and modes of thought—all the accumulated knowledge that comes from simply knowing an individual so well and living intimately with him. The art More used in these instances was an art that moved beyond itself toward an intensity of close personal experience.

Still other portions of the work seem not to have been addressed to any audience at all except the author himself, engaged not only in writing the book, but also, by writing it, in preparing himself to die. For those who come to know it well, *A Dialogue of Comfort* will be seen to contain certain chains of association that underlie the text for a number of pages and then flare out in a flash of intense personal revelation having to do with More's ambivalent attitude toward the king, the destitution of his family, or his own hidden fears of torture, demonic illusion, and death. Most of these personal associations arise from More's reflection on scripture.

There are almost five hundred quotations or specific references to scripture in *A Dialogue of Comfort*, an average of almost two to a page. Most of them seem to be used in the fashion of the time to prove or to exemplify a point. But as the book proceeds and the quotations accumulate, one begins to suspect that scripture stands in some more complex relation to the work. More's scriptural references are often linked together so as to form complex units of meaning. But the links are not usually present in the brief fragments of scripture More quotes, nor in the text of the *Dialogue* itself. The associative links are usually found in the context in which the quotations appear.

These chains of association tend to revolve about a number of crucial concerns of More in prison, but they do not come together to form a consistent pattern or "secret teaching." They flare out at times and then subside. But taken as a whole they constitute the most personal and private part of the book and are best seen perhaps as a prayer or prayerful meditation in which More applies what he is writing to his own tribulation and his own need for spiritual comfort. In becoming aware of these scriptural contexts we seem to step into More's cell more than four hundred years ago and participate to some degree in the actual process by which he prepared himself to die.

A typical example and one of the most starkly autobiographical occurs in a series of recurrent quotations from the apocryphal Book of Sapientia, or Wisdom. More alludes to the passage on three separate occasions, each time in relation to one of the temptations described in Psalm 90. The first allusion occurs in Book II. More is speaking of the second temptation, the arrow that flies by day, which he interprets as pride:

> Up we fly like an arrow that were shot up into the air. And yet when we be suddenly shotten up into the highest, ere we be well warm there, down we come unto the cold ground again, and then even there stick we still. And yet for the short while that we be upward and aloft, Lord, how lusty and how proud we be, buzzing above busily like as a bumblebee flieth about in summer, never ware that she shall die in winter. (p. 161)

Then, by a process of association, More links the arrow in Psalm 90 with a similar image in Sapientia, where an arrow is used explicitly as a metaphor for pride. Although More quotes Sapientia 5:8–9 and 12–14, he seems to have had in mind, here and in his subsequent allusions, the entire passage, in fact the entire first six chapters, which tell a continuous story. The Book of Sapientia is addressed to all the rulers of the earth and instructs them in the ways of wisdom. The instruction consists primarily of a moral exemplum, contrasting the just man with the rich and powerful of this world, who do not believe in God. "The breath of our nostrils is smoke," they say, "and speech is a spark kindled by the beating of our hearts. When it is extinguished, our body will be ashes, and our spirit will dissolve like gentle air" (2:2–3).[11] They resolve, therefore, to live for this world only and enjoy the good things of the

---

11. Translations are from the Revised Standard Version, corrected where necessary by reference to the Vulgate.

earth (2:6–11). And they turn against the just man because he rebukes them. "Let us see if his words are true," they say, "and let us test what will happen to him and see what his last days will be. For if he is the true son of God, He will help him and deliver him from the hand of his enemies. Let us examine him with insults and torture so that we may see how gentle he is and test his patience. Let us condemn him to a most shameful death, for according to what he says, he will be protected" (2:17–20). If More remembered such an insignificant detail in this section of Sapientia as the metaphor of pride as an arrow, it is difficult to believe that he was not also aware of the startling resemblance between himself and the just man whose only hope was in God. After persecuting the man of God and condemning him to an early death, the wicked rulers of the earth eventually die themselves and descend into hell. They see the man of God in glory and finally come to understand the vanity of their lives. Then follow the verses More quotes, as the wicked lament their folly: "What has our pride profited us, and what good has our boasted wealth brought us? All those things have vanished like a shadow . . . or like an arrow shot at a mark: the divided air presently comes together again, so that no one knows its passage. So we also, as soon as we were born, ceased to be, and we had no mark of virtue to show, but were consumed in our wickedness" (5:8–9, 12–13).

After connecting the arrow in Psalm 90 with the arrow of pride in Sapientia, More makes another associative link that proceeds partially from the text and partially from the context. In the text More moves from the arrow of pride to Lucifer, who committed the first sin of pride:

For when himself was in heaven and began to fly up a-cop-high, with that lusty light flight of pride, saying, *Ascendam super astra, et ponam solium meum ad latera Aquilonis, et ero similis altissimo*: I will sty up above the stars, and set my throne on the sides of the North and will be like unto the Highest. Long ere he could fly up half so high as he said in his heart he would, he was turned from a bright glorious angel into a dark deformed

devil, and from flying any farther upward, down was he
thrown into the deep dungeon of hell. (pp. 162–63)

The quotation is taken from the so-called taunt of the people of
Israel over the King of Babylon in the fourteenth chapter of Isaiah,
traditionally interpreted as an account of the fall of Lucifer. Although he makes use of this allegorical interpretation in the text,
More also seems aware of its literal significance, referring to the fall
of an unjust king. For the scene in Isaiah is surprisingly similar to
that of Sapientia: a mighty king whose power knew no limits on
earth awakens in hell. Those who see him ponder his fate and
remark on the vanity of his life. As More uses it, the entire passage
is applicable both to Lucifer and to temporal monarchs like Henry
VIII, joint rulers of this world of shadows. As the verses in Isaiah
continue, they seem strangely reminiscent, almost prophetic, of
the reign of Henry VIII: "Is this the man who disturbed the earth
and shook kingdoms, who made the world a desert and overthrew
its cities, who did not let his prisoners go home? . . . You have
destroyed your land, you have slain your people: the heirs of the
wicked will nevermore be named. Prepare his sons for slaughter
because of the iniquity of their fathers. They will not rise up; they
will not inherit the land" (14:16–17, 20–21).

A page or so later, in the next scriptural quotation, More once
again seems to allude to the king. The general discussion in the text
concerns wealth and authority. If a man feels that the possession of
great power and wealth endangers his soul, he should be willing to
give them up and turn to God alone. In any case it is always good to
stand in moderate fear, as it says in scripture: *"Beatus homo qui
semper est pavidus*: Blessed is the man that is alway fearful" (p. 165).
The quotation is from Proverbs 28:14. The context is almost identical to the sections of Sapientia and Isaiah we have been looking at,
and its application to Henry VIII seems inescapable. The entire
passage reads:

Blessed is the man who is alway fearful, but he who hardens his
heart will fall into evil. Like a roaring lion or a hungry bear is a
wicked king over a poor people. A ruler who lacks understand-

ing will oppress many through false accusations. . . . A man who brings false accusations against the blood of the soul, even if he flees to the pit, no one will help him. He who walks in simplicity of heart will be saved, but he who walks in crooked ways will fall at once. (28:14–18)

The final allusion to Sapientia occurs toward the end of Book III, in relation to the last of the four temptations in Psalm 90, the assault of the noonday devil, which More interprets as open persecution for the faith. In his previous references to Sapientia More emphasized the fate of the wicked when they awaken in hell. In this last quotation he stresses instead the glory of the just man in heaven. In Chapters 25 and 26 More contrasts the pains of hell with the joys of heaven. "Let us not so much with looking to have described what manner of joys they shall be," More says, "as with hearing what our Lord telleth us in holy scripture" (p. 313). He then quotes Sapientia 3:7: *"Fulgebunt justi sicut sol, et qui erudiunt ad justitiam tanquam scintillae in arundineto discurrent*: Righteous men shall shine as the sun and shall run about like sparks of fire among reeds" (p. 313). The verses immediately preceding More's quotation mention a time of trial or testing of the righteous, such as More himself was going through, whereby God finds them worthy:

The souls of the just are in the hand of God, and the torment of death will not touch them. In the eyes of the foolish they seemed to have died, and their departure was thought to be an affliction and their going from us utter destruction. But they are at peace. For though in the sight of men they suffered torture, their hope is full of immortality. Having suffered a little, they will receive great reward because God tested them and found them worthy of himself. Like gold in the furnace he tried them, and like a sacrificial offering he accepted them. And in time they will be respected. Just men will shine and run about like sparks of fire among the reeds. (3:1–7)

The passage continues by contrasting the reward of the righteous with the punishment of the wicked, whose offspring will be accursed, and again the verses seem like a warning to Henry VIII:

But the wicked, who despised the just man and turned away from God will receive the punishment they devised for themselves. For whoever rejects wisdom and discipline is miserable; their hope is vain, their labor unprofitable, and their work useless. Their wives are foolish and their children evil. Their offspring are accursed. For blessed is the barren woman who is undefiled, who has not entered into a sinful union. She will have fruit when God examines the souls of saints. . . . But the children of adulterers will not come to maturity, and the seed of an unlawful union will perish. . . . The prolific brood of the wicked will be of no use, and none of their legitimate offshoots will strike deep root or take firm hold. . . . For children born of unlawful unions are witnesses of evil against their parents when God examines them. But the just man, though he die early, will be at rest. (3:10–13, 16; 4:3, 6–7)

The entire passage in Sapientia, one must remember, is a moral exemplum addressed to kings, urging them to rule with justice. Within or below the fictional conversation of *A Dialogue of Comfort* in Buda on the eve of a Turkish invasion, we seem to hear in all these allusions to Sapientia the voice of Thomas More's own heart in meditation, murmuring to his former friend, remembering perhaps, in Robert Lowell's phrase, "the great king's bluff arm on his neck, / feeling that friend-slaying, terror-ridden heart / beating under the fat of Aretino"[12]—saying:

Listen, therefore, O kings, and understand; learn, O judges of the ends of the earth. . . . For your power was given to you by the Lord, and your strength from the Most High, who will inquire into your works and read your thoughts because as ministers of his kingdom you did not judge rightly, nor guard the law of justice, nor walk according to the will of God. He will appear to you terribly and swiftly, for severe judgment awaits those who rule. . . . To you then, O kings, my words are directed, that you may learn wisdom and not depart from it. (6:2, 4–6, 10)

12. "Sir Thomas More," in *Notebook 1967–68* (New York, 1969), p. 41.

A Dialogue of Comfort grows out of the total context of More's life. It is the final summing up, and for those who knew him well, it would have been impossible at times to distinguish it from the man himself.

II

Since *A Dialogue of Comfort* bears every sign of being More's ultimate spiritual testament, we may well believe that he would have lavished upon it all the care that his time would allow. The work itself bears out this conjecture, for it displays all the signs of More's finest literary skill, both in the details of its language and in the total command of its development. But we must, to appreciate its skill, adjust ourselves to its unhurried, deliberate pace, to its highly colloquial style, and to its curiously digressive manner, by which the work becomes a book of comfort against all kinds of tribulation, not only against that kind which Thomas More himself is suffering. The treatise seems written at random only if we insist on limiting its concerns to the special situation of More's own treatment at the hands of Henry VIII. More is aware of larger issues than his own fate. He sees his plight as involved in mankind's universal condition. At the same time the generalizing tendency of the treatise serves wittily to disguise its personal implications. "What are you writing there, Thomas?" "A book of comfort for those who are sick, or who are tempted by the devil, or who are living in Hungary." So the book escaped suspicion and somehow made its way out of the prison cell.

This general application and disguise is accomplished by means of deliberate garrulity and conscious digression, with the result that the topic of persecution for the faith is held in abeyance during the first two books of the treatise, while all the lesser kinds of tribulation are being covered. Then in the final book all strands are drawn together in a subtle, surprising, and powerful way that fulfills the underlying design. Let us see how this design is developed.

Each of the three books has its own peculiar theme and method, with a lapse in time before each renewal of the conversation: each book has the effect of a fresh attack upon the universal problem. Book I is chiefly composed of the reassertion of familiar, traditional views on the necessity of faith. If faith is maintained, tribulation serves to cure past sins and prevent sins to come. It is a gift of God, the mark of God's favor. But for all his wise utterances here, Uncle Antony finds his nephew hard to convince. Vincent listens respectfully and seems to be taking in the arguments, yet about three-fifths of the way through the first book he suddenly enters a startling objection:

> But yet, good uncle, though that some do thus, this answereth not full the matter. For we see that the whole church in the common service use divers collects, in which all men pray specially for the princes and prelates, and generally every man for other, and for himself too, that God would vouchsafe to send them all perpetual health and prosperity. And I can see no good man pray God send another sorrow, nor no such prayers are there put in the priest's portas [prayer book] as far as I can hear.
>
> And yet if it were as you say, good uncle, that perpetual prosperity were to the soul so perilous, and tribulation thereto so fruitful, then were as me seemeth every man bound of charity, not only to pray God send their neighbors sorrow, but also to help thereto himself, and when folk are sick, not pray God send them health, but when they come to comfort them they should say, "I am glad, good gossip, that you be so sick. I pray God keep you long therein." (pp. 48–49)

Antony quells this and other objections with an effect of main force, since in the end he takes the floor for twelve pages of an unbroken dissertation, closing with a "summary comfort" that lists all the benefits of tribulation. One might think that after this resounding catalogue (see Chapter 20) there would not be much more to say.

Yet an uneasy feeling persists that the problems of human suffering cannot be adequately met by the delivery of traditional apothegms. The wisdom of Book I, however eloquent, however sound, is not enough, we feel (as Vincent feels), to cover all the experiences of man in tribulation. The positions set forth by Antony remain too theoretical, too far removed from actual existence. Such wisdom is a basis to build upon, no more. Book I is appropriately the shortest of the three.

As the dialogue resumes in Book II, after a lapse of several days, we find ourselves abruptly moved out of the orderly world of theory and plunged into the chaotic world of everyday. Now Antony and Vincent begin by swapping worldly jests, and Antony at once signals a drastic change in tone and technique when he apologizes in a jocular way for having talked too much the other day, saying that he wished "the last time after you were gone, when I felt myself (to say the truth) even a little weary, that I had not so told you still a long tale alone, but that we had more often interchanged words, and parted the talk between us, with ofter enterparling upon your part, in such manner as learned men use between the persons whom they devise disputing in their feigned dialogues" (pp. 82–83). He immediately demonstrates the change in tone by an anecdote, comparing himself with the nun who lectured her brother at length at the convent grate, and then berated him for not giving her the benefit of his wisdom. Vincent responds with the "merry tale" concerning the "kinswoman" who loved to talk.

While they are thus jesting Antony declares that he will from now on force his nephew to talk half the time. This turns out to be quite a jest in itself, since some of Antony's unbroken disquisitions are in fact even longer than in the first book. Nevertheless, Book II works in quite a different way from Book I. It is thirty-five pages longer, and that extra length, we might say, is filled out with a remarkable array of racy, vivid, colloquial anecdotes. What we are watching here is a gradual process of adjusting theory to the world as it is, a process that More wittily heralds in the first chapter of Book II by having the nephew ask whether Antony really meant, in the previous day's conversation, to rule out all forms of worldly comfort, such as "a merry tale with a friend" or "proper pleasant talking." Antony allows that his theories cannot in fact be so strictly applied, considering that men are as they are: "a man to take now and then some honest worldly mirth, I dare not be so sore as utterly to forbid it" (p. 86). True, we ought to find all our joy and comfort in talking of heaven, but somehow men seem to be easily wearied by this topic, as Cassian, he says, shows in one of his *Collations*: "a certain holy father in making of a sermon spake of heaven and of heavenly things so celestially that much of his audience with the sweet sound thereof began to forget all the world and fall asleep. Which when the father beheld, he dissembled their sleeping and suddenly said unto them, 'I shall tell you a merry tale.' At which word they lift up their heads and hearkened unto that. And after the sleep therewith broken, heard him tell on of heaven again" (p. 87). Shortly after this Antony becomes so involved in recounting the strange tale of a fever of his, in which he felt hot and cold at once, that he loses his train of thought: "But see now what age is, lo, I have been so long in my tale that I have almost forgotten for what purpose I told it. Oh now I remember, lo" (p. 93).

We are moving ever more clearly and concretely into the world of actuality—the story of the fever includes an allusion to a young woman trained in medicine that almost certainly is a reference to More's adopted daughter, Margaret Giggs. Now the world's stage opens out suddenly with two long and brilliant tales involving religious satire. The first occurs when Vincent narrates at length his recent experiences in Saxony, during the early days of Luther's revolt ("nor Luther was not then wedded yet"). Vincent proceeds to give a brilliant parody of a Lutheran sermon that he has heard, in words that bring directly home the powerful appeal of the Reformers. Twenty pages later, however, we find the other side of the picture in the longest and most brilliant tale of the entire treatise, the beast fable which Antony says he heard from his old nurse, Mother Maud. This is, among other things, a hilarious piece of anti-clerical satire, with Father Reynard the confessor representing a parody of the worldly priest.

Thus far, nearly halfway through the second book, we have been within the realm of comical satire, but now, with Chapter 15, we move into a darker realm of tales concerning self-destruction. Some of these are savagely comic in their way, such as the opening anecdote of the carpenter's wife who was so fiendish that the devil tempted her to taunt her husband into chopping off her head with his axe: "There were standing other folk by, which had a good sport to hear her chide, but little they looked for this chance till it was done ere they could let it. They said they heard her tongue babble in her head and call 'whoreson, whoreson' twice, after that the head was fro the body" (p. 130).

Although some of the examples are thus touched with grim humor, the major part of the thirty-five-page discussion of suicide or self-destruction is given over to a serious discussion of the ways by which a man can distinguish the illusions of the devil from the true revelations of God (Chapter 16). This question of temptation by demons was a real and pressing issue for More, as we may see from the frequent notation *contra demones* which More wrote in the margins of the book of Psalms which he had with him in the Tower.[13] In this connection it is interesting to note that here in the dialogue More says: "Special verses may there by drawn out of the psalter against the devil's wicked temptations" (p. 159). There is no evidence that More was tempted toward suicide, in the ordinary sense of that word; but in a subtler way the possibility of such a devilish temptation may indeed have been close to More's mind. He dwells at some length upon the case of the "very special, holy man" who was by the devil "brought into such an high spiritual pride" that he became convinced it was God's will that he should destroy himself, "and that thereby should he go straight to heaven" (pp. 133–34). More in the Tower had chosen a course that was almost certain to lead to his death. How could he be sure that he was not being assailed by the temptation of spiritual pride? But of course the whole section on self-destruction is part of More's effort to make his book useful in comfort against all tribulations for every man.

Finally, for the last twenty pages of Book II, the discussion turns toward a very practical examination of the role of *business* in this

13. See *Thomas More's Prayer Book*, ed. L. L. Martz and R. S. Sylvester (New Haven, 1969), pp. 27, 29, 31, 32, 50, 59, 66, 67, 100, 101, 106, 111, 115.

world, a term under which More includes the busy search for pleasures of the flesh, along with business in the sense of seeking worldly wealth. In this connection More takes the occasion to explain the necessity of having men of substance in this world, in a passage that sounds like a rebuke to those who would take his *Utopia* as a blueprint for society. It is appropriate that after this reconciliation with the ways of the busy world, Book II should end with the bringing in of a good dinner.

In Book II nearly every aspect of the world as More knew it is vividly brought before us, in colloquial terms, until we may feel that the turmoil of human existence is in some danger of overwhelming the unity and direction of the dialogue. But, as the danger of disunity threatens, More quietly and firmly brings in the counter-force of reason to control these follies and evils. About a quarter of the way through the second book he brings in the great central text from Psalm 90 which runs like a refrain throughout the rest of Book II and on throughout Book III, forming the basis for a sustained set of considerations on the comfort to be found in "the truth of God":

> The prophet saith in the psalm, *Scuto circumdabit te veritas ejus, non timebis a timore nocturno, a sagitta volante in die, a negotio perambulante in tenebris, ab incursu et demonio meridiano*: The truth of God shall compass thee about with a pavis; thou shall not be afeard of the night's fear, nor of the arrow flying in the day, nor of the business walking about in the darknesses, nor of the incursion or invasion of the devil in the midday. (p. 109)

The intricacy of the discussion that lies ahead is at once shown here as More now proceeds to repeat, ten times within the space of one page, that key word *pavis*: the ancient term for a long shield protecting the whole body. With a winding, repetitive method of discourse, More then dissects the text, part by part, seeing in it four kinds of temptations or tribulations by which we are beset by the devil.

1. *"non timebis a timore nocturno:* Thou shalt not be afeard of the fear of the night" (p. 110)—which includes temptations that come

from an overly scrupulous conscience, from the pusillanimity of a "timorous mind." This is a fear that in its worst form leads to the temptation of suicide.

2. *"A sagitta volante in die*: From the arrow flying in the day"— that is, "the arrow of pride, with which the devil tempteth a man" in prosperity (p. 160).

3. *"negotium perambulans in tenebris*: business walking in the darkness" (p. 169)—business which includes both the busy seeking after fleshly pleasures and the busy seeking after worldly wealth.

Such are the three lesser fears that constitute the matter of Book II. This whole part of the treatise is pursued in a tantalizing manner of deliberate digression and casual divagation that is foreshadowed in Chapter 11, where the basic text is introduced, with Antony saying: "And therefore I shall peradventure, except any further thing fall in our way, with treating of those two verses finish and end all our matter" (p. 109). What falls in our way from here on happens to be about two-thirds of the entire treatise! This consciously ambling and rambling manner is openly maintained by many different asides, such as the explanation that occurs in the middle of the discussion of devilish delusions: "That were somewhat out of our purpose, cousin," says Antony, "sith as I told you before, the man were not then in sorrow and tribulation, whereof our matter speaketh, but in a perilous, merry, mortal temptation; so that if we should, beside our own matter that we have in hand, enter into that too, we might make a lenger work between both, than we could well finish this day. Howbeit, to be short . . . " (p. 136). Then he continues the admittedly "irrelevant" discussion for a dozen more pages. Similarly, Antony promises to "touch one word or twain of the third temptation . . . and then will we call for our dinner." At this suggestion Vincent, always concerned for his uncle's health, pleads: "for our Lord's sake, take good heed, uncle, that you forbear not your dinner over-long." "Fear not that, cousin, I warrant you," Antony replies, "for this piece will I make you but short" (pp. 168–69). The piece of course runs on for twenty more pages.

The whole of Book II thus serves as a variegated interlude, or as a leisurely prologue, before the main event, which now rushes upon us in the form of the fourth temptation, to which More devotes the whole of Book III, the longest book of all:

> The fourth temptation, cousin, that the prophet speaketh of in the foreremembered psalm ... is plain, open persecution, which is touched in these words, *ab incursu et demonio meridiano*. And of all his temptations this is the most perilous, the most bitter sharp, and the most rigorous. .... For in this temptation he showeth himself such as the prophet nameth him, *demonium meridianum*: the midday devil, he may be so lightsomely seen with the eye of a faithful soul by his fierce, furious assault and incursion. For therefore saith the prophet that the truth of God shall compass that man round about, that dwelleth in the faithful hope of his help, with a pavis, *ab incursu et demonio meridiano*: from the incursion and the devil of the midday. (pp. 204–05)

Here, twelve pages along in Book III, is the climax of the mode of repetitious winding by which More pursues his tenacious explication of the basic text; we are now ninety-five pages away from the point at which the text was introduced, and yet the word *pavis* is still ringing, and will continue to ring, as the keynote of the faithful man's belief. In this way the last two books are firmly tied together, while More's explication of the text gradually develops, through its network of repetitions, into an abiding proof that the *pavis* of God is always present to protect the faithful amid the apparent chaos of ordinary life. As the explication weaves its way among the illustrative, gossipy anecdotes of Book II, we come to feel that the disorder of life is being brought under the steady control of reason. More's biblical explication, we might say, gradually weaves a net that subdues the unruly world of anecdote. Yet even this is not enough for full comfort. The reasoning mind of man may do much, More seems to say, but the most difficult problem and the richest comfort remain to be explored.

As the third book opens, the problem is abruptly brought before us, as Vincent enters with the news (just received in a letter from

Constantinople) that the Turk is preparing a mighty army which may in all likelihood be aimed at Hungary. We are returned with a jolt to the threat with which the treatise began, a threat whose imminence had gradually receded as More's discourse turned to lesser matters. But now the historical situation, both for the Hungarians and for Thomas More, is brought in hard upon us, especially when Vincent says: "I hear at mine ear some of our own here among us, which within these few years could no more have borne the name of a Turk than the name of the devil, begin now to find little fault therein, yea, and some to praise them too, little and little as they may, more glad to find faults at every state of Christendom: priests, princes, rites, ceremonies, sacraments, laws and customs, spiritual, temporal and all" (p. 196). And there are, he says, even some who "talk as though they looked for a day when, with a turn unto the Turk's faith, they should be made masters here of true Christian men's bodies and owners of all their goods" (p. 199).

Here, then, in this incursion of the midday devil, lies the ultimate temptation by which the soul of a man will stand or fall. In such a plight the theoretical wisdom of the ages, as presented in Book I, will not suffice; nor will the toughest reasoning powers of man, struggling to subdue the world about him, as represented in Book II. There is, in this ultimate danger, only one resource: to turn within the self and give the mind to meditation on the great central facts of the faith: the vanity of worldly things; the facts of death, judgment, hell, and heaven; and above all the great central fact of Christ's passion.

Thus in Book III More presents what might be called a treatise on the art of meditation. He advises what topics to seek out, and he shows by brief examples how to meditate upon these ancient themes: *contemptus mundi*, the Last Things, and the Passion. By such meditation, More shows a man may move with the help of reason into a realm that includes and yet transcends reason: the realm of the affections, the emotions, where man may find his ultimate comfort in his love of God.

As the minds of uncle and nephew move toward this affectionate meditation, we notice that the nephew comes to play a greater part in the final book. He does not talk half the time, but he comes near to sharing a quarter of the talk; and there is throughout the final book much more true engagement and "enterparling" of minds than we have seen in the first two books. There Vincent was presented as callow, naive, badly in need of instruction. But here in Book III we note that it is the nephew who tells, with subtle insight, that story of the great man of the church who was never "satiate of hearing his own praise" (Chapter 10). One has the feeling from this tale of flattery, and from the nephew's frequent, vigorous, and highly intelligent intervention in the last book, that his mind has been aroused and strengthened, and that young and old have been truly brought together within the flexible and all-inclusive movement of the dialogue. This final accordance of human minds within the pavis of truth represents the carefully designed fulfillment of the anguished plea for help with which the nephew had entered upon the scene:

And sith that I now see the likelihood that when ye be gone we shall be sore destitute of any such other like, therefore thinketh me that God of duty bindeth me to sue to you now, good uncle, in this short time that we have you, that it may like you against these great storms of tribulations, with which both I and all mine are sore beaten already, and now upon the coming of this cruel Turk fear to fall in far mo, I may learn of you such plenty of good counsel and comfort that I may, with the same laid up in remembrance, govern and stay the ship of our kindred, and keep it afloat from peril of spiritual drowning. (p. 6)

III

What we have called the literary surface of the work is thus brilliantly executed, but, deep within, the work is created and sustained by a profound theological principle that is implicit in the definition of "comfort" that More provides near the end of Book I. "Comfort," he here says, is properly taken by them that take it right, rather for the consolation of good hope, that men take in their heart, of some good growing toward them, than for a present pleasure with which the body is delighted and tickled for the while. . . . And therefore . . . I speak but of such comfort as is very comfort indeed, by which a man hath hope of God's favor and remission of his sins, with minishing of his pain in purgatory or reward else in heaven, and such comfort cometh of tribulation and for tribulation well taken. (pp. 70–71)

Thus the virtue of hope appears near the close of a discussion stressing the virtue of faith, and the virtue of charity will ultimately follow. *A Dialogue of Comfort* draws its firm underlying structure from an interior trinity.

The first book is focused on faith and is divided into three primary sections: (1) a consideration of faith itself; (2) a catalogue of the major kinds of tribulation; (3) a series of objections by which our perspective is adjusted to accept tribulation in the light of faith as a gift of God. The first chapter is essentially negative. Ancient moral philosophers attempted to show men how to rise above the miseries of this world. They emphasized, More says, the freedom of the mind. Their teachings are extremely important, but they do not go far enough. For the philosophers of Greece and Rome lacked "the chief comfort of all, . . . without which . . . all other comforts are nothing." Since they lived before the coming of Christ, they lacked the necessary faith to refer "the final end of their comfort unto God" and the willingness to suffer tribulation on earth so as to obtain God's favor and eternal reward in heaven (pp. 10–11).

More makes it absolutely clear here at the beginning of the book that he is dealing not with the "consolations of philosophy," but with supernatural sources of comfort beyond the reach of reason alone. He is speaking not of man in a state of nature, but of man in a state of grace. For although faith, according to traditional theology, is an act of the intellect directing the will to the true and the good, it is also the first of the supernatural or theological virtues.

Since reason alone is insufficient, one must begin, More explains, with a firm foundation of faith. But faith is not in man's possession. One man cannot give it to another or even to himself. It is "the gracious gift of God" alone. If a man feels his faith weak, all he can do is to pray to God that it may please him to increase it. What More attempts here is to supply the reader with a realization, a full exploration, of truths to which the reader had perhaps given mere verbal or intellectual assent for most of his life. Remembering these things, men should not complain if they fall into tribulation. Rather they should turn it to their spiritual advantage by finding in it not anguish, diminishment, and desolation, but the glorification of their spirit. Even if it is God's will that we die in tribulation, we should give him thanks and long to go to him: "And then shall hope of heaven comfort our heaviness, and out of our transitory tribulation shall we go to everlasting glory" (p. 79). At a certain point faith is imperceptibly transformed into hope.

Book II is divided into four disproportionate parts: (1) an introduction that sets the tone for the conversation that follows and defends the use of merry tales and anecdotes; (2) a discussion, largely through objections, of penance or tribulation willingly assumed for the forgiveness of sins; (3) a discussion of tribulation not chosen, but accepted willingly, divided into two parts, temptation and persecution; and finally (4) a formal meditation on the 90th Psalm, which begins here and extends throughout the remainder of the book. The emphasis throughout is on the theological virtue of hope. Hope in general, Aquinas says, must have certain conditions accompanying it. It must be directed toward something good that lies in the future; the good must be arduous and difficult to obtain; and it must be possible to obtain.[14] Considered not in general terms, but as a theological virtue, the good we hope for is eternal happiness in heaven. It is not therefore something already possessed. And although it is arduous and difficult to gain, it is possible to obtain by means of God's assistance.[15] The object of

14. See Thomas Aquinas, *Summa Theologica*, ed. Institutum Studiorum Medievalium Ottaviensis (Ottawa, 1941), I–II, Q. 40, a. 1.

15. *Ibid.*, II–II, Q. 17, a. 1 and a. 7.

hope, in other words, is eternal happiness with God, and the means by which men obtain this hope is paradoxically the supernatural gift of hope itself, by which they trust in God's assistance to enable them to achieve it. "Now the object of hope is, in one way, eternal happiness, and, in another way, the divine assistance."[16] Hope, then, is inseparable from sanctifying grace, the strength man is given to see him through the trials and temptations of this world, and at the same time it is the supernatural trust that God will give that strength.

More also thinks of the virtue of hope in this dual sense. But the first aspect—the hope of eternal happiness in heaven—is posited, as it were, outside the book as its final cause. What More insists on within the work itself is the second aspect of hope—God's willingness to give man the strength to resist temptation so that he may at last attain the final object of hope. This is the main burden of the extended meditation on the 90th Psalm that begins in Book II and continues through Book III. In each of the various temptations considered—the night's fear, the arrow flying in the day, the business walking about in the darkness, and the incursion of the devil in the midday—the remedy is same: to hope and trust in God's assistance. The effect is repetitive, but it is also cumulative, as we come to realize in temptation after temptation that man is sustained by hope and that chance and necessity give way before it.

The most unusual feature of Book II is the change of tone that occurs as the book begins. From this point on merry tales and anecdotes crowd the conversation and, on the whole, form one of the most inexplicable features of the work—a genuine sense of humor and wit rising discordantly from the grim circumstances of fear, suffering, and death—tales of humorous suicide and prideful martyrdom side by side with playful anecdotes, thinly disguised, about the vagaries of Dame Alice, More's second wife, or the precocious brilliance of his adopted daughter, Margaret Giggs. According to what Antony says in the prefatory chapter, the merry tales and anecdotes that fill Book II with their strange levity are

16. *Ibid.*, II–II, Q. 17, a. 7.

designed as a form of relief to compensate for human weakness and are therefore entirely superficial compared with the grim business underneath the laughter. But surely this is wrong, for the anecdotes are not a superficial overlay. They are part of the very process of thought, inextricably fused with the material presented. They rise primarily from More's view of his own and all human nature.

More's mirth, which gives his literary works and his life their unique and most characteristic quality, is one of the most mysterious elements in the man. In one sense it is a matter of personal style, a mask with which to face the world—an intellectual strategy employed in the brilliant, complex ironies of *Utopia*; in conversation with his wife and the king's good servants, Wolsey, Cromwell, and the Lords at Lambeth; and even in his last, graceful remarks on the scaffold, which so outraged the chronicler Edward Hall.[17] But it also had to do with his view of his relationship with God, which allowed him to see the world with sufficient detachment to be aware of its insignificance in the face of eternity. Viewed from this perspective, the merry tales and anecdotes in *A Dialogue of Comfort* would seem to proceed directly from the structure of the work. The argument of Book II reasons the need in times of tribulation for the infused theological virtue of hope. Meanwhile the tone itself, created by the merry tales and anecdotes, demonstrates even more graphically than the argument the realization of the hope and trust in God that More is speaking of in the dialogue. In the anecdotes and merry tales the theological virtue of hope is realized as an emotional experience. The tone of Book II, indeed the essential tone of *A Dialogue of Comfort* in all its complexity, is a clear expression of the hope and trust in God and the detachment from worldly things that the dialogue itself is working to effect.

The overall form of the argument, the structural use of the three theological virtues, continues in Book III, but in a somewhat unexpected fashion. For charity is not approached directly, as hope was

17. See Chambers, *Thomas More*, pp. 347, 349.

in Book II. Although it suffuses the book and remains its goal throughout, charity emerges fully only in the last, cumulative chapter, in the meditation on Christ's passion and death. It is as if More, faced with the overwhelming question of violent death, felt that some new beginning must be made and extensive preparation laid down first. Hence the emphasis on reason and will, structure and logical organization, throughout the third book. The realization of charity in Book III, in other words, emerges from a rational process, from the very structure and organization of the work itself—the movement of the mind through rational forms, categories, and distinctions, attempting to control fear and direct the desires toward God. By considering all the possibilities clearly and foreseeing all the probable torments—even the chance that one might not be able to endure them—one is in a better position to control the instinctive fear of pain and death. But reason alone is not enough. At a certain point the mind proceeds beyond itself, the choice is made, and reason is absorbed in charity—the love of man for God.

More develops a rational structure in Book III so as to contain fear and subject it to the will. At the same time, however, within that rational process something else occurs, like the mysterious motion of grace in the soul, which leads directly to the full emergence of the theological virtue of charity in the final chapter of the book. Beginning with Chapter 16, the conclusion to the long middle section on the goods of fortune, More ends each step in the rational process with a formal allusion to an aspect of Christ's passion and death appropriate to the matter at hand. The pattern seems somewhat casual at first, but it is soon seen to embody a guiding principle, as though Christ's passion were the ultimate goal of the rational process itself. After considering the goods of fortune, for example, More refers in Chapter 16 to Christ's voluntary poverty and his lack of worldly power. From this point on these two forces, the power of reason in the frame and argument, and the power of love in the allusions to Christ's passion, operate alternately to affect the will and turn the mind and heart toward God. Reason remains the primary form or organizing principle, but as the book proceeds the recollection of Christ's passion becomes increasingly insistent. In Chapter 17, on fear, More refers to Christ's fear and anxiety in the agony in the garden; in Chapter 18, on captivity and servitude, to Christ's assumption of the form of a servant, "obedient unto death, even death on the cross"; in Chapters 19 and 20, to Christ's imprisonment; and in Chapter 23, on shame, to the crown of thorns, the mockery of the Roman soldiers, and the degradation of death on the cross. Finally, in Chapter 26 More concludes the series by identifying Christ's passion with the suffering of all those called upon to die in defense of the faith:

> Our head is Christ, and therefore to him must we be joined, and as members of his must we follow him, if we will come thither. He is our guide to guide us thither and is entered in before us, and he therefore that will enter in after, *Debet sicut ille ambulavit et ipse ambulare*: The same way that Christ walked, the same way must he walk, . . . *Nesciebatis quia oportebat Christum pati, et sic introire in regnum suum:* Knew you not that Christ must suffer passion, and by that way enter into his kingdom? Who can for very shame desire to enter into the kingdom of Christ with ease, when himself entered not into his own without pain? (pp. 317–18)

In the formal meditation on the passion with which the book ends, all its diverse strands are brought together. As a meditation, it reflects the traditional process of late medieval meditation, precursor to the Ignatian method. The first step is to release the imagination so as to recall as graphically as possible the pain and torment Christ suffered on the cross: "his lovely limbs drawn and stretched out upon the cross to the intolerable pain of his forbeaten and sore beaten veins and sinews, new feeling with the cruel stretching and straining pain, far passing any cramp, in every part of his blessed body at once. Then the great, long nails cruelly driven with hammers through his holy hands and feet" (p. 318). The second step is to apply the reason or understanding to what the imagination presents so as to arrive at an act of will. By understanding fully what the imagination has visualized, man arrives at a sense of God's love, which arouses the will with desire: "If we would . . . remember these things in such wise, as would God we would, I verily suppose that the consideration of his incomparable kindness could not fail in such wise to inflame our key-cold hearts and set them on fire in his love, that we should find ourself not only content, but also glad and desirous to suffer death for his sake, that so marvelously lovingly letted not to sustain so far passing painful death for ours" (p. 319).

In the act of meditation, such as More performs here, the mind rises to the emotional apprehension of the love of God and the "desire to be dissolved and to be with Christ," which Aquinas describes as the most perfect form of charity.[18] But it inevitably subsides and falls away. Only in the actual moment of death can one fully lose himself in the darkness of Christ's love. Until then, fearful and anxious, one remains in hope: "And therefore . . . let us well consider these things, and let us have sure hope in the help of God. . . . In our fear let us remember Christ's painful agony, that himself would for our comfort suffer before his passion to the intent that no fear should make us despair, and ever call for his help, such as himself list to send us, and then need we never to doubt but that either he shall keep us from the painful death, or shall not fail so to strength us in it that he shall joyously bring us to heaven by it" (pp. 322–25). As More's definition of comfort suggests, the ultimate consolation of *A Dialogue of Comfort* is "the consolation of good hope, that men take in their heart of some good growing toward them."

18. *Summa Theologica*, II–II, Q. 24, a. 9.

A NOTE ON THE TEXT

The text of *A Dialogue of Comfort* presented here is based on that given in Volume 12 of The Yale Edition of the Complete Works (New Haven, 1976), as established by Louis L. Martz. Spelling and punctuation have been modernized and glosses have been provided for words which have changed their meaning or become archaic since the early sixteenth century. An effort has been made, in modernizing the punctuation, to preserve More's long sentences with their involved, but colloquially effective, syntax. A few archaic spellings (e.g., "tone" and "tother," "ourself," "leese," "richesse") have been allowed to stand in the text in the belief that they help to catch something of the flavor of the original. When archaic words occur frequently in the text, glosses have been repeated at fairly regular intervals. Brief historical and explanatory notes are interwoven with the glosses. All references to the Psalms are to the Vulgate version. The reader who desires fuller annotation and a broadly based introduction to the *Dialogue* should consult Volume 12 of the Complete Works.

BIBLIOGRAPHY

I. TEXTS

The following volumes have already appeared in The Yale Edition of the Complete Works of St. Thomas More (New Haven and London, 1961–).

Vol. 2, *The History of King Richard III*, ed. R. S. Sylvester, 1963; second printing, 1975.

Vol. 3, Part I, *Translations of Lucian*, ed. C. R. Thompson, 1974.

Vol. 4, *Utopia*, ed. E. Surtz and J. H. Hexter, 1965; third printing, 1975.

Vol. 5, *Responsio ad Lutherum*, ed. J. M. Headley, 1969.

Vol. 8, *The Confutation of Tyndale's Answer*, ed. L. A. Schuster, R. C. Marius, J. P. Lusardi, and R. J. Schoeck, 1973.

Vol. 12, *A Dialogue of Comfort against Tribulation*, ed. L. L. Martz and F. Manley, 1976.

Vol. 13, *Treatise on the Passion*, etc., ed. Garry Haupt, 1976.

Vol. 14, *De Tristitia Christi*, ed. Clarence Miller, 1976.

It is expected that the entire series will be completed by 1985.

Two companion volumes to the Edition are:

R. W. Gibson and J. M. Patrick, *St. Thomas More: A Preliminary Bibliography of His Works and of Moreana to the Year 1750*, 1961.

Thomas More's Prayerbook, ed. L. L. Martz and R. S. Sylvester, 1969.

In the Selected Works of St. Thomas More series, the following modern-spelling texts are available in both clothbound and paperbound editions:

E. F. Rogers, ed., *St. Thomas More: Selected Letters*, 1961.

E. Surtz, ed., *Utopia*, 1964.

R. S. Sylvester, ed., *The History of King Richard III and Selections from the English and Latin Poems*, 1976.

The standard edition of More's correspondence is E. F. Rogers, ed., *The Correspondence of Sir Thomas More* (Princeton, 1947). An expanded and revised edition of this volume will be published as Volume 15 of the Yale Edition, ed. H. Schulte Herbrüggen.

II. BIOGRAPHIES

A. Sixteenth and Seventeenth Centuries

William Roper, *The Lyfe of Sir Thomas Moore, knighte* (1557), ed. E. V. Hitchcock, London, 1935, Early English Text Society. Roper's *Life*, together with Cavendish's *Life of Wolsey*, is conveniently available in paperback in *Two Early Tudor Lives*, ed. R. S. Sylvester and D. P. Harding, New Haven, 1962.

Nicholas Harpsfield, *The Life and Death of Sir Thomas Moore, knight* (1557), ed. E. V. Hitchcock and R. W. Chambers, London, 1932, Early English Text Society.

Thomas Stapleton, as Part III of his *Tres Thomae, The Life and Illustrious Martyrdom of Sir Thomas More* (1588), trans. P. E. Hallett, 1928, rev. ed. by E. E. Reynolds, London, 1966.

Ro. Ba., *The Lyfe of Syr Thomas More* (1599), ed. E. V. Hitchcock, P. E. Hallett, and A. W. Reed, London, 1950, Early English Text Society. (The author is not identified.)

Cresacre More, *The Life and Death of Sir Thomas More* (1626–31). The last of the family biographies, written by More's great-grandson. A modern edition is being prepared by Michael Anderegg.

B. Modern Biographies

T. E. Bridgett, *Life and Writings of Blessed Thomas More*, London, 1891, 3d ed. 1904.

R. W. Chambers, *Thomas More*, London, 1935.

E. E. Reynolds, *The Field Is Won*, London, 1968.

G. Marc'hadour, *Thomas More ou la sage folie*, Paris, 1971.

III. STUDIES AND COMPLEMENTARY MATERIALS

Adams, R.P., *The Better Part of Valor: More, Erasmus, Colet and Vives on Humanism, War, and Peace, 1496–1535*, Seattle, 1962.

Baumer, F. L., "England, the Turk, and the Common Corps of Christendom," *American Historical Review, 50* (1944), 26–48.

Bernard de Clairvaux, *Lent with Saint Bernard: A Devotional Commentary on Psalm Ninety-One*, trans. and ed. by a Religious of C.S.M.V., London, 1953.

Biblia Sacra, Vulgatae Editionis, Sixti V. et Clementis VIII. Jussu Recognita atque Edita, London, 1865.

Boland, Paschal, *The Concept of Discretio Spirituum in John Gerson's De Probatione Spirituum and De Distinctione Verarum Visionum a Falsis*, Washington, D.C., 1959.

Castelli, Alberto, trans. and ed., *Il Dialogo del Conforto nelle Tribolazioni*, Rome, 1970.

Chew, Samuel C., *The Crescent and the Rose*, New York, 1937.

Creasy, Edward S., *History of the Ottoman Turks*, ed. Zeine N. Zeine, Beirut, 1961.

Daly, James J., "A Neglected Classic," *Catholic World, 113* (1921), 514–23.

Daniel, N. A., *Islam and the West: The Making of an Image*, Edinburgh, 1960.

Fischer-Galati, S., *Ottoman Imperialism and German Protestantism, 1521–1555*, Cambridge, Mass., 1959.

Fowler, John, ed., *A Dialogue of Cumfort against Tribulation*, Antwerp, 1573.

Fumée, M., *The Historie of the Troubles of Hungarie*, trans. R. C., Gentleman, London, 1600.

Green, Paul D., "Suicide, Martyrdom, and Thomas More," *Studies in the Renaissance, 19* (1972), 135–55.

Hallett, Philip E., ed., *A Dialogue of Comfort against Tribulation*, London, 1937.

Inalcik, Halil, *The Ottoman Empire: The Classical Age, 1300–1600*, trans. N. Itzkowitz and C. Imber, London, 1973.

Jovius, Paulus, *A Shorte Treatise vpon the Turkes Chronicles*, trans. Peter Ashton, London, 1546.

Kuhn, Joaquin, "The Function of Psalm 90 in Thomas More's *A Dialogue of Comfort*," *Moreana, 22* (1969), 61–67.

LP. Letters and Papers, Foreign and Domestic, of the Reign of Henry VIII, ed. J. S. Brewer, James Gairdner, and R. H. Brodie, 21 vols., London, 1862–1932.

Marc'hadour, G., *The Bible in the Works of St. Thomas More*, 5 vols., Nieuwkoop, 1969–71.

Martz, Louis L., "The Design of More's *Dialogue of Comfort*," *Moreana, 15–16* (1967), 331–46.

Miles, Leland, ed., *A Dialogue of Comfort against Tribulation*, Bloomington and London, 1965.

———, "More's *Dialogue of Comfort* as a First Draft," *Studies in Philology, 63* (1966), 126–34.

———, "The Literary Artistry of Thomas More: *The Dialogue of Comfort*," *Studies in English Literature, 1500–1900, 6* (1966), 7–33.

More, Thomas, *The Workes . . . in the Englysh Tonge*, London, 1557.

Newton, Thomas, *A Notable Historie of the Saracens . . . Drawen out of Augustine Curio and sundry other good Authours*, London, 1575.

Patrides, C. A., " 'The Bloody and Cruell Turke': the Background of a Renaissance Commonplace," *Studies in the Renaissance, 10* (1963), 126–35.

PG. Patrologiae Cursus Completus: Series Graeca, ed. J. P. Migne, 161 vols., Paris, 1857–66. Cited by volume and column.

PL. Patrologiae Cursus Completus: Series Latina, ed. J. P. Migne, 221 vols., Paris, 1844–1903. Cited by volume and column.

Schoeck, R. J., "Thomas More's *Dialogue of Comfort* and the Problem of the Real Grand Turk," *English Miscellany, 20* (1969), 23–37.

Schwoebel, Robert, *The Shadow of the Crescent*, Nieuwkoop, 1967.

Southern, R. W., *Western Views of Islam in the Middle Ages*, Cambridge, Mass., 1962.

Sylvester, R.S., ed., *St. Thomas More: Action and Contemplation* (essays by R. J. Schoeck, G. Elton, L. L. Martz, and G. Marc'hadour), New Haven, 1972.

A DIALOGUE OF COMFORT
AGAINST TRIBULATION

A Dialogue of Comfort[1] against Tribulation, Made by an Hungarian in Latin, and Translated out of Latin into French, and out of French into English.

Antony and Vincent

Vincent

Who would have went,[2] O my good uncle, afore a few years passed, that such as in this country would visit their friends lying in disease and sickness, should come (as I do now) to seek and fetch comfort of them or, in giving comfort to them, use the way that I may well use to you. For albeit that the priests and friars be wont to call upon sick men to remember death, yet we worldly friends, for fear of discomforting them, have ever had a guise[3] in Hungary to lift up their hearts and put them in hope of life. But now, my good uncle, the world is here waxen[4] such, and so great perils appear here to fall at hand, that me thinketh the greatest comfort that a man can have is when he may see that he shall soon be gone. And we that are likely long to live here in wretchedness have need of some comfortable[5] counsel against tribulation to be given us by such as you be, good uncle, that have so long lived virtuously, and are so learned in the law of God, as very few be better in this country here, and have had of such things as we now do fear, good experience and assay[6] in yourself, as he that hath been taken

1. spiritual consolation.   2. supposed.   3. habit.   4. grown.
5. consoling.   6. trial.

prisoner in Turkey two times in your days and now likely to depart hence ere long. But that may be your great comfort, good uncle, sith[7] you depart to God. But us here shall you leave of your kindred a sort of very comfortless orphans, to all whom your good help and counsel and comfort hath long been a great stay, not as an uncle unto some, and to some as one further of kin, but as though unto us all, you had been a natural father.

Antony

Mine own good cousin,[8] I cannot much say nay, but that there is indeed, not here in Hungary only, but almost in all places of Christendom, such a customable manner[9] of unchristian comforting, which albeit that in any sick man it doth more harm than good, withdrawing him in time of sickness with the looking and longing for life, fro the meditation of death, judgment, heaven, and hell, whereof he should beset[1] much part of his time, even all his whole life in his best health, yet is that manner in my mind more than mad, where such kind of comfort is used to a man of mine age. For as we well wot[2] that a young man may die soon, so be we very sure that an old man cannot live long. And yet sith there is, as Tully saith,[3] no man for all that so old but that he hopeth yet that he may live one year more and of a frail folly delighteth to think thereon and comfort himself therewith, other men's words of like manner[4] comfort adding mo[5] sticks to that fire shall in a manner[6] burn up quite the pleasant moisture that most should refresh him: the wholesome dew, I mean, of God's grace, by which he should wish with God's will to be hence and long to be with him in heaven. Now where you take my departing fro you so heavily, as of him of whom ye recognize of your goodness to have had here before help and comfort: would God I had to you and other mo done half so much as myself reckoneth had been my duty to do. But whensoever God

7. since.
8. kinsman; often used in the sixteenth century for nephew or niece.
9. *customable manner:* customary kind.   1. devote.   2. know.
3. Cf. Cicero, *De Senectute,* 7, 24.   4. *like manner:* a similar kind of.
5. more.   6. sense.

take me hence, to reckon yourself then comfortless, as though your chief comfort stood in me, therein make ye, me thinketh, a reckoning very much like as though you would cast away a strong staff and lean upon a rotten reed, for God is and must be your comfort and not I. And he is a sure comfort that, as he said to his disciples, never leaveth his servants in case of comfortless orphans, not even when he departed from his disciples by death, but both, as he promised, sent them a comforter, the Holy Spirit of his Father and himself,[7] and made them also sure that to the world's end he would ever dwell with them himself.[8] And therefore if ye be part of his flock and believe his promise, how can ye be comfortless in any tribulation, when Christ and his Holy Spirit, and with them their unseparable Father, if you put full trust and confidence in them, be never one finger brede[9] of space nor one minute of time from you?

Vincent

O my good uncle, even these same self words, wherewith ye well prove that because of God's own gracious presence we cannot be left comfortless, make me now feel and perceive what a miss[1] of much comfort we shall have when ye be gone. For albeit, good uncle, that while ye do tell me this I cannot but grant it for true, yet if I now had not heard it of you I had not remembered it, nor it had not fallen in my mind. And over that, like as our tribulations shall in weight and number increase, so shall we need not only one such good word or twain, but a great heap thereof, to stable and strength[2] the walls of our hearts against the great surges of the tempestuous sea.

Antony

Good cousin, trust well in God, and he shall provide you teachers abroad[3] convenient in every time, or else shall himself sufficiently teach you within.

---

7. John 14:16–18, 25–26.   8. Matt. 28:20; John 14:16.
9. breadth.   1. loss.
2. *stable and strength:* stabilize and strengthen.   3. from without.

Vincent

Very well, good uncle. But yet if we would leave the seeking of outward learning, where we might have it, and look to be inwardly taught only by God, then should we thereby tempt God and displease him. And sith that I now see the likelihood that when ye be gone we shall be sore[4] destitute of any such other like, therefore thinketh me that God of duty bindeth me to sue to you now, good uncle, in this short time that we have you, that it may like[5] you against these great storms of tribulations, with which both I and all mine are sore beaten already, and now upon the coming of this cruel Turk[6] fear to fall in far mo, I may learn of you such plenty of good counsel and comfort that I may, with the same laid up in remembrance, govern and stay the ship of our kindred, and keep it afloat from peril of spiritual drowning.

You be not ignorant, good uncle, what heaps of heaviness hath of late fallen among us already, with which some of our poor family be fallen into such dumps that scantly[7] can any such comfort as my poor wit[8] can give them any thing[9] assuage their sorrow. And now, sith the tidings have come hither so breme[1] of the great Turk's enterprise into these parties[2] here, we can almost neither talk nor think of any other thing else than of his might and our mischief.[3] There falleth so continually before the eyen[4] of our heart, a fearful imagination of this terrible thing: his mighty strength and power, his high malice and hatred, and his incomparable cruelty, with robbing, spoiling, burning, and laying waste all the way that his army cometh; then killing or carrying away the people far hence fro home, and there sever the couples and kindred asunder, every one far from the other, some kept in thralldom, and some kept in prison, and some for a triumph tormented and killed in his presence; then send his people hither and his false faith therewith, so that such as are here and remain still shall either both leese[5] all and

---

4. severely.   5. please.
6. Suleiman the Magnificent. See the Introduction.   7. scarcely.
8. mental capacity.   9. *any thing:* to any extent.   1. much spoken of.
2. parts.   3. misfortune.   4. eyes.   5. lose.

be lost too, or forced to forsake the faith of our Savior Christ, and fall to the false sect of Mahomet. And yet, which we more fear than all the remnant, no small part of our own folk that dwell even here about us are (as we hear) fallen to him, or already confederate with him, which, if it so be, shall haply[6] keep this quarter fro the Turk's incursion. But then shall they that turn to his law leave all their neighbors nothing, but shall have our goods given them and our bodies both, but if[7] we turn as they do, and forsake our Savior too. And then (for there is no born Turk so cruel to Christian folk as is the false Christian that falleth fro the faith) we shall stand in peril if we persevere in the truth, to be more hardly handled and die more cruel death by our own countrymen at home than if we were taken hence and carried into Turkey.

These fearful heaps of peril lie so heavy at our hearts, while we wot not into which we shall fortune to fall, and therefore fear all the worst, that, as our Savior prophesied of the people of Jerusalem, many wish among us already before the peril come that the mountains would overwhelm them or the valleys open and swallow them up and cover them.[8]

Therefore, good uncle, against these horrible fears of these terrible tribulations, of which some you wot well our house already hath, and the remnant stand in dread of, give us, while God lendeth you us, such plenty of your comfortable counsel as I may write and keep with us to stay us when God shall call you hence.

Antony

O my good cousin, this is an heavy hearing, and likewise as we that dwell here in this part fear that thing so sore now which few years passed feared it not at all, so doubt[9] I that ere it long be, they shall fear it as much, that think themself now very sure because they dwell further off. Greece feared not the Turk when that I was

6. perhaps.   7. *but if:* unless.
8. Luke 23:28–30.   9. fear.

born, and within a while after, all the whole empire was his.[1] The great Soldan of Syria[2] thought himself more than his match, and long since ye were born hath he that empire, too. Then hath he taken Belgrade, the fortress of this realm.[3] And since hath he destroyed our noble, young goodly king.[4] And now strive there twain[5] for us. Our Lord send the grace that the third dog[6] carry not away the bone from them both. What should I speak of the noble strong city of Rhodes, the winning thereof he counteth as a victory against the whole corps of Christendom, sith all Christendom was not able to defend that strong town against him?[7] Howbeit if the princes of Christendom everywhere about would, where as need was, have set to their hands[8] in time, the Turk had never taken any one place of all these places. But partly dissensions fallen among ourselves, partly that no man careth what harm other folk feel, but each part suffer other[9] to shift for itself, the Turk is in few years wonderfully increased, and Christendom on the other side very sore decayed. And all this worketh our unkindness,[1] with which God is not content.

But now whereas you desire of me some plenty of comfortable things which ye may put in remembrance and comfort therewith your company, verily in the rehearsing and heaping of your mani-

1. In 1452 Mahomet II sacked Athens and in the following year took Constantinople and most of the Greek Isles.
2. Kansuh Ghuri, Sultan of the Circassian Mamelukes of Syria and Egypt. Defeated by Selim I in a battle fought near Aleppo (August 1516).
3. Captured by Suleiman the Magnificent in 1521.
4. Louis II of Hungary (1506–26), killed while fighting the Turks at the battle of Mohács (August 1526). See the Introduction.
5. John Zapolya, Voivode of Transylvania, and Ferdinand, Archduke of Austria, claimants to the Hungarian throne after the death of Louis II.
6. Suleiman the Magnificent.
7. Rhodes fell after a five-month siege to Suleiman the Magnificent in 1522.
8. *set to . . . hands:* become seriously involved.
9. *suffer other:* permits the other.
1. *worketh our unkindness:* is caused by our unnatural conduct.

fold fears, myself began to feel that there should much need against so many troubles, many comfortable counsels. For surely, cousin, a little before your coming, as I devised[2] with myself upon the Turk's coming, it happed[3] my mind to fall suddenly from that into the devising upon mine own departing. Wherein albeit that I fully put my trust and hope to be a saved soul by the great mercy of God, yet sith[4] there is here no man so sure that without revelation[5] may clean stand out of dread, I bethought me also upon the pains of hell, and after I bethought me then upon the Turk again. And first me thought his terror nothing, when I compared it with the joyful hope of heaven. Then compared I it on the tother[6] side with the fearful dread of hell; and therein[7] casting in my mind those terrible devilish tormentors, with the deep consideration of that furious endless fire, me thought that if the Turk with all his whole host, and all trumpets and his timbrels[8] too, were, to kill me in my bed, come to my chamber door, in respect of the tother reckoning,[9] I regard him not a rush.[1]

And yet when I now heard your lamentable words, laying forth, as it were present before my face, that heap of heavy sorrowful tribulations that, beside those that are already fallen, are in short space like to follow, I waxed therewith myself suddenly somewhat aflight.[2] And therefore I well allow your request in this behalf, that would have store of comfort[3] aforehand ready by you, to resort to and to lay up in your heart as a treacle[4] against the poison of all desperate[5] dread that might rise of occasion of sore tribulation. And herein shall I be glad (as my poor wit will serve me) to call to mind with you such things as I before have read, heard, or thought upon, that may conveniently serve us to this purpose.

2. considered.   3. happened.   4. since.
5. a personal message from God.   6. other.   7. in that way.
8. musical instruments similar to tambourines.
9. *in . . . reckoning:* in comparison with the other consideration.
1. *regard . . . rush:* take no account of him.
2. *waxed . . . aflight:* became distressed.   3. spiritual consolation.
4. antidote.   5. hopeless.

The First Chapter

That the comforts devised by the old paynim[6] philosophers were insufficient, and the cause wherefore.

First shall ye, good cousin, understand this: that the natural wise men[7] of this world, the old moral philosophers, labored much in this matter, and many natural reasons have they written whereby they might encourage men to set little by such goods, or such hurt either, the going and coming whereof are the matter and cause of tribulation: as are the goods of fortune, riches, favor, and friends, fame, worldly worship,[8] and such other things, or of the body as beauty, strength, agility, quickness,[9] and health. These things, ye wot well, coming to us are matter of worldly wealth, and taken from us by fortune or by force or the fear of the losing be matter of adversity or tribulation. For tribulation seemeth generally to signify nothing else but some kind of grief, either pain of the body or heaviness of the mind.

Now the body not to feel that[10] it feeleth, all the wit in the world cannot bring about. But that the mind should not be grieved, neither with the pain that the body feeleth, nor with the occasions of heaviness offered and given unto the soul itself, this thing labored the philosophers very much about, and many goodly sayings have they toward[1] the strength and comfort against tribulation, exhorting men to the full contempt of all worldly loss, and despising of sickness and all bodily grief, painful death and all. Howbeit in very deed, for anything that ever I read in them, I never could yet find that ever these natural reasons were able to give sufficient comfort of themself. For they never stretch so far but that they leave untouched, for lack of necessary knowledge, that special point which is not only the chief comfort of all, but

6. pagan.
7. i.e., classical philosophers, who relied only on their natural faculties, unaided by the supernatural gift of divine revelation.
8. honor.   9. liveliness.   10. that which.   1. in reference to.

without which also all other comforts are nothing: that is to wit, the referring the final end of their comfort unto God, and to repute and take for the special cause of comfort that by the patient sufferance[2] of their tribulation they shall attain his favor, and for their pain receive reward at his hand in heaven. And for lack of knowledge of this end they did (as they needs must) leave untouched also the very special mean[3] without which we can never attain to this comfort: that is to wit, the gracious help and aid of God, to move, stir, and guide us forward, in the referring all our ghostly[4] comfort, yea and our worldly comfort too, all unto that heavenly end. And therefore, as I say, for lack of these things, all their comfortable[5] counsels are very far unsufficient. Howbeit though they be far unable to cure our disease of themself, and therefore are not sufficient to be taken for our physicians, some good drugs have they yet in their shops, for which they may be suffered to dwell among our pothecaries,[6] if the medicines be not made of their own brains, but after the bills[7] made by the great physician, God, prescribing the medicines himself and correcting the faults of their erroneous receipts.[8] For without this way taken with them, they shall not fail to do as many bold blind pothecaries do, which either for lucre or of a foolish pride give sick folk medicines of their own devising, and therewith kill up in corners[9] many such simple folk as they find so foolish to put their lives in such lewd[1] and unlearned, blind bayards'[2] hands.

We shall therefore neither fully receive those philosophers' reasons in this matter nor yet utterly refuse them; but using them in such order as shall beseem[3] them, the principal and the effectual medicines against these diseases of tribulation shall we fetch from the high, great and excellent physician, without whom we could never be healed of our very deadly disease of damnation; for our necessity wherein, the Spirit of God spiritually speaketh of himself

---

2. endurance.   3. means.   4. spiritual.   5. encouraging.
6. pharmacists.   7. *after the bills:* according to the prescriptions.
8. prescriptions.   9. *kill up in corners:* kill privily, without notice.
1. ignorant.   2. reckless persons'.   3. suit.

to us, and biddeth us of all our health give him the honor, and therein thus saith unto us, *Honora medicum propter necessitatem enim ordinavit eum altissimus:* Honor thou the physician, for him hath the high God ordained for thy necessity.[4]

Therefore let us require[5] that high physician, our blessed Savior Christ, whose holy manhood[6] God ordained for our necessity to cure our deadly wounds with the medicine made of the most wholesome blood of his own blessed body, that likewise as he cured by that incomparable medicine our mortal malady, it may like[7] him to send us and put in our minds such medicines at this time, as against the sickness of sorrows and tribulations may so comfort and strength us in his grace as our deadly enemy the devil may never have the power by his poisoned dart of murmur, grudge, and impatience, to turn our short sickness of worldly tribulation into the endless, everlasting death of infernal damnation.

The Second Chapter

That for a foundation men must needs begin with faith.

Sith all our principal comfort must come of God, we must first presuppose in him to whom we shall with any ghostly counsel give any effectual[8] comfort one ground to begin withal, whereupon all that we shall build must be supported and stand; that is to wit, the ground and foundation of faith, without which had ready[9] before, all the spiritual comfort that any man may speak of can never avail[10] a fly. For likewise as it were utterly vain to lay natural reasons of comfort to him that hath no wit,[1] so were it undoubtedly frustrate to lay spiritual causes of comfort to him that hath no faith. For

---

4. Ecclus. 38:1.   5. ask.   6. manhood.   7. please.
8. effective.   9. *had ready:* possessed already.   10. benefit.
1. intelligence.

except a man first believe that holy scripture is the word of God, and that the word of God is true, how can a man take any comfort of that that the scripture telleth him therein? Needs must the man take little fruit of the scripture, if he either believe not that it were the word of God, or else ween[2] that though it were, it might yet be for all that untrue. This faith as it is more faint or more strong, so shall the comfortable words of holy scripture stand the man in more stead or less.[3] This virtue of faith can neither any man give himself, nor yet any one man another; but though men may with preaching be ministers unto God therein, and the man with his own free will, obeying freely the inward inspiration of God, be a weak worker with almighty God therein, yet is the faith indeed the gracious gift of God himself. For as Saint James saith, *Omne datum optimum et omne donum perfectum desursum est descendens a Patre luminum:* Every good gift and every perfect gift is given from above, descending from the Father of lights.[4] Therefore feeling our faith by many tokens very faint, let us pray to him that giveth it, that it may please him to help and increase it. And let us first say with him in the gospel, *Credo Domine, adjuva incredulitatem meam:* I believe, good Lord, but help thou the lack of my belief.[5] And after let us pray with the apostles, *Domine, adauge nobis fidem:* Lord, increase our faith.[6] And finally, let us consider, by Christ's saying unto them, that if we would not suffer[7] the strength and fervor of our faith to wax[8] lukewarm, or rather key-cold, and in manner[9] leese[1] his vigor by scattering our minds abroad about so many trifling things that of the matters of our faith we very seldom think, but that we would withdraw our thought fro the respect and regard of all worldly fantasies, and so gather our faith together into a little narrow room, and like the little grain of mustard seed, which is of nature hot, set it in the garden of our soul, all weeds pulled out for the better feeding of our faith. Then shall it grow, and so spread up in height that the birds—that is to wit, the holy angels of heaven—

---

2. suppose.   3. *stand . . . less:* benefit the man more or less.
4. James 1:17.   5. Mark 9:23.   6. Luke 17:5.   7. allow.
8. grow.   9. *in manner:* so to speak.   1. lose.

shall breed[2] in our soul, and bring forth virtues in the branches of our faith;[3] and then with the faithful trust that through the true belief of God's word we shall put in his promise, we shall be well able to command a great mountain of tribulation to void[4] from the place where he stood in our heart, whereas with a very feeble faith and a faint, we shall be scant[5] able to remove a little hillock.[6] And therefore, as for the first conclusion, as we must of necessity before any spiritual comfort presuppose the foundation of faith, so, sith no man can give us faith but only God, let us never cease to call upon God therefor.

Vincent

Forsooth, good uncle, me thinketh that this foundation of faith, which, as you say, must be laid first, is so necessarily requisite that without it all spiritual comfort were utterly given in vain. And therefore now shall we pray God for a full and a fast[7] faith. And I pray you, good uncle, proceed you farther in the process of your matter of spiritual comfort against tribulation.

Antony

That shall I, cousin, with good will.

The Third Chapter

The first comfort in tribulation may a man take in this: when he feeleth in himself a desire and longing to be comforted by God.

I will in my poor mind assign for the first comfort the desire and longing to be by God comforted, and not without some reason call I

2. dwell.   3. Luke 13:18–19.   4. withdraw.   5. scarcely.
6. Matt. 17:19–20 and Mark 11:21–23.   7. steadfast.

this the first cause of comfort. For like as the cure of that person is in a manner desperate[8] that hath no will to be cured, so is the discomfort of that person desperate that desireth not his own comfort.

And here shall I note you two kinds of folk that are in tribulation and heaviness—one sort that will seek for no comfort, another sort that will. And yet of these that will not are there also two sorts. For first one sort there are that are so drowned in sorrow that they fall into a careless, deadly dullness, regarding nothing, thinking almost on nothing, no more than if they lay on a lethargy, with which it may so fall that wit and remembrance will wear away and fall even fair[9] from them. And this comfortless kind of heaviness in tribulation is the highest kind of the deadly sin of sloth. Another sort are there that will seek for no comfort, nor yet none receive, but are in their tribulation (be it loss or sickness) so testy, so fumish, and so far out of all patience, that it booteth no man[1] to speak to them; and these are in a manner[2] with impatience so furious, as though they were half in a frenzy, and may with a custom of such fashioned behavior fall in thereto full and whole. And this kind of heaviness in tribulation is even a mischievous[3] high branch of the mortal sin of ire.

And then is there, as I told you, another kind of folk, which fain[4] would be comforted, and yet are they of two sorts, too. One sort are those that in their sorrow seek for worldly comfort, and of them shall we now speak the less, for the divers occasions that we shall after have to touch them in mo[5] places than one. But this will I here say that I learned of Saint Bernard: he that in tribulation turneth himself unto worldly vanities to get help and comfort by them, fareth like a man that in peril of drowning catcheth whatsoever cometh next to hand, and that holdeth he fast, be it never so simple a stick. But then that helpeth him not, for that stick he draweth

8. hopeless.   9. completely.
1. *it . . . man:* it is fruitless for anyone.
2. *in a manner:* so to speak.   3. calamitous.   4. gladly.
5. more.

down under the water with him, and there lie they drowned to-gether.[6] So surely if we custom ourself to put our trust of comfort in the delight of these peevish[7] worldly things, God shall for that foul fault suffer our tribulation to grow so great that all the pleasure of this world shall never bear us up, but all our peevish pleasure shall in the depth of tribulation drown with us.

The tother[8] sort is, I say, of those that long and desire to be comforted of God. And as I told you before, they have an undoubted great cause of comfort even in that point alone, that they consider themself to desire and long to be of almighty God comforted. This mind[9] of theirs may well be cause of great comfort[1] unto them for two great considerations. The one is that they see themself seek for their comfort where they cannot fail to find it. For God both can give them comfort and will. He can for he is almighty; he will for he is all good and hath promised himself, *Petite et accipietis:* Ask and you shall have.[2] He that hath faith (as he must needs have that shall take comfort) cannot doubt but God will surely keep this promise. And therefore hath he a great cause to be of good comfort, as I say, in that he considereth that he longeth to be comforted by him, which his faith maketh him sure he will not fail to comfort him.

But here consider this, that I speak here of him that in tribulation longeth to be comforted by God. And that is he that referreth the manner of his comforting to God, holding himself content, whether it be by taking away or minishment[3] of the tribulation itself, or by the giving of him patience and spiritual consolation therein. For him that only longeth to have God take his trouble fro him, we cannot so well warrant that mind for a cause of so great comfort; for both may he desire that that never mindeth[4] to be the better, and may miss also the effect of his desire, because his request is haply[5] not good for himself. And of this kind of longing and requiring we shall have occasion further to speak hereafter.

6. "In Adventu Domini," *Sermones de Tempore,* I, i (*PL 183,* 35).
7. foolish.   8. other.   9. intention.   1. consolation.
2. John 16:24.   3. diminishment.   4. intends.
5. perhaps.

But he that, referring the manner of his comfort unto God, desireth of God to be comforted, asketh a thing so lawful and so pleasant unto God that he cannot fail to speed;[6] and therefore hath he, as I say, great cause to take comfort in the very desire itself.

Another cause hath he to take of that desire a very great occasion of comfort. For sith[7] his desire is good and declareth unto himself that he hath in God a good faith, it is a good token unto him that he is not an abject,[8] cast out of God's gracious favor, while he perceiveth that God hath put such a virtuous well-ordered appetite in his mind. For as every evil mind cometh of the world and ourself and the devil, so is every such good mind, either immediately or by the mean[9] of our good angel or other gracious occasion, inspired into man's heart by the goodness of God himself. And what a comfort may then this be unto us, when we by that desire perceive a sure undoubted token, that toward our final salvation our Savior is himself so graciously busy about us.

The Fourth Chapter

That tribulation is a mean to draw man to that good mind, to desire and long for the comfort of God.

Vincent

Forsooth, good uncle, this good mind of longing for God's comfort is a good cause of great comfort indeed. Our Lord in tribulation send it us. But by this I see well that woe may they be which in tribulation lack that mind, and that desireth not to be comforted by God, but are either of[1] sloth or impatience discomfortless,[2] or of folly seek for their chief ease and comfort anywhere else.

6. attain his end.   7. since.   8. outcast.   9. means.
1. because of.   2. incapable of receiving comfort.

Antony

That is, good cousin, very true as long as they stand in that state. But then must ye consider that tribulation is yet a mean to drive him fro that state, and that is one of the causes for the which God sendeth it unto man. For albeit that pain was ordained of God for the punishment of sin (for which they that can never now but sin, can never be but ever punished in hell), yet in this world in which his high mercy giveth men space to be better, the punishment by tribulation that he sendeth serveth ordinarily for a mean of amendment. Saint Paul was himself sore[3] against Christ, till Christ gave him a great fall and threw him to the ground and struck him stark blind. And with that tribulation he turned to him at the first word, and God was his physician and healed him soon after both in body and soul, by his minister Ananias, and made him his blessed apostle.[4]

Some are in the beginning of tribulation very stubborn and stiff against God, and yet at length tribulation bringeth them home. The proud king Pharaoh did abide and endure two or three of the first plagues, and would not once stoop at[5] them, but then God laid on a sorer lash that made him cry to him for help. And then sent he for Moses and Aaron, and confessed himself for a sinner and God for good and righteous, and prayed them to pray for him and to withdraw that plague, and he would let them go. But when his tribulation was withdrawn, then was he nought[6] again. So was his tribulation occasion of his profit, and his help again cause of his harm; for his tribulation made him call to God, and his help made hard his heart again.

Many a man that in an easy tribulation falleth to seek his ease in the pastime of worldly fantasies findeth in a greater pain all these comforts so feeble that he is fain[7] to fall to the seeking of God's

3. extremely.   4. Acts 9:1–20. Cf. also Acts 22:4–16 and 26:9–18.
5. *stoop at:* bow before, give in to.
6. wicked. The allusion is to Exod. 7–9.   7. obliged.

help. And therefore is, as I say, the very tribulation itself many times a mean to bring the man to the taking of the afore-remembered comfort therein, that is to wit, to the desire of comfort given by God, which desire of God's comfort is, as I have proved you, great cause of comfort itself.

The Fifth Chapter

The special means to get this first comfort in tribulation.

Howbeit though the tribulation itself be a mean oftentimes to get man this first comfort in it, yet itself sometime alone bringeth not a man to it. And therefore, sith without this comfort first had, there can in tribulation none other good comfort come forth, we must labor the means that[8] this first comfort may come. And thereto seemeth me, that if the man of sloth or impatience or hope of worldly comfort have no mind to desire and seek for comfort of God, those that are his friends, that come to visit and comfort him, must afore all things put that point in his mind, and not spend the time, as they commonly do, in trifling and turning him to the fancies of the world. They must also move him to pray God to put this desire in his mind, which when he getteth once, he then hath the first comfort, and without doubt, if it be well considered, a comfort marvelous great. His friends also that thus counsel him must, unto the attaining thereof, help to pray for him themself, and cause him to desire good folk to help him to pray therefor. And then, if these ways be taken for the getting, I nothing doubt but the goodness of God shall give it.

8. *labor . . . that:* work for a way in which.

The Sixth Chapter

It sufficeth not that a man have a desire to be comforted by God only by the taking away of the tribulation.

Vincent

Verily me thinketh, good uncle, that this counsel is very good. For except[9] the person have first a desire to be comforted by God, else can I not see what can avail to give him any further counsel of any spiritual comfort. Howbeit, what if the man have this desire of God's comfort, that is to wit, that it may please God to comfort him in his tribulation by taking that tribulation from him? Is not this a good desire of God's comfort and a desire sufficient for him that is in tribulation?

Antony

No, cousin, that is it not. I touched before a word of this point, and passed it over because I thought it would fall in our way again, and so, wot[1] I well, it will ofter[2] than once. And now am I glad that ye move it me[3] here yourself.

A man may many times well and without sin desire of God the tribulation to be taken from him; but neither may we desire that in every case, not yet very well in no case (except very few), but under a certain condition either expressed or implied. For tribulations are, ye wot well, of many sundry kinds: some by loss of goods or possessions, and some by the sickness of ourself, and some by the loss of friends, or by some other pain put unto our bodies, some by the dread of the losing of those things that we fain[4] would save, under which fear fall all the same things that we have spoken before. For we may fear loss of goods or possessions, or the loss of our friends, their grief and trouble or our own, by sickness, impris-

9. unless.   1. know.   2. more often.
3. *move it me:* bring it up to me.   4. gladly.

onment, or other bodily pain; we may be troubled with the dread of death; and many a good man is troubled most of all with the fear of that thing which he that most need hath feareth least of all: that is to wit, the fear of losing through deadly sin the life of his silly[5] soul. And this last kind of tribulation is the sorest[6] tribulation of all. Though we touch here and there some pieces thereof before, yet the chief part and principal point will I reserve to treat apart effectually[7] that matter in the last end.[8]

But now, as I said, where the kinds of tribulations are so divers,[9] some of these tribulations a man may pray God to take from him, and take some comfort in the trust that God will so do. And therefore against hunger, sickness, and bodily hurt, and against the loss of either body or soul, men may lawfully many times pray to the goodness of God, either for themself or for their friend. And toward[1] this purpose are expressly prayed many devout orisons[2] in the common service of our mother, holy church. And toward our help in some of these things serve some of the petitions in the *pater noster,*[3] wherein we pray for our daily food, and to be preserved from the fall[4] in temptation, and to be delivered from evil.

But yet may we not alway[5] pray for the taking away from us of every kind of temptation. For if a man should in every sickness pray for his health again, when should he show himself content to die and depart unto God? And that mind[6] a man must have, ye wot well, or else it will not be well.

One tribulation is it unto good men to feel in themself the conflict of the flesh against the soul, the rebellion of sensuality against the rule and governance of reason, the relics[7] that remain in mankind of our old original sin of which Saint Paul so sore[8] complaineth in his epistle to the Romans.[9] And yet may we not pray

5. deserving of pity.   6. most grievous.
7. *apart effectually:* separately and explicitly.
8. *in . . . end:* in the last section of our discussion (Book III).
9. various.   1. in reference to, regarding.   2. prayers.
3. the Our Father.   4. lapse into sin.   5. always.
6. attitude.   7. surviving traces.   8. grievously.
9. Rom. 7–8.

while we stand[1] in this life to have this kind of tribulation utterly taken from us. For it is left us by God's ordinance to strive against it and fight withal, and by reason and grace to master it and use it for the matter of our merit.

For the salvation of our soul may we boldly pray; for grace may we boldly pray; for faith, for hope, and for charity, and for every such virtue as shall serve us to heavenward.[2] But as for all other things before remembered, in which is contained the matter of every kind of tribulation, we may never well make prayer so precisely, but that we must express or imply a condition therein: that is to wit, that if God see the contrary better for us, we refer it whole[3] to his will, and instead of our grief taken away, pray that God of his goodness may send us either spiritual comfort[4] to take it gladly, or strength at the least way[5] to take it patiently. For if we determine[6] with ourself that we will take no comfort in no thing but in the taking of our tribulation from us, then either prescribe we to God that we will[7] he shall no better turn do us, though he would, than we will ourself appoint him, or else do we declare that what thing is best for us ourself can better tell than he.

And therefore, I say, let us in tribulation desire this help and comfort, and let us remit[8] the manner of that comfort unto his own high pleasure, which when we do, let us nothing[9] doubt but that like as his high wisdom better seeth what is best for us than we can see ourself, so shall his sovereign goodness give us the thing that shall indeed be best. For else if we will presume to stand unto our own choice, except it so be that God offer us the choice himself, as he did to David in the choice of his own punishment after his high pride conceived in the numbering of his people,[1] we may foolishly choose the worse; and by the prescribing unto God ourself so precisely what we will that he shall do for us, except that of his gracious favor he reject our folly, he shall for indignation grant us our own request, and after shall we well find that it shall turn us to harm. How many men attain health of body, that were better for

---

1. remain.   2. *serve . . . heavenward:* help us in gaining heaven.
3. wholly.   4. strength, consolation.
5. *at . . . way:* at the very least.   6. decide.   7. desire.
8. resign.   9. not at all.   1. 2 Kings 24:1–16.

their soul-health their body were sick still? How many men get out of prison that hap[2] on such harms abroad as the prison should have kept them from? How many have there been, loath to leese[3] their worldly goods, [who] have in keeping of them soon after lost their life? So blind is our mortality, and so unware[4] what will fall, so unsure also what manner mind[5] we will ourself have tomorrow, that God could not lightly[6] do man a more[7] vengeance than in this world to grant him his own foolish wishes.

What wit have we poor fools to wit[8] what will serve us when the blessed apostle himself, in his sore tribulation praying thrice unto God to take it away from him, was answered again by God in a manner[9] that he was but a fool in asking that request, but that the help of God's grace in that tribulation to strength[1] him was far better for him than to take the tribulation from him. And therefore, by experience perceiving well the truth of that lesson, he giveth us good warning not to be too bold of our own mind when we require ought[2] of God, nor to be precise in our asking, but refer the choice to God as his own pleasure.[3] For his own Holy Spirit so sore desireth our weal that, as man might say, he groaneth for us in such wise as no tongue can tell. *Nos autem,* saith Saint Paul, *quid oremus ut oportet nescimus, sed ipse spiritus postulat pro nobis gemitibus inenarrabilibus:* What may we pray that were behovable[4] for us, cannot ourself tell, but the Spirit himself desireth for us with unspeakable groanings.[5]

And therefore I say for conclusion of this point: let us never ask of God precisely our own ease by delivery from our tribulation, but pray for his aid and comfort by which ways himself shall best like. And then may we take comfort even of our such request; for both are we sure that this mind cometh of God, and also be we very sure that as he beginneth to work with us, so, but if[6] ourself flit from him, he will not fail to tarry with us. And then, he dwelling with us,

2. happen.   3. lose.   4. unaware of.
5. *what . . . mind:* what sort of attitude.   6. easily.   7. greater.
8. know.   9. *in a manner:* in effect.   1. strengthen.
2. *require ought:* ask anything.   3. 2 Cor. 12:7–10.
4. advantageous.   5. Rom. 8:26.   6. unless.

what trouble can do us harm? *Si deus nobiscum quis contra nos:* If God
be with us, saith Saint Paul, who can stand against us?[7]

The Seventh Chapter

A great comfort it may be in tribulation, that every tribulation is (if we will ourself) a thing either medicinable,[8] or else more than medicinable.

Vincent

You have, good uncle, well opened and declared the question
that I demanded you, that is to wit, what manner[9] comfort a man
might pray for in tribulation. And now proceed forth, good uncle,
and show us yet further some other spiritual comfort in tribulation.

Antony

This may be, thinketh me, good cousin, great comfort in tribulation: that every tribulation which any time falleth unto us is either
sent to be medicinable, if men will so take it, or may become
medicinable, if men will so make it, or is better than medicinable,
but if we will forsake it.

Vincent

Surely this is very comfortable,[1] if we may well perceive it.

Antony

These three things that I tell you we shall consider thus. Every
tribulation that we fall in cometh either by our own known deserv-

7. Rom. 8:31.   8. possessed of healing properties.
9. kind of.   1. consoling.

ing deed bringing us thereunto, as the sickness that followeth our intemperate surfeit, or the prisonment or other punishment put upon a man for his heinous crime; or else it is sent us by God without any certain deserving cause open and known unto ourself, either for punishment of some sins passed, we certainly know not for which, or for preserving us from some sins in which we were else like to fall; or finally for no respect[2] of the man's sin at all, but for the profit of his patience and increase of his merit. In all the former causes, tribulation is (if we will) medicinable. In this latter case of all, it is yet better than medicinable.

The Eighth Chapter

The declaration larger concerning them that fall in tribulation by their own well-known fault, and that yet such tribulation is medicinable.

Vincent

This seemeth me very good, good uncle, saving that it seemeth somewhat brief and short, and thereby me thinketh somewhat obscure and dark.

Antony

We shall therefore, to give it light withal, touch every member[3] somewhat more at large.

One member is, ye wot well, of them that fall in tribulation through their own certain well-deserving deed open and known to themself, as where we fall in a sickness following upon our own gluttonous feasting, or a man that is punished for his own open fault. These tribulations, lo, and such other like, albeit that they may seem discomfortable in that a man may be sorry to think

2. consideration.   3. section.

himself the cause of his own harm, yet hath he good cause of comfort in them, if he consider that he may make them medicinable for himself, if himself will. For whereas there was due to that sin (except it were purged here) a far greater punishment after this world in another place, this worldly tribulation of pain and punishment by God's good provision for him put upon him here in this world before, shall by the mean of Christ's passion (if the man will in true faith and good hope by meek and patient sufferance of his tribulation so make it) serve him for a sure medicine to cure him and clearly discharge him of all his sickness and disease of those pains that else he should suffer after. For such is the great goodness of almighty God, that he punisheth not one thing twice. And albeit so that this punishment is put unto the man not of his own election and free choice, but so by force as he would fain[4] avoid it and falleth in it against his will, and therefore seemeth worthy no thank, yet so far passeth the great goodness of God the poor unperfect[5] goodness of man, that though men make their reckoning one here with another such, God yet of his bounty in man's account toward him alloweth it far otherwise. For though that a man fall in his pain by his own fault, and also first against his will, yet as soon as he confesseth his fault, and applieth his will to be content to suffer that pain and punishment for the same, and waxeth[6] sorry—not for that only that[7] he shall sustain such punishment, but for that also that he hath offended God and thereby deserved much more—our Lord from that time counteth it not for pain taken against his will, but it shall be a marvelous good medicine, and work as a willingly taken pain, the purgation and cleansing of his soul, with gracious remission of his sin and of the far greater pain that else had been prepared therefor, peradventure[8] forever in hell.

For many there are, undoubtedly, that would else drive forth[9] and die in their deadly sin, which yet in such tribulation, feeling

4. gladly.   5. imperfect.   6. grows.
7. *for . . . that:* only because.   8. perhaps.
9. *drive forth:* pass the time.

their own frailty so effectually,[1] and the false flattering world failing them so fully, turn goodly[2] to God and call for mercy, and by grace make virtue of necessity, and make a medicine of their malady, taking their trouble meekly, and make a right godly end.

Consider well the story of Achan, that committed sacrilege at the great city of Jericho; whereupon God took a great vengeance upon the children of Israel, and after told them the cause, and bade them go seek the fault and try it out by lots.[3] When the lot fell upon the very man that did it, being tried[4] by the falling first upon his tribe, and then upon his family, and then upon his house, and finally upon his person, he might well see that he was deprehended[5] and taken against his will. But yet at the good exhortation of Joshua saying unto him, *Fili mi da gloriam deo Israel, et confiteri et indica mihi quid feceris, et ne abscondas:* My own son, give glory to the God of Israel, and confess and show me what thou hast done and hide it not, he confessed humbly the theft and meekly took his death therefor,[6] and had, I doubt not, both strength and comfort in his pain, and died a very good man; which, if he had never come in the tribulation, had been in peril never haply[7] to have had just remorse thereof in all his whole life, but might have died wretchedly and gone to the devil eternally. And thus made this thief a good medicine of his well-deserved pain and tribulation.

Consider the well-converted thief that hung on Christ's right hand.[8] Did not he by his meek sufferance[9] and humble knowledge[10] of his fault, asking forgiveness of God and yet content to suffer for his sin, make of his just punishment and well-deserved tribulation a very good special medicine, to cure him of all the pain in the tother[1] world and win him eternal salvation? And thus I say that this kind of tribulation, though it seem the most base and the least comfortable, is yet (if the man will so make it) a very marvelous, wholesome medicine, and may therefore be to the man

1. powerfully.   2. fittingly.
3. *go . . . lots:* seek out the sin and discover who committed it by drawing lots.
4. ascertained.   5. detected.
6. Josh. 7:19.   7. perhaps.   8. See Luke 23:33, 39-43.
9. endurance.   10. acknowledgment.   1. other.

that will so consider it, a great cause of comfort and spiritual consolation.

The Ninth Chapter

The second point, that is to wit, that tribulation that is sent us by God without any open deserving cause known unto ourself; and that this kind of tribulation is medicinable if men will so take it and therefore great occasion of comfort.

Vincent

Verily, mine uncle, this first kind of tribulation have you to my mind opened sufficiently, and therefore I pray you resort now to the second.

Antony

The second kind was, ye wot[2] well, of such tribulation as is so sent us by God that we know no certain cause deserving that present trouble, as we certainly know that upon[3] such a surfeit we fell in such a sickness, or as the thief knoweth that for such a certain theft he is fallen into such a certain punishment.

But yet, sith[4] we seldom lack faults against God worthy and well deserving great punishment indeed, we may well think, and wisdom is so to do, that with sin we have deserved it, and that God for some sin sendeth it, though we certainly know not ourself for which. And therefore as yet thus far-forth[5] is this kind of tribulation somewhat in effect in comfort to be taken like unto the other. For this—as ye see if we will thus take it well, reckoning it to be sent for our sin and suffering it patiently therefore—is medicinable

2. know.   3. out of.   4. since.   5. far.

against the pain in the tother world to come, for our sins in this world passed, which is, as I showed you, a cause of right great comfort.

But yet may then this kind of tribulation be to some men of more sober living, and thereby of the more clear conscience, somewhat a little more comfortable, for though they may none otherwise reckon themselves than sinners (for as Saint Paul saith, *Nullius mihi conscius sum sed non in hoc justificatus sum:* My conscience grudgeth me not of any thing, but yet am I not thereby justified;[6] and Saint John saith, *Si dixerimus quia peccatum non habemus, ipsi nos seducimus, et veritas in nobis non est:* If we say that we have no sin in us, we beguile ourselves, and truth is there not in us[7]) yet forasmuch as the cause is to them not so certain as it is to the other afore-remembered in the first kind, and that it is also certain that God sometime sendeth tribulation for keeping and preserving a man fro such sin as he should else fall in, and sometime also for exercise of their patience and increase of merit, great cause of increase in comfort have these folk of the clearer conscience in the fervor of their tribulation, in that they may take the comfort of a double medicine, and of a thing also that is of the kind which we shall finally speak of, that I call better than medicinable. But as I have before spoken of this kind of tribulation, how it is medicinable in that it cureth the sin passed, and purchaseth remission of the pain due therefor, so let us somewhat consider how this tribulation sent us by God is medicinable, in that it preserveth us fro the sin into which we were else like to fall.

If that thing be a good medicine, that restoreth us our health when we leese[8] it, a good medicine must this needs be that preserveth our health while we have it, and suffereth[9] us not to fall into that painful sickness that must after drive us to a painful plaster.[1]

Now seeth God sometime that worldly wealth is, with one that is yet good, coming upon him too fast, that foreseeing how much weight of worldly wealth the man may bear, and how much will

6. 1 Cor. 4:4.   7. 1 John 1:8.   8. lose.
9. permits.   1. poultice.

overcharge[2] him and enhance[3] his heart up so high that grace should fall from him low, God of his goodness, I say, preventeth[4] his fall and sendeth his tribulation betime[5] while he is yet good, to gar[6] him to ken[7] his maker, and by less liking the false flattering world set a cross upon the ship of his heart, and bear a low sail thereon, that the boistous[8] blast of pride blow him not under the water.

Some young lovely lady, lo, that is yet good enough, God seeth a storm coming toward her that would (if her health and her fat feeding should a little lenger[9] last) strike her into some lecherous love, and instead of her old-acquainted knight, lay her abed with a new-acquainted knave. But God, loving her more tenderly than to suffer[1] her fall into such shameful beastly sin, sendeth her in season a goodly[2] fair fervent[3] fever, that maketh her bones to rattle, and wasteth away her wanton flesh, and beautifieth her fair fell[4] with the color of the kite's claw,[5] and maketh her look so lovely that her lover would have little lust[6] to look upon her, and maketh her also so lusty that if her lover lay in her lap,[7] she should so sore long to break unto him the very bottom of her stomach[8] that she should not be able to refrain it[9] from him, but suddenly lay it all in his neck.

Did not, as I before showed you,[1] the blessed apostle himself confess that the high revelations that God had given him might have enhanced[2] him into so high pride that he might have caught a foul fall, had not the provident goodness of God provided for his

---

2. overburden.   3. raise.   4. anticipates.
5. before it is too late.   6. make.   7. know.   8. violent.
9. longer.   1. allow.   2. splendid.   3. burning.   4. skin.
5. *color . . . claw:* i.e., whitish-yellow. The kite is a form of hawk, a scavenger and eater of dead flesh.   6. desire.
7. *lay . . . lap:* a common euphemism in the Renaissance for sexual intercourse.
8. *break . . . stomach:* to reveal one's inmost thoughts. More also uses the phrase to mean "vomit" at the same time that he glances at the sexual connotation (reveal to him the bottom of her stomach).
9. *refrain it:* keep it back.   1. See above, p. 23.   2. raised.

remedy? And what was his remedy but a painful tribulation, so sore[3] that he was fain[4] to call thrice to God to take the tribulation from him? And yet would God not grant his request, but let him lie so long therein till himself, that saw more in Saint Paul than Saint Paul saw in himself, wist[5] well the time was come in which he might well without his harm take it from him.[6]

And thus ye see, good cousin, that tribulation is double medicine: both a cure for the sin passed, and a preservative fro the sin that is to come. And therefore, in this kind of tribulation is there good occasion of a double comfort; but that is, I say, diversly[7] to sundry, divers folk, as their own conscience is with sin cumbered[8] or clear. Howbeit I will advise no man to be so bold as to think that their tribulation is sent them to keep them fro the pride of their holiness. Let men leave that kind of comfort hardily[9] to Saint Paul, till their living be like.[10] But of the remnant may men well take great comfort and good beside.

The Tenth Chapter

Of the third kind of tribulation, which is not sent a man for his sin, but for exercise of his patience and increase of his merit, which is better than medicinable.[1]

Vincent

The third kind, uncle, that remaineth now behind, that is to wit, which is sent a man by God, and not for his sin, neither committed nor which would else come, and therefore is not medicinable but sent for exercise of our patience and increase of our merit, and

3. grievous.   4. obliged.   5. knew.   6. 2 Cor. 12:1–10.
7. in various ways.   8. encumbered.   9. by all means.
10. *living be like:* lives be like St. Paul's.
1. possessed of healing properties.

therefore better than medicinable, though it be as you say (and as indeed it is) better for the man than any of the tother two kinds in another world where the reward shall be received, yet can I not see by what reason a man may in this world, where the tribulation is suffered, take any more comfort therein than in any of the tother twain that are sent a man for his sin, sith he cannot here know whether it be sent him for sins before committed or sin that else should fall,[2] or for increase of merit and reward after to come, namely[3] sith every man hath cause enough to fear and to think that his sin already passed hath deserved it, and that it is not without peril a man to think otherwise.

Antony

This that ye say, cousin, hath place of truth in far the most part of men, and therefore must they not envy nor disdain (sith they may take in their tribulation consolation for their part sufficient) that some other that more be worthy take yet a great deal mo.[4] For as I told you, cousin, though the best man must confess himself a sinner, yet be there many men (though to the multitude few) that for the kind of their living, and thereby the clearness of their conscience, may well and without sin have a good hope that God sendeth them some great grief for exercise of their patience and for increase of their merit, as it appeareth not only by Saint Paul in the place before remembered,[5] but also by that holy man Job, which in sundry places of his dispicions[6] with his burdenous[7] comforters letted[8] not to say that the clearness of his own conscience declared and showed unto himself that he deserved not the sore[9] tribulation that he then had.[1] Howbeit (as I told you before) I will not advise every man at adventure[2] to be bold upon this manner[3] of comfort. But yet some men know I such as[4] I durst,[5] for

---

2. *else should fall:* might otherwise happen.   3. particularly.
4. more.   5. 2 Cor. 12:1-10.   6. discussions.
7. burdensome.   8. hesitated.   9. grievous.
1. See Job 6, 23, 31.   2. *at adventure:* recklessly.   3. kind.
4. that.   5. dare.

their more ease and comfort in their great and grievous pain, put them in right good hope that God sendeth it unto them, not so much for their punishment as for exercise of their patience. And some tribulations are there also that grow upon[6] such causes, that in these cases I would never let,[7] but alway[8] would without any doubt give that counsel and comfort to any man.

Vincent

What causes, good uncle, be those?

Antony

Marry, cousin, wheresoever a man falleth in tribulation for the maintenance of justice or for the defense of God's cause. For if I should hap[9] to find a man that had long lived a very virtuous life, and had at last happened to fall into the Turk's hands, and there did abide by[1] the truth of his faith, and with the suffering of all kind of torments taken upon his body, still did teach and testify the truth, if I should in his passion[2] give him a spiritual comfort, might I be bold to tell him no further, but that he should take patience in this pain, and that God sendeth it him for his sin, and that he is well worthy to have it, although it were yet much more? He might well answer me and such other comforters as Job answered his, *Onerosi consolatores estis vos:* Burdenous and heavy comforters be you.[3] Nay, I would not fail to bid him boldly (while I should see him in his passion) cast sin and hell and purgatory and all upon the devil's pate, and doubt not but likewise as[4] if he gave over his hold all his merit were lost and he turned into misery, so if he stand and persevere still in the confession of his faith, all his whole pain shall turn all into glory.

Yea, more shall I yet say you than this: that if there were a

6. *grow upon:* arise from.   7. hesitate.   8. always.
9. chance.   1. *abide by:* remain true to.
2. suffering. In this context the word is also used to recall Christ's passion. Christ is traditionally believed to have been the first martyr.
3. Job 16:2.   4. that.

Christian man that had among those infidels committed a very deadly crime, such as were worthy death (not only by their law but by Christ's too, as manslaughter, adultery, or such other thing like), if when he were taken he were offered pardon of his life upon condition that he should forsake the faith of Christ, if this man would now rather suffer death than so do, should I comfort him in his pain but as[5] I would a malefactor? Nay, this man, though he should have died for his sin, dieth now for Christ's sake, while he might live still if he would forsake him. The bare[6] patient taking of his death should have served for the satisfaction of his sin, through the merit of Christ's passion, I mean, without help of which no pain of our own could be satisfactory. But now shall Christ, for his forsaking of his own life in the honor of his faith, forgive the pain of all his sins of his mere liberality,[7] and accept all the pain of his death for merit of reward in heaven, and shall assign no part thereof to the payment of his debt in purgatory, but shall take it all as an offering, and requite it all with glory. And this man among Christian men, all[8] had he been before a devil, nothing would I after doubt to take him for a martyr.

Vincent

Verily, good uncle, me thinketh this is said marvelous well; and it specially delighteth and comforteth me to hear it because of our principal fear that I first spake of, the Turk's cruel incursion into this country of ours.

Antony

Cousin, as for the matter of that fear, I purpose to touch last of all, nor I meant not here to speak thereof, had it not been that the vehemence of your objection brought it in my way. But rather would I else have put some sample[9] for this place of such as suffer tribulation for maintenance of right and justice, and that rather

5. *but as:* as.   6. mere.
7. *of . . . liberality:* out of his perfect generosity.
8. even if.   9. example.

choose to take harm than do wrong in any manner[10] of matter. For surely if a man may (as indeed he may) have great comfort in the clearness of his conscience, that hath a false crime put upon him, and by false witness proved upon him, and he falsely punished and put to worldly shame and pain therefor, an hundred times more comfort may he have in his heart that,[1] where white is called black and right is called wrong, abideth by the truth and is persecuted for justice.

Vincent

Then if a man sue me wrongfully for my land, in which myself have good right, it is a comfort yet to defend it well, sith[2] God shall give me thank therefor?

Antony

Nay, nay, cousin, nay, there walk ye somewhat wide,[3] for there you defend your own right for your temporal avail.[4] And sith Saint Paul counseleth, *Non vosmet defendentes charissimi:* Defend not yourselves, most dear friends,[5] and our Savior counseleth, *Si qui vult tecum in judicio contendere et tunicam tuam tollere dimitte ei et pallium:* If a man will strive with thee at law and take away thy coat, leave him thy gown too,[6] the defense therefore of our right asketh no reward. Say you speed well if ye get leave;[7] look hardily[8] for no thank. But, on the other side, if ye do as Saint Paul biddeth, *Quaerentes non quia sua sunt sed quia aliorum:* Seek not for your own profit but for other folks',[9] but defend therefore of pity a poor widow, or a poor fatherless child, and rather suffer sorrow by some strong extortion, than suffer them take wrong; or if ye be a judge and will have such zeal to justice that ye will rather abide[1] tribulation by the

10. kind.   1. who.   2. since.
3. *walk . . . wide:* you miss the point.   4. benefit.
5. Rom. 12:19.   6. Matt. 5:40.
7. *speed . . . leave:* attain your end if you be permitted.   8. certainly.
9. Cf. Phil. 2:4 and 1 Cor. 10:24. More's quotation is not exact.
1. put up with.

malice of some mighty man than judge wrong for his favor—such tribulations, lo, be those that are better than only medicinable. And every man upon whom they fall may be bold so to reckon them, and in his deep trouble may well say to himself the words that Christ hath taught him for his comfort, *Beati misericordes quia misericordiam consequentur:* Blessed be the merciful men, for they shall have mercy given them; *Beati qui persecutionem patiuntur propter justitiam, quoniam ipsorum est regnum caelorum:* Blessed be they that suffer persecution for justice, for theirs is the kingdom of heaven.[2] Here is an high comfort, lo, for them that are in the case. And in this case their own conscience can show it them, and so may fulfill their hearts with spiritual joy that the pleasure may far surmount the heaviness and the grief of all their temporal trouble. But God's nearer[3] cause of faith against the Turks hath yet a far passing[4] comfort, and by many degrees far excelleth this, which as I have said I purpose to treat last; and for this time this sufficeth concerning the special comfort that men may take in the third kind of tribulation.

The Eleventh Chapter

Another kind of comfort yet in the base kind of tribulation sent for our sin.

Vincent

Of truth, good uncle, albeit that every of these kinds of tribulation have cause of comfort in them, as ye have well declared, if men will so consider them, yet hath this third kind above all a special prerogative therein.

2. Matt. 5:7, 10.   3. more pertinent.
4. surpassing.

Antony

That is undoubtedly true. But yet is there not, good cousin, the most base kind of them all, but that yet hath mo causes of comfort than I have spoken of yet. For I have, ye wot[5] well, in that kind that is sent us for our sin spoken of no nother[6] comfort yet, but twain: that is to wit, one, that it refraineth[7] us from the sin that else we would fall in, and in that serveth us, through the merit of Christ's passion, as a mean[8] by which God keepeth us from hell, and serveth for the satisfaction of such pain as else we should endure in purgatory.

Howbeit there is therein another great cause of joy besides this. For surely these pains sent us here for our sins, in whatsoever wise they hap unto us, be our own sin never so sore,[9] nor never so open and evident unto ourself and all the world too, yet if we pray for grace to take it meekly and patiently, and, confessing to God that it is far over-little for our fault, beseech him yet nevertheless that sith we shall come hence so void of all good works whereof we should have any reward in heaven, to be not only so merciful unto us as to take that our present tribulation in release of our pain in purgatory, but also so gracious unto us as to take our patience therein for a matter of merit and reward in heaven, I verily trust and nothing doubt it but God shall of his high bounty grant us our boon. For likewise as in hell pain serveth only for punishment without any manner[1] of purging, because all possibility of purging is past and in purgatory punishment serveth for only purging because the place of deserving[2] is passed, so while we be yet in this world in which is our place and our time of merit and well-deserving, the tribulation that is sent us here for our sin shall, if we faithfully so desire, beside the cleansing and purging of our pain, serve us also for increase of reward.

And so shall I suppose[3] and trust in God's goodness all such

---

5. know.   6. other.   7. restrains.   8. means.   9. severe.
1. kind.   2. earning the right to reward.   3. believe as a fact.

penance and good works as a man willingly performeth enjoined[4]
by his ghostly[5] father in confession, or which he willingly further
doth of his own devotion beside. For though man's penance, with
all the good works that he can do, be not able to satisfy of themself
for the least sin that we do, yet the liberal goodness of God through
the merit of Christ's bitter passion (without which all our works
could neither satisfy nor deserve,[6] nor yet do not indeed neither
merit nor satisfy so much as a spoonful to[7] a great vessel full, in
comparison of the merit and satisfaction that Christ hath merited
and satisfied for us himself), this liberal goodness of God, I say,
shall yet at our faithful instance[8] and request cause our penance
and tribulation, patiently taken in this world, to serve us in the
tother[9] world both for release and reward tempered after such
rate[1] as his high goodness and wisdom shall see conveniently[2] for
us, whereof our blind mortality cannot here imagine nor devise the
stint.[3] And thus hath yet even the first kind of tribulation and the
most base, though not fully so great as the second, and very far less
than the third, far greater cause of comfort yet than I spake of
before.

The Twelfth Chapter

A certain objection against the things aforesaid.

Vincent

Verily, good uncle, this liketh[4] me very well, but yet is there, ye
wot well, some of these things now brought in question. For as for

4. when they are imposed.   5. spiritual.
6. be entitled to reward.   7. compared with.   8. entreaty.
9. other.
1. *tempered . . . rate:* made suitable according to whatever estimate.
2. appropriate.   3. *devise the stint:* gauge the amount.   4. pleases.

any pain due for our sins to be minished[5] in purgatory by the patient sufferance[6] of our tribulation here, there are, ye wot well, many that utterly deny that and affirm for a sure truth that there is no purgatory at all; and then is, if they say true, the cause of that comfort gone, if the comfort that we shall take[7] be but in vain and need not. They say, ye wot well also, that men merit nothing at all, but God giveth all for faith alone, and that it were sin and sacrilege to look for any reward in heaven, either for our patient and glad suffering for God's sake, or for any other good deed; and then is there gone, if this be thus, the tother cause of our further comfort too.

Antony

Cousin, if some things were as they be not, then should some things be as they shall not. I cannot indeed say nay but that some men of late[8] have brought up some such opinion, and many mo[9] than these beside, and have spread them abroad. And albeit that it is a right heavy thing to see such variance in our belief rise and grow among ourself to the great encouraging of the common enemies of us all, whereby they have our faith in derision and catch hope to overwhelm us all, yet do there three things not a little recomfort[1] my mind.

The first is that in some communications had of late together, hath appeared good likelihood of some good agreement to grow in one accord of our faith.[2]

The second, that in the meanwhile, till this may come to pass, contentions, dispicions,[3] with uncharitable behavior, is prohibited

5. diminished.
6. endurance.
7. receive.   8. recently.
9. more.   1. encourage.
2. The reference is vague, and More may intend the "communications" to be taken simply as mere rumors that never came to pass.
3. discussions.

and forboden[4] in effect upon all parties—all such parties, I mean, as fell before to fight for it.[5]

The third is that all Germany, for all their divers[6] opinions, yet as they agree together in profession of Christ's name, so agree they now together in preparation of a common power in defense of Christendom against our common enemy the Turk. And I trust in God that this shall not only help us here to strength[7] us in this war, but also that as God hath caused them to agree together in the defense of his name, so shall he graciously bring them to agree together in the truth of his faith.

Therefore will I let God work and leave off contention, and nothing shall I now say, but that with which they that are themself of the contrary mind shall in reason have no cause to be discontent. For first as for purgatory, though they think there be none, yet sith they deny not that all the corps of Christendom by so many hundred years have believed the contrary, and among them all the old interpreters of scripture from the apostles' days down to our own time, of whom they deny not many for holy saints, that I dare not now believe these men against all those, these men must of their courtesy hold my poor fear excused. And I beseech our Lord heartily for them that when they depart out of this wretched world, they find no purgatory at all, so God keep them from hell. And as for the merit of man in his good works, neither are they that deny it full agreed among themself, nor any man is there almost of them all, that sith he began to write, hath not somewhat changed and varied from himself. And far the more part are thus far agreed with us, that like as we grant them that no good work is ought worth to heavenward[8] without faith, and that no good work of man is

4. forbidden.
5. A reference perhaps to the Peace of Cadan (June 29, 1534), which reaffirmed the Peace of Nürnberg (1532) between the Emperor Charles V and the Protestant League of Schmalkalden. The Peace of Nürnberg called for an end to all war over religion and urged instead "true friendship and Christian charity."
6. various.   7. strengthen.
8. *ought . . . heavenward:* worth anything in gaining heaven.

rewardable in heaven of his[9] own nature, but through the mere [10] goodness of God that list[1] to set so high a price upon so poor a thing, and that this price God setteth through Christ's passion, and for that[2] also that they be his own works with us (for good works to Godward worketh no man without[3] God work with him), and as we grant them also that no man may be proud of his works for his own unperfect[4] working, and for that that in all that man may do he can do God no good, but is a servant unprofitable and doth but his bare duty;[5] as we, I say, grant unto them these things, so this one thing or twain do they grant us again: that men are bound to work good works if they have time and power, and that whoso worketh in true faith most, shall be most rewarded. But then set they thereto that all his reward shall be given him for his faith alone, and nothing for his works at all, because his faith is the thing (they say) that forceth him to work well. Strive will I not with them for this matter now, but yet this I trust to the great goodness of God, that if the question hang on that narrow point, while Christ saith in the scripture in so many places that men shall in heaven be rewarded for their works,[6] he shall never suffer our souls that are but mean-witted men, and can understand his words but as himself hath set them, and as old holy saints hath construed them before, and as all Christian people this thousand year have believed, to be damned for lack of perceiving such a sharp, subtle thing, specially sith[7] some men that have right good wits, and are beside that right well learned too, can in no wise[8] perceive for what cause or why these folk that fro good works take away the reward and give the reward all whole to faith alone, give the reward to faith rather than to charity. For this grant they themself, that faith serveth of[9] nothing but if she be companied[1] with her sister charity. And then saith the scripture too, *Fides, spes, charitas tria haec, major autem horum charitas:* Of the three virtues, faith, hope and charity, of all these three the greatest is charity,[2]

9. its.   10. absolute.   1. chooses.   2. *for that:* because.
3. unless.   4. imperfect.   5. Luke 17:10.
6. Cf. Mark 9:40; Matt. 5:3–11, 16:27, 25:31–46.   7. since.
8. way.   9. *serveth of:* counts for.
1. accompanied.   2. 1 Cor. 13:13.

and therefore as worthy to have the thank as faith. Howbeit, as I said, I will not strive therefor, nor indeed as our matter standeth, I shall not greatly need. For if they say that he which suffereth tribulation or martyrdom for the faith shall have his high reward, not for his work but for his well-working faith, yet sith they grant that have it he shall, the cause of the high comfort in the third kind of tribulation standeth. And that is, ye wot well, the effect[3] of all my purpose.

Vincent

Verily, good uncle, this is truly driven and tried out[4] to the uttermost as it seemeth me. I pray you proceed at your pleasure.

The Thirteenth Chapter

That a man ought to be comfortable to himself and have good hope and be joyful also in tribulation appeareth well by this: that a man hath great cause of fear and heaviness, that continueth alway still in wealth discontinued with[5] no tribulation.

Antony

Cousin, it were too long work to peruse every comfort that a man may well take in tribulation, for as many comforts, ye wot well, may a man take thereof as there be good commodities[6] therein, and that be there surely so many that it would be very long to rehearse and treat of them. But me seemeth we cannot lightly[7] better perceive what profit and commodity and thereby what comfort they may take of it that have it, than if we well consider what harm the lack is, and thereby what discomfort the lack thereof should be to them

---

3. fulfillment.   4. *driven . . . out:* deduced and ascertained.
5. *discontinued with:* interrupted by.   6. advantages.   7. easily.

that never have it. So it is now that all holy men agree, and all the scripture is full, and our own experience proveth at our eye that we be not come into this wretched world to dwell here, nor have not, as Saint Paul saith, our dwelling city here, but we be seeking for that city that is to come;[8] and therefore Saint Paul showeth us that we do seek for it, because he would put us in mind that we should seek for it, as they that are good folk and fain[9] would come thither do.

For surely whoso setteth so little thereby that he lusteth[1] not to seek therefor, it will be, I fear me, long ere he come thereat, and marvelous great grace if ever he come thither. *Sic currite*, saith Saint Paul, *ut comprehendatis*: Run so that ye may get it.[2] If it must then be gotten with running, when shall he come at it that list [3] not once to step toward it?

Now because this world is, as I tell you, not our eternal dwelling but our little while wandering, God would that we should in such wise use it as folk that were weary of it, and that we should in this vale of labor, toil, tears and misery not look for rest and ease, game, pleasure, wealth, and felicity. For they that so do fare like a fond[4] fellow that going toward his own house where he should be wealthy, would for a tapster's[5] pleasure become an hostler[6] by the way, and die in a stable and never come at home.

And would God that those that drown themself in the desire of this world's wretched wealth, were not yet more fools than so; but alas their folly as far passeth[7] the foolishness of that other fond fellow, as there is distance between the height of heaven and the very depth of hell. For as our Savior saith, *Vae vobis qui ridetis nunc, quia lugebitis et flebitis:* Woe may you be that laugh now, for you shall wail and weep.[8] *Est tempus flendi*, saith the scripture, *et est tempus ridendi:* There is time of weeping, and there is time of laughing.[9] But as you see, he setteth the weeping time before, for that is the time of this wretched world, and the laughing time shall come after in heaven. There is also a time of sowing and a time of reaping too.[1]

8. Heb. 13:14.   9. gladly.   1. desires.   2. 1 Cor. 9:24–25.
3. wishes.   4. foolish.   5. one who draws ale in a tavern.
6. stableman.   7. surpasses.   8. Luke 6:25.
9. Eccles. 3:4.   1. Eccles. 3:2.

Now must we in this world sow, that we may in the tother world reap. And in this short sowing time of this weeping world, must we water our seed with the showers of our tears, and then shall we have in heaven a merry laughing harvest forever. *Euntes ibant et flebant*, saith the prophet, *mittentes semina sua:* They went forth sowing their seeds weeping. But what saith he shall follow thereof? *Venientes autem venient cum exultatione portantes manipulos suos:* They shall come again more than laughing with great joy and exultation with their handfuls of corn in their hands.[2]

Lo, they that in their going home toward heaven sow their seeds with weeping shall at the day of judgment come to their bodies again with everlasting plentiful laughing. And for to prove that this life is no laughing time but rather the time of weeping, we find that our Savior himself wept twice or thrice,[3] but never find we that he laughed so much as once. I will not swear that he never did, but at the leastwise he left us no samples[4] of it, but on the other side he left us ensample of weeping. Of weeping have we matter enow[5] both for our own sins and other folks' too. For surely so should we do bewail[6] their wretched sins, and not be glad to detract[7] them nor envy them nother.[8] Alas, seely[9] souls, what cause is there to envy them, that are ever wealthy in this world and ever out of tribulation, which as Job saith, *Ducunt in bonis dies suos et in puncto ad inferna descendunt:* Lead all their days in wealth, and in a moment of an hour descend into their grave and be painfully buried in hell?[1] Saint Paul saith to the Hebrews that God those that he loveth he chastiseth; *Et flagellat omnem filium quem recipit:* And he scourgeth every son of his that he receiveth.[2] Saint Paul saith also, *Per multas tribulationes oportet nos introire in regnum dei:* By many tribulations must we go into the kingdom of God.[3] And no marvel, for as our Savior said of himself unto his two disciples that were going into the

2. Ps. 125:6.
3. John 11:35 and Luke 19:41. See also Heb. 5:7.   4. examples.
5. enough.   6. *do bewail:* lament.   7. disparage.   8. neither.
9. deserving of pity.   1. Job 21:13.   2. Heb. 12:6.
3. Acts 14:21.

castle[4] of Emmaus, *An nesciebatis quia oportebat Christum pati et sic introire in regnum suum:* Know you not that Christ must suffer and so go into his kingdom?[5] And would we that are servants look for more privilege in our master's house than our master himself?[6] Would we get into his kingdom with ease, when himself got not into his own but by pain? His kingdom hath he ordained for his disciples, and he saith unto us all, *Qui vult meus esse discipulus, tollat crucem suam et sequatur me:* If any man will be my disciple, let him learn at me to do as I have done, take his cross of tribulation upon his back and follow me.[7] He saith not here, lo, let him laugh and make merry.

Now if heaven serve but for Christ's disciples, and they be those that take their cross of tribulation, when shall these folk come there that never have tribulation? And[8] it be true that Saint Paul saith, that God chastiseth all them that he loveth, and scourgeth every child that he receiveth and to heaven shall none come but such as he loveth and receiveth, when shall they then come thither whom he never chastiseth, nor never do vouchsafe to file[9] his hands upon them and give them so much as one lash? And if we cannot, as Saint Paul saith we cannot, come to heaven but by many tribulations, how shall they come thither then that never have none at all?

Thus see we well by the very scripture itself, how true the words are of the old holy saints, that with one voice in a manner[10] say all one thing: that is to wit, that we shall not have both continual wealth in this world and in the tother[1] too. And therefore sith[2] that they that in this world without any tribulation enjoy their long continual course of never-interrupted prosperity, have a great cause of fear and of discomfort, lest they be far fallen out of God's favor and stand deep in his indignation and displeasure, while he never send them tribulation, which he is ever wont to send them whom he loveth—they therefore, I say, that are in tribulation have on the

4. village.   5. Luke 24:26.   6. John 15:19–20; Matt. 10:24–25.
7. A combination of Matt. 16:24 and Luke 14:27.   8. If.
9. *do . . . file:* be willing to defile.   10. sense.
1. other.   2. since.

tother side a great cause to take in their grief great inward comfort and spiritual consolation.

The Fourteenth Chapter
A certain objection and the answer thereto.

Vincent

Verily, good uncle, this seemeth so indeed. Howbeit, yet me thinketh that you say very sore[3] in some thing, concerning such persons as are in continual prosperity, and they be, ye wot[4] well, not a few. And those are they also that have the rule and authority of this world in their hand; and I wot well that when they talk with such great cunning[5] men as I trow[6] can tell the truth, and when they ask them whether, while they make merry here in earth all their life, they may not yet for all that have heaven after too, they do tell them, "Yes, yes well enough," for I have heard them tell them so myself.

Antony

I suppose, good cousin, that no very wise men, and specially none that very good is therewith, will tell any man fully of that fashion. But surely such as so say to them, I fear me that they flatter them either for lucre or fear. Some of them think peradventure[7] thus: "This man maketh much of me now, and giveth me money also to fast and watch and pray for him, but so I fear me would he do no more, if I should go tell him now that all that I do for him will not serve him, but if[8] he go fast and watch and pray for himself too. For if I should set thereto[9] and say further that my diligent intercession for him should, I trust, be the mean[1] that God should the

3. harshly.   4. know.   5. wise.   6. trust.   7. perhaps.
8. *but if:* unless.   9. *set thereto:* add to that.   1. means.

sooner give him grace to amend, and fast and watch and pray and take affliction in his own body for the bettering of his sinful soul, he would be wondrous wroth[2] with that; for he would be loath to have any such grace at all as should make him go leave off any of his mirth and so sit and mourn for his sin." Such mind[3] as this is, lo, have there some of those that are not unlearned and have worldly wit at will,[4] which tell great men such tales as perilously beguile them, rather than the flatterer that so telleth them would with a true tale jeopard[5] to lose his lucre.

Some are there also that such tales tell them for consideration of another fear: for seeing the man so sore[6] set on his pleasure that they despair any amendment of him whatsoever they should show him, and then seeing also besides that the man doth no great harm, but of a gentle[7] nature doth some good men some good, they pray God themself to send him grace. And so they let him lie lame still in his fleshly lusts, *ad probaticam piscinam expectantes aquae motum,* at the pool that the gospel speaketh of, beside the temple wherein they washed their sheep for the sacrifice, and they tarry to see the water stirred.[8] And when his good angel coming from God shall once begin to stir the water of his heart, and move him to the lowly meekness of a simple sheep, then if he call them to him they will tell him another tale, and help to bear him and plunge him into the pool of penance over the hard[1] ears. But in the meanwhile, for fear lest when he would wax[2] never the better, he would wax much the worse, and fro gentle, smooth, sweet, and courteous, wax angry, rough, froward, and sour, and thereupon be troublous[3] and tedious to the world—to make fair weather withal, they give him fair words for the while, and put him in good comfort,[4] and let him for the remnant[5] stand at his own adventure.[6] And in such wise[7] deal they with him as the mother doth sometime with her child, which when the little boy would not rise for her in time but lie still abed

2. angry.   3. an intention.   4. *at will:* at their disposal.
5. risk.   6. extremely.   7. well-born, belonging to the gentry.
8. John 5:2–4.   1. very.   2. become.   3. troublesome.
4. encouragement.   5. remainder.
6. *stand . . . adventure:* take his own chances.   7. a way.

and slug,[8] and when he is up weepeth because he hath lain so long, fearing to be beaten at school for his late coming thither, she telleth him it is but early days,[9] and he shall come time enough, and biddeth, "Go, good son, I warrant thee I have sent to thy master myself. Take thy bread and butter with thee. Thou shalt not be beaten at all." And so thus she may send him merry forth at door, that he weep not in her sight at home; she studieth not much upon the matter, though he be taken tardy and beaten when he cometh to school. Surely thus, I fear me, fare there many friars and state's chaplains[1] too, in comfort-giving to great men, when they be loath to displease them. I cannot commend their thus doing, but surely thus I fear me they do.

The Fifteenth Chapter

Other objections.

Vincent

But yet, good uncle, though that some do thus, this answereth not full the matter. For we see that the whole church in the common service use divers collects,[2] in which all men pray specially for the princes and prelates, and generally every man for other,[3] and for himself too, that God would vouchsafe to send them all perpetual health and prosperity. And I can see no good man pray God send another sorrow, nor no such prayers are there put in the priest's portas[4] as far as I can hear.

And yet if it were as you say, good uncle, that perpetual prosperity were to the soul so perilous, and tribulation thereto so fruitful,

8. be lazy.   9. *early days:* early in the day.
1. *state's chaplains:* chaplains to nobility.
2. The prayers in the mass, varying with the day, between the gloria and the epistle, as well as the secrets and post-communions.
3. the other.   4. breviary.

then were as me seemeth every man bound of charity, not only to pray God send their neighbors sorrow, but also to help thereto themself, and when folk are sick, not pray God send them health, but when they come to comfort them they should say, "I am glad, good gossip,[5] that ye be so sick. I pray God keep you long therein." And neither should any man give any medicine to other, nor take any medicine himself neither, for by the minishing[6] of the tribulation, he taketh away part of the profit from his soul, which can by no bodily profit be sufficiently recompensed.

And also this wot ye well, good uncle, that we read in holy scripture of men that were wealthy and rich and yet very good withal. Solomon was, ye wot well, the richest and wealthiest king that any man could in his time tell of, and yet was he well beloved with God.[7] Job was also no beggar, pardie,[8] nor no wretch otherwise, nor lost his riches and his wealth for that[9] God would not that his friend should have wealth, but for the show of his patience to the increase of his merit and confusion of the devil, and for proof that prosperity may stand with God's favor. *Reddidit deus Job omnia duplicia:* God restored him double of all that ever he lost, and gave him after long life to take his pleasure long.[1] Abraham was eke,[2] ye wot well, a man of great substance and so continued all his life in honor and in wealth. Yea, and when he died too, he went unto such wealth that Lazarus, which died in tribulation and poverty, the best place that he came to was that rich man's bosom.[3] Finally, good uncle, this we find at our eye, and every day we perceive it by plain experience, that many a man is right wealthy, and yet therewith right good, and many a man a miserable wretch, as evil as he is wretched. And therefore it seemeth hard, good uncle, that between prosperity and tribulation the matter should go thus: that tribulation should alway[4] be given by God to all those he loveth for a sign of salvation, and prosperity sent for displeasure as a token of eternal damnation.

5. friend.   6. diminishing.
7. See 3 Kings 10:14–29.   8. an oath: "by God."
9. *for that:* because.   1. Job 42:10, 16–17.   2. also.
3. Luke 16:22.   4. always.

The Sixteenth Chapter
The answer to the objections.

Antony

Either I said not, cousin, or else meant I not to say, that for an undoubted rule worldly pleasure were alway displeasant to God, or tribulation evermore wholesome to every man. For well wot I that our Lord giveth in this world unto every sort of folk either sort of fortune. *Et facit solem suum oriri super bonos et malos et pluit super justos et injustos:* He maketh his sun to shine both upon the good and the bad, and the rain to rain both upon the just and unjust.[5] And on the tother side *Flagellat omnem filium quem recipit:* He scourgeth every son that he receiveth.[6] And yet he beateth not only good folk that he loveth but *multa flagella peccatoris* too: there are many scourges for sinners also.[7]

He giveth evil folk good fortune in this world, both to call them by kindness, and if they thereby come not, the more is their unkindness.[8] And yet where wealth will not bring them he giveth them sometime sorrow. And some that in prosperity cannot to God creep forward, in tribulation they run toward him apace.[9] *Multiplicate sunt infirmitates eorum postea acceleraverunt:* Their infirmities were multiplied, saith the prophet, and after that they made haste.[1]

To some that are good men God showeth wealth here also, and they give him great thank for his gift, and he rewardeth them for that thank too. To some good folk he sendeth sorrow, and they thank him thereof too. If God should give the goods of this world only to evil folk, then would men ween[2] that God were not lord thereof. If God would give the goods only to good men, then would folk take occasion to serve him but for them. Some will in wealth fall to folly. *Homo cum in honore esset non intellexit comparatus est jumentis insipientibus, et similis factus est illis:* When man was in honor, his understanding failed him; then was he compared with beasts

5. Matt. 5:45.   6. Heb. 12:6.   7. Ps. 31:10.
8. unnatural conduct.   9. quickly.
1. Ps. 15:4.   2. think.

and made like unto them.[3] Some man with tribulation will fall into sin, and therefore saith the prophet, *Non relinquet dominus virgam peccatorum super sortem justorum ut non extendant justi ad iniquitatem manus suas:* God will not leave the rod of wicked men upon the lot of righteous men, lest the righteous peradventure hap[4] to extend and stretch out their hands to iniquity.[5]

So say I not nay, but that in either state, wealth or tribulation, may be matter of virtue and matter of vice also. But this is the point, lo, that standeth here in question between you and me: not whether every prosperity be a perilous token, but whether continual wealth in this world without any tribulation be a fearful sign of God's indignation. And therefore this mark[6] that we must shoot at set up well in our sight, we shall now mete for the shot,[7] and consider how near toward or how far off your arrows are from the prick.[8]

Vincent

Some of my bolts,[9] uncle, will I now take up myself, and prettily[1] put them under your belt again. For some of them I see well be not worth the meting,[2] and no great marvel though I shoot wide, while I somewhat mistake the mark.

Antony

These that make toward the mark and light far too short, when the shot is met[3] shall I take up for you. To prove that perpetual wealth should be no evil token, you lay first that for princes and prelates and every man for other,[4] we pray all for perpetual prosperity, and that in the common prayers of the church too. Then say you secondly that if prosperity were so perilous, and tribulation so profitable, every man ought then to pray God to send other sorrow.

3. Ps. 48:12, 20.   4. happen.   5. Ps. 124:3.   6. target.
7. *mete . . . shoot:* determine the success of the various shots by measuring the closeness of the arrows to the center of the target.
8. bull's eye.   9. arrows.   1. without fanfare.   2. measuring.
3. measured.   4. the other.

Thirdly ye further your objections with examples of Solomon, Job, and Abraham. And fourthly in the end of all, you prove by experience of our own time daily before our face, that some wealthy folk are good, and some needy very nought.[5] That last bolt, sith I lie the same myself,[6] you may be content to take up, it lieth so far wide.

Vincent

That will I with good will, uncle.

Antony

Well, do so then, cousin, and we shall mete for the remnant. First must you, cousin, be sure that you look well to the mark. And that can you not, but if ye know what thing tribulation is; for sith that is one of the things that we principally speak of, but if you consider well what thing that is, you may miss the mark again.

I suppose now that you will agree that tribulation is every such thing as troubleth and grieveth the man, either in body or in mind, and is as it were the prick of a thorn, a bramble, or a briar thrust into his flesh or into his mind. And surely, cousin, the prick that very sore[7] pricketh the mind, as far almost passeth[8] in pain the grief that paineth the body, as doth a thorn that sticketh in the heart, pass and exceed in pain the thorn that is thrust in the heel.

Now, cousin, if tribulation be this that I call it, then shall you soon consider this: that there be mo[9] kinds of tribulation than peradventure ye thought on before. And thereupon it followeth also, that sith every kind of tribulation is an interruption of wealth, prosperity, which is but of wealth another name, may be discontinued by mo ways than you would before have went.[1]

Then say I thus unto you, cousin, that sith tribulation is not only such pains as pain the body, but every trouble also that grieveth the mind, many good men have many tribulations that every man marketh not, and consequently their wealth interrupted therewith

---

5. wicked.
6. *sith . . . myself:* since I agree with you.   7. grievously.
8. surpasses.   9. more.   1. believed.

when other men are not ware.[2] For trow[3] you, cousin, that the temptations of the devil, the world, and the flesh soliciting the mind of a good man to sin, is not a great inward trouble and secret grief in his heart?

To such wretches as care not for their conscience but like unreasonable beasts follow their foul affections, many of these temptations be no trouble at all, but matter of their beastly pleasure. But unto him, cousin, that standeth in the dread of God, the tribulation of temptation is so painful that to be rid thereof or sure of the victory therein, be his substance never so great, he would gladly give more than half.

Now if he that careth not for God think this trouble but a trifle, and with such tribulation prosperity not interrupted, let him cast[4] in his mind if himself hap upon a fervent longing for the thing which get he cannot, and as a good man will not, as percase[5] his pleasure of some certain good woman that will not be nought,[6] and then let him tell me whether the ruffle[7] of his desire shall so torment his mind, as all the pleasure that he can take beside, shall for lack of that one, not please him of a pin. And I dare be bold to warrant him, that the pain in resisting and the great fear of falling, that many a good man hath in his temptation, is an anguish and a grief every deal as great as his.

Now say I further, cousin, that if this be true, as in very deed true it is, that such trouble is tribulation, and thereby consequently an interruption of prosperous wealth, no man precisely meaneth to pray for other[8] to keep him in continual prosperity without any manner[9] of discontinuance or change in this world; for that prayer, without any other condition added or implied, were inordinate and were very childish, for it were to pray that either they should never have temptation, or else that if they had, they might follow it and fulfill their affection.

Who dare, good cousin, for shame or for sin, for himself or any man else make this manner kind of prayer? Besides this, cousin,

2. aware.   3. suppose.   4. consider.
5. perchance.   6. unchaste.   7. perturbation.
8. any other man.   9. kind.

the church, ye wot[1] well, adviseth every man to fast, to watch and pray, both for taming of his fleshly lusts, and also to mourn and lament his sin before committed, and to bewail his offenses done against God, and as they did at the city of Nineveh,[2] and as the prophet David did,[3] for their sin put affliction unto their flesh. And when a man so doth, cousin, is this no tribulation to him because he doth it himself? For I wot well ye would agree that it were if another man did it against his will. Then is tribulation, ye wot well, tribulation still, though it be taken well in worth;[4] yea, and though it be taken with very right good will, yet is pain, ye wot well, pain, and therefore so is it though a man do it himself.

Then sith the church adviseth every man to take tribulation for his sin, whatsoever words you find in any prayer they never mean ye may be fast and sure, to pray God to keep every good man nor every bad man neither, from every manner kind[5] of tribulation.

Now he that is not in some kind of tribulation, as peradventure[6] in sickness or in loss of goods, is not yet out of tribulation if he have his ease of body or of mind inquieted,[7] and thereby his wealth interrupted with another kind of tribulation, as is either temptation to a good man, or voluntary affliction, either of body by penance or of mind by contrition and heaviness for his sin and offense against God.

And thus I say that for precise,[8] perpetual wealth and prosperity in this wretched world, that is to say, for the perpetual lack of all trouble and all tribulation, there is no wise man that either prayeth for himself or for any man else. And thus answer I your first objection.

Now before I meddle with your second, your third will I join unto this, for upon this answer will the solution of your ensamples[9] conveniently[1] depend. As for Solomon, [he] was, as you say, all his days a marvelous wealthy king, and much was he beloved with God,

1. know.   2. Jon. 3:6–9.   3. 2 Kings 12:1–24.
4. *taken . . . worth:* considered valuable.
5. *every . . . kind:* every kind of.
6. perhaps.   7. disquieted.   8. complete.
9. examples.   1. properly.

I wot well, in the beginning of his reign; but that the favor of God persevered with him as his prosperity did, that can I not tell. And therefore will I not warrant it. But surely we see that his continual wealth made him fall first into such wanton folly, in multiplying wives to an horrible number, contrary to the commandment of God given in the law by Moses, and secondly taking to wife among other such as were infidels, contrary to another commandment of God's written law also, that finally by the mean[2] of his miscreant[3] wife he fell into the maintenance of idolatry himself, and of this find we none amendment or repentance, as we find of his father.[4] And therefore though he were buried where his father was, yet whether he went to the rest that his father did, through some secret sorrow for his sin at last—that is to say, by some kind of tribulation—I cannot tell, and am therefore content to trust well, and pray God he did so. But surely we be not sure.[5] And therefore the ensample of Solomon can very little serve you, for you might as well lay it for a proof that God favored idolatry as that he favored prosperity, for Solomon was, ye wot well, in both.

As for Job, sith our question hangeth upon perpetual prosperity, the wealth of Job that was with so great adversity so sore[6] interrupted, can as yourself seeth serve you for no sample.[7] And that God gave him here in this world all thing double that he lost, little toucheth my matter, which did deny not prosperity to be God's gift and given to some good men too, namely[8] such as have tribulation too.

But Abraham, cousin, I suppose is all your chief hold, because

2. means.   3. unbelieving.

4. Solomon's wealth is recounted in 3 Kings 10:14–27, his early favor with God in 3 Kings 3:3–14, and his foreign wives in 3 Kings 11:1–2. In his old age he was corrupted by his wives and is said to have worshipped foreign gods (11:4–9). For the commandment forbidding marriage to foreign women, see Exod. 34:14–16 and Deut. 7:3–4.

5. The biblical accounts of Solomon break off before his death by saying that the rest of his deeds have already been recounted in other works. These works are no longer extant, hence More's doubts. See 3 Kings 11:43; 2 Par. 9:31.

6. grievously.   7. example.   8. especially

that you not only show riches and prosperity perpetual in him through the course of all his whole life in this world, but that after his death also Lazarus, the poor man that lived in tribulation and died for pure hunger and thirst, had after his death his place, comfort, and rest in Abraham the wealthy rich man's bosom. But here must you consider that Abraham had not such continual prosperity, but that yet it was discontinued[9] with divers tribulations. Was it nothing to him, trow ye, to leave his own country, and at God's sending, to go into a strange land, which God promised him and his seed forever, but in all his whole life he gave himself never a foot?[1]

Was it no trouble that his cousin Lot and himself were fain[2] to part company because their servants could not agree together?[3]

Though he recovered Lot again from the three kings, was his taking no trouble to him, trow you, in the meanwhile?[4]

Was the destruction of the five cities none heaviness to his heart? A man would ween yes, that readeth in the story what labor he made to save them.[5]

His heart was, I dare say, in no little sorrow when he was fain to let Abimelech the king have his wife; whom, though God provided to keep undefiled and turned all to wealth, yet was it no little woe to him for the meantime.[6]

What a continual grief was it to his heart many a long day, that he had no child of his own body begotten? He that doubteth thereof shall find it in Genesis of his own moan made unto God.[7]

No man doubteth but Ishmael was great comfort to him at his birth, and was it no grief then when he was cast out, the mother and the child both?[8]

Isaac that was the child of promission,[9] although God kept his life which was unlooked for, yet while the loving father bound him and went about to behead him and offer him up in sacrifice, who but himself can conceive what heaviness his heart had then?[1] I

9. interrupted.   1. Gen. 12:1.   2. obliged.   3. Gen. 13:5–11.
4. Gen. 14:1–16. More's reference to *three* kings is a mistake.
5. Gen. 18:22–23.   6. Gen. 20:1–16.   7. Gen. 15:2–3.
8. Gen. 16:1–16; 21:1–21.   9. promise.   1. Gen. 22:1–15.

would ween[2] in my mind, because you speak of Lazarus, that Lazarus' own death panged not him so sore.[3]

Then as Lazarus' pain was patiently borne, so was Abraham's taken not only patiently, but which is a thing much more meritorious, of obedience willingly. And therefore though[4] Abraham had not, as he did indeed, far excel Lazarus in merit of reward for many other things beside, and specially for that[5] he was a special patriarch of the faith, yet had he far passed him even by the merit of tribulation well taken here for God's sake, too. And so serveth for your purpose no man less than Abraham.

But now, good cousin, let us look a little lenger[6] here upon the rich Abraham and Lazarus the poor, and as we shall see Lazarus sit in wealth somewhat under the rich Abraham, so shall we see another rich man lie full low beneath Lazarus, crying and calling out of his fiery couch, that Lazarus might with a drop of water falling from his finger's end a little cool and refresh the tip of his burning tongue.[7]

Consider well now what Abraham answered to the rich wretch. *Fili recordare, quia recipisti bona in vita tua et Lazarus similiter mala nunc autem hic consolatur tu vero cruciaris:* Son, remember that thou hast in the life received wealth, and Lazarus in likewise pain, but now receiveth he comfort, and thou sorrow, pain, and torment.[8]

Christ describeth his wealth and his prosperity, gay and soft apparel, with royal delicate fare continually day by day. *Epulabatur,* saith our Savior, *quotidie splendide:* He did fare royally every day.[9] His wealth was continual, lo, no time of tribulation between. And Abraham telleth him the same tale, that he had taken his wealth in this world, and Lazarus in likewise his pain, and that they had now changed each to the clean contrary: poor Lazarus from tribulation into wealth, and the rich man from this continual prosperity into perpetual pain.

Here was laid expressly to Lazarus no very great virtue by name,[1]

2. suppose.   3. severely.
4. even if.   5. *specially for that:* especially because.
6. longer.   7. Luke 16:22–31.   8. Luke 16:25.
9. Luke 16:19.   1. *by name:* particularly.

nor to this rich glutton no great heinous crime, but the taking of his own continual ease and pleasure, without any tribulation or grief, whereof grew sloth and negligence to think upon the poor man's pain; for that ever himself saw Lazarus and wist him die[2] for hunger at his door, that laid neither Christ nor Abraham to his charge. And therefore, cousin, this story, lo, of which by occasion of Abraham and Lazarus you put me in remembrance, well declareth what peril is in continual worldly wealth, and contrariwise what comfort cometh of tribulation. And thus as your other samples of Solomon and Job nothing for the matter further you, so your ensample of the rich Abraham and poor Lazarus have not a little hindered you.

The Seventeenth Chapter
An answer to the second objection.

Vincent

Surely, uncle, you have shaken mine example sore,[3] and have in meting of your shoot[4] removed me these arrows, me think, farther from the prick[5] than me thought they stack[6] when I shot them; and I shall now be content to take them up again. But yet me seemeth surely that my second shaft may stand; for of truth if every kind of tribulation be so profitable that it be good to have it as you say it is: I cannot see wherefore any man should either wish or pray or any manner[7] thing do, to have any kind of tribulation withdrawn, either from himself or any friend of his.

---

2. *wist him die:* knew that he was dying.   3. severely.
4. *meting . . . shoot:* measuring the success of your shots.
5. bull's eye.   6. stuck.   7. kind of.

Antony

I think in very deed tribulation so good and so profitable, that I should haply[8] doubt as ye do, wherefore[9] a man might labor or pray to be delivered of it, saving that God which teacheth us the one teacheth us also the tother,[1] and as he biddeth us take our pain patiently, and exhort our neighbor to do also the same, so biddeth he us also not let[2] to do our devoir,[3] to remove the pain from us both. And then when it is God that teacheth both, I shall not need to break our brain in devising[4] wherefore he would bid us do both, the tone[5] seeming to resist the tother.

If he send the scourge of scarcity and great famine, he will[6] we shall bear it patiently, but yet would he that we should eat our meat when we can hap[7] to get it. If he send us the plague of pestilence, he will we shall patiently take it, but yet will he that we let us blood and lay plasters[8] to draw it, and rip it, and lance it, and so get it away. Both these points teacheth God in scripture in mo[9] than many places.

Fasting is better than eating, and more thank hath of God, and yet will God that we shall eat. Praying is better than drinking, and much more pleasant to God, and yet will God that we drink. Waking in good business is much more acceptable to God than sleeping, and yet will God that we shall sleep. God hath given us our bodies here to keep, and will that we maintain them to do him service with till he send for us hence. Now can we not surely tell how much tribulation may mar it, or peradventure hurt the soul also. Wherefore the apostle, after that he had commanded the Corinthians to deliver to the devil the abominable fornicator that forbare not[1] the bed of his own father's wife,[2] yet after that he had been awhile accursed and punished for his sin, the apostle commanded them charitably to receive him again, and give him conso-

8. perhaps.   9. why.   1. other.   2. hesitate.   3. duty.
4. wondering.   5. one.   6. wishes.   7. happen.
8. poultices.   9. more.   1. *forbare not:* did not refrain from.
2. 1 Cor. 5:1–5.

lation, *ut non a magnitudine doloris absorbeatur:* that the greatness of his sorrow should not swallow him up.[3]

And therefore when God sendeth the tempest, he will that the shipmen shall get them to their tackling and do the best they can for themself, that the sea eat them not up. For help ourself as well as we can, he can make his plague as sore[4] and as long lasting as himself list.[5] And as he will that we do for ourself, so will he that we do for our neighbor too, and that we shall in this world be each to other piteous and not *sine affectione*.[6] For which the apostle rebuketh them that lack their tender affections, so that of charity sorry should we be for their pains too, upon whom for cause necessary we be driven ourselves to put it.[7] And whoso saith that for pity of his neighbor's soul he will have none of his body, let him be sure that, as Saint John saith, he that loveth not his neighbor whom he seeth, loveth God but a little whom he seeth not.[8] So he that hath no pity on the pain that he feeleth his neighbor feel afore him, pitieth little, whatsoever he saith, the pain of his soul that he seeth not yet.

God sendeth us also such tribulation sometime because his pleasure is to have us pray unto him for help. And therefore when Saint Peter was in prison, the scripture showeth that the whole church without intermission prayed incessantly for him; and at their fervent prayer God by miracle delivered him.[9] When the disciples in the tempest stood in fear of drowning, they prayed unto Christ and said, *Salva nos domine perimus:* Save us, Lord, we perish; and then at their prayer he shortly ceased the tempest.[1] And now see we proved often that in sore[2] weather or sickness, by general proces-

---

3. 2 Cor. 2:7. More's identification of the fornicator mentioned in 1 Cor. 5 with the sinner referred to in this passage is dependent on tradition, such as the *Glossa Ordinaria* (*PL 114*, 553). They are no longer believed to be the same man.

4. severe.   5. wishes.

6. without feeling. The phrase is taken from 2 Tim. 3:3.

7. 2 Cor. 2:5–11.   8. 1 John 4:20.   9. Acts 12:1–11.

1. Matt. 8:25–26.   2. extreme.

sions[3] God giveth gracious help. And many a man in his great pain and sickness by calling upon God is marvelously made whole.

This is God's goodness, that because in wealth we remember him not but forget to pray to him, sendeth us sorrow and sickness to force us to draw toward him, and compelleth us to call upon him and pray for release of our pain, whereby when we learn to know him and seek to him, we take a good occasion to fall after into a further grace.

The Eighteenth Chapter

Of them that in tribulation seek not unto God, but some to the flesh and some to the world and some to the devil himself.

Vincent

Verily, good uncle, with this good answer am I well content.

Antony

Yea, cousin, but many men are there, with whom God is not content, which abuse this great high goodness of his, whom neither fair treating nor hard handling can cause them to remember their maker, but in wealth they be wanton, forget God, and follow their lust.[4] And when God with tribulation draweth them toward him, then wax they wood[5] and draw back all that ever they may, and rather run and seek help at any other hand, than to go fet[6] it at his. Some for comfort seek to the flesh, some to the world, and some to the devil himself.

3. i.e., the "extraordinary" processions of the church: a form of public supplication in time of great need or distress.
4. desire.   5. wax they wood: they become insane.
6. receive.

Some man that in worldly prosperity is very full of wealth, and hath deep stepped into many a sore[7] sin, which sins when he did them, he counted for part of his pleasure, God willing of his goodness to call the man to grace, casteth a remorse into his mind among[8] after his first sleep, and maketh him lie a little while and bethink him.[9] Then beginneth he to remember his life, and from that he falleth to think upon his death, and how he must leave all this worldly wealth within a while behind here in this world, and walk hence alone he woteth[1] not whither, nor how soon he shall take his journey thither, nor can tell what company he shall meet there. And then beginneth he to think that it were good to make sure and to be merry, so that we be wise therewith lest there hap to be such black bugs[2] indeed as folk call devils, whose torments he was wont to take for poets' tales.

Those thoughts, if they sink deep, are a sore[3] tribulation, and surely if he take hold of the grace that God therein offereth him, his tribulation is wholesome and shall be full comfortable[4] to remember that God by this tribulation calleth him and biddeth him come home out of the country of sin that he was bred and brought up so long in, and come into the land of behest[5] that floweth milk and honey. And then if he follow this calling (as many one full well doth) joyful shall his sorrow be, and glad shall he be to change his life, leave his wanton lusts, and do penance for his sins, bestowing his time upon better business.

But some men now when this calling of God causeth them to be sad, they be loath to leave their sinful lusts that hang in their hearts, and specially if they have any such kind of living as they must leave off or fall deeper in sin, or if they have done so many great wrongs that they have many amends to make that must (if they follow God) minish[6] much their money. Then are those folk, alas, woefully bewrapped,[7] for God pricketh upon them oft of his great goodness still, and the grief of this great pang pincheth them by the heart,

7. grievous. 8. occasionally. 9. *bethink him:* collect his thoughts.
1. knows. 2. *black bugs:* bogies, objects of terror. 3. severe.
4. encouraging. 5. *land of behest:* promised land.
6. diminish. 7. enveloped, involved.

and of wickedness they wry[8] away, and fro this tribulation they turn to their flesh for help and labor to shake off this thought. And then they amend[9] their pillow and lay their head softer and assay[1] to sleep; and when that will not be, then they find a talk awhile with them that lie by them; if that cannot be neither, then they lie and long for day, and then get them forth about their worldly wretchedness, the matter of their prosperity, the selfsame sinful things with which they displease God most. And at length with many times using this manner, God utterly casteth them off, and then they set nought neither by God nor devil. *Peccator cum in profundum venerit contemnit:* When the sinner cometh into the depth, then he contemneth[2] and setteth nought by no thing saving worldly fear that may fall by chance or that needs must, they wot well, fall once by death.

But alas, when death cometh, then cometh again their sorrow. Then will no soft bed serve, nor no company make him merry. Then must he leave his outward worship and comfort of his glory, and lie panting in his bed as he were on a pinebank.[3] Then cometh his fear of his evil life, and of his dreadful death. Then cometh the torment: his cumbered[4] conscience and fear of his heavy judgment. Then the devil draweth him to despair with imagination of hell and suffereth[5] him not then to take it for a fable. And yet if he do, then findeth it the wretch no fable. Ah, woe worth the while[6] that folk think not of this in time.

God sendeth to some man great trouble in his mind, and great tribulation about his worldly goods, because he would of his goodness take his delight and his confidence from them; and yet the man withdraweth no part of his fond[7] fantasies, but falleth more fervently to them than before, and setteth his whole heart like a fool more upon them. And then he taketh him all to the devices of his worldly counsellors, and without any counsel of God or any trust put in him, maketh many wise ways, as he weeneth,[8] and all

---

8. swerve.   9. rearrange.   1. try.   2. Prov. 18:3.
3. rack.   4. burdened.   5. allows.
6. *woe . . . while:* may evil befall the time.   7. foolish.   8. thinks.

turn at length to folly, and one subtle drift[9] driveth another to nought.

Some have I seen even in their last sickness, sit up in their deathbed underpropped with pillows, take their playfellows to them, and comfort themselves with cards. And this they said did ease them well to put fancies out of their head. And what fantasies, trow you? Such as I told you right now, of their own lewd[1] life and peril of their soul, of heaven and of hell, that irked them to think of, and therefore cast it out with cardsplay as long as ever they might, till the pure pangs of death pulled their heart fro their play, and put them in the case they could not reckon[2] their game. And then left them their gamners[3] and slyly slunk away, and long was it not ere they galped[4] up the ghost. And what game they came then to, that God knoweth and not I. I pray God it were good, but I fear it very sore.[5]

Some men are there also, that do as did King Saul: in their tribulation go seek unto the devil. This king had commanded all such to be destroyed as use the false abominable superstition of this ungracious witchcraft and necromancy.[6] And yet fell he to such folly afterward himself, that ere he went to battle, he sought unto a witch and besought her to raise up a dead man to tell him how he should speed.[7]

Now had God showed him before by Samuel that he should come to nought,[8] and he went about none amendment, but waxed worse and worse, so that God list not to look to him; and when he sought by the prophet to have answer of God, there came none answer to him, which thing he thought strange, and because he was not with God heard at his pleasure, he made suit to the devil, desiring a woman by witchcraft to raise up dead Samuel. But speed had he such thereof as commonly they have all that in their business meddle with such matters. For an evil answer had he and an evil speed thereafter, his army discomfit[9] and himself slain.[1] And as

9. scheme.   1. wicked.   2. pay attention to.   3. gamesters.
4. vomited; i.e., gave up the ghost, died.   5. severely.
6. 1 Kings 28:3, 9.   7. succeed.   8. 1 Kings 15:23, 28.
9. defeated.   1. 1 Kings 28:3–19.

it is rehearsed in Paralipomenon, the tenth chapter of the first book, one cause of his fall was for lack of trust in God, for which he left to take counsel of God and fell to seek counsel of the witch, against God's prohibition in the law, and against his own good deed by which he punished and put out all witches so late afore.[2] Such speed let them look for that play the same part, as I see many do, that in a great loss send to seek a conjuror to get their gear[3] again; and marvelous things there they see sometime, but never groat[4] of their good. And many fond fools are there that, when they be sick, will meddle with no physick[5] in no manner wise,[6] nor send his water to no cunning[7] man, but send his cap or his hose to some wise woman otherwise called a witch. Then sendeth she word again that she hath spied in his hose, where when he took none heed, he was taken with a spirit between two doors as he went in the twilight, but the spirit would not let him feel it in[8] five days after, and it hath the while festered in his body, and that is the grief that paineth him so sore.[9] But let him go to no leech-craft,[1] nor any manner physick other than good meat and strong drink, for syrups should sour him up; but he shall have five leaves of valerian, that she enchanted with a charm and gathered with her left hand. Let him lay those five leaves to his right thumb, not binded fast to, but let it hang loose thereat, by a green thread. He shall never need to change it, look it fall not away, but let it hang till he be whole, and he shall need no more.

In such wise witches and in such mad medicines have their souls more faith a great deal than in God. And thus, cousin, as I tell you, all these kind of folk in their tribulation call not upon God, but seek for their ease and help otherwise to the flesh and the world and to the flinging[2] fiend. The tribulation that God's goodness sendeth them for good, themself by their folly turn into their harm. And

---

2. *so . . . afore:* a short while before. Cf. 1 Par. 10:13.
3. property.   4. a particle. The groat was worth fourpence.
5. medical treatment.   6. *in . . . wise:* in no way.   7. learned.
8. before.   9. grievously.   1. medical treatment.
2. raging.

they that on the tother[3] side seek into God therein, both comfort and profit they greatly take thereby.

The Nineteenth Chapter

Another objection with the answer thereunto.

Vincent

I like well, good uncle, all your answer herein. But one doubt yet remaineth there in my mind which riseth upon this answer that you make, and that doubt soiled,[4] I will as for this time, mine own good uncle, encumber you no further; for me think I do you very much wrong to give you occasion to labor yourself so much, in matter of some study with long talking at once. I will therefore at this time move you[5] but one thing, and seek some other time for the remnant at your more ease.

My doubt, good uncle, is this. I perceive well by your answers gathered and considered together, that you will well agree that a man may both have worldly wealth and yet well go to God; and that on the tother side, a man may be miserable and live in tribulation and yet go to the devil. And as a man may please God by patience in adversity, so may he please God by thanksgiving in prosperity.

Now sith[6] you grant these things to be such, that either of them both may be matter of virtue or else matter of sin, matter of damnation or matter of salvation, they seem neither good nor bad of their own nature, but things of themself egall[7] and indifferent, turning to good or the contrary, after as[8] they be taken. And then if this be thus, I can perceive no cause why you should give the preeminence unto tribulation, or wherefore you should reckon more cause of comfort therein, than you should reckon to stand in prosperity, but rather a great deal less by in a manner[9] half; sith

---

3. other.   4. resolved.   5. *move you:* bring up.
6. since.   7. equal.
8. *after as:* according to the way in which.
9. *in a manner:* so to speak.

that in prosperity the man is well at ease, and may also by giving thank to God get good unto his soul, whereas in tribulation, though he may merit by patience (as in abundance of worldly wealth the tother may by thank), yet lacketh he much comfort that the wealthy man hath, in that he is sore[1] grieved with heaviness and pain; beside this also that a wealthy man, well at ease, may pray to God quietly and merrily with alacrity and great quietness of mind, whereas he that lieth groaning in his grief cannot endure to pray nor think almost upon nothing but upon his pain.

Antony

To begin, cousin, where you leave: the prayers of him that is in wealth and him that is in woe, if the men be both nought,[2] their prayers be both like. For neither hath the tone list[3] to pray nor the tother neither, and as the tone is let[4] with his pain, so is the tother with his pleasure, saving that the pain stirreth him sometime to call upon God in his grief though the man be right bad, where the pleasure pulleth his mind another way, though the man be meetly[5] good.

And this point I think there are few that can (if they say true) say that they find it otherwise. For in tribulation, which cometh, you wot well, in many sundry kinds, any man that is not a dull beast or a desperate wretch calleth upon God, not hoverly[6] but right heartily, and setteth his heart full whole upon his request, so sore[7] he longeth for ease and help of his heaviness. But when men are wealthy and well at their ease, while our tongue pattereth[8] upon our prayers apace,[9] good God, how many mad ways our mind wandereth the while.

Yet wot I well that in some tribulation, the while such sore[1] sickness there is, or other grievous bodily pain, that hard it were for a man to say a long pair of matins.[2] And yet some that lie a-dying

1. severely.   2. wicked.   3. desire.   4. hindered.   5. suitably.
6. lightly.   7. greatly.   8. recites rapidly and mechanically.
9. quickly.   1. severe.
2. the night office of the church, noted for its length. It consists of anywhere from twelve to eighteen psalms plus readings and responses. "Pair" is used in a collective sense, as in "a pair of trousers."

say full devoutly the seven psalms[3] and other prayers with the priest at their own aneling.[4] But those that for the grief of their pain cannot endure to do it, or that be more tender and lack that strong heart and stomach that some other have, God requireth no such long prayers of them; but the lifting up of their heart alone without any word at all is more acceptable to him of one in such case than long service so said as folk use[5] to say it in health. The martyrs in their agony made no long prayers aloud, but one inch of such a prayer, so prayed in that pain, was worth an whole ell[6] and more even of their own prayers prayed at some other time.

Great learned men say that Christ, albeit that he was very[7] God, and as God was in eternal, equal bliss with his Father, yet as man merited not for us only but for himself too. For proof whereof they lay in these words the authority of Saint Paul, *Christus humiliavit semetipsum factus obediens usque ad mortem, mortem autem crucis, propter quod et deus exaltavit illum, et donavit illi nomen quod est super omne nomen ut in nomine Jesu omne genu flectatur celestium terrestrium et infernorum, et omnis lingua confitiatur, quia dominus Jesus Christus in gloria est dei patris:* Christ hath humbled himself and become obedient unto the death, and that unto the death of the cross, for which thing God hath also exalted him and given him a name which is above all names, that in the name of Jesus every knee be bowed, both of the celestial creatures and the terrestrial, and of the infernal too, and that every tongue shall confess that our Lord Jesus Christ is in the glory of God his Father.[8]

Now if it so be as these great learned men upon such authority of holy scripture say, that our Savior merited as man, and as man deserved reward, not for us only but for himself also, then were there in his deeds, as it seemeth, sundry degrees and difference of

3. the seven penitential psalms, numbers 6, 31, 37, 50, 101, 129, and 142 in the Vulgate.
4. anointing; i.e., the sacrament of extreme unction.
5. are accustomed.
6. unit of length, roughly equivalent to one yard. More puns on "hell."
7. true.   8. Phil. 2:8–11.

deserving, and not his maundy like merit as his passion,[9] nor his sleep like merit as his watch and his prayer, no, nor his prayers peradventure[1] all of like merit neither, but though there none was nor none could be in his most blessed person, but excellent and uncomparable, passing the prayer of any pure creature, yet his own not all alike, but some one far above some other.

And then if it thus be, of all his holy prayers the chief seemeth me those that he made in his great agony and pain of his bitter passion. The first when he thrice fell prostrate in his agony, when the heaviness of his heart, with fear of death at hand so painful and so cruel as he well beheld it, made such a fervent commotion in his blessed body, that the bloody sweat of his holy flesh dropped down on the ground.[2] The tother were the painful prayers that he made upon the cross, where for all the torment that he hanged in, of beating, nailing and stretching out all his limbs, with the wresting of his sinews, and breaking of his tender veins, and the sharp crown of thorn so pricking him into the head that his blessed blood streamed down all his face. In all these hideous pains, in all their cruel despites,[3] yet two very devout and fervent prayers he made: the tone for their pardon that so despiteously put him to this pain, and the tother about his own deliverance, commending his own soul unto his holy Father in heaven.[4] These prayers of his, among all that ever he made, made in his most pain, reckon I for the chief. And these prayers of our Savior at his bitter passion, and of his holy martyrs in the fervor of their torment, shall serve us to see that there is no prayer made at pleasure so strong and effectual as in tribulation.

Now come I to the touching of the reason you make, where you tell me that I grant you that both in wealth and in woe some man may be nought and offend God, the tone by impatience, the tother by fleshly lust, and on the tother side both in tribulation and

9. *and not . . . passion:* i.e., Christ's washing of his apostles' feet (*maundy*) did not have the same degree of merit as his passion.

1. perhaps.

2. Matt. 26:36–44; Luke 22:44.   3. scorn.

4. Luke 23:34, 46.

prosperity too, some man may also do very well and deserve thank of God by thanksgiving to God, as well of his gift of riches, worship and wealth, as of need, penury, prisonment, sickness, and pain; and that therefore you cannot see for what cause I should give any preeminence in comfort unto tribulation, but rather allow prosperity for the thing more comfortable, and that not a little but in a manner by double, sith therein hath the soul comfort and the body both: the soul by thankgiving unto God for his gift, and then the body by being well at ease, where the person pained in tribulation taketh no comfort but in his soul alone.

First, as for your double comfort, cousin, you may cut off the tone.[5] For a man in prosperity, though he be bound to thank God of his gift wherein he feeleth ease, and may be glad also that he giveth thank to God, yet for that he taketh his ease here, hath he little cause of comfort, except that the sensual feeling of bodily pleasure, you list for to call by the name of comfort. Nor I say not nay but that sometime men use so to take it, when they say, "This good drink comforteth well my heart." But comfort, cousin, is properly taken by them that take it right, rather for the consolation of good hope, that men take in their heart, of some good growing toward them, than for a present pleasure with which the body is delighted and tickled for the while. Now though a man without patience can have no reward for his pain, yet when his pain is patiently taken for God's sake, and his will conformed to God's pleasure therein, God rewardeth the sufferer after the rate of his pain. And this thing appeareth by many a place in scripture, of which some have I showed you and yet shall I show you mo.[6] But never found I any place in scripture that I remember, in which, though the wealthy man thank God for his gift, our Lord promised any reward in heaven because the man took his ease and pleasure here. And therefore, sith I speak but of such comfort as is very comfort indeed, by which a man hath hope of God's favor and remission of his sins, with minishing[7] of his pain in purgatory or

5. first one.   6. more.   7. diminishing.

reward else in heaven, and such comfort cometh of tribulation and for tribulation well taken, but not for pleasure though it be well taken, therefore of your comfort that you double by prosperity, you may, as I told you, cut very well away the half.

Now why I give prerogative in comfort unto tribulation, far above prosperity, though a man may do well in both, of this thing will I show you causes two or three. For as I before have at length showed you, out of all question continual wealth interrupted with no tribulation is a very discomfortable[8] token of everlasting damnation; whereupon it followeth that tribulation is one cause of comfort unto a man's heart, in that it dischargeth him of the discomfort that he might of reason take of over long-lasting wealth.

Another is that scripture much commendeth tribulation, as occasion of more profit than wealth and prosperity, not to them only that are therein, but to them too that resort unto them. And therefore saith Ecclesiastes, *Melius est ire ad domum luctus quam ad domum convivii. In illa enim finis cunctorum admonetur homo, et vivens cogitat quid futurum sit:* Better it is to go to the house of weeping and wailing for some man's death, than to the house of a feast. For in that house of heaviness is a man put in remembrance of the end of every man, and while he yet liveth he thinketh what shall come after[9]. And yet he further saith, *Cor sapientium ubi tristitia est, et cor stultorum ubi laetitia:* The heart of wise men is thereas[1] heaviness is, and the heart of fools is thereas is mirth and gladness.[2] And verily thereas you shall hear worldly mirth seem to be commended in scripture, it is either commonly spoken as in the person of some worldly disposed people, or understonden[3] of rejoicing spiritual, or meant of some small moderate refreshing of the mind against an heavy discomfortable dullness.

Now whereas prosperity was to the children of Israel promised in the old law as a special gift of God, that was for their imperfection at that time, to draw them to God with gay things and pleasant,

8. discouraging.   9. Eccles. 7:3.   1. in the place where.
2. Eccles. 7:5.   3. understood

as men, to make children learn, give them cakebread[4] and butter; for as the scripture maketh mention, that people were much after the manner of[5] children in lack of wit and in waywardness,[6] and therefore was their master Moses called *pedagogus,* that is, a teacher of children, or as they call such one in the grammar schools, an usher[7] or a master of the petits.[8] For as Saint Paul saith, *Nihil ad perfectum duxit lex:* The old law brought nothing to perfection.[9]

And God also threateneth folk with tribulation in this world for sin, not for that[1] worldly tribulation is evil, but for that we should be well ware[2] of the sickness of sin for fear of that thing to follow, which, though it be indeed a very good wholesome thing, if we will well take it, is yet because it is painful the thing that we be loath to have.

But this I say yet again and again, that as for the far better thing in this world toward the getting of the very good that God giveth in the world to come, the scripture undoubtedly so commendeth tribulation that in respect and comparison thereof it discommendeth[3] this worldly wretched wealth and discomfortable comfort utterly. For to what other thing soundeth[4] the words of Ecclesiastes that I rehearsed[5] you now, that it is better to be in the house of heaviness than to be at a feast? Whereto soundeth this comparison of his, that the wise man's heart draweth thither as[6] folk are in sadness, and the heart of a fool is thereas he may find mirth? Whereto draweth[7] this threat of the wise man, that he that delighteth in wealth shall fall into woe?[8] *Risus,* saith he, *dolore miscebitur, et extrema gaudii luctus occupat:* Laughter shall be mingled with sorrow, and the end of mirth is taken up with heaviness.[9] And our Savior

---

4. bread made in flattened cakes.
5. *after . . . of:* of the same nature as.
6. Cf. Deut. 33:26–29; Exod. 32:9–14.
7. teacher acting under another.
8. schoolboys. See Gal. 3:24–25.   9. Heb. 7:19.
1. *for that:* because.   2. aware.
3. finds fault with.   4. refer.
5. repeated to.   6. *thither as:* to the place where.   7. tends.
8. Prov. 11:28.   9. Prov. 14:13.

saith himself, *Vae vobis qui ridetis quia lugebitis et flebitis:* Woe be to you that laugh, for you shall weep and wail.[1] But he saith on the tother side, *Beati qui lugent, quoniam illi consolabuntur:* Blessed be they that weep and wail, for they shall be comforted.[2] And he saith to his disciples, *Mundus gaudebit; vos autem dolebitis, sed tristitia vestra vertetur in gaudium:* The world shall joy and you shall be sorry, but your sorrow shall be turned into joy.[3] And so is it, ye wot well, now, and the mirth of many that then were in joy is now turned all to sorrow. And thus you see by the scripture plain, that in matter of very comfort tribulation is as far above prosperity as the day is above the night.

Another preeminence of tribulation over wealth in occasion of merit and reward shall well appear upon certain considerations well marked in them both. Tribulation meriteth in patience and in the obedient conforming of the man's will unto God, and in thanksgiving to God for his visitation. If you reckon me[4] now against these many other good deeds that a wealthy man may do, as by riches give alms, by authority labor in doing many men justice, or if you find further any such other thing like, first I say that the patient person in tribulation hath in all those virtues of a wealthy man an occasion of merit too, the which a wealthy man hath not againward[5] in the fore-rehearsed virtues of his; for it is easy for the person that is in tribulation to be well willing to do the selfsame if he could, and then shall his good will, where the power lacketh, go very near to the merit of the deed.

But now is not the wealthy man in a like case with the will of patience and conformity and thanks given to God for tribulation, sith it is not so ready[6] for the wealthy man to be content to be in the tribulation that is the occasion of the patient's desert,[7] as for the troubled to be content to be in prosperity to do the good deeds that the wealthy man doth.

Besides this, all that the wealthy man doth, though he could not

1. Luke 6:25.   2. Matt. 5:5.   3. John 16:20.
4. *reckon me:* estimate for me.   5. on the contrary.   6. likely.
7. *patient's desert:* patient man's merit.

do them without those things that are accounted for wealth and called by that name, as not do great alms without great riches, nor do those many men right by his labor without authority, yet may he do these things being not in wealth indeed, as where he taketh his wealth for no wealth, nor his riches for no riches, nor in heart setteth by neither nother,[8] but secretly liveth in a contrite heart and a life penitential, as many times did the prophet David, being a great king, so that worldly wealth was no wealth unto him. And therefore it is not of necessity worldly wealth to be cause of these good deeds, sith he may do them and doth them best indeed to whom the thing that worldly folk call wealth is yet, for his godly set mind drawn fro the delight thereof, no pleasure in manner[9] nor no wealth at all.

Finally, whensoever the wealthy man doth those good virtuous deeds (if we consider the nature of them right), we shall perceive that in the doing of them, he doth ever for the rate and portion[1] of those deeds, minish the matter of his worldly wealth; as in giving great alms, he departeth[2] with so much of his worldly goods which are in that part the matter of his wealth. In laboring about the doing of many good deeds, his labor minisheth his quiet and his rest, and for the rate of so much,[3] it minisheth his wealth, if pain and wealth be each to other contrary, as I ween[4] ye will agree they be.

Now whosoever then will well consider the thing, he shall, I doubt not, perceive and see therein in these good deeds that the wealthy man doth, though he doth it by that that his wealth maketh him able, yet in the doing of them he departeth, for the portion,[5] from the nature of wealth toward the nature of some part of tribulation. And therefore even in those good deeds themself that prosperity doth in goodness, the prerogative of tribulation above wealth appears. Now if it hap[6] that some man cannot perceive this

8. the one nor the other.   9. *in manner:* so to speak.
1. *for . . . portion:* according to the amount and portion. That is, the rich man diminishes his wealth to the extent that he uses it to do good deeds.
2. parts.   3. *for . . . much:* to that degree.   4. suppose.
5. *for the portion:* with regard to the part.   6. chance.

point, because the wealthy man for all his alms abideth rich still, and for all his good labor abideth still in his authority, let him consider that I speak but after[7] the portion. And because the portion of all that he giveth of his goods is very little in respect of that he leaveth, therefore is the reason haply with some folk little perceived, but if[8] it so were that he went forth with giving till he had given out all and left himself nothing, then would a very[9] blind man see it; for as he were from riches come to poverty, so were he from wealth willingly fallen into tribulation. And between labor and rest the reason goeth alike, which who can so consider shall see that for the portion in every good deed done by the wealthy man, the matter is all one. Then sith we have somewhat weighed the virtues of prosperity, let us consider on the tother side the afore-named things that are the matter of merit and reward in tribulation: that is to wit, patience, conformity, and thanks.

Patience, the wealthy man hath not in that he is wealthy; for if he be pinched in any point wherein he taketh patience, in that part he suffereth some tribulation, and so not by his prosperity but by his tribulation hath the man that merit. Like is it if we would say that if the wealthy man hath another virtue in the stead of patience, that is to wit, to keep himself from pride, and from such other sins as wealth would bring him to; for the resisting of such motions[1] is, as I before told you, without any doubt a minishing of fleshly wealth, and is a very true kind and one of the most profitable kinds of tribulation. So that all that good merit groweth to the wealthy man not by his wealth but by the minishing of his wealth with wholesome tribulation.

The most color[2] of comparison is in the tother twain,[3] that is to wit, in the conformity of man's will unto God, and in the thanksgiving unto God; for like as the good man in tribulation sent him by God, conformeth his will to God's will in that behalf, and giveth God thank therefor, so doth the wealthy man in his wealth which God giveth him conform his will to God's in that point, sith he is

7. according to.   8. *but if:* unless.   9. *a very:* even a.
1. inclinations.   2. plausible reason.   3. *tother twain:* other two.

well content to take it of his gift, and giveth God again also right
hearty thank therefor. And thus, as I said, in these two things may
you catch the most color to compare the wealthy man's merit with
the merit of tribulation. But yet that they be not matches you may
soon see by this; for in tribulation can there none conform his will
unto God's and give him thank therefor but such a man as hath in
that point a very special good mind.[4] But he that is very nought,[5] or
hath in his heart but very little good, may well be content to take
wealth at God's hand and say, "Marry,[6] I thank you sir for this with
all mine heart, and will not fail to love you well while you let me fare
no worse." *Confitebimur tibi cum benefeceris ei.*[7]

Now if the wealthy man be very good, yet in conformity of his will
and thanks given to God for his wealth, his virtue is not like yet to
his that doth the same in tribulation. For as the philosophers said in
that thing very well of old, virtue standeth in things of hardness
and difficulty.[8] And then, as I told you, much less hardness and less
difficulty there is, by a great deal, to be content and to conform our
will to God's will, and to give him thanks too for our ease than for
our pain, for our wealth than for our woe. And therefore is the
conforming of our will unto God's, and the thanks that we give him
for our tribulation, more worthy thank again, and more reward
meriteth in the very fast[9] wealth and felicity of heaven than our
conformity with our thanks given for and in our worldly wealth
here.

And this thing saw the devil when he said unto our Lord of Job,
that it was no marvel though Job had a reverent fear unto God—
God had done so much for him and kept him in prosperity. But the
devil wist[1] well that it was an hard thing for Job to be so loving and
so to give thanks to God in tribulation and adversity.[2] And therefore was he glad to get leave[3] of God to put him in tribulation, and

4. attitude.   5. wicked.   6. Indeed.
7. Ps. 48:19. "We will praise you when you help him out." The agreement
of the pronouns is confused. The Vulgate reads *Confitebitur.*
8. A common idea among a variety of philosophers. Cf. Seneca, *De Pro-
videntia,* V, 9–10 and Aristotle, *Nicomachean Ethics,* II, iii (1105a, 9–13).
9. steadfast.   1. knew.   2. Job 1:9–12.   3. permission.

thereby trusted to cause him murmur and grudge[4] against God with impatience. But the devil had there a fall in his own turn. For the patience of Job in the short time of his adversity gat[5] him much more favor and thank of God, and more is he renowned and commended in scripture for that than for all the goodness of his long prosperous life. Our Savior saith himself also, that if we say well by them or yield them thank that doth us good, we do no great thing therein, and therefore can we with reason look for no great thank again.[6]

And thus have I showed you, lo, no little preeminence that tribulation hath in merit, and therefore no little preeminence of comfort in hope of heavenly reward above the virtues, the merit, and cause of good hope and comfort that cometh of wealth and prosperity.

The Twentieth Chapter

A summary comfort of tribulation.

And therefore, good cousin, to finish our talking for this time, lest I should be too long a let[7] unto your other business, if we lay first for a sure ground a very fast faith, whereby we believe to be true all that the scripture saith, understanding truly as the old holy doctors declare it, and as the Spirit of God instructeth his catholic church, then shall we consider tribulation as a gracious gift of God: a gift that he specially gave his special friends; the thing that in scripture is highly commended and praised; a thing whereof the contrary long continued is perilous; a thing which, but if God send it, men have need by penance to put upon themself and seek it; a thing that helpeth to purge our sins passed; a thing that preserveth us fro sin that else would come; a thing that causeth us set less by

4. complain.   5. gained.
6. Luke 6:32–35; Matt. 5:44–47.
7. hindrance.

the world; a thing that exciteth us to draw more toward God; a thing that much minisheth[8] our pains in purgatory; a thing that much increaseth our final reward in heaven; the thing by which our Savior entered his own kingdom; the thing with which all his apostles followed him thither; the thing which our Savior exhorteth all men to; the thing without which, he saith, we be not his disciples; the thing without which no man can get to heaven.

Whoso these things thinketh on and remembereth well, shall in his tribulation neither murmur nor grudge, but first by patience take his pain in worth,[9] and then shall he grow in goodness and think himself well worthy. Then shall he consider that God sendeth it for his weal, and thereby shall he be moved to give God thank therefor.

Therewith shall his grace increase, and God shall give him such comfort by considering that God is in his trouble evermore near unto him. *Quia deus juxta est üs qui tribulato sunt corde:* God is near, saith the prophet, to them that have their heart in trouble, that his joy thereof shall minish much of his pain.[1] And he shall not seek for vain comfort elsewhere, but specially trust in God and seek for help of him, submitting his own will wholly to God's pleasure, and pray to God in his heart, and pray his friends to pray for him, and specially the priests, as Saint James biddeth.[2] And begin first with confession, and make us clean to God and ready to depart and be glad to go to God, putting purgatory in his pleasure. If we this do, this dare I boldly say: we shall neither live here the less of half an hour, but shall with this comfort find our hearts lighted,[3] and thereby the grief of our tribulation lessed,[4] and the more likelihood to recover and to live the lenger.[5] Now if God will, we shall hence; then doth he much more for us, for he that this way taketh cannot go but well. For of him that is loath to leave this wretched world, mine heart is much in fear lest he die not well. Hard it is for him to be welcome that cometh against his will, that saith unto God when he cometh to fetch him, "Welcome my maker, maugre my teeth."[6] But he that so loveth him that he longeth to go to him, mine

8. diminishes.   9. *take . . . worth:* consider his pain worthwile.
1. Ps. 33:19.   2. James 5:14.   3. cheered.   4. lessened.
5. longer.   6. *maugre my teeth:* in spite of everything I could do.

heart cannot give[7] me but he shall be welcome, all were it[8] so that he should come or[9] he were well purged. For charity covereth a multitude of sins,[1] and he that trusteth in God cannot be confounded.[2] And Christ saith, He that cometh to me I will not cast him out.[3] And therefore let us never make our reckoning of long life. Keep it while we may, because God hath so commanded, but if God give the occasion that with his goodness we may go, let us be glad thereof and long to go to him. And then shall hope of heaven comfort our heaviness, and out of our transitory tribulation shall we go to everlasting glory, to which, my good cousin, I pray God bring us both.

Vincent

Mine own good uncle, I pray God reward you. And at this time will I no longer trouble you. I trow[4] I have this day done you much tribulation with mine importune[5] objections of very little substance, and you have even showed me a sample[6] of sufferance[7] in bearing my folly so long and so patiently. And yet shall be so bold upon you further as to seek some time to talk forth of the remnant, the most profitable point of tribulation, which you said you reserved to treat of last of all.

Antony

Let that be hardily[8] very shortly, cousin, while this is fresh in mind.

Vincent

I trust, good uncle, so to put this in remembrance that it shall never be forgotten with me. Our Lord send you such comfort[9] as he knoweth to be best.

---

7. misgive.   8. *all were it:* even if it were.   9. before.
1. 1 Pet. 4:8.   2. Rom. 10:11 (where Paul paraphrases Prov. 29:25).
3. John 6:37.   4. believe.   5. importunate.
6. *a sample:* an example.   7. forbearance.
8. by all means.   9. spiritual consolation.

Antony

That is well said, good cousin, and I pray the same good for you, and for all our other friends that have need of comfort, for whom, I think, more than for yourself, you needed of some counsel.

Vincent

I shall with this good counsel that I have heard of you do them some comfort, I trust in God, to whose keeping I commit you.

Antony

And I you also. Farewell, mine own good cousin.

The Second Book

Vincent

It is to me, good uncle, no little comfort that, as I came in here, I heard of your folk[1] that you have had since my last being here (God be thanked) meetly[2] good rest, and your stomach[3] somewhat more come to you. For verily, albeit I had heard before that in respect of the great grief[4] that for a month space had holden you, you were a little before my last coming to you somewhat eased and relieved, for else would I not for no good have put you to the pain to talk so much as you then did; yet after my departing from you, remembering how long we tarried together, and that we were all that while in talking, and all the labor yours in talking so long together without interpausing between, and that of matter studious and displeasant, all of disease and sickness and other pain and tribulation, I was in good faith very sorry, and not a little wroth with myself for mine own oversight, that I had so little considered your pain. And very feared I was till I heard other word, lest you should have waxed[5] weaker and more sick thereafter. But now I thank our Lord that hath sent the contrary, for else a little casting back[6] were in this great age of yours no little danger and peril.

Antony

Nay, nay, good cousin. To talk much, except some other pain let[7] me, is to me little grief. A fond[8] old man is often so full of words as a

---

1. *of your folk:* from your servants. 2. fairly. 3. appetite.
4. illness. 5. become. 6. *casting back:* relapse. 7. prevent.
8. foolish.

woman. It is, you wot[9] well, as some poets paint us,[1] all the lust[2] of an old fool's life to sit well and warm with a cup and a roasted crab[3] and drivel and drink and talk.

But in earnest, cousin, our talking was to me great comfort, and nothing displeasant at all. For though we communed of sorrow and heaviness, yet was the thing that we chiefly thought upon not the tribulation itself, but the comfort that may grow thereon. And therefore am I now very glad that you be come to finish up the remnant.

Vincent

Of truth, my good uncle, it was comfortable to me and hath been since to some other of your friends, to whom as my poor wit[4] and remembrance would serve me, I did (and not needless[5]) report and rehearse[6] your most comfortable counsel. And now come I for the remnant, and am very joyful that I find you so well refreshed and so ready thereto. But yet this one thing, good uncle, I beseech you heartily, that if I for delight to hear you speak in the matter, forget myself and you both, and put you to too much pain, remember you your own ease and, when you list[7] to leave, command me to go my way and seek some other time.

Antony

Forsooth, cousin, many words, if a man were very weak, spoken (as you said right now) without interpausing, would peradventure[8] at length somewhat weary him. And therefore wished I the last time after you were gone, when I felt myself (to say the truth) even a little weary, that I had not so told you still a long tale alone, but that we had more often interchanged words, and parted the talk between us, with ofter enterparling[9] upon your part, in such man-

9. know.
1. Cf. Juvenal, *Sat. X,* 188–245 and Horace, *De Arte Poet.,* 169–76.
2. desire.   3. wild apple.   4. intelligence.   5. unnecessarily.
6. repeat.   7. choose.   8. perhaps.
9. *ofter enterparling:* more often sharing in the conversation.

ner as learned men use between the persons whom they devise disputing in their feigned dialogues. But yet in that point I soon excused you, and laid the lack even where I found it, and that was even upon mine own neck. For I remembered that between you and me, it fared as it did once between a nun and her brother.

Very virtuous was this lady, and of a very virtuous place, a close religion,[1] and therein had been long. In all which time she had never seen her brother, which was in likewise very virtuous too, and had been far off at an university, and had there take the degree of doctor in divinity. When he was come home, he went to see his sister, as he that highly rejoiced in her virtue. So came she to the grate that they call, I trow,[2] the locutory.[3] And after their holy watchword[4] spoken on both the sides, after the manner used in that place, the tone[5] took the tother by the tip of the finger, for hand would there none be wrongen[6] through the grate. And forthwith began my lady to give her brother a sermon of the wretchedness of this world, and the frailty of the flesh, and the subtle sleight[7] of the wicked fiend, and gave him surely good counsel (saving somewhat too long) how he should be well ware[8] in his living, and master well his body for saving of his soul. And yet ere her own tale came all at an end, she began to find a little fault with him and said, "In good faith, brother, I do somewhat marvel that you that have been at learning so long, and are a doctor and so learned in the law of God, do not now at our meeting (while we meet so seld[9]) to me that am your sister and a simple unlearned soul, give of your charity some fruitful exhortation, and as I doubt not but you can say some good thing yourself." "By my troth, good sister," quoth her brother, "I cannot for you, for your tongue have never ceased, but said enough for us both." And so, cousin, I remembered that when I was once fall[1] in, I left you little space to

1. *close religion:* cloistered religious order or house.
2. believe.
3. the "speaking place" or grate at which nuns of contemplative orders are allowed to speak to visitors.
4. customary greeting.   5. one.   6. squeezed.   7. trickery.
8. wary.   9. seldom.   1. drawn.

say aught between. But now will I therefore take another way with you, for I shall of our talking drive you to the tone half.

Vincent

Now forsooth, uncle, this was a merry tale. But now if you make me take the tone half, then shall you be contented far otherwise than there was of late a kinswoman of your own, but which will I not tell you—guess there and[2] you can. Her husband had much pleasure in the manner and behavior of another honest man, and kept him therefore much company, by the reason whereof he was at his mealtime the more oft from home. So happed it on a time that his wife and he together dined or supped with that neighbor of theirs. And then she made a merry quarrel to him, for making her husband so good cheer out at door that she could not have him at home. "Forsooth, mistress," quod he (as he was a dry, merry man), "in my company nothing keepeth him but one.[3] Serve you him with the same, and he will never be from you." "What gay thing may that be?" quoth our cousin then. "Forsooth, mistress," quod he, "your husband loveth well to talk, and when he sitteth with me I let him have all the words." "All the words?" quoth she. "Marry, that am I content he shall have all the words with good will as he hath ever had, but I speak them all myself, and give them all to him, and for aught that I care for them, so shall he have them still. But otherwise to say that he shall have them all, you shall keep him still rather than he get the half."

Antony

Forsooth, cousin, I can soon guess which of our kin she was.[4] I would we had none therein, for all her merry words, that less would let[5] their husbands for to talk.

---

2. if.   3. i.e., one thing.
4. Hallett (p. viii) sees this story as a personal anecdote involving More himself and his wife, Dame Alice.
5. hinder. The sense is obscure. Antony seems to be saying through the negative involutions that he wishes there were more women who would hinder their husbands less.

Vincent

Forsooth, she is not so merry but she is as good. But where you find fault, uncle, that I speak not enough, I was in good faith ashamed that I spake so much, and moved you such questions as I found upon your answer might better have been spared, they were so little worth. But now sith[6] I see you be so well content that I shall not forbear boldly to show my folly, I will be no more so shamefast,[7] but ask you what me list.

The First Chapter

Whether a man may not in tribulation use some worldly recreation for his comfort.

And first, good uncle, ere we proceed further, I will be bold to move[8] you one thing more of that we talked when I was here before. For when I revolved in my mind again the things that were here concluded by you, me thought you would in no wise[9] that in any tribulation men should seek for comfort either in worldly thing or fleshly, which mind,[1] uncle, of yours seemeth somewhat hard. For a merry tale with a friend refresheth a man much, and without any harm lighteth his mind[2] and amendeth his courage and his stomach,[3] so that it seemeth but well done to take such recreation. And Solomon saith, I trow, that men should in heaviness give the sorry[4] man wine to make him forget his sorrow.[5] And Saint Thomas saith[6] that proper pleasant talking, which is called $\epsilon\dot{v}\tau\rho\alpha\pi\epsilon\lambda\dot{\iota}\alpha$, is a good virtue, serving to refresh the mind and make it quick and lusty to labor and study again, where continual fatigation[7] would make it dull and deadly.

6. since.   7. bashful.   8. bring up with.
9. *would . . . wise:* in no way wished.   1. attitude.
2. *lighteth his mind:* raises his spirits.   3. disposition.   4. sorrowful.
5. Prov. 31:6–7.   6. See *Summa Theologica*, II–II, Q. 168, a. 2.
7. exhausting toil.

Antony

Cousin, I forgot not that point, but I longed not much to touch it. For neither might I well utterly forbear it where the case might hap to fall that it should not hurt. And on the tother side, if the case so should fall, me thought yet it should little need to give any man counsel to it. Folk are prone enough to such fancies of their own mind. You may see this by ourself, which coming now together to talk of as earnest sad matter as men can devise, were fallen yet even at the first into wanton[8] idle tales. And of truth, cousin, as you know very well, myself am of nature even half a giglet[9] and more. I would I could as easily mend my fault as I well know it. But scant can I refrain[1] it, as old a fool as I am; howbeit so partial will I not be to my fault as to praise it.

But for that you require[2] my mind in the matter, whether men in tribulation may not lawfully seek recreation, and comfort themself with some honest mirth: first agreed that our chief comfort must be of God, and that with him we must begin, and with him continue, and with him end also; a man[3] to take now and then some honest worldly mirth, I dare not be so sore[4] as utterly to forbid it, sith good men and well-learned have in some case allowed it, specially for[5] the diversity of divers men's minds. For else if we were all such as I would God we were, and such as natural wisdom would we should be, and is not all clean excusable that we be not indeed, I would then put no doubt but that unto any man the most comfortable talking that could be, were to hear of heaven; whereas now (God help us) our wretchedness is such, that in talking awhile thereof, men wax almost weary, and as though to hear of heaven were an heavy burden, they must refresh themself after with a foolish tale.

Our affection toward heavenly joys waxeth wonderful cold. If dread of hell were as far gone, very few would fear God, but that yet a little sticketh in our stomachs. Mark me, cousin, at the sermon, and commonly toward the end somewhat, the preacher speaketh

8. frivolous.   9. a person given to excessive merriment.
1. *scant . . . refrain:* scarcely . . . control.
2. *for . . . require:* because you ask.
3. i.e., in that case for a man, etc.   4. harsh.   5. because of.

of hell and of heaven. Now while he preacheth of the pains of hell, still they stand and yet give him the hearing, but as soon as he cometh to the joys of heaven, they be busking[6] them backward and flockmeale[7] fall away. It is in the soul somewhat as it is in the body. Some are there of nature or of evil custom come to that point, that a worse thing sometime more steadeth[8] them than a better. Some man, if he be sick, can away with no wholesome meat nor no medicine can go down with them, but if[9] it be tempered with some such thing for his fancy as maketh the meat or the medicine less wholesome than it should be. And yet while it will be no better, we must let him have it so.

Cassianus, that very good virtuous man, rehearseth[1] in a certain collation[2] of his, that a certain holy father in making of a sermon spake of heaven and of heavenly things so celestially that much of his audience with the sweet sound thereof began to forget all the world and fall asleep. Which when the father beheld, he dissembled[3] their sleeping and suddenly said unto them, "I shall tell you a merry tale." At which word they lift up their heads and hearkened unto that. And after the sleep therewith broken, heard him tell on of heaven again. In what wise[4] that good father rebuked then their untoward[5] minds, so dull unto the thing that all our life we labor for, and so quick and lusty[6] toward other trifles, I neither bear in mind nor shall here need to rehearse.[7] But thus much of that matter sufficeth for our purpose: that whereas you demand[8] me whether in tribulation men may not sometime refresh themself with worldly mirth and recreation, I can no more say but he that cannot long endure to hold up his head and hear talking of heaven, except he be now and then between (as though heaven were heaviness) refreshed with a foolish merry tale, there is none other

6. hastening.   7. in droves.   8. helps.   9. *but if:* unless.
1. relates.
2. discourse or treatise; also the title of a work by Cassian.
3. pretended not to notice.   4. way.   5. perverse.   6. vigorous.
7. The story is told not in the *Collationes,* but in Cassian's *De Coenobiorum Institutis,* V, 31 (*PL 49*, 247–48).
8. ask.

remedy, but you must let him have it. Better would I wish it but I cannot help it.

Howbeit let us, by mine advice, at the least wise make these kinds of recreation as short and seld[9] as we can. Let them serve us but for sauce and make them not our meat. And let us pray unto God, and all our good friends for us, that we may feel such a savor in the delight of heaven, that in respect of the talking of the joys thereof, all worldly recreation be but a grief to think on. And be sure, cousin, that if we might once purchase the grace to come to that point, we never of worldly recreation had so much comfort in a year, as we should find in bethinking us of heaven in less than half an hour.

Vincent

In faith, uncle, I can well agree to this, and I pray God bring us once to take such a savor in it. And surely as you began the tother day, by faith we must come to it, and to faith by prayer. But now I pray you, good uncle, vouchsafe[1] to proceed in our principal matter.

The Second Chapter

Of the short uncertain life in extreme age or sickness.

Antony

Cousin, I have bethought me somewhat of this matter since we were last together, and I find it (if we should go some way to work) a thing that would require many mo days to treat of, than we should haply[2] find meet[3] thereto in so few as myself ween[4] that I have now to live. While every time is not like[5] with me, and among many painful in which I look every day to depart, my mending days come

9. infrequent.   1. be willing.   2. perhaps.   3. appropriate.
4. think.   5. alike.

very seld and are very shortly gone. For surely, cousin, I cannot liken myself more meetly now than to the snuff[6] of a candle that burneth within the candlestick nose.[7] For as that snuff burneth down so low that who that looketh on it would ween it were quite out, and yet suddenly lifteth a leam[8] half an inch above the nose, and giveth a pretty, short light again, and thus playeth divers times till at last, or it be looked for,[9] out it goeth altogether: so have I, cousin, divers such days together, as every day of them I look even for to die; and yet have I then after that some such few days again as you see me now have yourself, in which a man would ween that I might it well continue. But I know my lingering not likely to last long, but out will my soul suddenly someday within a while. And therefore will I with God's help (seem I never so well amended)[1] nevertheless reckon every day for my last. For though that to the repressing of the bold courage of blind youth there is a very true proverb, that as soon cometh a young sheep's skin to the market as an old, yet this difference there is at the least between them: that as the young man may hap sometime to die soon, so the old man can never live long. And therefore, cousin, in our matter here, leaving out many things that I would else treat of, I shall for this time speak but of very few; howbeit hereafter if God send me mo[2] such days, then will we, when you list,[3] further talk of mo.

The Third Chapter

He divideth tribulation into three kinds, of which three the last he shortly passeth over.

All manner of tribulation, cousin, that any man can have, as far as for this time cometh to my mind, falleth under some one at the

6. wick.   7. socket.   8. flame.
9. *or . . . for:* before it is expected.   1. improved.   2. more.
3. wish.

least of these three kinds: either is it such as himself willingly taketh, or secondly such as himself willingly suffereth,[4] or finally such as he cannot put from him.

This third kind I purpose not much more to speak of now, for thereof shall as for this time suffice these things that we have treated between us this other day. What kind of tribulation this is I am sure yourself perceive. For sickness, imprisonment, loss of good,[5] loss of friends, or such bodily harm as a man hath already caught and can in no wise avoid: these things and such like are the third kind of tribulation that I speak of, which a man neither willingly taketh in the beginning, nor can, though he would, put willingly away. Now think I that as to the man that lacketh wit[6] and faith, no comfort can serve whatsoever counsel be given, so to them that have both, I have as to this kind said in manner enough already. And considering that suffer it needs he must, while he can by no manner of mean[7] put it from him, the very necessity is half counsel enough to take it in good worth[8] and bear it patiently, and rather of his patience to take both ease and thank than by fretting and by fuming to increase his present pain, and by murmur and grudge[9] to fall into further danger after, by displeasing of God with his froward[1] behavior. And yet, albeit that I think that that is said[2] sufficeth, yet here and there I shall in the second kind show some such comforts as shall well serve unto this last kind too.

The Fourth Chapter

The first kind also will I shortly pass.[3] For the tribulation that a man taketh himself willingly, which no man putteth upon him

---

4. endures.   5. property.   6. intelligence.
7. *by . . . mean:* by no means of any kind.
8. *take . . . worth:* consider it valuable.
9. complaint.   1. unruly.
2. *that that is said:* that what has been said.
3. *shortly pass:* treat only briefly.

against his own will, is, you wot[4] well, as I somewhat touched the last day, such affliction of the flesh or expense of his goods as a man taketh himself, or willingly bestoweth in punishment of his own sin and for devotion to God.

Now in this tribulation needeth the man none to comfort him. For while no man troubleth him but himself, which feeleth how farforth he may conveniently bear, and of reason and good discretion shall not pass[5] that (wherein if any doubt arise, counsel needeth,[6] and not comfort), the courage that for God's sake and his soul health kindleth his heart and inflameth thereto, shall by the same grace that put it in his mind, give him such comfort and such joy therein, that the pleasure of his soul shall pass the pain of his body. Yea, and while he hath in heart also some great heaviness for his sin, yet when he considereth the joy that shall come of it, his soul shall not fail to feel then that strange case which my body felt once in a great fever.

Vincent

What strange case was that, uncle?

Antony

Forsooth, cousin, even in this same bed—it is now more than fifteen years ago—I lay in a tertian[7] and had passed, I trow, three or four fits. But after fell there on me one fit out of course,[8] so strange and so marvelous that I would in good faith have thought it unpossible. For I suddenly felt myself verily both hot and cold throughout all my body, not in some part the tone[9] and in some part the tother (for that had been, you wot well, no very strange thing to feel the head hot while the hands were cold), but the selfsame parts, I say, so God save my soul, I sensibly felt, and right painfully too, all in one instant both hot and cold at once.

---

4. know.   5. surpass.   6. is needed.
7. a form of fever in which the onslaughts occur every third day.
8. sequence.   9. one.

Vincent

By my faith, uncle, this was a wonderful thing, and such as I never heard happen any man else in my days. And few men are there of whose mouths I could have believed it.

Antony

Courtesy, cousin, peradventure[1] letteth[2] you to say that you believe it not yet of my mouth neither. And surely, for fear of that, you should not have heard it of me neither, had there not happed me[3] another thing soon after.

Vincent

I pray you, what was that, uncle?

Antony

Forsooth, cousin, this: I asked a physician or twain that then looked unto me, how this should be possible, and they twain told me both that it could not be so, but that I was fallen in some slumber and dreamed that I felt it so.

Vincent

This hap[4] hold I little cause you[5] to tell the tale the more boldly.

Antony

No, cousin, that is true. Lo, but then happed there another, that a young girl here in this town, whom a kinsman of hers had begun to teach physic, told me that there was such a kind of fever indeed.[6]

---

1. perhaps.   2. prevents.   3. *happed me:* happened to me.
4. event.   5. i.e., for you.
6. According to Harpsfield (pp. 90–91), the fever was More's own, and the young girl was Margaret Giggs, More's adopted daughter.

Vincent

By our Lady, uncle, save for the credence of you, the tale would I not tell again upon that hap of the maid. For though I know her now for such as I durst well believe her, it might hap her very well at that time to lie, because she would ye should take her for cunning.[7]

Antony

Yea, but yet happed there another hap thereon, cousin, that a work of Galen, *De Differentiis Febrium*, is ready to be sold in the booksellers' shops, in which work she showed me then the chapter where Galen saith the same.[8]

Vincent

Marry, uncle, as you say, that hap happed well, and that maid had, as hap was, in that one point more cunning than had both your physicians beside, and hath, I ween, at this day in many points mo.

Antony

In faith, so ween I, too, and that is well wared[9] on her. For she is very wise and well-learned and very virtuous too.

But see now what age is, lo; I have been so long in my tale that I have almost forgotten for what purpose I told it. Oh now I remember, lo. Likewise I say, as myself felt my body then both hot and cold at once, so he that is contrite and heavy for his sin shall have cause to be and shall be indeed both sad and glad, and both twain at once, and shall do as I remember holy Saint Jerome biddeth, *Et doleas et de dolere gaudeas:* Both be thou sorry, saith he,

7. learned.

8. See Galen, *De Differentiis Febrium,* II, 6: "Of the fever called 'epiala.'" The Greek *editio princeps* of Galen was published at Venice by the Aldine Press in 1525. Margaret's husband, John Clement, helped edit the work, and More's reference is probably intended as a compliment to him as well as to Margaret.

9. *that . . . her:* that compliment is well spent upon her.

and be thou also of thy sorrow joyful.[1] And thus as I began to say, of comfort to be given unto him that is in this tribulation, that is to wit, in fruitful heaviness and penance for his sin, shall we none need to give, other than only to remember and consider well the goodness of God's excellent mercy, that infinitely passeth the malice of all men's sins, by which he is ready to receive every man, and did spread his arms abroad upon the cross lovingly to embrace all them that will come; and even there accepted the thief at his last end that turned not to God till he might steal no lenger;[2] and yet maketh more feast in heaven at one that fro sin turneth, than of four score and nineteen good men that sinned not at all.[3] And therefore of that first kind will I make no longer tale.

The Fifth Chapter

An objection concerning them that turn not to God till they come at the last cast.[4]

Vincent

Forsooth, uncle, this is unto that kind, comfort very great, and so great also that it may make many a man bold to abide in his sin even unto his end, trusting to be then saved as that thief was.

Antony

Very sooth you say, cousin, that some wretches are there such, that in such wise abuse the great goodness of God, that the better that he is the worse again be they. But, cousin, though there be more joy made of his turning that from the point of perdition cometh to salvation, for pity that God had and his saints all of the

---

1. The saying is not by Jerome; it appears in the *Liber de Vera et Falsa Poenitentia*, XIII, 28 (*PL 40*, 1124), formerly attributed to Augustine.
2. Luke 23:39–43.   3. Luke 15:4–7.
4. *at the last cast:* near to death.

peril of perishing that the man stood in, yet is he not set in like state
in heaven, as he should have been if he had lived better before,
except it so fall that he live so well after, and do so much good that
he therein outrun in the shorter time, those good folk that yet did
not so much in much lenger. As it proved in the blessed apostle
Saint Paul, which of a persecutor became an apostle, and last of all
came in into that office, and yet in the labor of sowing the seed of
Christ's faith outran all the remnant, and so farforth that he letted[5]
not to say of himself, *plus omnibus laboravi:* I have labored more
than all the remnant have.[6]

But yet, my cousin, though God, I doubt not, be so merciful unto
them that in any time of their life turn and ask his mercy and trust
therein, though it be at the last end of a man's life, and hireth him
as well for heaven that cometh to work in his vineyard toward
night, at such time as workmen leave work and go home, being
then in will to work if the time would serve, as he hireth him that
cometh in the morning,[7] yet may there no man upon the trust of
this parable be bold all his life to lie still in sin. For let him remember that into God's vineyard there goeth no man but he that is
called thither. Now he that in hope to be called toward night, will
sleep out the morning and drink out the day, is full likely to pass at
night unspoken to, and then shall he with shrewd[8] rest go supper-
less to bed.

They tell of one that was wont alway to say, that all the while he
lived he would do what he list.[9] For three words when he died
should make all safe enough. But then so happed it that long or[1] he
were old, his horse once stumbled upon a broken bridge, and as he
labored to recover him, when he saw it would not be, but down into
the flood headling[2] needs he should in a sudden flight, he cried out
in the falling, "Have all to the devil!" And there was he drowned
with his three words ere he died, whereon his hope hung all his
wretched life. And therefore let no man sin in hope of grace. Grace

5. hesitated.   6. 1 Cor. 15:10.   7. Matt. 20:1–16.   8. ill.
9. wished.   1. before.
2. headlong. For analogues to this story, cf. Caesarius of Heisterbach,
Dialogue of Miracles, V, xi–xii; Chaucer, *The Friar's Tale,* 1539–70.

cometh but at God's will, and that mind[3] may be the let[4] that grace
of fruitful repenting shall never after be offered him, but that he
shall either graceless go linger on careless, or with a care fruitless,
fall into despair.

The Sixth Chapter

An objection of them that say the tribulation of penance needeth not[5] but is a superstitious folly.

Vincent

Forsooth, uncle, in this point me thinketh you say very well. But
then are there some again that say on the tother side, that heaviness
for our sins we shall need none at all, but only change our intent
and purpose to do better, and for all that that is past take no
thought at all.

And as for fasting and other affliction of the body, they say we
should not do it, but only to tame the flesh when we feel it wax[6]
wanton and begin to rebel; for fasting, they say, serveth to keep the
body in temperance. But for to fast for penance, or to do any other
good work, almsdeed or other, toward satisfaction of our own sin,
this thing they call plain injury to the passion of Christ, by which
only are our sins forgiven freely without any recompense of our
own. And they that would do penance for their own sins, look to be
their own Christs and pay their own ransoms, and save their souls
themself. And with these reasons in Saxony many cast fasting off,
and all other bodily affliction, save only where need requireth to
bring the body to temperance; for other good they say can it none
do to ourself, and then to our neighbor can it do none at all. And
therefore they condemn it for superstitious folly.

Now heaviness of heart and weeping for our sins, this they

3. attitude.   4. hindrance.   5. *needeth not:* is not necessary.
6. grow.

reckon shame almost and womanish peevishness;[7] howbeit, thanked be God, their women wax there now so mannish that they be not so peevish nor so poor of spirit, but that they can sin on as men do, and be neither afeard nor ashamed, nor weep for their sins at all.

And surely, mine uncle, I have marveled the less ever since I heard the manner of their preachers there. For as you remember, when I was in Saxony, these matters were in manner[8] but in a mammering,[9] nor Luther was not then wedded yet,[1] nor religious men[2] out of their habit, but suffered were those that would be of the sect, freely to preach what they would unto the people. And forsooth, I heard a religious man there myself, one that had been reputed and taken for very good, and which as far as the folk perceived was of his own living somewhat austere and sharp. But his preaching was wonderful; me think I hear him yet, his voice was so loud and shirl,[3] his learning less than mean.[4] But whereas his matter was much part again fasting and all affliction for any penance, which he called men's inventions, he cried ever out upon them to keep well the laws of Christ, let go their peevish penance and purpose them to amend, and seek nothing to salvation but the death of Christ. "For he is our justice, and he is our Savior, and our whole satisfaction for all our deadly sins. He did full penance for us all upon his painful cross; he washed us there all clean with the water of his sweet side, and brought us out of the devil's danger with his dear precious blood. Leave, therefore, leave, I beseech you, these inventions of men, your foolish Lenten fasts and your peevish penance. Minish never Christ's thanks[5] nor look to save yourself. It is Christ's death, I tell you, that must save us all, Christ's death, I tell you yet again, and not our own deeds. Leave your own fasting, therefore, and lean to Christ alone, good Christian people, for Christ's dear bitter passion."

7. foolishness.   8. *in manner:* so to speak.
9. stuttering; i.e., in a state of doubt.   1. Luther married in June 1525.
2. *religious men:* those bound by monastic vows, monks or friars.
3. shrill.   4. average.
5. *Minish . . . thanks:* Do not diminish the gratitude due to Christ.

Now so loud and so shirl he cried Christ in their ears, and so thick he came forth with Christ's bitter passion, and that so bitterly spoken, with the sweat dropping down his cheeks, that I marveled not though I saw the poor women weep. For he made mine hair stand up upon mine head. And with such preaching were the people so brought in,[6] that some fell to break the fasts on the fasting days, not of frailty or of malice first, but almost of devotion, lest they should take fro Christ the thank of[7] his bitter passion. But when they were a while nuzzled[8] in that point first, they could endure and abide after many things mo, with which had he begun, they would have pulled him down.

Antony

Cousin, God amend that man whatsoever he be, and God keep all good folk fro such manner of preachers. Such one preacher much more abuseth the name of Christ and of his bitter passion than five hundred hazarders[9] that in their idle business swear and forswear themself by his holy bitter passion at the dice. They carry the minds of the people fro the perceiving of their craft,[1] by the continual naming of the name of Christ, and crying his passion so shirl into their ears.

They forget that the church hath ever taught them that all our penance without Christ's passion were not worth a pease.[2] And they make the people ween[3] that we would be saved by our own deeds without Christ's death, where[4] we confess that his only passion meriteth incomparable more for us than all our own deeds do. But his pleasure is that we shall also take pain our ownself with him. And therefore he biddeth all that will be his disciples take their crosses on their back as he did and with their crosses follow him.[5]

And where they say that fasting serveth but for temperance to tame the flesh and keep it from wantonness, I would in good faith

---

6. *brought in:* deceived.   7. *thank of:* gratitude for.   8. trained.
9. gamblers.   1. trickery.   2. pea, thing of little value.
3. believe.   4. whereas on the contrary.   5. Luke 9:23.

have went[6] that Moses had not been so wild, that for taming of his flesh he should have needed to fast whole forty days together.[7] No, nor Elijah neither.[8] Nor yet our Savior himself,[9] which began and the apostles followed and all Christendom have kept the Lenten forty days' fast that these folk now call so foolish. King Ahab was not disposed to be wanton in his flesh, when he fasted and went clothed in sackcloth and all besprent[1] with ashes.[2]

No, no more was in Nineveh the king and all the city, but they wailed and did painful penance for their sin, to procure God to pity them and withdraw his indignation.[3] Anna, that in her widowhead abode so many years with fasting and praying in the temple till the birth of Christ, was not, I ween, in her old age so sore disposed to the wantonness of her flesh, that she fasted all therefor.[4] Nor Saint Paul, that fasted so much, fasted not all therefor neither.[5]

The scripture is full of places that prove the fasting not to be the invention of man, but the institution of God, and that it hath many mo prophets than one. And that the fasting of one man may do good to another our Savior showeth himself, where he saith that some kind of devils cannot be by one man cast out of another, *nisi in oratione et jejunio:* without prayer and fasting.[6] And therefore I marvel that they take this way against fasting and other bodily penance.

And yet much more I marvel that they mislike the sorrow and heaviness and displeasure of mind that a man should take in forthinking[1] of his sin. The prophet saith, *Scindite corda vestra et non vestimenta:* Tear your hearts, saith he, and not your clothes.[2] And the prophet David saith, *Cor contritum et humiliatum deus non despicies:* A contrite heart and an humbled, that is to say, an heart broken, torn, and with tribulation of heaviness for his sin laid alow under foot, shall thou not, good Lord, despise.[3] He saith also of his own contrition, *Laboravi in gemitu meo, lavabo per singulas noctes lectum meum, lacrimis meis stratum meum rigabo:* I have labored in my

6. thought.   7. Exod. 34:28.   8. 3 Kings 19:8.
9. Luke 4:1–2.   1. besprinkled.   2. 3 Kings 21:27.
3. Jon. 3:6–9.   4. Luke 2:37.   5. 2 Cor. 11:27.
6. Mark 9:28.   1. repenting.   2. Joel 2:13.   3. Ps. 50:19.

wailing; I shall every night wash my bed with my tears, my couch will I water.[4]

But what should I need in this matter lay forth one place or twain? The scripture is full of those places by which it plain appeareth, that God looketh of duty[5] not only that we should amend and be better in the time to come, but also be sorry and weep and bewail our sins committed before. And all the old holy doctors be full and whole of that mind[6] that men must have for their sins contrition and sorrow in heart.

The Seventh Chapter

What if a man cannot weep, nor in his heart be sorry for his sins?

Vincent

Forsooth, uncle, yet seemeth me this thing somewhat a sore sentence,[7] not for that[8] that I think otherwise but that there is good cause and great wherefore a man so should, but for that of truth some man cannot be sorry and heavy for his sin that he hath done, though he never so fain[9] would. But though he can be content for God's sake to forbear it from thenceforth, yet for every sin that is past can he not only not weep, but some were haply[1] so wanton that when he happeth to remember them, he can scantly[2] forbear to laugh. Now if contrition and sorrow of heart be so requisite of necessity to remission, many a man should stand, as it seemeth, in very perilous case.

---

4. Ps. 6:7.   5. *looketh of duty:* considers it our duty.
6. *whole . . . mind:* completely of that opinion.
7. *sore sentence:* severe judgment.   8. *for that:* because.
9. gladly.   1. perhaps.   2. scarcely.

Antony

Many so should indeed, cousin, and indeed many so do, and the old saints write very sore in this point. Howbeit, *Misericordia domini super omnia opera ejus:* The mercy of God is above all his works,[3] and he standeth not bounden unto common rule; *Et ipse cognovit figmentum suum, et propiciatur infirmitatibus nostris:* And he knoweth the frailty of his earthen vessel that is of his own making, and is merciful and hath pity upon our feeble infirmities,[4] and shall not exact of us above the thing that we may do.

But yet, cousin, he that findeth himself in that case, in that he is minded to do well hereafter, let him give God thank that he is no worse, but in that he cannot be sorry for his sin passed, let him be sorry hardily[5] that he is no better. And as Saint Jerome biddeth him that for his sin sorroweth in his heart, be glad and rejoice in his sorrow,[6] so would I counsel him that cannot be sad for his sin, to be sorry yet at the least that he cannot be sorry. Besides this, though I would in no wise[7] any man should despair, yet would I counsel such a man while that affection[8] lasteth not to be too bold of courage, but live in double fear. First, for it is a token either of faint faith or of a dull diligence. For surely if we well believe in God, and therewith deeply consider his majesty, with the peril of our sin and the great goodness of God also, either should dread make us tremble and break our stony heart, or love should for sorrow relent[9] it into tears.

Besides this, sith[1] I can scant believe but sith so little misliking of our old sin is an affection not very pure and clean, and none unclean thing shall enter into heaven,[2] cleansed shall it be and purified before that we come there. And therefore would I further

---

3. Ps. 144:9.

4. Ps. 102, a combination of verses 14 and 3.

5. by all means.

6. The attribution to Jerome is incorrect. See above, pp. 93–94 and p. 94, n. 1.

7. *though . . . wise:* though I would not wish in any way.

8. state of mind.   9. soften.   1. since.   2. Rev. 21:27.

advise one in that case the counsel which Master Gerson[3] giveth every man: that sith the body and the soul together make the whole man, the less affliction that he feeleth in his soul, the more pain in recompense let him put upon his body, and purge the spirit by the affliction of the flesh. And he that so doth, I dare lay my life, shall have his hard heart after relent into tears, and his soul in an wholesome heaviness and heavenly gladness too, specially if (which must be joined with every good thing) he join faithful prayer therewith.

But, cousin, as I told you the tother[4] day before, in these matters with these new men[5] I will not dispute. But surely for mine own part I cannot well hold with them, for as far as mine own poor wit[6] can perceive, the holy scripture of God is very plain against them. And the whole corps of Christendom in every Christian region, and the very places in which they dwell themself, have ever unto their own days clearly believed against them. And all the old holy doctors have evermore taught against them; and all the old holy interpreters have construed the scripture against them. And therefore if these men have now perceived so late that the scripture hath be misunderstanden all this while, and that of all those old holy doctors no man could understand it, then am I too old at this age to begin to study it now. And trust these men's cunning,[7] cousin, that dare I not in no wise, sith I cannot see nor perceive no cause wherefore I should think that these men might not now in the understanding of scripture as well be deceived themself as they bear us in hand[8] that all those other have been all this while before.

Howbeit, cousin, if it so be that their way be not wrong, but that they have found out so easy a way to heaven, as to take no thought,

3. In *The Imitation of Christ*, II, xii, formerly attributed to Jean Gerson, but now known to have been written by Thomas à Kempis.
4. other.
5. *new men:* upstarts, parvenus; in this case, heretics such as Luther and Tyndale.
6. intelligence.   7. knowledge, wisdom.
8. *bear . . . hand:* maintain.

but make merry, nor take no penance at all, but sit them down and drink well for our Savior's sake, set cock-a-hoop[9] and fill in all the cups at once, and then let Christ's passion pay for all the scot,[1] I am not he that will envy their good hap,[2] but surely counsel dare I give no man to adventure that way with them. But such as fear lest that way be not sure, and take upon them willingly tribulation of penance, what comfort they do take and well may take therein, that have I somewhat told you already. And sith these other folk sit so merry without such tribulation, we need to talk to them, you wot[3] well, of no such manner[4] comfort. And therefore of this kind of tribulation will I make an end.

The Eighth Chapter

Of that kind of tribulation which, though they not willingly take,[5] yet they willingly suffer.

Vincent

Verily, good uncle, so may you well do, for you have brought it unto a very good pass. And now I require[6] you come to the tother kind, of which you purposed alway to treat last.

Antony

That shall I, cousin, very gladly do. The tother kind is this, which I rehearsed[7] second, and sorting out the tother twain have kept it for the last. This kind of tribulation is, you wot well, of them that willingly suffer tribulation though that of their own choice they took it not at the first. This kind, cousin, divide we shall into twain. The first might we call temptation, the second persecution. But

9. *set cock-a-hoop:* let the liquor flow.   1. reckoning, bill.   2. fortune.
3. know.   4. kind of.   5. i.e., take upon themselves.
6. request.   7. related.

here must you consider that I mean not every kind of persecution, but that kind only, which though the sufferer would be loath to fall in, yet will he rather abide it and suffer, than by the fleeting[8] from it fall in the displeasure of God, or leave God's pleasure unprocured. Howbeit if we well consider these two things, temptation and persecution, we may find that either of them is incident[9] to the tother. For both by temptation the devil persecuteth us, and by persecution the devil also tempteth us; and as persecution is tribulation to every man, so is temptation tribulation to every good man. Now though the devil, our spiritual enemy, fight against man in both, yet this difference hath the common temptation from the persecution: that temptation is as it were the fiend's train,[1] and persecution his plain open fight. And therefore will I now call all this kind of tribulation here by the name of temptation, and that shall I divide into two parts. The first shall I call the devil's trains, the tother his open fight.

The Ninth Chapter

First of temptation in general, as it is common to both.

To speak of every kind of temptation particularly by itself, this were, ye wot well, in manner[2] an infinite thing, for under that as I told you fall persecutions and all. And the devil hath of his trains a thousand subtle ways, and of his open fight as many poisoned darts.

He tempteth us by the world; he tempteth us by our own flesh; he tempteth us by pleasure; he tempteth us by pain; he tempteth us by our foes; he tempteth us by our own friends; and under color[3]

8. shifting, moving away.   9. naturally pertaining or attached.
1. trap, ambush.   2. *in manner:* so to speak.
3. semblance, pretext.

of kindred, he maketh many times our next[4] friends our most foes. For as our Savior saith, *Inimici hominis domestici ejus.*[5]

But in all manner of so divers temptations, one marvelous comfort is this: that with the mo we be tempted, the gladder have we cause to be. For as Saint James saith, *Omne gaudium existimate fratres quum in tentationes varias incideritis:* Esteem it and take it, saith he, my brethren, for a thing of all joy when you fall into divers and sundry manner of temptations.[6] And no marvel, for there is in this world set up as it were a game of wrestling, wherein the people of God come in on the tone side, and on the tother side come mighty strong wrestlers and wily, that is to wit, the devils, the cursed, proud, damned spirits. For it is not our flesh alone that we must wrestle with, but with the devil too. *Non est nobis colluctatio adversus carnem et sanguinem sed adversus principes et potestates tenebrarum harum, adversus spiritualia nequitiae in caelestibus:* Our wrestling is not here, saith Saint Paul, against flesh and blood, but against the princes and potestates[7] of these dark regions, against the spiritual wicked ghosts of the air.[8]

But as God unto them that on his part[9] give his adversary the fall, hath prepared a crown, so he that will not wrestle shall none have. For as Saint Paul saith, *Nemo coronabitur nisi qui legitime certaverit:* There shall no man have the crown but he that doth his devoir[1] therefor according to the law of the game.[2] And then as holy Saint Bernard saith, how couldst thou fight or wrestle therefor, if there were no challenger against thee that would provoke thee thereto?[3] And therefore may it be a great comfort, as Saint James saith, to every man that seeth himself challenged and provoked by tempta-

---

4. nearest.
5. Matt. 10:36. The passage reads: "I have come to set a man against his father, and a daughter-in-law against her mother-in-law. And a man's enemies will be the members of his own household."
6. James 1:2.   7. potentates.   8. Eph. 6:12.
9. *on his part:* for his sake.   1. duty.   2. 2 Tim. 2:5.
3. Cf. *Meditationes de Cognitione Humanae Conditionis,* XII, 34 (*PL 184,* 504) and *Sermones in Cantica, Sermo* XVII (*PL 183,* 858).

tion. For thereby perceiveth he that it cometh to his course[4] to wrestle, which shall be, but if he willing[5] will play the coward or the fool, the matter of his eternal reward.[6]

The Tenth Chapter
A special comfort in all temptation.

But now must this needs be to man an inestimable comfort in all temptation, if his faith fail him not; that is to wit, that he may be sure that God is alway ready to give him strength against the devil's might, and wisdom against the devil's trains. For as the prophet saith, *Fortitudo mea et laus mea est dominus, factus est mihi in salutem:* My strength and my praise is our Lord, he hath been my safeguard.[7] And the scripture saith, *Pete a deo sapientiam et dabit tibi:* Ask wisdom of God, and he shall give it thee,[8] *ut possitis* (as Saint Paul saith) *deprehendere omnes artes:* that you may spy and perceive all the crafts.[9] A great comfort may this be in all kinds of temptation, that God hath so his hand upon him that is willing to stand and will trust in him and call upon him, that he hath made him sure by many faithful promises in holy scripture, that either he shall not fall, or if he sometime through faintness of faith stagger or hap[1] to fall, yet if he call upon God betimes,[2] his fall shall be no sore bruising to him, but as the scripture saith, *Justus si ceciderit non collidetur, quia dominus supponit manum:* The just man, though he fall, shall not be bruised, for our Lord holdeth under his hand.[3]

The prophet expresseth a plain comfortable promise of God against all temptation, where he saith, *Qui habitat in adjutorio altis-*

4. turn.
5. *but . . . willing:* unless he willingly.
6. James 1:2. Cf. also James 1:12.   7. Ps. 117:14.
8. James 1:5. Cf. also Matt. 7:7–8.
9. A summary in paraphrase of Eph. 3:18, which More evidently meant to expand, leaving a blank space in the MS.
1. happen.   2. without delay.   3. Ps. 36:24.

simi, in protectione dei caeli commorabitur: Whoso dwelleth in the help of the highest God, he shall abide in the protection or defense of the God of heaven.[4] Who dwelleth now, good cousin, in the help of the high God? Surely he that through a good faith abideth in the trust and confidence of God's help, and never for lack of that faith and trust in his help falleth desperate of all help, nor departeth from the hope of his help, to seek himself help, as I told you the tother day, of the flesh, the world, or the devil.

Now he then that by fast faith and sure hope dwelleth in God's help and hangeth alway thereupon, never falling fro that hope, he shall, saith the prophet, ever dwell and abide in God's defense and protection; that is to say, that while he faileth not to believe well and hope well, God will never fail in all temptation to defend him. For unto such a faithful well-hoping man, the prophet in the same psalm saith further, *Scapulis suis obumbrabit tibi, et sub pennis ejus sperabis:* With his shoulders shall he shadow thee, and under his feathers shalt thou trust.[5] Lo, here hath every faithful man a sure promise, that in the fervent heat of temptation or tribulation (for as I have said divers times before, they be in such wise concident[6] that every tribulation the devil useth for temptation to bring us to impatience, and thereby to murmur and grudge and blasphemy; and every kind of temptation, to a good man that fighteth against it and will not follow it, is a very painful tribulation)—in the fervent heat, I say therefore, of every temptation, God giveth the faithful man that hopeth in him the shadow of his holy shoulders, which are broad and large, sufficient to refrigerate[7] and refresh the man in that heat; and in every tribulation he putteth his shoulders for a defense between. And then what weapon of the devil may give us any deadly wound, while that impenetrable pavis[8] of the shoulder of God standeth alway between?

Then goeth the verse further and saith unto such a faithful man, *Et sub pennis ejus sperabis:* Thine hope shall be under his feathers,

4. Ps. 90:1.   5. Ps. 90:4.   6. of the same nature.   7. cool.
8. convex shield large enough to cover the whole body. Used primarily as a defense against archery.

that is to wit, for the good hope thou hast in his help, he will take thee so near him into his protection that as the hen, to keep her young chickens from the kite,[9] nestleth them together under her own wings, so fro the devil's claws, the ravenous kite of this dark air, will the God of heaven gather the faithful trusting folk near unto his own sides, and set them in surety very well and warm, under the covering of his heavenly wings.

And of this defense and protection, our Savior spake himself unto the Jews, as mention is made in the twenty-third chapter of Saint Matthew, to whom he said in this wise: *Jerusalem, Jerusalem, quae occidis prophetas et lapidas eos qui ad te missi sunt, quoties volui congregare te quemadmodum gallina congregat pullos suos sub alas suas et noluisti?* That is to say, Jerusalem, Jerusalem, that killest the prophets and stonest unto death them that are sent unto thee, how often would I have gathered thy sons together as the hen gathereth her chickens under her wings, and thou wouldest not?[1]

Here are, cousin Vincent, words of no little comfort unto every Christian man, by which we may see with how tender affection God of his great goodness longeth to gather under the protection of his wings, and how often like a loving hen he clucketh home unto him, even those chickens of his that willfully walk abroad into the kite's danger, and will not come at his clucking, but ever the more he clucketh for them, the farther they go from him. And therefore can we not doubt if we will follow him, and with faithful hope come run to him, but that he shall in all matter of temptation, take us near unto him and set us even under his wing. And then are we safe, if we will tarry there, for against our will can there no power pull us thence, nor hurt our souls there. *Pone me,* saith the prophet, *juxta te, et cujusvis manus pugnet contra me:* Set me near unto thee, and fight against me whose hand that will.[2]

And to show the grave safeguard and surety that we shall have while we sit under his heavenly feathers, the prophet saith yet a

9. a kind of hawk.   1. Matt. 23:37.
2. The verse is not from the Psalms, as More's ascription to "the prophet" would seem to indicate, but from Job 17:3.

great deal further, *Sub umbra alarum tuarum exultabo;* that is to wit, that we shall not only when we sit by his sweet side under his holy wing sit in safeguard, but that we shall also under the covering of his heavenly wings with great exultation rejoice.[3]

The Eleventh Chapter

Of four kinds of temptation, and therein both the parts of that kind of tribulation that men willingly suffer touched in the two verses of the psalter.

Now in the two next verses following, the prophet briefly comprehendeth four kinds of temptations, and therein all the tribulation that we shall now speak of, and also some part of that which we have spoken of before. And therefore I shall peradventure,[4] except any further thing fall in our way, with treating of those two verses finish and end all our matter.

The prophet saith in the psalm, *Scuto circumdabit te veritas ejus, non timebis a timore nocturno, a sagitta volante in die, a negotio perambulante in tenebris, ab incursu et demonio meridiano:* The truth of God shall compass thee about with a pavis; thou shall not be afeard of the night's fear, nor of the arrow flying in the day, nor of the business walking about in the darknesses, nor of the incursion or invasion of the devil in the midday.[5]

First, cousin, in these words, "The truth of God shall compass thee about with a pavis," the prophet for the comfort of every good man in all temptation and in all tribulation, beside those other things that he said before, that the shoulders of God should shadow them, and that also they should sit under his wing, here saith he further that the truth of God shall compass thee with a pavis; that is to wit, that as God hath faithfully promised to protect

3. Ps. 62:8.   4. perhaps.   5. Ps. 90:5–6.

and defend those that faithfully will dwell in the trust of his help, so will he truly perform it. And thee that such one art, will the truth of his promise defend, not with a little round buckler[6] that scant[7] can cover the head, but with a long large pavis that covereth all along the body, made, as holy Saint Bernard saith, broad above with the Godhead, and narrow beneath with the manhead; so that this pavis is our Savior Christ himself.[8]

And yet is not this pavis like other pavises of this world, which are not made but in such wise as while it defendeth one part, the man may be wounded upon the tother;[9] but this pavis is such that, as the prophet saith, it shall round about enclose and compass thee, so that thine enemy shall hurt thy soul on no side. For *scuto*, saith he, *circumdabit te veritas ejus:* With a pavis shall his truth environ and compass thee round about. And then continently[1] following, to the intent that we should see that it is not without necessity, that the pavis of God should compass us about upon every side, he showeth in what wise we be by the devil, with trains[2] and assaults, by four kinds of temptations and tribulations environed upon every side, against all which compass of temptations and tribulations that round, compassing pavis of God's truth shall in such wise defend us and keep us safe, that we shall need to dread none of them all.

The Twelfth Chapter
The first kind of the four temptations.

First he saith, *Non timebis a timore nocturno:* Thou shalt not be afeard of the fear of the night. By the night is there in scripture sometime understanden tribulation, as appeareth in [the] thirty-fourth chapter of Job, *Novit enim Deus opera eorum, idcirco inducet noctem:* God hath known the work of them, and therefore shall he

6. small, round shield.   7. scarcely.
8. *In Psalmum XC*,V, 2 (*PL 183*, 196).   9. other.
1. continuously, without interruption.   2. traps, ambushes.

bring night upon them, that is to wit, tribulation for their wickedness.[3] And well you wot[4] that the night is of the nature self[5]
discomfortable[6] and full of fear. And therefore by the night's fear,
here I understand the tribulations by which the devil through the
sufferance of God, either by himself or other that are his instruments, tempteth good folk to impatience, as he did Job. But he
that, as the prophet saith, dwelleth and continueth faithfully in the
hope of God's help, shall so be clipped in[7] on every side with the
shield or pavis of God, that he shall have no need to be afeard of
such tribulation that is here called the night's fear. And it may be
also conveniently called the night's fear for two causes: the tone
for that[8] many times the cause of his tribulation is unto him that
suffereth dark and unknown, and therein varieth it and differeth
fro that tribulation by which the devil tempteth a man by open fight
and assault, for a good known thing from which he would withdraw him, or for some known evil thing, into which he would drive
him by force of such persecution. Another cause for which it is
called the night's fear may be for that that the night is so far out of
courage, and naturally so casteth folk in fear, that of everything
whereof they perceive any manner[9] dread, their fantasy doubleth
their fear, and maketh them often ween[1] that it were much worse
than indeed it is.

The prophet saith in the psalter, *Posuisti tenebras, et facta est nox, in
illa pertransibunt omnes bestiae silvarum, catuli leonis rugientes
quaerentes a deo escam sibi:* Thou hast, good Lord, set the darkness,
and made was the night, and in the night walken all the beasts of
the woods, the whelps of the lions roaring and calling unto God for
their meat.[2] Now though that the lions' whelps walk about roaring
in the night and seek for their prey, yet can they not get such meat
as they would[3] alway, but must hold themself content with such as
God suffereth to fall in their way, and though they be not ware[4]
thereof, yet of God they ask it and of him they have it.

3. Job 34:25–26.   4. know.   5. *of . . . self:* by its very nature.
6. disheartening.   7. *clipped in:* surrounded.   8. *for that:* because.
9. kind of.   1. think.   2. Ps. 103:20–21.   3. desire.
4. aware.

And this may be comfort to all good men in their night's fear, in their dark tribulation, that though they fall into the claws or the teeth of those lions' whelps, yet shall all that they can do not pass beyond the body, which is but as the garment of the soul. For the soul itself which is the substance of the man is so surely fenced in round about with the shield or pavis of God, that as long as he will abide faithfully in *adjutorio altissimi,* in the hope of God's help, the lions' whelps shall not be able to hurt it. For the great lion himself could never be suffered to go further in the tribulation of Job than God from time to time gave him leave. And therefore the deep darkness of the midnight maketh men that standeth out of faith and out of good hope in God to be in their tribulation far in the greater fear, for lack of the light of faith, whereby they might perceive that the uttermost of their peril is a far less thing than they take it for.

But we be so wont to set so much by our body, which we see and feel, and in the feeding and fostering whereof we set our delight and our wealth, and so little alas and so seld[5] we think upon our soul, because we cannot see that but by spiritual understanding, and most special by the eye of our faith (in the meditation whereof we bestow, God wot, little time), that the loss of our body we take for a sorer[6] thing and for a greater tribulation a great deal, than we do the loss of our soul. And where our Savior biddeth us that we should not fear those lions' whelps that can but kill our bodies, and when that is done, have no further thing in their power wherewith they can do us harm, but biddeth us stand in dread of him which, when he hath slain the body, is able then beside to cast the soul into everlasting fire:[7] we be so blind in the dark night of tribulation, for lack of full and fast belief of God's word, that whereas in the day of prosperity we very little fear God for our soul, our night's fear of adversity maketh us very sore to fear the lion and his whelps for dread of loss of our bodies.

And whereas Saint Paul in sundry places showeth us that our

5. seldom.   6. more severe.   7. Matt. 10:28, Luke 12:4–5.

body is but as the garment of the soul,[8] yet the faintness of our faith to the scripture of God maketh us with the night's fear of tribulation more to dread, not only the loss of our body than of our soul, that is to wit, of the clothing than of the substance that is clothed therewith, but also of the very outward goods that serve for the clothing of the body. And much more foolish are we in that dark night's fear, than were he that would forget the saving of his body, for fear of leesing[9] of his old rainbeaten cloak that is but the covering of his gown or his coat.

Now consider further yet that the prophet in the fore-rehearsed verses saith not that in the night walk only the lions' whelps, but also *omnes bestiae silvarum:* all the beasts of the wood.[1] Now wot you well that if a man walk through the wood in the night, many things may make him afeard, of which in the day he would not be afeard a whit. For in the night every bush to him that waxeth[2] once afeard seemeth a thief.

I remember that when I was a young man, I was once in the war with the king my master (God assoil[3] his soul), and we were camped within the Turk's ground many a mile beyond Belgrade (which would God were ours now as well as it was then). But so happed[4] it that in our camp about midnight, there suddenly rose a rumor and a scry[5] that the Turk's whole army was secretly stealing upon us. Wherewith our whole host was warned to arm them in haste and set themself in array to fight, and then were the scourers[6] of ours that brought those sudden tidings examined more leisurely by the council, what surety or what likelihead they had perceived therein. Of whom one showed that by the glimmering of the moon, he had espied and perceived and seen them himself, coming on softly and soberly in a long range[7] all in good order, not one farther forth than the other in the forefront, but as even as a thread and in breadth farther than he could see in length.

8. Cf. 2 Cor. 5:1–4; 1 Cor. 15:40–50, 53.   9. losing.
1. Ps. 103:20.   2. becomes.   3. absolve.   4. chanced.
5. clamor.   6. scouts.   7. line.

His fellows, being examined, said that he was somewhat pricked[8] forth before them, and came so fast back to tell it them, that they thought it rather time to make haste and give warning to the camp, than to go near unto them. For they were not so far off, but that they had yet themself somewhat an unperfect sight of them too.

Thus stood we watching all the remnant of the night, evermore hearkening when we should hear them come, with "Hush. Stand still. Me think I hear a trampling." So that at last many of us thought we heard them ourself also. But when the day was sprungen[9] and that we saw no man, out was our scourer sent again, and some of our captains with him, to show whereabout the place was in which he perceived them. And when they came thither, they found that the great fearful army of the Turks so soberly coming on, turned (God be thanked) into a fair long hedge standing even stone-still.

And thus fareth it in the night's fear of tribulation, in which the devil, to bear down and overwhelm with dread the faithful hope that we should have in God, casteth in our imagination much more fear than cause. For while there walk in that night not only the lions' whelps, but over that all the beasts of the wood beside, the beast that we hear roar in the dark night of tribulation, and fear it for a lion, we sometime find well afterward in the day that it was no lion at all, but a seely[1] rude roaring ass.[2] And the thing that on the sea seemeth sometime a rock is indeed nothing else but a mist. Howbeit, as the prophet saith, he that faithfully dwelleth in the hope of God's help, the pavis of his truth shall so fence him roundabout, that be it ass, colt, or a lion's whelp, or a rock of stone, or a mist, *Non timebit a timore nocturno:* The night's fear thereof shall he nothing need to dread.

8. spurred; i.e., he had ridden ahead.   9. sprung, risen.
1. harmless, foolish.
2. More combines Ps. 103:20–21 with Aesop's fable of the Ass in the Lion's Skin. In the fable the ass put on a lion's skin and frightened all the beasts in the forest but gave himself away at last with his braying.

The Thirteenth Chapter
Of pusillanimity.

Therefore find I that in the night's fear, one great part is the fault of pusillanimity, that is to wit, faint and feeble stomach,[3] by which a man for faint heart is afeard where he needeth not, by the reason whereof he fleeth oftentimes for fear of that thing of which (if he fled not) he should take none harm. And some man doth sometime by his fleeing make his enemy bold on him, which would if he fled not, but durst[4] abide thereby, give over and flee from him.

This fault of pusillanimity maketh a man in his tribulation for feeble heart first impatient, and afterward oftentimes driveth him by impatience into a contrary affection,[5] making frowardly[6] stubborn and angry against God, and thereby to fall into blasphemy as do the damned souls in hell.

This fault of pusillanimity and timorous mind letteth[7] a man also many times from the doing of many good things, which if he took a good stomach to him in the trust of God's help, he were well able to do. But the devil casteth him in a cowardice, and maketh him take it for humility to think himself unmeet[8] and unable thereto, and therefore to leave the good thing undone, whereof God offereth him occasion and had made him convenient[9] thereto.

But such folk have need to lift up their hearts and call upon God, and by the counsel of other good ghostly[1] folk, cast away the cowardice of their own conceit,[2] which the night's fear by the devil hath framed in their fantasy, and look in the gospel upon him which laid up his talent and left it unoccupied, and therefore utterly lost it, with a great reproach of his pusillanimity, by which he had went[3] he should have excused himself in that he was afeard

3. spirit, disposition.   4. dared.   5. state of mind.
6. *making frowardly:* i.e., making him perversely.   7. prevents.
8. unfit.   9. suitable.   1. spiritual.   2. imagining.
3. thought.

to put it forth in ure[4] and occupy it.[5] And all this fear cometh by the devil's drift,[6] wherein he taketh occasion of the faintness of our good and sure trust in God. And therefore let us faithfully dwell in the good hope of his help, and then shall the pavis of his truth so compass us about, that of this night's fear we shall have no fear at all.

The Fourteenth Chapter

Of the daughter of pusillanimity, a scrupulous conscience.

This pusillanimity bringeth forth by the night's fear a very timorous daughter, a seely wretched girl and ever puling,[7] that is called scrupulosity or a scrupulous conscience. This girl is a meetly[8] good posil[9] in an house, never idle but ever occupied and busy. But albeit she hath a very gentle mistress that loveth her well and is well content with that she doth, or if it be not all well, as all cannot alway be well, content to pardon her, as she doth other of her fellows, and so letteth her know that she will; yet can this peevish[1] girl never cease whining and puling[2] for fear lest her mistress be alway angry with her, and that she shall shrewdly[3] be shent:[4] were her mistress, ween you,[5] like to be content with this condition? Nay, surely.

I knew such one myself whose mistress was a very wise woman (which is in women very rare), very mild also and meek, and liked very well such service as she did her in the house. But this continual discomfortable[6] fashion of hers she so much misliked that she would sometime say "Ay! what aileth this girl? The elvish[7] urchin weeneth I were a devil, I trow. Surely if she did me ten times better

4. *in ure:* into use.   5. Matt. 25:14–30.   6. scheme.
7. whining.   8. tolerably.   9. maid.   1. foolish.
2. crying faintly.   3. harshly.   4. scolded.
5. *ween you:* do you think.   6. miserable.   7. troublesome.

service than she doth, yet with this fantastical fear of hers, I would be loath to have her in my house."

Thus fareth, lo, the scrupulous person, which frameth himself many times double the fear that he hath cause, and many times a great fear where there is no cause at all. And of that that is indeed no sin, maketh a venial, and that that is venial, imagineth to be deadly. And yet for all that, falleth in them,[8] being namely[9] of their nature such as no man long liveth without.[1] And then he feareth that he be never full confessed, nor never full contrite, and then that his sins be never full forgiven him. And then he confesseth and confesseth again, and cumbereth himself and his confessor both. And then every prayer that he saith, though he say it as well as the frail infirmity of the man will suffer,[2] yet is he not satisfied but if[3] he say it again and yet after that again. And when he hath said one thing thrice, as little is he satisfied at the last as with the first. And then is his heart evermore in heaviness, unquiet and in fear, full of doubt and of dullness, without comfort or spiritual consolation.

With this night's fear the devil sore[4] troubleth the mind of many a right good man, and that doth he to bring him to some great inconvenience.[5] For he will, if he can, drive him so much to the minding[6] of God's rigorous justice, that he will keep him from the comfortable[7] remembrance of God's great, mighty mercy, and so make him do all his good works wearily, and without consolation or quickness.[8]

Moreover, he maketh him to take for sin something that is none, and for deadly some such as are but venial, to the intent that when he shall fall into them, he shall by reason of his scruple, sin, where else he should not, or sin deadly while his conscience in the deed doing so gave[9] him, where indeed he had offended but venially.

---

8. *falleth in them:* i.e., commits both venial and mortal sins.

9. especially.

1. *And yet . . . without:* i.e., venial sins (which the scrupulous take to be mortal) are by their very nature such that no one lives long without committing them.

2. permit.   3. *but if:* unless.   4. severely.   5. harm.
6. consideration.   7. consoling.   8. liveliness.   9. misgave.

Yea, and further the devil longeth to make all his good works and spiritual exercise so painful and so tedious unto him, that with some other suggestion or false wily doctrine of a false spiritual liberty, he should for the false ease and pleasure that he should suddenly find therein, be easily conveyed from that evil fault into a much worse, and have his conscience as wide and as large after as ever it was narrow and strait before. For better is yet of truth a conscience[a] little too strait than a little too large.

My mother had, when I was a little boy, a good old woman that took heed to[1] her children; they called her Mother Maud. I trow you have heard of her.

Vincent

Yea, yea, very much.

Antony

She was wont when she sat by the fire with us, to tell us that were children many childish tales. But as Plinius saith that there is no book lightly[2] so bad, but that some good thing a man may pick out thereof,[3] so think I that there is almost no tale so foolish, but that yet in one matter or other, to some purpose it may hap[4] to serve. For I remember me that among other of her fond[5] tales, she told us once that the ass and the wolf came upon a time to confession to the fox. The poor ass came to shrift[6] in the Shrovetide,[7] a day or two before Ash Wednesday, but the wolf would not come to confession till he saw first Palm Sunday past, and then foded[8] yet forth farther till Good Friday.[9] The fox asked the ass before he began *benedicite*[1]

1. *heed to:* care of.   2. frivolously.
3. Pliny the Younger, *Epistles,* III, 5.   4. happen.   5. foolish.
6. confession.
7. The Sunday, Monday, and Tuesday preceding Ash Wednesday, a period when members of the church were urged to go to confession to prepare themselves for Lent.
8. postponed by evasive excuses.
9. The wolf delays until Lent is almost over.
1. The standard formula for the beginning of confession.

wherefore he came to confession before Lent began so soon. The poor beast answered him again: for fear of deadly sin, if he should lose his part of any of those prayers that the priest in the cleansing days[2] pray for them that are then confessed already.

Then in his shrift he had a marvelous grudge[3] in his inward conscience, that he had one day given his master a cause of anger, in that that with his rude roaring before his master arose, he had awaked him out of his sleep and bereaved him of his rest

The fox for that fault, like a good discreet confessor, charged him to do so no more, but lie still and sleep like a good son himself till his master were up and ready to go to work, and so should he be sure that he should not wake him no more.

To tell you all the poor ass's confession it were a long work, for everything that he did was deadly sin with him, the poor soul was so scrupulous. But his wise, wily[4] confessor accounted them for trifles, as they were, and sware after unto the badger that he was so weary to sit so long and hear him, that, saving for the manner sake,[5] he had liever[6] have sitten all that while at breakfast with a good fat goose.

But when it came to the penance giving, the fox found that the most weighty sin in all his shrift was gluttony, and therefore he discreetly gave him in penance, that he should never for greediness of his meat[7] do any other beast any harm or hindrance, and then eat his meat and study[8] for no more.

Now as good Mother Maud told us, when the wolf came to Father Reynard[9] (that was, she said, the fox's name) to confession upon Good Friday, his confessor shook his great pair of beads upon him almost as big as bowls[1] and asked him wherefore he came so late. "Forsooth, Father Reynard," quoth he, "I must needs tell

2. *cleansing days:* the period of Shrovetide, when Lenten penitents had a special prayer said over them.
3. scruple.   4. clever.
5. *manner sake:* sake of appearances.   6. rather.
7. food in general.   8. search.
9. The name alludes to the unscrupulous hero of the popular medieval beast epic, *Reynard the Fox.*
1. bowling balls.

you the truth. I come you wot[2] well, therefor:[3] I durst[4] come no sooner for fear lest you would for my gluttony have given me in penance to fast some part of this Lent."

"Nay, nay," quoth the Father Fox," I am not so unreasonable, for I fast none of it myself. For I may say to thee, son, here in confession between us twain, it is no commandment of God this fasting, but an invention of man. The priests make folk fast and put them to pain about the moonshine in the water,[5] and do but make folk fools, but they shall make me no such fool, I warrant thee, son. For I eat flesh all this Lent myself, I. Howbeit indeed, because I will not be occasion of slander, I therefore eat it secretly in my chamber out of sight of all such foolish brethren as for their weak scrupulous conscience would wax[6] offended withal. And so would I counsel you to do."[7]

"Forsooth, Father Fox," quoth the wolf, "and so, I thank God, I do as near as I can; for when I go to my meat I take none other company with me but such sure brethren as are of mine own nature, whose conscience are not weak, I warrant you, but their stomachs as strong as mine."

"Well then, no force,"[8] quoth Father Fox.

But when he heard after by his confession, that he was so great a ravener[9] that he devoured and spent sometime so much victual at one meal, as the price thereof would well find[1] some poor man with his wife and his children almost all the week, then he prudently reproved that point in him, and preached him a process[2] of his own temperance, which never used, as he said, to pass upon himself[3] the valure[4] of sixpence at a meal—no, nor yet so much neither.

"For when I bring home a goose," quoth he, "not out of the poulter's shop, where folk find them out of the feathers ready plucked, and see which is the fattest, and yet for sixpence buy and

2. know.   3. for this reason.   4. dared.
5. *moonshine . . . water:* unreal, illusory things that cannot be attained.
6. become.
7. The fox's opinions parody protestant views. Fasting was required every day in Lent except Sunday.
8. *no force:* it does not matter.   9. plunderer.   1. provide for.
2. story.   3. *pass . . . himself:* exceed.   4. value.

choose the best, but out of the housewife's house at the first hand, which may somewhat better cheap aforth them,[5] you wot well, than the poulter may, nor yet cannot be suffered[6] to see them plucked, and stand and choose them by day, but am fain[7] by night to take at a venture,[8] and when I come home am fain to do the labor to pluck her myself too. Yet for all this, though it be but lean, and I ween not well worth a groat, serveth it me sometime, for all that, both dinner and supper too. And therefore as for that you live of ravin,[9] therein can I find no fault. You have used it so long that I think you can do none other. And therefore were it folly to forbid it you, and to say the truth against good conscience too. For live you must, I wot well, and other craft can[1] you none. And therefore (as reason is) must you live by that. But yet, you wot well, too much is too much, and measure[2] is a merry mean, which I perceive by your shrift you have never used to keep. And therefore surely this shall be your penance: that you shall all this year never pass upon yourself the price of sixpence at a meal as near as your conscience can guess the price."

Their shrift have I showed you as Mother Maud showed it us. But now serveth for our matter the conscience of them both in the true performing of their penance.

The poor ass, after his shrift, when he waxed anhungered, saw a sow lie with her pigs well lapped[3] in new straw, and near he drew and thought to have eaten of the straw, but anon[4] his scrupulous conscience began therein to grudge[5] him, for while his penance was, that for greediness of his meat, he should do none other body none harm, he thought he might not eat one straw there, lest for lack of that straw some of those pigs might hap to die for cold. So held he still his hunger till one brought him meat. But when he should fall thereto, then fell he yet in a far further scruple. For then it came in his mind that he should yet break his penance if he should eat any of that either, sith[6] he was commanded by his ghostly father[7] that he should not for his own meat hinder any

5. *better . . . them:* supply them more cheaply.   6. allowed.
7. obliged.   8. *a venture:* random.   9. rapine, robbery.
1. know.   2. moderation.   3. bedded.   4. soon.
5. trouble.   6. since.   7. *ghostly father:* confessor.

other beast. For he thought that if he ate not that meat, some other beast might hap to have it, and so should he by the eating of it peradventure[8] hinder another. And thus stood he still fasting till when he told the cause, his ghostly father came and informed him better, and then he cast off that scruple and fell mannerly[9] to his meat, and was a right honest ass many a fair day after.

The wolf, now coming from shrift clean soiled[1] from his sins, went about to do as a shrewd[2] wife once told her husband that she would do when she came from shrift.

"Be merry, man," quoth she now, "for this day I thank God was I well shriven, and I purpose now therefore to leave off all my old shrewdness and begin even afresh."

Vincent

Ah well, uncle, can you report her so? That word heard I her speak, but she said it in sport to make her husband laugh.

Antony

Indeed, it seemed she spake it half in sport. For that she said she would cast away all her shrewdness, therein I trow[3] she sported, but in that she said she would begin it all afresh, her husband found that good earnest.[4]

Vincent

Well, I shall show her what you say, I warrant you.

Antony

Then will you make me make my word good.[5] But whatsoever she did, at the leastwise so fared now this wolf, which had cast out in confession all his old ravin, and then hunger pricked him forward

8. perhaps.   9. properly.   1. absolved.   2. shrewish.
3. believe.   4. *good earnest:* actual fact.
5. *Then . . . good:* i.e., you will see she was not entirely joking. Harpsfield (p. 94) identifies this as an anecdote about Dame Alice.

that as the shrewd wife said, he should begin all afresh. But yet the prick of conscience withdrew and held him back, because he would not for breaking of his penance, take any prey for his mealtide that should pass the price of sixpence.

It happed him then as he walked prowling for his gere[6] about, he came where a man had in few days before cast off two old lean and lame horses, so sick that no flesh was there left upon them. And the tone,[7] when the wolf came by, could scant stand on his legs, and the tother already dead and his skin ripped off and carried away. And as he looked upon them suddenly, he was first about to feed upon them and whet his teeth on their bones. But as he looked aside, he spied a fair cow in a close,[8] walking with her young calf by her side, and as soon as he saw them, his conscience began to grudge him against both those two horses. And then he sighed and said to himself, "Alas, wicked wretch that I am, I had almost broken my penance ere I was ware.[9] For yonder dead horse, because I never saw dead horse sold in the market, and I should die therefor by the way that my sinful soul shall to,[1] I cannot devise what price I should set upon him, but in my conscience I set him far above sixpence, and therefore I dare not meddle with him.

"Now then is yonder quick[2] horse of likelihood worth a great deal of money. For horse be dear in this country, especially such soft amblers,[3] for I see by his pace he trotteth not, nor can scant[4] shift a foot, and therefore I may not meddle with him, for he very far passeth my sixpence. But kine[5] this country here hath enough, but money have they very little. And therefore, considering the plenty of the kine and the scarcity of the money, as for yonder peevish[6] cow, seemeth unto me in my conscience worth not past a groat,[7] and[8] she be worth so much. Now then, as for her calf is not so much as she by half, and therefore while the cow is in my conscience worth but fourpence, my conscience cannot serve me

6. sustenance.   7. one.   8. enclosed field.   9. aware.
1. *and if . . . to:* i.e., even if I should die because of the way in which my sinful soul is tending.
2. live.   3. *soft amblers:* easygoing pacers.   4. barely.
5. cattle.   6. foolish.   7. fourpence.   8. if.

for sin of my soul to praise[9] her calf above twopence, and so pass
they not sixpence between them both. And therefore they twain
may I well eat at this one meal and break not my penance at all."
And so thereupon he did without any scruple of conscience.

If such beasts could speak now as Mother Maud said they could
then, some of them would, I ween,[1] tell a tale almost as wise as this,
wherein, save for the minishing[2] of old Mother Maud's tale, else
would a shorter process[3] have served.

But yet as peevish as the parable is, in this it serveth for our
purpose; that the night's fear of a conscience somewhat scrupulous, though it be painful and troublous to him that hath it, like as
this poor ass had here, is less harm yet than a conscience over large,
or such as for his own fantasy the man list[4] to frame himself, now
drawing it narrow, now stretching it in breadth after the manner of
a cheverel point,[5] to serve on every side for his own commodity, as
did here the wily wolf.[6] But such folk are out of tribulation, and
comfort need they none, and therefore are they out of our matter.

But those that are in the night's fear of their own scrupulous
conscience, let them be well ware, as I said, that the devil, for
weariness of the tone, draw them not into the tother; and while he
would flee fro Scylla, drive him into Charybdis.[7] He must do as
doth a ship that should come into an haven, in the mouth whereof
lie secret rocks under the water on both the sides. If he be by
mishap entered in among them that are on the tone side and
cannot tell how to get out, he must get a substantial,[8] cunning[9]
pilot, that so can conduce[1] him from the rocks on that side, that yet

9. appraise.   1. think.   2. cutting short.   3. discourse.
4. chooses.
5. *cheverel point:* leather cord used to fasten clothing.
6. Shorter, medieval versions of Mother Maud's tale are reprinted in *Les
Fabulistes Latins,* ed. L. Hervieux (Paris, 1893–99), IV, 255; II, 313. More's
direct source, however, seems to have been the conversation between his
stepdaughter, Alice Alington, and Sir Thomas Audley, as reported in her
letter to Margaret Roper. See the Introduction.
7. For the story of the rock of Scylla and the whirlpool Charybdis, see the
Odyssey, XII, 85–110, 234–54.
8. sound, solid.   9. knowledgeable.   1. lead.

he bring him not into those that are on the tother side, but can guide him in the midway. Let them, I say therefore, that are in the troublous fear of their own scrupulous conscience, submit the rule of their own conscience to the counsel of some other good man, which after the variety and the nature of the scruples may temper the advice. Yea, although a man be very well learned himself, yet let him in this case learn the custom used among physicians. For be one of them never so cunning, yet in his own disease and sickness he never useth to trust all to himself, but send for such of his fellows as he knoweth meet,[2] and putteth himself in their hands, for many considerations whereof they assign the causes. And one of the causes is fear, whereof upon some tokens[3] he may conceive in his own passion[4] a great deal more than needeth and than were good for his health, that for the time that he knew no such thing at all.

I knew once in this town one of the most cunning men in that faculty and the best expert, and therewith the most famous too, and he that the greatest cures did upon other men. And yet when he was himself once very sore[5] sick, I heard his fellows that then looked unto him, of all which every one would in their own disease have used his help before any other man, wish yet that for the time of his own sickness, being so sore as it was, he had known no physic at all, he took so great heed unto every suspicious token, and feared so far the worst, that his fear did him sometime much more harm than the sickness gave him cause.

And therefore, as I say, whoso hath such a trouble of his scrupulous conscience, let him for a while forbear the judgment of himself, and follow the counsel of some other, whom he knoweth for well learned and virtuous, and specially in the place of confession. For there is God specially present with his grace assisting his sacrament. And let him not doubt to acquiet[6] his mind, and follow that that he is there bode,[7] and think for awhile less of the fear of God's justice, and be more merry in remembrance of his mercy, and persevere in prayer for grace, and abide and dwell faithfully in

2. suitable.   3. symptoms.   4. pain.   5. seriously.
6. quiet.   7. advised.

the sure hope of his help, and then shall he find without any doubt, that the pavis[8] of God's truth shall (as the prophet saith) so compass him about, that he shall not dread this night's fear of scrupulosity, but shall have his conscience stablished in good quiet and rest.

The Fifteenth Chapter

Another kind of the night's fear, another daughter of pusillanimity, that is to wit, that horrible temptation by which some folk are tempted to kill and destroy themself.

Vincent

Verily, good uncle, you have in my mind well declared these kinds of the night's fear.

Antony

Surely, cousin, but yet are there many mo than I can either remember or find. Howbeit, one yet cometh now to my mind, of which I before nothing thought, and which is yet in mine opinion of all the other fears the most horrible, that is to wit, cousin, where the devil tempteth a man to kill and destroy himself.

Vincent

Undoubtedly this kind of tribulation is marvelous and strange, and the temptation is of such a sort, that some men have opinion that such as once fall in that fantasy can never full cast it off.

Antony

Yes, yes, cousin, many an hundred and else God forbid. But the thing that maketh men so say is because that of those which finally

8. large shield.

do destroy themself, there is much speech and much wondering (as it is well worthy). But many a good man and woman hath sometime, yea, divers years one after other continually be tempted thereto, and yet have by grace and good counsel well and virtuously withstand it, and been in conclusion clearly delivered of it, and their tribulation nothing known abroad and therefore nothing talked of. But surely, cousin, an horrible sore trouble it is to any man or woman that the devil tempteth therewith. Many have I heard of and with some have I talked myself, that have been sore cumbered with that temptation, and marked have I not a little the manner of them.

Vincent

I require[9] you, good uncle, show me somewhat of such things as you perceive therein. For first where you call this kind of temptation the daughter of pusillanimity and thereby so near of sib[1] unto the night's fear, me thinketh on the tother[2] side that it is rather a thing that cometh of a great courage and boldness, when they dare their own hands put themself to death, from which we see almost every man shrink and flee, and that many such as we know by good proof and plain experience for men of great heart and excellent hardy courage.

Antony

I said, Cousin Vincent, that of pusillanimity cometh this temptation, and very truth it is that indeed so it doth, but I meant it not that of only faint heart and fear it cometh and groweth alway, for the devil tempteth sundry folks by sundry ways. But the cause wherefore I spake of none other kind of that temptation, than of only that which is the daughter that the devil begetteth upon pusillanimity, was for that[3] that those other kinds of that temptation fall not under the nature of tribulation and fear, and therefore fall they far out of our matter here, and are such temptations as only need counsel and not comfort or consolation, for that the

9. ask.   1. kin.   2. other.   3. *for that:* because.

persons therewith tempted be, with that kind of tribulation not troubled in their mind, but verily well content both in the tempting and following. For some hath there been, cousin, such that they have be tempted thereto by mean of a foolish pride, and some by the mean of anger, without any dread at all, and very glad to go thereto. To this I say not nay. But where you ween[4] that none fall thereto by fear, but that they have all a strong mighty stomach,[5] that shall ye well see the contrary, and that peradventure[6] in those of whom you would ween the stomach most strong and their heart and courage most hardy.

Vincent

Yet is it marvel unto me that it should be as you say it is, that this temptation is unto them that do it for pride or for anger no tribulation, nor that they should need, in so great a distress and peril both of body and soul to be lost, no manner of good ghostly[7] comfort.

Antony

Let us therefore, cousin, consider a sample or two, for thereby shall we the better perceive it. There was here in Buda[8] in King Ladislaus'[9] days a good, poor, honest man's wife. This woman was so fiendish that the devil, perceiving her nature, put her in the mind that she should anger her husband so sore that she might give him occasion to kill her, and then should he be hanged for her.

Vincent

This was a strange temptation indeed. What the devil should she be the better then?

4. think.   5. disposition.   6. perhaps.   7. spiritual.
8. Fortress and surrounding town on a high bluff of the Danube, opposite the town of Pest on the low west bank of the river. They were incorporated into the present city of Budapest in 1872.
9. Vladislav II, King of Bohemia, elected to the Hungarian throne in 1490. After his death in 1516, he was succeeded by his ten-year-old son, Louis II.

Antony

Nothing, but that it eased her shrewd stomach[1] before, to think that her husband should be hanged after. And peradventure if you look about the world and consider it well, you shall find mo such stomachs than a few. Have you never heard no furious body plainly say that to see some such man have a mischief, he would with good will be content to lie as long in hell as God liveth in heaven?

Vincent

Forsooth and some such have I heard of.

Antony

This mind[2] of his was not much less mad than hers, but rather haply[3] more mad of the twain, for the woman peradventure did not cast so far peril[4] therein. But to tell you now to what good pass the charitable purpose came: as her husband (the man was a carpenter) stood hewing with his chip-ax[5] upon a piece of timber, she began after her old guise[6] so to revile him that the man waxed wroth[7] at last and bode[8] her get her in, or he would lay the helm[9] of his ax about her back, and said also that it were little sin even with that ax-head to chop off that unhappy head of hers that carried such an ungracious tongue therein. At that word the devil took his time[1] and whetted her tongue against her teeth, and when it was well sharped, she sware to him in very fierce anger, "By the mass, whoreson husband, I would thou wouldest; here lieth mine head, lo." And therewith down she laid her head upon the same timber log. "If thou smite it not off, I beshrew[2] thine whoreson's heart." With that, likewise as the devil stood at her elbow, so stood, as I heard say, his good angel at his, and gave him ghostly courage, and

1. *shrewd stomach:* bad disposition.   2. attitude.   3. perhaps.
4. *cast . . . peril:* anticipate such a perilous outcome.
5. small hand ax.   6. practice.   7. *waxed wroth:* became angry.
8. commanded.   9. handle.
1. *took his time:* took advantage of his opportunity.   2. curse.

bode him be bold and do it. And so the good man up with his chip-ax and at a chop chopped off her head indeed.

There were standing other folk by, which had a good sport to hear her chide, but little they looked for this chance till it was done ere they could let[3] it. They said they heard her tongue babble in her head and call "whoreson, whoreson" twice, after that the head was fro the body. At the leastwise, afterward unto the king thus they reported all, except only one, and that was a woman; and she said that she heard it not.

Vincent

Forsooth, this was a wonderful work. What became, uncle, of the man?

Antony

The king gave him his pardon.

Vincent

Verily, he might in conscience do no less.

Antony

But then was farther,[4] almost at another point, that there should have been a statute made, that in such case there should never after pardon be granted, but the truth being able to be proved, none husband should need any pardon, but should have leave by the law to follow the sample of the carpenter and do the same.

Vincent

How happed[5] it, uncle, that that good law was left unmade?

Antony

How happed it? As it happeth, cousin, that many mo be left unmade as well as it, and within a little as good as it too, both here

3. prevent.   4. *But . . . farther:* i.e., the case carried farther.
5. happened.

and in other countries, and sometime some worse made in their stead. But as they say, the let of that law was the queen's grace,[6] God forgive her soul. It was the greatest thing I ween, good lady, that she had to answer for when she died. For surely, save for that one thing, she was a full blessed woman.

But letting now that law pass, this temptation in procuring her own death was unto this carpenter's wife no tribulation at all, as far as ever men could perceive, for it liked her well to think thereon, and she even longed therefor. And therefore if she had told you or me before her mind and that she would so fain[7] bring it so to pass, we could have had none occasion to comfort her as one that were in tribulation, but marry, counsel her (as I told you before) we might, to refrain and amend that malicious, devilish mind.

Vincent

Verily that is truth. But such as are well willing to do any purpose that is so shameful will never tell their mind to nobody for very shame.

Antony

Some will not indeed, and yet are there some again that, be their intent never so shameful, find some yet whom their heart serveth them to make of their counsel therein. Some of my own folk here can tell you that no longer ago than even yesterday, one that came out of Vienna showed us among other talking that a rich widow (but I forgot to ask him where it happed), having all her life an high proud mind and a fell[8] (as those two virtues are wont alway to keep company together), was at debate[9] with another neighbor of hers in the town. And on a time she made of her counsel a poor neighbor of hers, whom she thought for money she might induce to follow her mind. With him she secretly brake[1] and offered him

---

6. *the let . . . grace:* i.e., the queen blocked the passage of the law. Vladislav's queen was Anne de Candale of France, niece of Louis XII and sister of Gaston de Foix.
7. willingly.   8. fierce.   9. *at debate:* at odds.
1. revealed her mind.

ten ducats for his labor, to do so much for her as in a morning early to come to her house, and with an ax unknown privily strike off her head; and when he had so done then convey the bloody ax into the house of him with whom she was at debate, in some such manner wise[2] as it might be thought that he had murdered her for malice—and then she thought she should be taken for a martyr. And yet had she further devised that another sum of money should after be sent to Rome and there should be means made to the pope that she might in all haste be canonized.

This poor man promised, but intended not to perform it. Howbeit, when he deferred it, she provided the ax herself, and he appointed with her the morning when he should come and do it, and thereupon into her house he came. But then set he such other folk as he would should know her frantic fantasy, in such place appointed as they might well hear her and him talk together. And after that he had talked with her thereof what he would, so much as [he] thought was enough, he made her lie down and took up the ax in his own hand, and with the tother hand he felt the edge and found a fault that it was not sharp, and that therefore he would in no wise do it till he had grounden it sharper. He could not else, he said, for pity, it would put her to so much pain. And so full sore[3] against her will for that time she kept her head still, but because she would no more suffer any mo deceive her so, and feed her forth[4] with delays, ere it was very long after, she hung herself her[5] own hands.

Vincent

Forsooth here was a tragical story, whereof I never heard the like.

Antony

Forsooth the party that told it me swore that he knew it for a truth. And himself is, I promise you, such as I reckon for right honest and of substantial truth.

---

2. *manner wise:* way.   3. *full sore:* very strongly.
4. *feed . . . forth:* beguile her.   5. i.e., with her.

Now here she letted[6] not, as shameful a mind as she had, to make one of her counsel yet, and yet as I remember another too, whom she trusted with the money that should procure her canonization. And here I wot[7] well that her temptation came not of fear, but of high malice and pride. But then was she so glad in the pleasant device[8] thereof, that as I showed you, she took it for no tribulation, and therefore comforting of her could have no place; but if men should anything give her toward her help, it must have been, as I told you, good counsel. And therefore, as I said, this kind of temptation to a man's own destruction, which requireth counsel and is out of tribulation, was out of our matter, that is to treat of comfort in tribulation.

The Sixteenth Chapter

Of him that were moved to kill himself by illusion of the devil, which he reckoneth for a revelation.

But lest you might reject both these samples, weening they were but feigned[9] tales, I shall put you in remembrance of one which I reckon yourself have read in the *Collations* of Cassianus, and if you have not, there may you soon find it. For myself have half forgotten the thing, it is so long since I read it. But thus much I remember that he telleth there of one that was many days a very special, holy man in his living, and among the other virtuous monks and anchors[1] that lived there in wilderness, was marvelously much esteemed, saving that some were not all out of fear of him, lest his revelations, whereof he told many by himself, would prove illusions of the devil. And so proved it after indeed. For the man was by the devil's subtle suggestions brought into such an high spiritual pride, that in conclusion the devil brought him to that horrible point, that he made him go kill himself. And as far as my mind

6. hesitated.   7. know.   8. devising.   9. imaginary.
1. anchorites, hermits.

giveth me[2] now, without new sight of the book, he brought him to it by this persuasion: that he made him believe that it was God's will he should so do, and that thereby should he go straight to heaven.[3]

And then if it were by that persuasion, with which he took very great comfort in his own mind himself, then was it, as I said, out of our case, and needed not comfort, but counsel against giving credence to the devil's persuasion. But marry,[4] if he made him first perceive how he had been deluded, and then tempted him to his own death by shame and by despair, then was it within our matter, lo, for then was his temptation fallen down fro pride to pusillanimity, and was waxen[5] that kind of the night's fear that I speak of, wherein a good part of the counsel that were to be given him should have need to stand in[6] good comforting. For then was he brought into right sore tribulation.

But as I was about to tell you, strength of heart and courage is there none therein, not only for that[7] very[8] strength, as it hath the name of virtue in a reasonable creature, can never be without prudence,[9] but also for that, as I said, even in them that seem men of most hardiness,[1] it shall well appear to them that well weigh the matter, that the mind[2] whereby they be led to destroy themself groweth of pusillanimity and very foolish fear.

Take for the sample Cato Uticensis, which in Africa killed himself after the great victory that Julius Caesar had. Saint Austin well declareth in his work *De Civitate Dei* that there was no strength nor magnanimity therein, but plain pusillanimity and impotency of stomach,[3] whereby he was forced to the destruction of himself,

---

2. *as far . . . me:* as well as I can remember.
3. *Collationes,* II, 5 (*PL 49*, 529–30). Cassian tells the story of the old monk Hero who refused to join his brothers at the Easter feast and was visited by an "angel of Satan as an angel of light" who commanded him to throw himself into a bottomless well, where he died still believing that no harm would come to him.
4. indeed, to be sure.   5. become.   6. *stand in:* consist of.
7. *for that:* because.   8. true.
9. Cf. Aquinas, *Summa Theologica,* I–II, Q. 58, a. 4.   1. daring.
2. intention.   3. spirit.

because his heart was too feeble for to bear the beholding of another man's glory, or the suffering of other worldly calamities that he feared should fall on himself.[4] So that, as Saint Austin well proveth, that horrible deed is none act of strength, but an act of a mind either drawn from the consideration of itself with some devilish fantasy, wherein the man hath need to be called home by good counsel, or else oppressed by faint heart and fear, wherein a good part of the counsel must stand in lifting up his courage with good consolation and comfort.

And therefore if we found any such religious person, as was that father which Cassian writeth of, that were of such austerity and apparent ghostly[5] living, that he were with such as well knew him reputed for a man of singular virtue, and that it were perceived that he had many strange visions appearing unto him—if it should now be perceived after that, that the man went about secretly to destroy himself, whoso should hap to come to the knowledge thereof, and intended to do his devoir in the let,[6] first must he find the means to search and find out whether the man be, in his manner and his countenance, lightsome, glad, and joyful, or dumpish, heavy, and sad, and whether he go thereabout as one that were full of the glad hope of heaven, or as one that had his breast farced[7] full of tediousness and weariness of the world. If he were found in the first fashion, it were a token that the devil hath by his fantastical apparitions puffed him up in such a peevish[8] pride that he hath finally persuaded him by some illusion showed him for the proof, that God's pleasure is that he shall for his sake with his own hands kill himself.

Vincent

Now if a man so found it, uncle, what counsel should a man give him then?

4. *De Civitate Dei,* I, xxiii (*PL 41,* 36–37). Cato's death had been widely praised by Plutarch (*Cato Minor,* 65–70), Dio Cassius (*Hist. Rom.,* 42, x–xiii), Cicero (*De Off.,* I, xxxi), and others.
5. spiritual.   6. *do . . . let:* make an effort to prevent it.
7. stuffed.   8. foolish.

Antony

That were somewhat out of our purpose, cousin, sith[9] as I told you before, the man were not then in sorrow and tribulation, whereof our matter speaketh, but in a perilous, merry, mortal temptation; so that if we should, beside our own matter that we have in hand, enter into that too, we might make a lenger[1] work between both, than we could well finish this day. Howbeit, to be short, it is soon seen that therein the sum of the effect of the counsel must in manner[2] rest in giving him warning of the devil's sleights, and that must be done under such sweet, pleasant manner as the man should not abhor to hear it. For while it could lightly[3] be none other, but that the man were rocked and sung asleep by the devil's craft, and his mind occupied as it were in a delectable dream, he should never have good audience[4] for him that would rudely and boistously[5] shog[6] him and wake him, and so shake him out thereof. Therefore must you fair and easily touch him, and with some pleasant speech awake him, so that he wax not wayward as children do that are waked ere they list[7] to rise.

But when a man hath first begun with his praise, for if he be proud, ye shall much better please him with a commendation than with a dirige,[8] then after favor won therewithal, a man may little and little insinuate the doubt of such revelations, not at the first as it were for any doubt of his, but of some other that men in some other places talk of. And peradventure[9] it shall not miscontent himself to show great perils that may fall therein in another man's case than his own, and shall begin to preach upon it.

Or if you were a man that had not so very great scrupulous conscience of an harmless lie devised to do good withal, which kind Saint Austin, though he take alway for sin, yet he taketh but for venial, and Saint Jerome (as by divers places in his books appeareth) taketh not fully for so much;[1] then may you feign some

---

9. since.   1. longer.   2. *in manner:* so to speak.   3. easily.
4. hearing, attention.   5. roughly.   6. shake.   7. wish.
8. First word of the Office for the Dead; a dirge.   9. perhaps.
1. Augustine, *De Mendacio,* xiv, 25 (*PL 40,* 505–16); Jerome, *Commentarii in Epistolam ad Galatas,* I, ii (*PL 26,* 339–40).

secret friend of yours to be in such case, and that yourself somewhat fear his peril and have made of charity this voyage[2] for his
sake, to ask this good father's counsel. And in that communication
upon these words of Saint John, *Nolite omni spiritui credere, sed
probate spiritus si ex deo sint:* Give not credence to every spirit, but
prove the spirits whether they be of God;[3] and these words of Saint
Paul, *Angelus sathanae transfigurat se in angelum lucis:* The angel of
Satan transfigureth himself into the angel of the light;[4] you shall
take occasion the better if they hap[5] to come in on his side, but yet
not lack occasion neither if those texts, for lack of his offer, come in
upon your own. Occasion, I say, you shall not lack, to inquire by
what sure and undeceivable tokens a man may discern the true
revelations from the false illusions, whereof a man shall find many
both here and there in divers other authors, and whole together
divers goodly treatise of that good godly doctor, Master John
Gerson, entitled *De Probatione Spirituum;*[6] as whether the party be
natural wise, or anything seem fantastical; whether the party be
poor-spirited or proud, which will somewhat appear by his delight
in his own praise, or if of wiliness or of another pride for to be
praised of humility, he refuse to hear thereof, yet any little fault
found in himself, or diffidence declared and mistrust of his own
revelations and doubtful tokens told, wherefor himself should fear
lest they be the devil's illusions—such things (as Master Gerson
saith) will make him spete[7] out somewhat of his spirit, if the devil lie
in his breast.[8]

Or if the devil be yet so subtle that he keep himself close in his
warm den, and blow out never an hot word, yet is it to be considered what end his revelations draw to, whether to any spiritual
profit to himself or other folk, or only to vain marvels and wonders.
Also whether they withdraw him from such other good virtuous

2. journey, undertaking.   3. 1 John 4:1.   4. 2 Cor. 11:14.
5. happen.
6. Gerson actually wrote two treatises on the subject, which are reprinted
in his *Opera Omnia* (Antwerp, 1706), III, 37–59. More refers to them both
under the title of *De Probatione Spirituum.*
7. spit.   8. *De Probatione Spirituum, Opera Omnia,* III, 39.

business, as by the common rules of Christendom, or any rules of his profession, he was wont to use or were bound to be occupied in. Or whether he fall into any singularity of opinions against the scripture of God, or against the common faith of Christ's catholic church.

Many other tokens are there in that work of Master Gerson spoken of, to consider by[9] whether the person, never having revelations of God, nor illusions fro the devil, do either for winning of money or worldly favor feign his revelations himself and delude the people withal.[1]

But now for our purpose: if among any of the marks by which the true revelations may be known from false illusions, that man himself bring forth for one mark, the doing or teaching of anything against the scripture of God, or the common faith of the church, then have you an entry made you, by which when you list[2] you may enter into the special matter, wherein he can never well flit[3] from you.

Or else may you yet, if you list, feign that your secret friend (for whose sake you come to him for counsel) is brought in that mind by a certain apparition showed unto him, as himself saith, by an angel, as you fear, by the devil, that he can be by you none otherwise persuaded as yet, but that the pleasure of God is that he shall go kill himself, and that if he so do, then shall he be thereby so specially participant of Christ's passion, that he shall forthwith be carried up with angels into heaven. For which is he so joyful that he firmly purposeth upon[4] it, no less glad to do it than another man would be glad to avoid it. And therefore may you desire his good counsel, to instruct you with some substantial good advice, wherewith you may turn him from this error, that he be not, under hope of God's true revelation, in body and soul destroyed by the devil's false illusion.

If he will in this thing study and labor to instruct you, the thing that himself shall find of his own invention, though they be less

9. *consider by:* determine.
1. *De Probatione Spirituum, Opera Omnia,* III, 39, 41.   2. choose.
3. flee.   4. *purposeth upon:* intends to do.

effectual, shall peradventure more work with himself toward his own amendment, sith he shall of likelihead better like them, than shall double so substantial told him by another man.

If he be loath to think upon that side, and therefore shrink fro the matter, then is there none other way but adventure[5] after the plain fashion to fall into the matter and show what you hear, and to give him counsel and exhortation to the contrary, but if[6] you list to say that thus and thus hath the matter been reasoned already between your friend and you. And therein may you rehearse such things as should prove that the vision which moveth him is no true revelation, but a very false illusion.

Vincent

Verily, uncle, I well allow this, that a man should as well in this thing, as every other wherein he longeth to do another man good, seek such a pleasant way as the party should be likely to like, or at the leastwise well to take in worth[7] his communication, and not so to enter in thereunto as he whom he would help should abhor him and be loath to hear him, and therefore take no profit by him. But now, uncle, if it come by the tone way or the tother[8] to the point that hear me he will or shall, what be the reasons effectual with which I should by my counsel convert him?

Antony

All those by which you may make him perceive that himself is deceived, and that his visions be no godly revelations, but very devilish illusions. And those reasons must you gather of the man, of the matter, and of the law of God, or of some one of these. Of the man, if you can peradventure show him that in such a point or such he is waxen worse, since such revelations have haunted him, than he was before, as in those that are deluded, whoso be well acquainted with them shall well mark and perceive; for they wax more proud, more wayward, more envious, suspicious—misjudg-

5. venture.   6. *but if:* unless.
7. *take in worth:* consider valuable.   8. *tone . . . tother:* one . . . other.

ing and depraving[9] other men with the delight of their own praise, and such other spiritual vices of the soul.

Of the matter may you gather, if it have happed his revelations before to prove false, or that they be things rather strange than profitable, for that is a good mark between God's miracles and the devil's wonders. For Christ and his saints have their miracles alway tending to fruit and profit;[1] the devil and his witches and necromancers, all their wonderful works draw to no fruitful end, but to a fruitless ostentation and show, as it were a juggler that would for a show before the people play masteries[2] at a feast.

Of the law of God you must draw your reasons in showing by the scripture that the thing which he weeneth[3] God by his angel biddeth, God hath his[4] own mouth forbidden. And that is, you wot well, in the case that we speak of so easily to find that I need not to rehearse it to you, sith[5] there is plain among the commandments forbidden, the unlawful killing of any man, and therefore of himself, as Saint Austin saith all the church teacheth, except[6] himself be no man.[7]

Vincent

This is very true, good uncle, nor I will not dispute upon any glozing[8] of that prohibition. But sith we find not the contrary but that God may dispense with that commandment himself, and both license and command also, if himself list,[9] any man to go kill either another man or himself either: this man that is now by such a marvelous vision induced to believe that God so biddeth him, and therefore thinketh himself in that case of that prohibition discharged, and charged with the contrary commandment—with what reason may we make him perceive that his vision is but an illusion and not a true revelation?

---

9. vilifying.   1. Cf. Matt. 7:16–20.
2. conjuring feats, magic tricks.   3. thinks.   4. i.e., by his.
5. since.   6. unless.   7. *De Civitate Dei*, I, xx (*PL 41*, 34–35).
8. explaining away.   9. pleases.

Antony

Nay, Cousin Vincent, ye shall in this case not need to require[1] those reasons of me. But taking the scripture of God for a ground for this matter, you know very well yourself you shall go somewhat a shorter way to work, if you ask this question of him: that sith God hath once forboden[2] the thing himself, though he may dispense therewith if he will, yet sith the devil may feign himself God, and with a marvelous vision delude one and make as though God did it, and sith the devil is also more likely to speak against God's commandment than God against his own, you shall have good cause, I say, to demand of the man himself whereby he knoweth that his vision is God's true revelation and not the devil's false delusion.

Vincent

Indeed, uncle, I think that would be an hard question to him. May a man, uncle, have in such a thing even a very sure knowledge of his own mind?

Antony

Yea, cousin, God may cast into the mind of man, I suppose, such an inward light of understanding that he cannot fail but be sure thereof. And yet he that is deluded by the devil may think himself as sure, and yet be deceived indeed. And such a difference is there in a manner[3] between them, as is between the sight of a thing while we be waking and look thereon, and the sight with which we see a thing in our sleep while we dream thereof.

Vincent

This is a pretty similitude, uncle, in this thing. And then is it easy for the monk that we speak of,[4] to declare how he knoweth his vision for a true revelation and not a false delusion, if there be so great difference between them.

1. ask.   2. forbidden.   3. *in a manner:* so to speak.
4. The old monk in Cassian (above, p. 133), whom More has here confused with the example of the "secret friend" (above, p. 138).

Antony

Not so easy, cousin, as you ween it were. For how can you now prove unto me that you be awake?

Vincent

Marry, lo, do I not now wag my hand, shake my head, and stamp with my foot here in the floor?

Antony

Have you never dreamed ere this that you have done the same?

Vincent

Yes, that have I, and more too than that. For I have ere this in my sleep dreamed that I doubted whether I were asleep or awake, and have in good faith thought that I did thereupon even the same things that I do now indeed, and thereby determined that I was not asleep. And yet have I dreamed in good faith further that I have been afterward at dinner, and there making merry with good company, have told the same dream at the table, and laughed well thereat, that while I was asleep I had, by such means of moving the parts of my body and considering thereof, so verily thought myself waking.

Antony

And will you not now soon, trow[5] you, when you wake and rise, laugh as well at yourself, when you see that you lie now in your warm bed asleep again, and dream all this time, while you ween so verily that you be waking and talking of these matters with me?

Vincent

God's lord, uncle, you go now merrily to work with me indeed, when you look and speak so sadly,[6] and would make me ween I were asleep.

5. believe.   6. seriously.

Antony

It may be that you be so, for anything that you can say or do, whereby you may with any reason that you make, drive me to confess that yourself be sure of the contrary, sith you can do nor say nothing now whereby you be sure to be waking, but that you have ere this or hereafter may think yourself as surely to do the selfsame things indeed, while you be all the while asleep and nothing do but lie dreaming.

Vincent

Well, well, uncle, though I have ere this thought myself awake while I was indeed asleep, yet for all that, this I know well enough: that I am awake now, and so do you too, though I cannot find the words by which I may with reason force you to confess it, but that alway you may drive me off by the sample of my dream.

Antony

This is, cousin, as me seemeth, very true. And likewise seemeth me the manner and difference between some kind of true revelations and some kind of false illusions, as it standeth between the things that are done waking and the things that in our dreams seem to be done while we be sleeping: that is to wit, that he which hath that kind of revelation fro God is as sure of the truth as we be of our own deed while we be waking, and he that is illuded[7] by the devil is in such wise[8] deceived and worse too, than be they by their dream, and yet reckoneth for the time himself as sure as the tother, saving that the tone falsely weeneth, the tother truly knoweth.

But I say not, cousin, that this kind of sure knowledge cometh in every kind of revelation, for there are many kinds, whereof were too long to talk now; but I say that God doth or may do to man in some thing certainly send some such.

7. tricked.   8. a way.

Vincent

Yet then may this religious man of whom we speak, when I show him the scripture against his revelation and therefore call it an illusion, bid me with reason go care for myself. For he knoweth well and surely himself that his revelation is very good and true, and not any false illusion, sith for all the general commandment of God in the scripture, God may dispense where he will and when he will, and may command him to do the contrary, as he commanded Abraham to kill his own son,[9] and as Samson had by inspiration of God, commandment to kill himself, with pulling down the house upon his own head at the feast of the Philistines.[1]

Now if I would then do as you bode[2] me right now, tell him that such apparitions may be illusions, and sith God's word is in the scripture against him plain for the prohibitions, he must prove me the truth of his revelation, whereby that I may know it is not a false illusion: then shall he bid me again[3] tell him whereby that I can prove myself to be awake and talk with him, and not to be asleep and dream so, sith in my dream I may as surely ween so as I know that I do so. And thus shall he drive me to the same bay to which I would bring him.

Antony

This is well said, cousin, but yet could he not scape you so. For the dispensation of God's common precept, which dispensation he must say that he hath by his private revelation, is a thing of such sort as showeth itself naught[4] and false. For it never hath had any sample like,[5] since the world began unto now, that ever man hath read or heard of among faithful people commended.

First in Abraham, touching the death of his son, God intended it not, but only tempted the towardness[6] of the father's obedience. In Samson, all men make not the matter very sure, whether he be saved or not, but yet therein some matter appeareth. For the

9. Gen. 22:1–4.   1. Judg. 16:28–30.   2. ask.   3. in return.
4. wicked.   5. *it . . . like:* there has never been any similar example.
6. willingness, docility.

Philistines, being enemies to God and using Samson for their mocking-stock in scorn of God, it is well likely that God gave him the mind[7] to bestow his own life upon the revenging of the displeasure that those blasphemous Philistines did unto God. And that appeareth meetly[8] clear by this: that though his strength failed him when he wanted[9] his hair, yet had he not, as it seemeth, that strength evermore at hand while he had his hair, but at such times as it pleased God to give it him; which thing appeareth by these words that the scripture in some place of that matter, saith, *Irruit virtus domini in Samsonem:* The power or might of God rushed into Samson.[1] And so therefore while this thing that he did in the pulling down of the house, was done by the special gift of strength then at that point given him by God, it well declareth that the strength of God, and therewith the Spirit of God, entered into him therefor.[2]

Saint Austin also rehearseth that certain holy virtuous virgins in time of persecution, being by God's enemies, infidels, pursued upon to be deflowered by force, ran into a water and drowned themself, rather than they would be bereaved of their virginity. And albeit that he thinketh it is not lawful for any other maid to follow their sample, but rather suffer other to do her any manner violence by force, and commit sin of his own upon her against her will, than willingly and thereby sinfully herself become an homicide of herself, yet he thinketh that in them it happed by the special instinct of the Spirit of God, that for causes seen unto himself, would rather that they should avoid it with their own temporal death, than abide the defoiling[3] and violation of their chastity.[4]

But now this good man neither hath any of God's enemies to be

---

7. intention.   8. fairly, tolerably.   9. lacked.
1. Judg. 14:6 or 15:14; the phrasing is the same in each.
2. Augustine uses the same examples of Abraham and Samson in his section on suicide in *De Civitate Dei*, I, xxi (*PL 41*, 35).
3. defiling.
4. *De Civitate Dei*, I, xxvi (*PL 41*, 39), which More combines with Augustine's discussion of the rape of Lucrece in *De Civitate Dei*, I, xix (*PL 41*, 32).

by his own death revenged on, nor any woman that violently
pursue him by force to bereave him of his virginity, nor never find
we that God proved any man's obedient mind by the commandment of his own slaughter of himself. Therefore is his case both
plain against God's open precept, and the dispensation strange and
without sample,[5] no cause appearing or well imaginable but if he
would think that he could neither any longer live without him, or
take him to him in such wise as he doth other men, but command
him to come by a forboden way, by which without other cause we
never heard that ever he bode[6] any man else before.

Now whether you think if you should after this bid him tell you
by what way he knoweth that his intent riseth upon a true revelation and not upon a false illusion, he would bid you then again tell
him by what mean you know that you be talking with him well
waking, and not dream it sleeping: you may tell him again that men
thus to talk together as you do, and in such manner wise,[7] and to
prove and perceive that they so do by the moving of themself, with
putting the question thereof unto themself for their pleasure and
the marking and considering thereof, is in waking a daily common
thing that every man doth or may do when he will, and when they
do it, they do it but of pleasure; but in sleep it happeth very seld[8]
that men dream they so do, nor in the dream never put the
question but for doubt. And therefore it is more reason, that sith
his revelation is such also as happeth so seld, and ofter happeth that
men dream of such than have such indeed—therefore is it more
reason, you may tell him, that he show you whereby he knoweth in
such a rare thing, and a thing more like a dream, that himself is not
asleep, than you, in such a common thing among folk that are
waking and so seldom happing in a dream, should need to show
him whereby you know that you be not asleep.

Besides this, himself to whom you should show it seeth and
perceiveth the thing that he would bid you prove, but the thing that
he would make you believe, the truth of his revelation, which you

5. precedent.   6. commanded.   7. *in . . . wise:* in such a way.
8. seldom.

bid him prove, you see not, he woteth[9] well himself. And therefore ere you believe it against the scripture, it were well consonant unto reason that he should show you whereby he knoweth it for a true waking revelation, and not a false dreaming delusion.

Vincent

Then shall he peradventure say to me again, that whether I believe him or not, maketh him no matter; the thing toucheth himself and not me, and himself is in himself as sure that it is a true revelation, as that he can tell that he dreameth not but talketh with me waking.

Antony

Without doubt, cousin, if he abide at that point, and can be by no reason brought to do so much as doubt, nor can by no means be shogged[1] out of his deep sleep, but will needs take his dream for a very truth, and as some by night rise and walk about their chamber in their sleep, will so rise and hang himself: I can then none other way see but either bind him fast in his bed, or else assay[2] whether that might hap to help him with which the common tale goeth that a carver's wife in such a frantic fantasy holp[3] her husband.

To whom, when he would upon a Good Friday needs have killed himself for Christ's sake, as Christ was killed for him, she would not in vain plead against his mind, but well and wisely put him in remembrance that if he would die for Christ as Christ did for him, it were then convenient[4] for him to die even after the same fashion, and that might not be by his own hands, but by the hand of some other, for Christ pardie[5] killed not himself. And because her husband should need to make no mo of counsel,[6] (for that would he not in no wise) she offered him that, for God's sake, she would secretly crucify him herself upon a great cross, that he had made to nail a new carved crucifix upon. Whereof when he was very glad,

9. knows.   1. shaken.   2. test.   3. helped.
4. suitable, proper.   5. an oath: "by God."
6. *make . . . counsel:* take no one else into his confidence.

yet she bethought her that Christ was bounden to a pillar and beaten first, and after crowned with thorn. Whereupon, when she had by his own assent bound him fast to a post, she left not beating with holy exhortation to suffer so much and so long, that ere ever she left work and unbound him, praying nevertheless that she might put on his head and drive it well down, a crown of thorn that she had wreathen for him and brought him, he said he thought this was enough for that year. He would pray God forbear him of the remnant[7] till Good Friday come again. But when it came again the next year, then was his lust past; he longed to follow Christ no further.

Vincent

Indeed, uncle, if this help him not, then will nothing help him, I trow.

Antony

And yet, cousin, the devil may peradventure make him toward such a purpose first gladly to suffer other pain, yea, and minish his feeling too therein, that he may thereby the less fear his death. And yet are peradventure sometime such things and many mo to be assayed, for as the devil may hap to make him suffer, so may he hap to miss, namely if his friends fall to prayer for him against his temptation, for that can himself never do while he taketh it for none. But for conclusion, if the man be surely proved so inflexibly set upon the purpose to destroy himself, as commanded thereto by God, that no good counsel that men can give him, nor any other thing that men may do to him can refrain[8] him, but that he would surely shortly kill himself, then except only good prayer by his friends made for him, I can find no further shift,[9] but either have him ever in sight, or bind him fast in his bed. And so must he needs of reason be content to be ordered. For though himself take his

---

7. *forbear . . . remnant:* spare him the rest.   8. restrain.
9. expedient

fantasy for a true revelation, yet sith[1] he cannot make us perceive it for such, likewise as he thinketh himself by his secret commandment bounden to follow it, so must he needs agree that, sith it is against the plain open prohibition of God, we be by the plain open precept bounden to keep him from it.

Vincent

In this point, uncle, I can go no further. But now if he were, upon the tother[2] side, perceived to mind[3] his destruction and go thereabout with heaviness of heart, and thought, and dullness, what way were there to be used to him then?

Antony

Then were his temptation, as I told you before, properly pertaining to our matter, for then were he in a sore[4] tribulation and a very perilous. For then were it a token that the devil had either by bringing him into some great sin, brought him in despair, or peradventure by his revelations, founden false and reproved, or by some secret sin of his deprehended[5] and divulged, cast him both in despair of heaven through fear, and in a weariness of this life for shame, sith he seeth his estimation lost among other folk, of whose praise he was wont to be proud. And therefore, cousin, in such case as this is, the man is to be fair handled and sweetly, and with douce[6] and tender loving words to be put in good courage and comfort in all that men goodly may.

Here must they put him in mind that if he despair not, but pull up his courage and trust in God's great mercy, he shall have in conclusion great cause to be glad of this fall. For before he stood in greater peril than he was ware of, while he took himself for better than he was. And God, for favor that he beareth him, hath suffered him to fall deep into the devil's danger, to make him thereby know what he was while he took himself for so sure.[7] And therefore as he

1. since.   2. other.   3. intend   4. severe.   5. detected
6. sweet.   7. safe.

suffered him then to fall for a remedy against over-bold pride, so
will God now (if the man meek[8] himself, not with fruitless despair,
but with fruitful penance) so set him up again upon his feet, and so
strength him with his grace, that for this one fall that the devil hath
given him, he shall give the devil an hundred. And here must he be
put in remembrance of Mary Magdalen, of the prophet David, and
specially of Saint Peter,[9] whose high bold courage took a foul fall,
and yet because he despaired not of God's mercy, but wept and
called upon it, how highly God took him into his favor again in his
holy scripture is well testified and well through Christendom
known.

And now shall it be charitably done if some good virtuous folk,
such as himself somewhat esteemeth and hath afore longed to
stand in estimation with, do resort sometime unto him, not only to
give him counsel, but also to ask advice and counsel of him in some
cases of their own conscience, to let him thereby perceive that they
no less esteem him now, but rather more than they did before, sith
they think him now by his fall better expert of the devil's craft, and
thereby not only better instructed himself, but also better able to
give good advice and counsel unto other. This thing will, in my
mind, well amend and lift up his courage from the peril of that
desperate shame.

Vincent

Me think, uncle, that this were a perilous thing, for it may
peradventure make him set the less by his fall, and thereby cast him
into his first pride or into his other sin again, the falling whereinto
drave him into this despair.

Antony

I do not mean, cousin, that every fool should at adventure fall in
hand[1] with him, for so, lo, might it hap for to do harm indeed. But,

8. humble.
9. Cf. Luke 7:36–50; 1 Kings 11–12; and Matt. 26:69–75.
1. *at . . . hand:* recklessly deal with.

cousin, if a cunning[2] physician have a man in hand, he can well discern when and how long some certain medicine is necessary, which at another time ministered, or at that time over-long continued, might put the patient to peril.

If he have his patient in an ague,[3] to the cure whereof he needeth his medicines in their working cold, yet if he hap ere that fever be full cured to fall in some such other disease, as except[4] it were holpen[5] with hot medicines, were likely to kill the body before the fever could be cured, he would for the while have his most care to the cure of that thing wherein were most present peril, and when that were once out of jeopardy, do then the more exact diligence after about the further cure of the fever.

And likewise if the ship were in peril to fall into Scylla, the fear of falling into Charybdis on the tother side shall never let any wise master thereof to draw him from Scylla toward Charybdis first, in all that ever he may.[6] But when he hath him once so far away fro Scylla that he seeth him safe out of that danger, then will he begin to take good heed to keep him well fro the tother. And in like wise while this man is falling down to despair and to the final destruction of himself, a good wise spiritual leech,[7] will first look unto that, and by good comfort lift up his courage, and when he seeth that peril well past, care for the cure of his other faults after. Howbeit, even in the giving of his comfort, he may find ways enough in such wise to temper his words, that the man may take occasion of good courage, and yet far from occasion giving of new recidivation into his former sin, sith the great part of his counsel shall be to courage him to amendment, and that is pardie far fro falling unto sin again.

Vincent

I think, uncle, that folk fall into this ungracious[8] mind through the devil's temptation by many mo ways than one.

---

2. knowledgeable.   3. violent fever.   4. unless.   5. helped.
6. See above, p. 124, n. 7.   7. physician.   8. wicked.

Antony

That is, cousin, very true, for the devil taketh his occasion as he seeth them fall meet[9] for him. Some he stirreth to it for weariness of themself after some great loss, some for fear of horrible bodily harm and some, as I said, for fear of worldly shame.

One wist[1] I myself that had been long reputed for a right honest man, which had fallen in such a fantasy that he was well near worn away therewith, but what he was tempted to do, that would he not tell no man. But he told unto me that he was sore cumbered, and that it alway ran in his mind that folks' fantasies[2] were fallen from him, and that they esteemed not his wit[3] as they were wont to do, but ever his mind gave[4] him that the people began to take him for a fool. And folk of truth nothing so did at all, but reputed him both for wise and honest.

Two other knew I that were marvelous feared that they should kill themself and could tell me no cause wherefore they so feared it, but only that their own mind so gave them. Neither loss had they any had, nor no such thing toward[5] them, nor none occasion of any worldly shame—the tone in body very well liking[6] and lusty,[7] but wondrous weary were they both twain of that mind.[8] And alway they thought that do it they would not for nothing. And nevertheless ever they feared they should, and wherefore they so feared neither of them both could tell; and the tone lest he should do it desired his friends to bind him.

Vincent

This is, uncle, a marvelous strange manner.

Antony

Forsooth, cousin, I suppose many of them are in this case. The devil, as I said before, seeketh his occasions, for as Saint Peter saith,

9. favorable.   1. knew.   2. affections.   3. intelligence.
4. suggested to.   5. regarding.   6. pleasing.   7. healthy.
8. intention.

Adversarius vester diabolus quasi leo rugiens circuit quaerens quem devoret: Your adversary, the devil, as a roaring lion goeth about seeking whom he may devour.[9] He marketh well therefore the state and condition that every man standeth in, not only concerning these outward things, lands, possessions, goods, authority, fame, favor, or hatred of the world, but also men's complexions[1] within them, health or sickness, good humors or bad, by which they be light-hearted or lumpish, strong-hearted or faint and feeble of spirit, bold and hardy or timorous and fearful of courage.[2] And after as[3] these things minister him matter of temptation, so useth he himself in the manner of his temptation.

Now likewise as such folk as are full of young warm lusty blood and other humors exciting the flesh to filthy voluptuous living, the devil useth to make those things his instruments in tempting them and provoking them thereunto. And where he findeth some folk full of hot blood and choler, he maketh those humors his instruments to set their heart on fire in wrath and fierce furious anger: so where he findeth some folk which through some dull melancholious humors are naturally disposed to fear, he casteth sometime such a fearful imagination in their mind that without help of God they can never cast it out of their heart. Some at the sudden falling of some horrible thought into their mind, have not only had a great abomination thereat (which abomination they well and virtuously had thereat), but the devil, using their malicious humor, and thereby their natural inclination to fear, for his instrument, hath caused them to conceive therewith such a deep dread beside, that they ween[4] themself with that abominable thought to be fallen into such an outrageous sin, that they be ready to fall into despair of grace, weening that God hath given them over forever; whereas that thought, were it never so horrible and never so abominable, is

9. 1 Pet. 5:8.
1. The makeup or combination of a person's four humors: blood, phlegm, black bile, and yellow bile. Differences of personality and temperament were ascribed to varying proportions of humors in the body. Health was defined as a reasonable balance of one's four humors.
2. spirit.   3. *after as:* according to the way in which.   4. think.

yet unto them that never like it, but ever still abhor it and strive still thereagainst, matter of conscience and merit, and not any sin at all.

Some have, with holding a knife in their hand, suddenly thought upon the killing of themself, and forthwith in devising what an horrible thing it were, if they should mishap[5] so to do, have fallen in a fear that they should so do indeed, and have with long and often thinking thereon imprinted that fear so sore[6] in their imagination, that some of them have not after cast it off without great difficulty, and some could never in their life be rid thereof, but have after in conclusion miserably done it indeed. But likewise as where the devil useth the blood of a man's own body toward his purpose in provoking him to lechery, the man must and doth with grace and wisdom resist it: so must that man do, whose malicious humors the devil abuseth toward the casting of such a desperate[7] dread into his heart.

Vincent

I pray you, uncle, what advice were to be given him in such case?

Antony

Surely me thinketh his help standeth in two things, counsel and prayer. First as concerning counsel: likewise as it may be that he hath two things that hold him in his temptation, that is to wit, some evil humors of his own body and the cursed devil that abuseth them to his pernicious purpose, so must he need again[8] them twain the counsel of two manner[9] of folk, that is to wit, physicians for the body and physicians for the soul. The bodily physician shall consider what abundance the man hath of those evil humors that the devil maketh his instrument in moving the man toward that fearful affection,[1] and as well by diet convenient and medicines meet[2] therefor to resist them, as by purgations to disburden the body of them.

---

5. have the misfortune.   6. strongly.   7. hopeless.   8. against.
9. kinds.   1. state of mind.   2. suitable.

Nor let no man think strange that I would advise a man to take counsel of a physician for the body in such a spiritual passion.[3] For sith[4] the soul and the body be so knit and joined together that they both make between them one person, the distemperance[5] of either other engendereth sometime the distemperance of both twain. And therefore like[6] as I would advise every man in every sickness of the body, be[7] shriven and seek of a good spiritual physician the sure health of his soul, which shall not only serve against peril that may peradventure[8] further grow by that sickness than in the beginning men would ween were likely, but the comfort thereof and God's favor increasing therewith shall also do the body good, for which cause the blessed apostle, Saint James, exhorteth men that they shall in their bodily sickness induce[9] the priests, and saith that it shall do them good both in body and soul;[1] so would I sometime advise some men in some sickness of the soul, beside their spiritual leech, take also some counsel of the physician for the body.

Some that are wretchedly disposed and yet long to be more vicious than they be, go to physicians and pothecaries and inquire what things may serve to make them more lusty to their foul fleshly delight. And were it then any folly upon the tother[2] side, if he that feeleth himself against his will much moved unto such uncleanness should inquire of the physician what thing, without minishing[3] of his health, were meet for the minishing of such foul fleshly motion? Of spiritual counsel the first is to be shriven, that by reason of his other sins, the devil have not the more power upon him.

Vincent

I have heard some say, uncle, that when such folk have been at shrift,[4] their temptation hath been the more breme[5] upon them than it was before.

3. pain, suffering.   4. since.   5. bodily or mental disorder.
6. just.   7. i.e., to be.   8. perhaps.   9. bring in, summon.
1. James 5:14–15.   2. other.   3. diminishing.
4. confession.   5. fierce, raging.

Antony

That think I very well, but that is a special token that shrift is wholesome for them, while the devil is with that most wroth. You find in some places of the gospel that the devil, the person whom he possessed, did most trouble, when he saw that Christ would cast him out.[6] We must else let the devil do what he will, if we fear his anger, for with every good deed will he wax[7] angry.

Then is it in his shrift to be showed him that he not only feareth more than he needeth, but also feareth where he needeth not, and over that is sorry of that thing whereof, but if[8] he will willingly turn his good into his harm, he hath more cause to be glad.

First, if he have cause to fear, yet feareth he more than he needeth. For there is no devil so diligent to destroy him as God is to preserve him, nor no devil so near him to do him harm, as God is to do him good, nor all the devils in hell so strong to invade and assault him, as God is to defend him, if he distrust him not but faithfully put his trust in him.

He feareth also where he needeth not. For where he dreadeth that he were out of God's favor, because such horrible thoughts fall in his mind against his will, they be not imputed unto him.

He is, finally, sad of that he may be glad. For sith he taketh such thoughts displeasantly and striveth and fighteth against them, he hath thereby a good token that he is in God's favor, and that God assisteth him and helpeth him, and may make himself sure that so will God never cease to do, but if himself fail and fall from him first. And over that, this conflict that he hath against his temptation shall (if he will not fall where he need not) be an occasion of his merit and of a right great reward in heaven, and the pain that he taketh therein shall for so much (as Master Gerson well showeth) stand him in stead of his purgatory.[9]

The manner of the fight against this temptation must stand in

---

6. Cf. Mark 1:23–26 and 9:25–27; Matt. 8:28–32; Luke, 4:33–35.
7. grow.
8. *but if:* unless.
9. *The Imitation of Christ,* I, xxiv. Formerly attributed to Gerson.

three things, that is to wit, in resisting, and in contemning, and in the invocation of help.

Resist must a man for his own part with reason, considering what a folly it were to fall where he need not, while he is not driven to it in avoiding of any other pain, or in hope of winning any manner of pleasure, but contrariwise, should by that pain leese[1] everlasting life and fall into everlasting pain. And if it were in avoiding of other great pain, yet could he void[2] none so great thereby as he should thereby fall into.

He must also consider that a great part of this temptation is in effect but the fear of his own fantasy: the dread that he hath lest he shall once be driven to it, which thing he may be sure that (but if himself will of his own folly) all the devils in hell can never drive him to, but his own foolish imagination may. For likewise as some man, going over an high bridge, waxeth so feared through his own fantasy that he falleth down indeed, which were else able enough to pass over without any danger; and as some man shall upon such a bridge, if folk call upon him, "You fall, you fall," fall with the fantasy that he taketh thereof, which bridge, if folk looked merely upon him and said, "There is no danger therein," he would pass over well enough, and would not let[3] to run thereon if[4] it were but a foot from the ground: thus fareth it in this temptation. The devil findeth the man of his own fond[5] fantasy afeard, and then crieth he in the ear of his heart, "Thou fallest, thou fallest," and maketh the fond man afeard that he should at every foot fall indeed. And the devil so wearieth him with that continual fear (if he give the ear of his heart unto him) that at the last he withdraweth his mind from due remembrance of God, and then driveth him to that deadly mischief[6] indeed.

Therefore like as against the vice of the flesh, the victory standeth not all whole in the fight, but sometime also in the flight, saving that it is indeed a part of a wise warrior's fight to flee from his enemy's trains:[7] so must a man in this temptation too, not only

1. lose.   2. avoid.   3. hesitate.   4. as if.   5. foolish.
6. misfortune.   7. ambushes.

resist it alway with reasoning thereagainst, but sometime set it clear
at right nought, and cast it off when it cometh, and not once regard
it so much as to vouchsafe to think thereon. Some folk have been
clearly rid of such pestilent fantasies with very full contempt
thereof, making a cross upon their heart, and bidding the devil
avaunt,[8] and sometime laugh him to scorn too, and then turn their
mind to some other manner. And when the devil hath seen that
they have set so little by him, after certain assays[9] made in such
times as he thought most meet, he hath given that temptation quite
over, both for that[1] the proud spirit cannot endure to be mocked,
and also lest with much tempting the man to the sin whereto he
could not in conclusion bring him, he should much increase his
merit.

The final fight is by invocation of help unto God, both praying
for himself and desiring other also to pray for him, both poor folk
for his almoise[2] and other good folk of their charity, specially good
priests in that holy sacred service of the mass; and not only them,
but also his own good angel and other holy saints, such as his
devotion specially stand unto.[3] Or if he be learned, use then the
litany with the holy suffrages[4] that follow, which is a prayer in the
church of marvelous old antiquity, not made first, as some ween it
were, by that holy man, Saint Gregory, which opinion rose of that
that[5] in the time of a great pestilence in Rome, he caused the whole
city go in solemn procession therewith; but it was in use in the
church many years before Saint Gregory's days, as well appeareth
by the books of other holy doctors and saints that were dead
hundreds of years before Saint Gregory was born.[6] And holy Saint
Bernard giveth counsel that every man should make suit unto

---

8. be off.   9. attempts.   1. *for that:* because.   2. alms.
3. *stand unto:* is inclined toward.   4. prayers of intercession.
5. *of that that:* because.
6. Gregory the Great introduced the *Litania Septiformis* during a time of
flood and pestilence at Rome in 590 A.D. Modern scholars agree with More,
however, that the origins of the litany are obscure. References to Christian
litanies appear as early as the fourth century A.D. in the epistles of St. Basil
and the sermons of St. John Chrysostom.

angels and saints to pray for him to God in the things that he would have sped at his holy hand.[7]

If any man will stick at that, and say it need not[8] because God can hear us himself, and will also say that it is perilous so to do because, they say, we be not so counseled by no scripture, I will not dispute the matter here. He that will not do it, I let[9] him not to leave it undone. But yet for mine own part I will as well trust to the counsel of Saint Bernard, and reckon him for as good and as well learned in the scripture as any man that I hear say the contrary. And better dare I jeopard[1] my soul with the soul of Saint Bernard, than with his that findeth that fault in his doctrine.

Unto God himself every good man counseleth to have recourse above all, and in this temptation to have special remembrance of Christ's passion, and pray him for the honor of his death, the ground of man's salvation, keep this person thus tempted fro that damnable death.

Special verses may there be drawn out of the psalter against the devil's wicked temptations, as for example, *Exurgat deus et dissipentur inimici ejus, et fugiant qui oderunt eum a facie ejus*,[2] and many other which are in such horrible temptation, to God pleasant, and to the devil very terrible. But none more terrible nor more odious to the devil than the words with which our Savior drave him away himself: *Vade satana*,[3] nor no prayer more acceptable unto God, nor more effectual for the matter, than those words which our Savior hath taught us himself: *Ne nos inducas in tentationem sed libera nos a malo*.[4]

---

7. Cf. *De Triplici Genere Bonarum, Sermones de Diversis*, xvi, 3–4 (*PL 183*, 580–81) and *In Festo Omnium Sanctorum, Sermo V* (*PL 183*, 480).
8. *need not:* is not necessary.   9. prevent, hinder.
1. endanger.
2. Ps. 67:2: "Let God arise, and let his enemies be scattered, and let those who hate him flee from his face."
3. Matt. 4:10: "Begone, Satan," Christ's words in the temptation in the wilderness.
4. Matt. 6:13: "And lead us not into temptation, but deliver us from evil."

And I doubt not, by God's grace, but he that in such a temptation will use good counsel and prayer, and keep himself in good virtuous business and good, virtuous company, and abide in the faithful hope of God's help, shall have the truth of God (as the prophet saith in the verse aforerehearsed) so compass him about with a pavis,[5] that he shall not need to dread this night's fear of this wicked temptation. And thus will I finish this piece of the night's fear. And glad am I that we be past it and comen once unto the day, to those other words of the prophet: *A sagitta volante in die;*[6] for me thinketh I have made it a long night.

Vincent

Forsooth, uncle, so have you, but we have not slept in it but been very well occupied. But now I fear that except you make here a pause till you have dined, you shall keep yourself from your dinner over-long.

Antony

Nay, nay, cousin, for both brake I my fast even as you came in, and also you shall find this night and this day like a winter day and a winter night; for as the winter hath short days and long nights, so shall you find that I made you not this fearful night so long, but I shall make you this light courageous day as short. And so shall the matter require[7] well of itself indeed, for in those words of the prophet, *Scuto circumdabit te veritas ejus a sagitta volante in die:* The truth of God shall compass thee roundabout with a pavis from the arrow flying in the day.[8] I understand the arrow of pride, with which the devil tempteth a man, not in the night, that is to wit, in tribulation and adversity, for that time is too discomfortable and too fearful for pride, but in the day, that is to wit, in prosperity, for that time is full of lightsome lust and courage.[9]

---

5. large shield.   6. Ps. 90:6: "From the arrow that flies by day."
7. ask, request.   8. Ps. 90:5–6.
9. *lightsome . . . courage:* lighthearted vigor and boldness.

But surely this worldly prosperity, wherein a man so rejoiceth and whereof the devil maketh him so proud, is but even a very short winter day. For we begin many full poor and cold, and up we fly like an arrow that were shot up into the air. And yet when we be suddenly shotten up into the highest, ere we be well warm there, down we come unto the cold ground again, and then even there stick we still.[1] And yet for the short while that we be upward and aloft, Lord, how lusty[2] and how proud we be, buzzing above busily like as a bumblebee flieth about in summer, never ware that she shall die in winter. And so fare many of us (God help us), for in the short winter day of worldly wealth and prosperity, this flying arrow of the devil, this high spirit of pride, shot out of the devil's bow and piercing through our heart, beareth us up in our affection[3] aloft into the clouds, where we ween[4] we sit on the rainbow and overlook the world under us, accounting in the regard of[5] our own glory, such other poor souls as were peradventure[6] wont to be our fellows, for seely,[7] poor pismires and ants.

But this arrow of pride, fly it never so high in the clouds, and be the man that it carrieth up so high never so joyful thereof, yet let him remember that be this arrow never so light, it hath yet an heavy iron head, and therefore fly it never so high, down must it needs come and on the ground must it light, and falleth sometime not in a very cleanly place, but the pride turneth into rebuke and shame, and there is then all the glory gone.

Of this arrow speaketh the wise man in the fifth chapter of Sapience, where he saith, in the person of them that in pride and vanity passed the time of this present life, and after that so spent, passed hence into hell: *Quid profuit nobis superbia aut divitiarum jactantia, quid contulit nobis, transierunt omnia illa tanquam umbra etc., aut tanquam sagitta emissa in locum destinatum, divisus aer continuo in se reclusus est, ut ignoretur transitus illius sic et nos nati continuo desinimus esse, et virtutis quidem nullum signum valuimus ostendere in malignitate*

---

1. continuously.   2. vigorous.   3. emotion, passion.   4. think.
5. *in . . . of:* in comparison with.   6. perhaps.
7. deserving of pity.

*autem nostra consumpti sumus. Talia dixerunt in inferno ii qui peccav-
erunt:* What hath pride profit us, or what good hath the glory of our
riches done unto us? Passed are all those things like a shadow etc.,
or like an arrow shot out into the place appointed. The air that was
divided is by and by[8] returned into the place, and in such wise
closed together again that the way is not perceived in which the
arrow went. And in likewise we, as soon as we were born, be by and
by vanished away, and have left no token of any good virtue behind
us, but are consumed and wasted and come to nought in our
malignity. They, lo, that have lived here in sin, such words have
they spoken when they lay in hell.[9]

Here shall you, good cousin, consider that whereas the scripture
here speaketh of the arrow shot into his place appointed or intended, in shooting of this arrow of pride there be divers purpos-
ings and appointings. For the proud man himself hath no certain
purpose or appointment at any mark, butt, or prick[1] upon earth,
whereat he determineth to shoot and there to strike and tarry, but
ever he shooteth as children do that love to shoot up a-cop-high,[2] to
see how high their arrow can fly up.

But now doth the devil intend and appoint a certain prick, surely
set in a place into which he purposeth, fly this arrow never so high
and the proud heart thereon, to have them light both at last. And
that place is in the very pit of hell. There is set the devil's well
acquainted prick and his very just mark down, upon which prick
with his pricking[3] shaft of pride he hath by himself a plain proof
and experience that (but if[4] it be stopped by some grace of God by
the way) the soul that flieth up therewith can never fail to fall. For
when himself was in heaven and began to fly up a-cop-high, with
that lusty light flight of pride, saying, *Ascendam super astra, et ponam*

---

8. *by and by:* immediately.
9. Sap. 5:8–9, 12–14, where the scene is not hell, but the time of judgment.
1. A "mark" is any kind of target; "butt" has the same general meaning;
"prick" refers to a round target with a bull's eye and, more specifically, to
the bull's eye itself.
2. *a-cop-high:* as high as possible.   3. piercing.   4. *but if:* unless.

solium meum ad latera Aquilonis, et ero similis altissimo: I will sty[5] up above the stars, and set my throne on the sides of the North and will be like unto the Highest.[6] Long ere he could fly up half so high as he said in his heart he would, he was turned from a bright glorious angel into a dark deformed devil, and from flying any farther upward, down was he thrown into the deep dungeon of hell.

Now may it peradventure, cousin, seem that sith[7] this kind of temptation of pride is no tribulation or pain, all this that we speak of this arrow of pride, flying forth in the day of prosperity, were beside our matter.

Vincent

Verily, mine uncle, and so seemed it unto me, and somewhat was I minded so to say to you too, saving that were it properly pertaining to the present matter or somewhat disgressing therefro, good matter me thought it was, and such as I had no lust to let.[8]

Antony

But now must you, cousin, consider that though prosperity be contrary to tribulation, yet unto many a good man the devil's temptation unto pride in prosperity is a greater tribulation, and more need hath of good comfort and good counsel both, than he that never felt it would ween. And that is the thing, cousin, that maketh me speak thereof, as of a thing proper to this matter. For, cousin, as it is a thing right hard to touch pitch and never file[9] the fingers,[1] to put flax unto fire and yet keep them fro burning, to keep a serpent in thy bosom and yet be safe fro stinging, to put young men with young women without danger of foul fleshly desire: so is it hard for any person, either man or woman, in great

5. mount.
6. Part of the taunt of the people of Israel over the king of Babylon in Isa. 14:13–14, traditionally interpreted as an account of the fall of Lucifer.
7. since.   8. *lust to let:* desire to stop.   9. defile.
1. Cf. Ecclus. 13:1. By the Renaissance the saying had become a common proverb, similar to those that follow.

worldly wealth and much prosperity, so to withstand the suggestions of the devil and occasions given by the world, that they keep
themself from the deadly desire of ambitious glory. Whereupon
there followeth (if a man fall thereto) an whole flood of all unhappy
mischief: arrogant manner, high,[2] solein,[3] solemn port overlook-
ing the poor in word and countenance, displeasant and disdainous
behavior, ravin,[4] extortion, oppression, hatred and cruelty.

Now many a good man, cousin, comen into great authority,
casting in his mind the peril of such occasions of pride as the devil
taketh of prosperity to make his instruments of, wherewith to move
men to such high point of presumption as engendereth so many
great inconveniences,[5] and feeling the devil therewith offering to
themself suggestions thereunto: they be so sore[6] troubled therewith, and some fall so feared thereof, that even in the day of
prosperity they fall into the night's fear of pusillanimity; and
doubting[7] overmuch lest they should misuse themselves, leave the
things undone wherein they might use themself well, and mistrust-
ing the aid and help of God in holding them upright in their
temptations, give place to the devil in the contrary temptation.
Whereby for faint heart they leave off good business, wherein they
were well occupied, and under pretext (as it seemeth to themself)
of humble heart and meekness, and serving God in contemplation
and silence, they seek their own ease and earthly rest unware;
wherewith, if it so be, God is not well content.

Howbeit if it so be that a man feel himself such indeed, as by the
experience that he hath of himself, he perceiveth that in wealth
and authority he doth his own soul harm, and cannot do therein
the good that to his part appertaineth, but seeth the things that he
should set his hands to sustain, decay through his default and fall to
ruin under him, and that to the amendment thereof he leaveth his
own duty undone: then would I in any wise[8] advise him to leave off
that thing, be it spiritual benefice that he have, parsonage or
bishopric or temporal room[9] and authority, and rather give it over

2. proud.   3. sullen.   4. rapine.   5. misfortunes.
6. severely.   7. fearing.   8. case.   9. office

quite and draw himself aside and serve God, than take the worldly worship and commodity for himself, with incommodity to them whom his duty were to profit.

But on the tother[1] side, if he see not the contrary, but that he may do his duty conveniently well, and feareth nothing but that the temptations of ambition and pride may peradventure turn his good purpose and make him decline unto sin, I say not nay, but that well done it is to stand in moderate fear alway. Whereof the scripture saith, *Beatus homo qui semper est pavidus:* Blessed is the man that is alway fearful;[2] and Saint Paul saith, *Qui stat videat ne cadat:* He that standeth, let him look that he fall not.[3] Yet is overmuch fear perilous and draweth toward the mistrust of God's gracious help, which immoderate fear and faint heart holy scripture forbiddeth saying, *Noli esse pusillanimis:* Be not feeblehearted or timorous.[4] Let such a man therefore temper his fear with good hope and think that sith God hath set him in that place (if he think that God have set him therein) God will assist him with his grace to the well using thereof. Howbeit if he came thereto by simony or some such other evil mean, then were that thing one good reason wherefore he should the rather leave it off. But else let him continue in his good business, and against the devil's provocation unto evil, bless himself and call unto God and pray, and look, what[5] thing the devil tempteth him to, lean the more to the contrary. Let him be piteous and comfortable[6] to those that are in distress and affliction. I mean not to let every malefactor pass forth unpunished and freely run out and rob at rovers,[7] but in his heart be sorry to see that of necessity, for fear of decaying the common weal, men are driven to put malefactors to pain; and yet where he findeth good tokens and likelihead of amendment, there in all that he may, help, that mercy may be had. There shall never lack desperately disposed wretches enough beside, upon whom for ensample[8] justice may proceed. Let him think in his own heart every poor beggar his fellow.

1. other.   2. Prov. 28:14.   3. 1 Cor. 10:12.
4. Ecclus. 7:9.   5. whatever.   6. encouraging.
7. *at rovers:* indiscriminately.   8. *for ensample:* as a warning to others.

Vincent

That will be very hard, uncle, for an honorable man to do, when he beholdeth himself richly apparelled and the beggar rigged[9] in his rags.

Antony

If here were, cousin, two men that were beggars both, and afterward a great rich man would take the tone[1] unto him and tell him that for a little time he would have him in his house, and thereupon arrayed him in silk and give him a great bag by his side filled even full of gold, but giving him this knot[2] therewith, that within a little while, out he should in his old rags again and bear never a penny with him: if this beggar met his fellow now while his gay gown were on, might he not for all his gay gear take him for his fellow still? And were he not a very fool, if for a wealth of a few weeks, he would ween himself far his better?

Vincent

Yes, uncle, if the difference of their state were none other.

Antony

Surely, cousin, me thinketh that in this world, between the richest and the most poor, the difference is scant[3] so much. For let the highest look on the most base and consider how poor they came both into this world, and then consider further therewith how rich soever he be now, he shall yet within a while, peradventure less than one week, walk out again as poor as that beggar shall. And then by my troth, me thinketh this rich man much more than mad, if for the wealth of a little while, haply[4] less than one week, he reckon himself in earnest any better than the beggar's fellow. And

9. dressed.   1. one.   2. condition.   3. hardly.
4. perhaps.

less than thus can no man think that hath any natural wit[5] and well useth it.

But now a Christian man, cousin, that hath the light of faith, he cannot fail to think in this thing much further. For he will not think only upon his bare coming hither and his bare going hence again, but also upon the dreadful judgment of God, and upon the fearful pains of hell, and the inestimable joys of heaven. And in the considering of these things, he will call to remembrance that peradventure when this beggar and he be both departed hence, the beggar may be suddenly set up in such royalty that well were himself that ever was he born if he might be made his fellow. And he that well bethinketh him, cousin, upon these things, I verily think that the arrow of pride, flying forth in the day of worldly wealth, shall never so wound his heart that ever it shall bear him up one foot.

But now to the intent he may think on such things the better, let him use often to resort to confession, and there open his heart, and by the mouth of some virtuous ghostly[6] father, have such things oft renewed in his remembrance.

Let him also choose himself some secret solitary place in his own house, as far fro noise and company as he conveniently can, and thither let him sometime secretly resort alone, imagining himself as one going out of the world, even straight unto the giving up his reckoning unto God of his sinful living.[7] Then let him there before an altar or some pitiful image of Christ's bitter passion (the beholding whereof may put him in remembrance of the thing and move him to devout compassion) kneel down or fall prostrate as at the feet of almighty God, verily believing him to be there invisibly present, as without any doubt he is. There let him open his heart to God and confess his faults, such as he can call to mind, and pray

5. intelligence.   6. spiritual.
7. Reminiscent of More's own "new building" at Chelsea, where he spent each Friday alone in prayer and meditation. See Roper, pp. 25–26.

God of forgiveness. Let him call to remembrance the benefits that God hath given him, either in general among other men, or privately to himself, and give him humble hearty thanks therefor. There let him declare unto God the temptations of the devil, the suggestions of the flesh, the occasions of the world, and of his worldly friends—much worse many times in drawing a man from God than are his most mortal enemies, which thing our Savior witnesseth himself where he saith, *Inimici hominis domestici ejus:* The enemies of a man are they that are his own familiars.[8] There let him lament and bewail unto God his own frailty, negligence, and sloth in resisting and withstanding of temptation, his readiness and pronity[9] to fall thereunto. There let him lamentably beseech God of his gracious aid and help, to strength his infirmity withal, both in keeping himself fro falling, and when he by his own fault misfortuneth to fall, then with the helping hand of his merciful grace, to lift him up and set him on his feet in the state of his grace again.

And let this man not doubt but that God heareth him and granteth him gladly his boon. And so, dwelling in the faithful trust of God's help, he shall well use his prosperity and persevere in his good profitable business, and shall have therein the truth of God so compass him about with a pavis[1] of his heavenly defense, that of the devil's arrow flying in the day of worldly wealth, he shall not need to dread.

Vincent

Forsooth, uncle, I like this good counsel well, and I would ween[2] that such as are in prosperity, and take such order[3] therein, may do both to themself and other folk about much good.

Antony

I beseech our Lord, cousin, put this and better in the mind of every man that needeth it. And now will I touch one word or twain

---

8. Matt. 10:36.   9. propensity.   1. large shield.   2. think.
3. *take such order:* arrange matters in such a way.

of the third temptation, whereof the prophet speaketh in these words, *a negotio perambulante in tenebris:* from the business walking in the darkness; and then will we call for our dinner, leaving the last temptation, that is to wit, *ab incursu et demonio meridiano:* From the incursion and the devil of the midday,[4] till afternoon, and then shall we therewith, God willing, make an end of all this matter.

Vincent

Our Lord reward you, good uncle, for your good labor with me. But for our Lord's sake, take good heed, uncle, that you forbear not your dinner over-long.

Antony

Fear not that, cousin, I warrant you, for this piece will I make you but short.

The Seventeenth Chapter

Of the devil named
negotium perambulans in tenebris,
that is to wit, business walking in the darkness.

The prophet saith in the said psalm, *Qui habitat in adjutorio altissimi, in protectione dei caeli commorabitur scuto circumdabit te veritas ejus, non timebis a timore etc., A negotio perambulante in tenebris:* He that dwelleth in the faithful hope of God's help, he shall abide in the protection and safeguard of God of heaven. And thou that art such one, shall the truth of him so compass about with a pavis, that

4. Ps. 90:6.

thou shall not be afeard of the business walking about in the darknesses.[5]

Negotium is here, cousin, the name of a devil that is ever full of busyness in tempting folk to much evil business. His time of tempting is in the darknesses. For you wot well that beside the very full night, which is the deep dark, there are two times of darknesses: the tone ere the morning wax[6] light, the tother when the evening waxeth dark.

Two times of like manner[7] darkness are there also in the soul of man: the tone ere the light of grace be well in the heart sprongen up, the tother when the light of grace out of the soul beginneth to walk fast away.

In these two darknesses the devil that is called business busily walketh about, and such folk as will follow him, he carrieth about with him, and setteth them awork with many manner[8] bumbling[9] business. He setteth, I say, some to seek the pleasures of the flesh, in eating, drinking, and other filthy delight. And some he setteth about incessant seeking for these worldly goods.

And of such busy folk whom this devil called business, walking about in the darknesses, setteth awork with such business, our Savior saith in the gospel, *Qui ambulat in tenebris nescit quo vadit:* He that walketh in darknesses woteth[1] not whither he goeth.[2] And surely in such case are they. They neither wot which way they go nor whither, for verily they walk roundabout as it were in a round maze. When they ween themself at an end of their business, they be but at the beginning again. For is not the going about the serving of the flesh a business that hath none end, but evermore from the end cometh to the beginning again? Go they never so full fed to bed, yet evermore on the morrow as new[3] be they to be fed again as they were the day before.

Thus fareth it by the belly; thus fareth it by those parts that are beneath the belly. And as for covetise,[4] fareth[5] like the fire: the

---

5. Ps. 90:1, 5–6.   6. becomes.
7. *of like manner:* similar kinds of.   8. kinds of.   9. buzzing.
1. knows.   2. John 12:35.   3. ready.
4. covetousness.   5. i.e., it fareth.

more wood that cometh thereto, the more fervent and the more greedy it is.

But now hath this maze a center or a middle place, into which sometime they be conveyed suddenly, when they ween they were not yet far fro the brink. The center or middle place of this maze is hell, and into that place be these busy folk, that with this devil of business walk about in this busy maze in the darknesses, suddenly sometime conveyed, nothing ware whither they be going, and even while they ween that they were not far walked fro the beginning, and that they had yet a great way to walk about before they should come to the end. But of these fleshly folk walking in this busy pleasant maze, the scripture declareth the end, *Ducunt in bonis dies suos, et in puncto ad inferna descendunt:* They lead their life in pleasure, and at a pop down they descend into hell.[6]

Of the covetous men saith Saint Paul, *Qui volunt divites fieri, incidunt in tentationem et in laqueum diaboli, et desideria multa inutilia et nociva, quae mergunt homines in interitum et perditionem:* They that long to be rich do fall into temptation, and into the grin[7] of the devil, and into many desires unprofitable and harmful, which drown men into death and into destruction.[8] Lo, here is the middle place of this busy maze, the grin of the devil, the place of perdition and destruction that they fall and be caught and drowned in ere they be ware.

The covetous rich man also that our Savior speaketh of in the gospel, that had so great plenty of corn that his barns would not receive it, but intended to make his barns larger, and said unto himself that he would make merry many days, had went,[9] you wot well, that he had had a great way yet to walk; but God said unto him, *Stulte, hac nocte tollent a te animam tuam, quae autem parasti cujus erunt:* Fool, this night shall they take thy soul from thee, and then all this good that thou has gathered, whose shall it be?[10] Here you see that he fell suddenly into the deep center of this busy maze, so that he was fallen full therein long ere ever he had went he should have come near thereto.

6. Job. 21:13.   7. snare.   8. 1 Tim. 6:9.   9. thought.
10. Luke 12:20.

Now this wot I very well, that those that are walking about in this busy maze take not their business for any tribulation, and yet are there many of them forwearied[1] as sore,[2] and as sore panged and pained therein, their pleasures being so short, so little and so few, and their displeasures and their griefs so great, so continual and so many. That maketh me think upon a good, worshipful[3] man, which when he divers times beheld his wife what pain she took in strait binding up her hair to make her a fair large forehead, and with strait bracing in her body to make her middle small, both twain to her great pain, for the pride of a little foolish praise: he said unto her, "Forsooth, madame, if God give you not hell, he shall do you great wrong. For it must needs be your own of very right, for you buy it very dear and take great pain therefor."[4]

They that now lie in hell for their wretched living here do now perceive their folly in the more pain that they took here for the less pleasure. There confess they now their folly and cry out. *Lassati sumus in via iniquitatis:* We have been wearied in the way of wickedness.[5] And yet while they were walking therein, they would not rest themself, but run on still in their weariness and put themself still unto more pain and more, for that little, peevish[6] pleasure, short and soon gone, that they took all that labor and pain for, beside the everlasting pain that followed it for their further advantage after. So help me God, and none otherwise but as I verily think that many a man buyeth hell here with so much pain, that he might have bought heaven with less than the tone[7] half.

But yet as I say, while these fleshly and worldly busy folk are walking about in this round busy maze of this devil that is called business, that walketh about in these two times of darkness, their wits are so by the secret enchantment of the devil bewitched that they mark not the great long miserable weariness and pain that the devil maketh them take and endure about nought, and therefore they take it for no tribulation, so that they need no comfort. And

---

1. worn out.   2. severely.   3. distinguished, honorable.
4. Harpsfield (p. 94) again identifies this as a personal anecdote concerning More and Dame Alice.
5. Sap. 5:7.   6. foolish.   7. one.

therefore it is not for their sakes that I speak all this, saving that it may serve them for counsel toward the perceiving of their own foolish misery, through the good help of God's grace beginning to shine upon them again. But there are very good folk and virtuous that are in the daylight of grace, and yet because the devil tempteth them busily to such fleshly delight, and sith[8] they see plenty of worldly substance fall unto them, and feel the devil in likewise[9] busily tempt them to set their heart thereupon, they be sore troubled therewith, and begin to fear thereby that they be not with God in the light, but with this devil that the prophet calleth *Negotium*, that is to say, business walking about in these two times of darknesses.

Howbeit, as I said before of those good folk and gracious that are in the worldly wealth of great power and authority, and thereby fear the devil's arrow of pride, so say I now here again of these that stand in dread of fleshly foul sin and covetise: sith they be but tempted therewith and follow it not, albeit that they do well to stand ever in moderate fear, lest with waxing over-bold and setting the thing over-light they might peradventure mishap[1] to fall in thereto, yet sore to vex and trouble themself with the fear of loss of God's favor therefor, is without necessity and not alway without peril. For as I said before, that withdraweth the mind of a man far fro spiritual consolation of the good hope that he should have in God's help. And as for those temptations, while he that is tempted followeth them not, the fight against them serveth a man for matter of merit and reward in heaven, if he not only fly the deed, the consent, and the delectation, but also, in that he conveniently may, fly from all occasions thereof.

And this point is in those fleshly temptations eath[2] to perceive and meetly[3] plain enough. But in these worldly business pertaining unto covetise, therein is the thing somewhat more dark, and in the perceiving more difficulty. And very great troublous fear doth

8. since.   9. *in likewise:* in the same manner.
1. *peradventure mishap:* perhaps have the misfortune.
2. easy.   3. tolerably.

there oftentimes arise thereof in the hearts of very good folk, when
the world falleth fast unto them, because of the sore words and
terrible threats that God in holy scripture speaketh against those
that are rich, as where Saint Paul saith, *Qui volunt divites fieri incidunt
in tentationem, et in laqueum diaboli:* They that will be rich fall into
temptation and into the grin[4] of the devil;[5] and where our Savior
saith himself, *Facilius est camelum per foramen acus transire quam
divitem intrare in regnum dei:* It is more easy for a camel, or as some
say (for *camelus* so signifieth in the Greek tongue) for a great cable
rope, to go through an needle's eye, than for a rich man to enter
into the kingdom of God.[6]

No marvel now though good folk that fear God take occasion of
great dread at so dreadful words, when they see the worldly goods
fall to them. And some stand in doubt whether it be leeful[7] for
them to keep any good or no. But evermore in all those places of
scripture, the having of the worldly goods is not the thing that is
rebuked and threatened, but the affection that the haver unlee-
fully beareth thereto. For where Saint Paul saith, *Qui volunt divites
fieri etc.:* They that will be made rich, he speaketh not of the having,
but of the will and the desire and affection to have and the longing
for it. For that cannot be lightly[8] without sin. For the thing that folk
sore long for, they will make many shifts to get and jeopard[9]
themself therefor. And to declare that the having of richesse[1] is not
forboden, but the inordinate affection of the mind sore set thereupon, the prophet saith, *Divitiae si affluant nolite cor apponere:* If
riches flow unto you, set not your heart thereupon.[2] And albeit that
our Lord, by the said ensample of the camel or cable rope to come
through the needle's eye, said that it is not only hard, but also
impossible for a rich man to enter into the kingdom of heaven, yet

4. snare.   5. 1 Tim. 6:9.
6. Mark 10:25; Luke 18:25. Erasmus in his *New Testament* has an extended
discussion of the *camel/cable* crux More refers to here. More was apparently
unable to make up his mind about the reading since he usually gives both
versions whenever he cites the verse.
7. lawful.   8. easily.   9. endanger.   1. wealth.
2. Ps. 61:11.

he declared that though the rich man cannot get into heaven of himself, yet God, he said, can get him in well enough. For unto men, he said, it was impossible, but not unto God; for unto God, he said, all things are possible.[3] Yet over that he told of which manner[4] rich men he meant that could not get into the kingdom of heaven, saying, *Filioli, quam difficile est confidentes in pecuniis regnum dei introire:* My babes, how hard is it for them that put their trust and confidence in their money to enter into the kingdom of God.[5]

Vincent

This I suppose very true, and else God forbid; for else were the world in a very hard case, if every rich man were in such danger and peril.

Antony

That were it, cousin, indeed, and so I ween is it yet. For I fear me that to the multitude there be very few but that they long sore to be rich, and of those that so long to be, very few reserved[6] also but that they set their heart very sore thereon.

Vincent

This is, uncle, I fear me, very true, but yet not the thing that I was about to speak of. But the thing that I would have said was this: that I cannot well perceive (the world being such as it is, and so many poor people therein) how any man may be rich and keep him rich, without danger of damnation therefor. For all the while that he seeth poor people so many that lack, while himself hath to give them, and whose necessity (while he hath therewith) he is bound in such case of duty to relieve so farforth[7] that holy Saint Ambrose saith that whoso that die for default[8] where we might help them, we kill them:[9] I cannot see but that every rich man hath great cause to

3. Mark 10:23-27.   4. kind of.   5. Mark 10:24.
6. excepted.   7. *so farforth:* to such an extent.   8. neglect.
9. More is apparently mistaken. The passage occurs not in Ambrose, but in Zeno's "De Justitia," *Tractatus* I, iii (*PL II,* 287).

stand in great fear of damnation, nor I cannot perceive, as I say, how he can be delivered of that fear, as long as he keepeth his riches. And therefore, though he might keep his riches if there lacked poor men, and yet stand in God's favor therewith, as Abraham did and many another holy rich man since, yet in such abundance of poor men as there be now in every country, any man that keepeth any riches, it must needs be that he hath an inordinate affection thereunto, while he giveth it not out unto the poor needy persons, that the duty of charity bindeth and straineth[1] him to. And thus, uncle, in this world, at this day, me seemeth your comfort unto good men that are rich and troubled with fear of damnation for the keeping can very scantly serve.[2]

Antony

Hard is it, cousin, in many manner things, to bid or forbid, affirm or deny, reprove or allow a matter nakedly proposed[3] and put forth, or precisely to say this thing is good or this thing is nought, without consideration of the circumstances.

Holy Saint Austin telleth of a physician that gave a man a medicine in a certain disease that holp[4] him. The selfsame man at another time in the selfsame disease took the selfsame medicine himself and had thereof more harm than good, which thing when he showed unto the physician and asked him whereof that harm should hap,[5] "That medicine," quod he, "did thee no good but harm, because thou tookest it when I gave it thee not."

This answer Saint Austin very well alloweth. For that[6] though the medicine were one, yet might there be peradventure in the sickness some such difference as the patient perceived not, yea, or in the man himself, or in the place, or the time of the year; many things might make the let,[7] for which the physician would not then have given him the selfsame medicine that he gave him before.[8]

To peruse every circumstance that might, cousin, in this matter

---

1. forces.   2. *very . . . serve:* serve only in a very poor way.
3. proposed.   4. helped.   5. happen.   6. *For that:* Because.
7. obstacle.   8. *Epistola* 138, *Ad Marcellinum* (*PL 33,* 526–27).

be touched, and were to be considered and weighed, would indeed make this part of this devil of business a very busy piece of work and a long. But I shall a little open the point that you speak of, and shall show you what I think therein, with as few words as I conveniently can, and then will we go to dinner.

First, cousin, he that is a rich man and keepeth all his good, he hath, I think, very good cause to be very feared indeed. And yet I fear me that such folk fear least. For they be very far fro the state of good men, sith if they keep still all, then are they very far fro charity and do, you wot[9] well, almoise[1] either little or none at all. But now is our question, cousin, not in what case the rich man standeth that keepeth all, but whether we should suffer men to stand in a perilous dread and fear for the keeping of any great part. For that if by the keeping still of so much as maketh a rich man still, they stand in the state of damnation, then are the curates bounden plainly to tell them so, according to the commandment of God given unto them all in the person of Ezekiel: *Si dicente me ad impium morte morieris non annunciaveris ei etc.:* If when I say to the wicked man, "Thou shalt die," thou do not show it unto him, nor speak unto him, that he may be turned from his wicked way and may live, he shall soothly[2] die in his wickedness, and his blood shall I verily require of thine hand.[3]

But, cousin, though God invited men unto the following of himself in willful poverty, by the leaving of all together at once for his sake, as the thing whereby, with being out of the solicitude of worldly business and far fro the desire of earthly commodities, they may the more speedily get and attain the state of spiritual perfection and the hungry desire and longing for celestial things, yet doth he not command every man so to do upon the peril of damnation. For where he saith, *Qui non renunciaverit omnibus quae possidet non potest meus esse discipulus:* He that forsake not all that ever he hath cannot be my disciple,[4] he declareth well by other words of his own in the selfsame place a little before, what he meaneth. For there saith he more, *Si quis venit ad me, et non odit patrem suum et*

9. know.   1. *do . . . almoise:* give . . . alms.   2. truly.
3. Ezek. 3:18; cf. also Ezek. 33:8–9.   4. Luke 14:33.

matrem, et uxorem et filios et fratres et sorores, adhuc autem et animam suam, non potest meus esse discipulus: He that cometh to me, and hateth not his father and his mother, and his wife and his children, and his brethren and his sisters, yea, and his own life too, cannot be my disciple.[5]

Here meaneth our Savior Christ, that none can be his disciple but if[6] he love him so far above all his kin, and above his own life too, that for the love of him, rather than to forsake him, he shall forsake them all. And so meaneth he by those other words, that whosoever do not renounce and forsake all that ever he hath in his own heart and affection, that he will rather leese[7] it all and let it go every whit, than deadly displease God with the reserving of any one part thereof: he cannot be Christ's disciple, sith Christ teacheth us to love God above all thing, and he loveth not God above all thing that, contrary to God's pleasure, keepeth anything that he hath; for that thing he showeth himself to set more by than by God, while he is better content to leese God than it. But, as I said, to give away all, or that no man should be rich or have substance, that find I no commandment of. There are, as our Savior saith, in the house of his Father many mansions;[8] and happy shall he be that shall have the grace to dwell even in the lowest.

It seemeth very[9] by the gospel that those which for God's sake patiently suffer penury shall not only dwell above those in heaven that live here in plenty in earth, but also that heaven in some manner of wise[1] more properly belongeth unto them,[2] and is more specially prepared for them than it is for the rich, by that that[3] God in the gospel counseleth the rich folk to buy in a manner[4] heaven of them, where he saith unto the rich men, *Facite vobis amicos de mammona iniquitatis, ut quum defeceritis recipiant vos in aeterna tabernacula:* Make you friends of[5] the wicked riches, that when you fail here, they may receive you into the everlasting tabernacles.[6]

But now, although this be thus in respect of the riches and the

---

5. Luke 14:26.   6. *but if:* unless.   7. lose.   8. John 14:2.
9. true.   1. *in . . . wise:* in some kind of way.
2. Cf. Luke 6:20–21.   3. *by that that:* because.   4. way.
5. by means of.   6. Luke 16:9.

poverty compared together, yet they being good men both, there may be some other virtue beside, wherein the rich man may so peradventure[7] excel, that he may in heaven be far above that poor man that was here in earth in other virtues far under him, as the proof appeareth clear in Lazarus and Abraham.[8]

Nor I say not this to the intent to comfort[9] rich men in heaping up of riches. For a little comfort is bent[1] enough thereto for them that be not so proudhearted and obstinate but that they would, I ween,[2] to that counsel be with right little exhortation very conformable. But I say this for[3] those good men to whom God giveth substance and the mind[4] to dispose it well, and yet not the mind to give it all away at once, but for good causes to keep some substance still, should not despair of God's favor for the not doing of the thing which God hath given them no commandment of, nor drawn by any special calling thereunto.

Zacchaeus, lo, that climbed up into the tree for desire that he had to behold our Savior, at such time as Christ called aloud unto him and said, "Zacchaeus make haste and come down, for this day must I dwell in thine house,"[5] was so glad thereof and so touched inwardly with special grace to the profit of his soul, that whereas all the people murmured much that Christ would call him and be so familiar with him as of his own offer to come unto his house, considering that they knew him for the chief of the publicans, that were customers[6] or toll gatherers of the emperor's duties (all which whole company were among the people sore infamed of ravin,[7] extortion, and bribery), and then Zacchaeus not only the chief of that fellowship, but also grown greatly rich, whereby the people accounted him in their own opinion for a man very sinful and nought:[8] he forthwith by the instinct of the Spirit of God, in reproach of all such temerarious, bold,[9] and blind judgment, given upon a man whose inward mind and so sudden change they cannot

7. perhaps.   8. Luke 16:19–31.   9. encourage.
1. incentive.   2. think.   3. in order that.   4. intention.
5. Luke 19:5.   6. customs agents.
7. *sore . . . ravin:* extremely infamous for rapine.   8. wicked.
9. presumptuous.

see, shortly proved them all deceived, and that our Lord had at
those few words outwardly spoken to him, so wrought in his heart
within, that whatsoever he was before, he was then, unware unto
them all, suddenly waxen[1] good. For he made haste and came
down, and gladly received Christ and said, "Lo, Lord, the tone[2]
half of my goods here I give unto the poor people; and yet over
that, if I have in anything deceived any man, here am I ready to
recompense him fourfold as much."[3]

Vincent

This was, uncle, a gracious hearing. But I marvel me somewhat
wherefore Zacchaeus used his words in that manner of order. For
me thinketh he should first have spoken of making restitution unto
those whom he had beguiled, and speak of giving of his alms after.
For restitution is, you wot well, duty and a thing of such necessity
that in respect of restitution, alms-deed is but voluntary. Therefore
it might seem that to put men in mind of their duty in making
restitution first and doing their alms after, Zacchaeus should have
said more conveniently,[4] if he had said first that he would make
every man restitution whom he had wronged, and then give half in
alms of that that remained after, for only that might he call clearly
his own.

Antony

This is true, cousin, where a man hath not enough to suffice
both. But he that hath is not bounden to leave his alms ungiven to
the poor man that is at his hand and peradventure calleth upon
him, till he go seek up all his creditors and all those that he hath
wronged, so far peradventure asunder[5] that, leaving the tone good
deed undone the while, he may before they come together change
that good mind again and do neither the tone nor the tother.[6] It is
good alway to be doing some good out of hand[7] while we think
thereon; grace shall the better stand with us and increase also to go

1. become.   2. one.   3. Luke 19:8.   4. properly.
5. scattered, dispersed.   6. other.   7. *out of hand:* at once.

the farther in the tother after. And this I answer if the man had there done the tone out of hand, the giving, I mean, half in alms and not so much as speak of restitution till after; whereas now, though he spake the tone in order before the tother, and yet all at one time, the thing remained still in his liberty to put them both in execution, after such order as he should then think expedient.

But now, cousin, did the Spirit of God temper the tongue of Zacchaeus in the utterance of these words, in such wise[8] as it may well appear the saying of the wise man to be verified in them where he saith, *Domini est gubernare linguam:* To God it belongeth govern[9] the tongue.[1] For here when he said he would give half of his whole good unto poor people, and yet beside that not only recompense any man whom he had wronged, but more and recompense him by three times as much again, he double reproved the false suspicion of the people that accounted him for so evil that they reckoned in their mind all his good gotten in effect with wrong, because he was grown to substance in that office that was commonly misused extortiously.[2] But his words declared that he was ripe enough in his reckoning,[3] that if half his good were given away, yet were he well able to yield every man his duty with the tother half, and yet leave himself no beggar neither, for he said not he would give away all.

Would God, cousin, that every rich Christian man that is reputed right worshipful, yea, and (which yet in my mind more is) reckoned for right honest too, would and were able to do the thing that little Zacchaeus,[4] that same great publican (were he Jew or were he paynim[5]) said, that is to wit, with less than half his goods recompense every man whom he had wronged four times as much; yea, yea, cousin, as much for as much hardly,[6] and then they[7] shall receive it, shall be content, I dare promise for them, to let the tother thrice as much go and forgive it, because it was one of the hard

8. a way.   9. i.e., to govern.   1. Prov. 16:1.
2. by reliance on extortion.
3. *ripe . . . reckoning:* familiar enough with his accounts.
4. Luke 19:3 mentions that Zacchaeus was very short, which was why he climbed the sycamore tree to see Christ over the heads of the crowd.
5. pagan.   6. scarcely.   7. i.e., they who.

points of the old law, whereas Christian men must be full of forgiving, and not use to require[8] and exact their amends[9] to the uttermost.[1]

But now for our purpose here, notwithstanding that he promised not neither to give away all, nor to become a beggar neither, no, nor yet to leave off his office neither, which albeit that he had not used before peradventure in every point so pure as Saint John the Baptist had taught them the lesson, *Nihil amplius quam constitutum est vobis faciatis:* Do no more than is appointed unto you;[2] yet for as much as he might both lawfully use his substance that he minded to reserve, and lawfully might use his office too in receiving the prince's duty according to Christ's express commandment, *Reddite quae sunt Caesaris Caesari:* Give the emperor those things that be his,[3] refusing all extortion and bribery beside; our Lord, well allowing his good purpose, and exacting no further forth of him concerning his worldly behavior, answered and said, *Hodie salus facta est huic domui, eo quod et ipse filius sit Abrahae:* This day is health comen to this house, for that he too is the son of Abraham.[4]

But now forget I not, cousin, that in effect thus far you condescended unto[5] me that a man may be rich and yet not out of the state of grace, nor out of God's favor. Howbeit, you think that though it may be so in some time or in some place, yet at this time and in this place or any such other like, wherein be so many poor people upon whom they be, you think, bounden to bestow their good, they can keep no riches with conscience.

Verily, cousin, if that reason would hold, I ween the world was never such anywhere, in which any man might have kept any substance without the danger of damnation, as for[6] since Christ's

8. *use to require:* accustomed to ask.   9. restitution.
1. Cf. Exod. 22:1, 7, 9; Deut. 19:21; and Matt. 5:38–39.
2. Luke 3:13, the reply of John the Baptist to the publicans who came to be baptized and asked what they should do.
3. Mark 12:17.
4. Luke 19:9. Jesus' words to Zacchaeus after he promised to distribute his money.
5. *condescended unto:* agreed with.   6. *as for:* for.

days to the world's end, we have the witness of his own word that there hath never lacked poor men, nor never shall. For he said himself, *Pauperes semper habebitis vobiscum, quibus cum vultis benefacere potestis:* Poor men shall you alway have with you, whom when you will you may do good unto.[7] So that, as I tell you, if your rule should hold, then were there, I ween, no place in no time since Christ's days hither, nor, as I think, in as long before that neither, nor never shall there hereafter, in which there would abide any man rich without the danger of eternal damnation, even for his riches alone, though he demeaned[8] it never so well.

But, cousin, men of substance must there be, for else mo beggars shall you have pardie[9] than there be, and no man left able to relieve another. For this I think in my mind a very sure conclusion, that if all the money that is in this country were tomorrow next brought together out of every man's hand, and laid all upon one heap, and then divided out unto every man alike, it would be on the morrow after worse than it was the day before. For I suppose when it were all egally[1] thus divided among all, the best should be left little better then than almost a beggar is now, and yet he that was a beggar before, all that he shall be the richer for that he should thereby receive, shall not make him much above a beggar still; but many one of the rich men, if their riches stood but in movable substance, shall be safe enough from riches haply[2] for all their life after.

Men cannot, you wot well, live here in this world, but if that[3] some one man provide a mean of living for some other many. Every man cannot have a ship of his own, nor every man be a merchant without a stock. And these things, you wot well, must needs be had. Nor every man cannot have a plough by himself. And who might live by the tailor's craft if no man were able to put a gown to make?[4] Who by the masonry, or who could live a carpenter, if no man were able to build neither church or house? Who should be the makers of any manner[5] cloth, if there lacked men of

7. Mark 14:7.   8. managed.   9. an oath: "by God."
1. equally.   2. perhaps.   3. *but if that:* unless.
4. *put . . . to make:* request . . . to be made.   5. kind of.

substance to set sundry sorts awork. Some man that hath not two
ducats in his house were better forbear[6] them both and leave
himself not a farthing, but utterly lose all his own, than that some
rich man by whom he is weekly set awork should of his money lose
the tone half, for then were himself like to lack work; for surely the
rich man's substance is the well-spring of the poor man's living.

And therefore here would it fare by the poor man as it fared by
the woman in one of Aesop's fables, which had an hen that laid her
every day a golden egg, till on a day she thought she would have a
great many eggs at once. And therefore she killed her hen and
found but one or twain in her belly so that for a few she lost many.[7]

But now, cousin, to come to your doubt, how it may be that a man
may with conscience keep riches with him, when he seeth so many
poor men upon whom he may bestow it; verily, that might he not
with conscience do, if he must bestow it upon as many as he may.
And so must of truth every rich man do, if all the poor folk that he
seeth be so specially by God's commandment committed unto his
charge alone that, because our Savior saith, *Omni petenti te da:* Give
every man that asketh thee,[8] therefore he be bounden to give out
still to every beggar that will ask him, as long as any penny lasteth in
his purse. But verily, cousin, that saying hath (as Saint Austin[9] saith
other places in scripture hath) need of interpretation. For as Saint
Austin saith, Though Christ saith, Give every man that asketh thee,
he saith not yet give them all that they will ask thee.[1] But surely all
were one if he meant to bind me by commandment to give every
man without exception somewhat, for so should I leave myself
nothing.

6. give up.
7. The fable of the goose (or hen) that laid the golden eggs is attributed by
Caxton and others in the Renaissance to Avianus, not Aesop. Avianus
translated into Latin forty-two of the Greek fables of Babrius, dating from
the first century A.D.
8. A combination of Luke 6:30 and Matt. 5:42.
9. The idea is common in Augustine; see, for example, *Enarratio in Psalmum X (PL 36, 136)* and *De Civitate Dei,* XI, xix *(PL 41, 332–33)*.
1. Augustine, *De Sermone Domini in Monte,* II, xx *(PL 34, 1263–64)*.

Our Savior in that place of the sixth chapter of Saint Luke speaketh both of the contempt that we should in heart have of these worldly things, and also of the manner that men should use toward their enemies. For there he biddeth us love our enemies, give good words for evil, and not only suffer injuries patiently, both by taking away of our good and harm done unto our body, but also be ready to suffer the double,[2] and over that to do them good again that do us the harm.[3] And among these things he biddeth us give every man that asketh, meaning that in the thing that we may conveniently do a man good, we should not refuse it, what manner of man soever he be, though he were our mortal enemy; namely,[4] where we see that but if we help him ourself, the person of the man should stand in peril of perishing, and therefore saith, *Si esurierit inimicus tuus, da illi cibum:* If thine enemy be in hunger, give him meat.[5]

But now though I be bound to give every manner man in some manner of his necessity, were he my friend or my foe, Christian man or heathen, yet am I not unto all men bound alike, nor unto any man in every case alike, but, as I began to tell you, the differences of the circumstances make great change in the matter. Saint Paul saith, *Qui non providet suis, est infidelis deterior:* He that provideth not for those that are his is worse than an infidel.[6] Those are ours that are belonging to our charge, either by nature or by law, or any commandment of God—by nature as our children, by law as our servants in our household—so that albeit these two sorts be not ours all alike, yet would I think that the least ours of the twain, that is to wit, our servants, if they need or lack, we be bounden to look to them and provide for their need and see so farforth[7] as we may that they lack not the things that should serve for their necessity, while they dwell in our service. Me seemeth also if they fall sick in our service so that they cannot do the service that we retain them for, yet may we not in any wise turn them then out-of-doors and cast

---

2. *the double:* i.e., twice as much.

3. More paraphrases Luke 6:27-30.   4. especially.

5. Rom. 12:20, where Paul paraphrases Prov. 25:21.

6. 1 Tim. 5:8.   7. far.

them up comfortless,[8] while they be not able to labor and help themself; for this thing were a thing against all humanity. And surely, if he were but a wayfaring man that I received into my house as a guest, if he fall sick therein and his money gone, I reckon myself bounden to keep him still, and rather to beg about for his relief than cast him out in that case to the peril of his life, what loss soever I should hap[9] to sustain in the keeping of him. For when God hath by such chance sent him to me, and there once matched me with him, I reckon myself surely charged with him till I may without peril of his life be well and conveniently discharged of him.

By God's commandment are in our charge our parents,[1] for by nature we be in theirs sith as Saint Paul saith, it is not the children's part to provide for the parents, but the parents to provide for the children[2]—provide, I mean, conveniently good learning or good occupations to get their living by, with truth and the favor of God, but not to make provision for them of such manner living as to Godward they should live the worse for, but rather, if they see by their manner that too much would make them nought,[3] the father should then give them a great deal the less. But although that nature put not the parents in the charge of the children, yet not only God commandeth, but the order of nature also compelleth that the children should both in reverent behavior honor their father and mother and also in all their necessity maintain them. And yet as much as God and nature both bindeth us to the sustenance of our own father, his need may be so little, though it be somewhat, and a fremd[4] man's so great that both nature and God also would I should in such unequal need relieve that urgent necessity of a stranger, yea, my foe and God's enemy, too, the very Turk or Saracen, before a little need and unlikely to do great harm in my father and my mother too. For so ought they both twain themself to be well content I should.

But now, cousin, out of[5] the case of such extreme needs, well

---

8. without hope or consolation.   9. happen.
1. Cf. Exod. 20:12, the fourth commandment.   2. 2 Cor. 12:14.
3. wicked.   4. strange, unrelated.   5. *out of:* except in.

perceived and known unto myself, I am not bound to give every beggar that will ask, nor to believe every faitour[6] that I meet in the street, that will say himself that he is very sick, nor to reckon all the poor folk committed by God only so to my charge alone, that none other man should give them nothing of his till I have first given out all mine, nor am not bounden neither to have so evil opinion of all other folk save myself as to think that but if I help, the poor folk shall all fail at once, for God hath left in all this quarter no mo good folks now but me. I may think better by my neighbors and worse by myself than so, and yet come to heaven by God's grace well enough.

Vincent

Marry, uncle, but some man will peradventure be right well content in such case to think his neighbors very charitable to the intent that he may think himself at liberty to give nothing at all.

Antony

That is, cousin, very true. So will there some be content either to think or make as though they thought, but those are they that are content to give nought because they be nought. But our question is, cousin, not of them, but of good folk that by the keeping of worldly good stand in great fear to offend God. For the acquieting of their conscience speak we now, to the intent that they may perceive what manner of having of worldly good and keeping thereof may stand with the state of grace. Now think I, cousin, that if a man keep riches about him for a glory and rialty[7] of the world, in the consideration whereof he taketh a great delight and liketh himself therefor, taking the poorer for the lack thereof as one far worse than himself—such a mind[8] is very vain, foolish pride, and such a man is very nought indeed.

But on the tother[9] side if there be a man, such as would God were many, that hath unto riches no love, but having it fall abundantly unto him taketh to his own part no great pleasure thereof, but as

6. impostor.   7. regal splendor   8. attitude.   9. other.

though he had it not, keepeth himself in like abstinence and penance privily, as he would do in case he had it not; and in such things as he doth openly bestow somewhat more liberally upon himself in his house after some manner of the world, lest he should give other folk occasion to marvel and muse and talk of his manner and misreport him for an hypocrite, therein between God and him doth truly protest and testify, as did the good Queen Esther,[1] that he doth it not for any desire thereof in the satisfying of his own pleasure, but would with as good will or better forbear[2] the possession of riches, saving for the commodity that other men have by his possessing thereof, as percase[3] in keeping a good household in good Christian order and fashion, and in setting other folk awork with such things as they gain their living the better by his means— this man's having of riches I might, me thinketh, in merit match in a manner[4] with another man's forsaking of all, if there were none other circumstances more pleasant unto God added further unto the forsaking beside, as percase far the more fervent contemplation, by reason of the solicitude of all worldly business left off, which was the thing that made Mary Magdalen's part the better. For else would Christ have canned her much more thank[5] to go about and be busy in the helping her sister, Martha, to dress[6] his dinner, than to take her stool and sit down at her ease and do nought.[7]

Now if he that have this good and riches by him have not haply fully so perfect a mind, but somewhat loveth to keep himself from lack, and not so fully as a pure Christian fashion requireth, determined to abandon his pleasure—well, what will you more? The man is so much the less perfect than I would he were, and haply than himself would wish, if it were as easy to be it as to wish it, but yet not by and by in state of damnation for all that, no more than every man is forthwith in state of damnation that, forsaking all and entering into religion, is not yet alway so clear depured[8] from all

1. Esther 14:16–19.　　2. refrain from.　　3. for example.
4. *in a manner:* so to speak.
5. *canned . . . thank:* expressed much greater thanks.
6. prepare.　　7. Luke 10:38–42.　　8. purified.

worldly affections as he himself would very fain[9] he were and much bewaileth that he is not. Of whom some man that hath in the world willingly forsaken the likelihood of right worshipful rooms[1] hath afterward had much ado to keep himself from the desire of the office of cellarer[2] or sexton,[3] to bear yet at the leastwise some rule and authority, though it were but among the bells. But God is more merciful to man's imperfection if the man know it and knowledge it and mislike it and little and little labor to amend it, than to reject and cast to the devil him that after, as his frailty can bear and suffer, hath a general intent and purpose to please him, and to prefer or set by nothing in all this world before him.

And therefore, cousin, to make an end of this piece withal—*a negotio perambulante in tenebris,* of this devil, I mean, that the prophet calleth business walking in the darkness—if a man have a mind to serve God and please him, and rather lose all the good he hath than wittingly to do deadly sin, and would without murmur or grudge[4] give it every whit away in case that God should so command him, and intend to take it patiently if God would take it from him, and glad would be to use it unto God's pleasure, and do his diligence to know and to be taught what manner[5] using thereof God would be pleased with, and therein fro time to time be glad to follow the counsel of good, virtuous men, though he neither give away all at once, nor give every man that asketh him neither. Let every man fear and think in this world that all the good that he doth or can do is a great deal too little, but yet for all that fear, let him dwell therewith in the faithful hope of God's help, and then shall the truth of God so compass him about, as the prophet saith, with a pavis[6] that he shall not so need to dread the trains[7] and the temptations of the devil, that the prophet calleth business walking about in the darkness, but that he shall for all the having of riches and worldly substance so avoid his trains and his temptations that he

9. *would . . . fain:* would very gladly wish.
1. *worshipful rooms:* distinguished offices.
2. officer in a monastery in charge of the cellar or provisions.
3. officer in charge of maintenance of a church, bellringing, graves, etc.
4. complaint.   5. kind of.   6. large shield.   7. snares.

shall in conclusion, by the great grace and almighty mercy of God, get into heaven well enough. And now was I, cousin, about, lo, after this piece thus ended, to bid them bring in our dinner, but now shall I not need. Lo, for here they come with it already.

Vincent

Forsooth, good uncle, God disposeth and timeth your matter and your dinner both, I trust. For the end of your good tale, for which our Lord reward you, and the beginning here of your good dinner too, from which it were more than pity that you should any longer have tarried, meet even at the close together.

Antony

Well, cousin, now will we say grace, and then for a while will we leave talking and assay[8] how our dinner shall like us, and how fair we can fall to feeding, which done, you know my customable guise,[9] for manner[1] I may not call it because the guise is unmannerly, to bid you not farewell, but steal away fro you to sleep. But you wot[2] well I am not wont at afternoon to sleep long, but even a little to forget the world. And when I wake I will again come to you, and then is, God willing, all this long day ours, wherein we shall have time enough to talk much more than shall suffice for the finishing of this one part of our matter which only now remaineth.

Vincent

I pray you, good uncle, keep your customable manner, for manner may you call it well enough, for as it were against good manner to look that a man should kneel down for courtesy when his knee is sore, so is it very good manner that a man of your age, aggrieved with such sundry sicknesses beside that suffer[3] you not alway to sleep when you should, let this sleep not slip away, but take

8. try.   9. *customable guise:* customary practice.   1. custom.
2. know.   3. permit.

it when you may. And I will, uncle, in the meanwhile steal from you
too and speed⁴ a little errand, and return to you again.

Antony

Tarry while you will, and when you have dined go at your
pleasure, but I pray you tarry not long.

Vincent

You shall not need, uncle, to put me in mind of that; I would so
fain have up⁵ the remnant of our matter.

4. take care of.   5. *fain have up:* willingly take up.

The Third Book and the last
of consolation and comfort
in tribulation.

Vincent

Somewhat have I tarried the longer, uncle, partly for that I was
loath to come oversoon, lest my soon coming might have happed[1]
to have made you wake too soon, but specially by reason that I was
letted with[2] one that showed me a letter dated at Constantinople,
by which letter it appeareth that the great Turk prepareth a marvelous mighty army. And yet whither he will therewith, that can
there yet no man tell. But I fear in good faith, uncle, that his voyage
shall be hither. Howbeit he that wrote the letter saith it is secretly
said in Constantinople that great part of his army shall be shipped
and sent either into Naples or into Sicily.

Antony

It may fortune, cousin, that the letter of the Venetian dated at
Constantinople was devised at Venice. From thence come there
some among, and sometime fro Rome too, and sometime also fro
some other places letters all farced[3] full of such tidings that the
Turk is ready to do some great exploit, which tidings they blow
about for the furtherance of some such affairs as they then have
themself in hand.

The Turk hath also so many men of arms in his retinue at his
continual charge that lest they should lie still and do nothing, but

---

1. happened.   2. *letted with:* detained by.   3. crammed.

peradventure[4] fall in devising of some newelties[5] among themself, he is fain[6] yearly to make some assemblies and some changing of them from one place unto another, and part some sort asunder that they wax[7] not overwell acquainted by dwelling overlong together.

By these ways also he maketh those that he mindeth[8] suddenly to invade indeed the less to look therefor, and thereby the less preparation to make before while they see him so many times make a great visage[9] of war when he mindeth it not. But then at one time or other they suddenly feel it when they fear it not.

Howbeit full likely, cousin, it is of very truth that into this realm of Hungary he will not fail to come, for neither is there any country through Christendom that lieth for him so meet,[1] nor never was there any time till now in which he might so well and surely win it. For now call we him in ourself, God save us, as Aesop telleth that the sheep took in the wolf unto them to keep them fro the dogs.[2]

Vincent

Then are there very like, good uncle, all those tribulations to fall upon us here that I spake of in the beginning of our first communication here the tother[3] day.

Antony

Very truth it is, cousin, that so there will of likelihood in a while, but not forthwith all at the first. For while he cometh under the color[4] of aid for the tone[5] against the tother, he will somewhat see the proof before he fully show himself. But in conclusion, if he be able to get it for him, you shall see him so handle it that he shall not

4. perhaps.   5. new or unusual activities.   6. obliged.
7. become.   8. intends.
9. assumed appearance, outward show.   1. suitable.
2. A reference to the supporters of John Zapolya; see the Introduction. For the fable of the sheep and the dogs, cf. Erasmus, *Adagia,* "Ovem lupo commisisti," sig. k₃v (I. IV. x).
3. other.   4. semblance.   5. one.

fail to get it from him, and that forthwith out of hand[6] ere ever he suffer him settle himself oversure therein.[7]

Vincent

Yet say they, uncle, that he useth not to force any man to forsake his faith.

Antony

Not any man, cousin? They say more than they can make good that tell you so. He maketh a solemn oath among the ceremonies of the feast in which he first taketh upon him his authority that he shall in all that he possibly may minish[8] the faith of Christ and dilate the faith of Mahomet. But yet hath he not used to force every whole country at once to forsake their faith, for of some countries hath he been content only to take a tribute yearly and let them then live as they list.[9]

Out of some he taketh the whole people away, dispersing them for slaves among many sundry countries of his, very far fro their own, without any sufferance of regress.[1] Some country, so great and populous that they can not well be carried and conveyed thence, he destroyeth the gentlemen and giveth the lands, part to such as he bringeth, and part to such as willingly will renay[2] their faith, and keepeth the tother in such misery that they were in manner[3] as good be dead at once. In rest[4] he suffereth else no Christian man almost but those that resort as merchants, or those that offer themself to serve him in his war.

But as for those Christian countries that he useth not for only tributaries as he doth Chios,[5] Cyprus, or Candia,[6] but reckoneth

6. *forthwith . . . hand:* immediately.
7. Antony believes that if Suleiman ever gets the throne for Zapolya, he will not turn it over to him, but keep it for himself. Turkey eventually annexed a large portion of Hungary in 1547.
8. diminish.   9. please.
1. *sufferance of regress:* allowing of return.   2. deny.
3. *in manner:* so to speak.   4. *In rest:* As for the remainder.
5. One of the Greek Isles, about ten miles off the coast of Asia Minor.
6. Crete.

for clear conquest and utterly taketh for his own as Morea,[7] Greece, and Macedonia, and such other like (and as I verily think he will Hungary if he get it), in all those useth he Christian people after sundry fashions. He letteth them dwell there indeed, because they were too many to carry all away and too many to kill them all too, but if[8] he should either leave the land dispeopled and desolate, or else some other countries of his own from whence he should (which would not well be done) convey the people thither to people that land withal.

There, lo, those that will not be turned fro their faith, of which God keepeth (lauded be his holy name) very many, he suffereth to dwell still in peace, but yet is their peace for all that not very peaceable. For lands, he suffereth them to have none of their own; office or honest room[9] they bear none. With occasions of his wars he pilleth[1] them with taxes and tallages[2] unto the bare bones. Their children he chooseth where he list in their youth and taketh them fro their parents, conveying them whither he list, where their friends never see them after, and abuseth them as he list; some young maidens maketh harlots, some young men he bringeth up in war, and some young children he causeth to be gelded, not their stones[3] cut out as the custom was of old, but cutteth off their whole members by the body. How few scape and live he little forceth,[4] for he will have enough. And all that he so taketh young to any use of his own are betaken to such Turks or false renegades to keep, that they be turned fro the faith of Christ every one, or else so handled that as for this world they come to an evil cheving.[5] For beside many other contumelies and despites[6] that the Turks and the false renegade Christians many times do to good Christian people that still persevere and abide by the faith, they find the mean sometime to make some false shrews[7] say that they heard such a Christian man speak opprobrious words against Mahomet. And upon that

7. The Peloponnesus, that portion of Greece below the Isthmus of Corinth.
8. *but if:* unless.   9. office.   1. despoils, robs.
2. taxes levied upon feudal dependants by their lords.   3. testicles.
4. cares.   5. end.   6. scornful actions.   7. villains.

point falsely testified will they take occasion to compel him forsake
the faith of Christ and turn to the profession of their shameful,
superstitious sect, or else will they put him unto death with cruel,
intolerable torments.

Vincent

Our Lord, uncle, for his mighty mercy keep those wretches
hence. For by my truth if they hap to come hither, methink I see
many mo tokens than one that we shall have our own folk here
ready to fall in unto them. For like as before a great storm, the sea
beginneth sometime to work and roar in himself ere ever the wind
waxeth boistous,[8] so me think I hear at mine ear some of our own
here among us, which within these few years could no more have
borne the name of a Turk than the name of the devil, begin now to
find little fault therein, yea, and some to praise them too, little and
little as they may, more glad to find faults at every state[9] of Christendom: priests, princes, rites, ceremonies, sacraments, laws and
customs, spiritual, temporal and all.

Antony

In good faith, cousin, so begin we to fare here indeed, and that
but even now of late. For since the title of the crown hath comen in
question, the good rule of this realm hath very sore decayed, as
little while as it is.[1] And undoubtedly Hungary shall never do well,
as long as it standeth in this case, that men's minds hearken after
newelties[2] and have their hearts hanging upon a change. And
much the worse I like it when their words walk so large[3] toward the
favor of the Turk's sect, which they were ever wont to have in so
great abomination, as every true-minded Christian man and Christian woman too must have.

I am of such age as you see, and verily from as far as I can

8. rough.   9. estate, social rank.
1. The question of title to the Hungarian throne arose on the death of
Louis II in August 1526. See the Introduction.
2. novelties.   3. *walk so large:* tend so unrestrainedly.

remember it hath been marked and oftentime proved true that when children have in Buda fallen in a fantasy by themself to draw together, and in their playing make as it were corses[4] carried to church, and sing after their childish fashion the tune of the dirge, there hath great death there shortly followed after. And twice or thrice I may remember in my days, when children in divers parts of this realm have gathered themself in sundry companies and made as it were parties and battles, and after their battles in sport, wherein some children have yet taken great hurt, there hath fallen very[5] battle and deadly war indeed.

These tokens were somewhat like your ensample of the sea sith[6] they be of things that after follow tokens foregoing through some secret motion or instinct, whereof the cause is unknown. But by Saint Mary, cousin, these tokens like I much worse—these tokens, I say, not of children's plays, nor of children's songs, but old shrews' large, open words, so boldly spoken in the favor of Mahomet's sect in this realm of Hungary that hath been ever hitherto a very sure key of Christendom. And out of doubt if Hungary be lost, and that the Turk have it once fast in his possession, he shall ere it be long after have an open, ready way into almost the remnant of all Christendom. Though he win it not all in a week, the great part will be won after, I fear me, within very few years.

Vincent

But yet evermore I trust in Christ, good uncle, that he shall not suffer that abominable sect of his mortal enemies in such wise to prevail against his Christian country.

Antony

That is very well said, cousin. Let us have our sure hope in him, and then shall we be very sure that we shall not be deceived. For either shall we have the thing that we hope for or a better thing in the stead; for as for the thing itself that we pray for and hope to have, God will not alway send us. And therefore as I said in our first

4. corpses.   5. real.   6. since.

communication,[7] in all thing save only for heaven our prayer nor our hope may never be too precise, although the thing be leeful to require.[8]

Verily if we people of the Christian nations were such as would God we were, I would little fear all the preparations that the great Turk could make. No, nor yet being as bad as we be, I nothing doubt at all but that in conclusion, how base soever Christendom be brought, it shall spring up again till the time be come very near to the day of doom, whereof some tokens, as me thinketh, are not comen yet. But somewhat before that time shall Christendom be straited[9] sore and brought into so narrow a compass that, according to Christ's words, *Filius hominis quum venerit putas inveniet fidem in terra?* When the Son of Man shall come again, that is to wit, to the day of general judgment, weenest[1] thou that he shall find faith in the earth?[2] As who say,[3] but a little. For as appeareth in the Apocalypse and other places of scripture, the faith shall be at that time so far vaded[4] that he shall for the love of his elects, lest they should fall and perish too, abridge those days and accelerate his coming.[5]

But as I say, me thinketh I miss yet in my mind some of those tokens that shall by the scripture come a good while before that, and among other the coming in[6] of the Jews and the dilating[7] of Christendom again before the world come to that strait. So that I say for mine own mind, I little doubt but that this ungracious[8] sect of Mahomet shall have a foul fall, and Christendom spring and spread, flower and increase again. Howbeit, the pleasure and the comfort shall they see that shall be born after that we be buried, I fear me both twain. For God giveth us great likelihood that for our sinful, wretched living, he goeth about to make these infidels, that are his open, professed enemies, the sorrowful scourge of correc-

---

7. conversation.   8. *leeful to require:* lawful to ask.
9. forced into a narrow space.   1. thinkest.   2. Luke 18:8.
3. *As who say:* That is to say.   4. decayed.
5. Rev. 3:18–22, but More paraphrases Matt. 24:22.
6. *coming in:* conversion, as prophesied by Paul in Rom. 11:1–32.
7. expansion. See Rev. 3:9.   8. wicked, without grace.

tion over evil Christian people, that should be faithful and are of truth his falsely professed friends. And surely, cousin, albeit that me thinketh I see divers evil tokens of this misery coming to us, yet can there not in my mind be a worse prognostication thereof than this ungracious token that you note here yourself. For undoubtedly, cousin, this new manner here of men's favorable fashion in their language toward these ungracious Turks declareth plainly that not only their minds give[9] them that hither in shall he come, but also that they can be content both to live under him, and over that, fro the true faith of Christ to fall into Mahomet's false, abominable sect.

Vincent

Verily, mine uncle, as I go more about than you, so must I needs more hear, which is an heavy hearing in mine ear, the manner of men in this matter, which increaseth about us here. I trust in other places of this realm by God's grace it is otherwise, but in this quarter here about us, many of these fellows that are meet[1] for the war first were wont as it were in sport, and in a while after, half between game and earnest, and, by our Lady, now not far from fair, flat earnest indeed, talk as though they looked for a day when, with a turn unto the Turk's faith, they should be made masters here of true Christian men's bodies and owners of all their goods.

Antony

Though I go little abroad, cousin, yet hear I sometime when I say little almost as much as that. But while there is no man to complain to for the redress, what remedy but patience and fain[2] to sit still and hold my peace? For of these two that strive whither of them both shall reign upon us, and each of them calleth himself king, and both twain put the people to pain, the tone[3] is, you wot well, too far from our quarter here to help us in this behalf,[4] and the tother,[5]

9. suggest to.   1. fit.   2. being willing.   3. one.
4. Although Ferdinand invaded Hungary with a German-Bohemian army and defeated Zapolya in 1527, his base of operations remained in Austria.
5. other.

while he looketh for the Turk's aid, either will not, or I ween well dare not, find any fault with them that favor the Turk and his sect.[6] For of Turks natural this country lacketh none now, which are here conversant[7] under divers pretexts and of[8] everything advertise the great Turk full surely. And therefore, cousin, albeit I would advise every man pray still and call unto God to hold his gracious hand over us and keep away this wretchedness, if his pleasure be, yet would I further advise every good Christian body to remember and consider that it is very likely to come, and therefore make his reckoning, and cast his pennyworth's[9] before, and every man and every woman both, appoint with God's help in their own mind beforehand what thing they intend to do if the very worst fall.

The First Chapter

Whither[10] a man should cast[1] in his mind and appoint in his heart before that, if he were taken with Turks, he would rather die than forsake the faith.

Vincent

Well fare your heart, good uncle, for this good counsel of yours. For surely me thinketh that this is marvelous good. But yet heard I once a right cunning[2] and a very good man say that it were great folly and very perilous too that a man should think upon any such thing for fear of double peril that may follow thereupon. For either shall he be likely to answer himself to that case put by himself that

6. Zapolya was commonly recognized as a Turkish puppet, chosen by Suleiman immediately after the death of Louis II at Mohács. After his defeat by Ferdinand in 1527, Zapolya escaped to Poland, where he treated with Suleiman for the restoration of his throne. It was not until Suleiman's invasion of 1529 that Zapolya returned to Hungarian soil.
7. dwelling.   8. in.
9. *cast his pennyworth's:* count what it will cost him.   10. Whether.
1. determine.   2. wise.

he will rather suffer any painful death than forsake his faith, and by that bold appointment[3] should he fall in the fault of Saint Peter, that of oversight made a proud promise and soon had a foul fall,[4] or else were he likely to think that rather than abide the pain, he would forsake God indeed, and by that mind[5] should sin deadly through his own folly, whereas he needeth not, as he that shall peradventure[6] never come in the peril to be put thereunto. And that therefore it were most wisdom never to think upon any such manner[7] case.

Antony

I believe well, cousin, that you have heard some man that would so say, for I can show almost as much as that left of a very good man and a great, solemn doctor in writing. But yet, cousin, although I should hap[8] to find one or two mo as good men and as well learned too, that would both twain say and write the same, yet would I not fear for my part to counsel my friend to the contrary. For, cousin, if his mind answer him as Saint Peter answered Christ, that he would rather die than forsake him, though he say therein more unto himself than he should be peradventure able to make good if it came to the point, yet perceive I not that he doth in that thought any deadly displeasure unto God, nor Saint Peter, though he said more than he could perform, yet in his so saying offended not God greatly neither. But his offense was when he did not after so well as he said before.

But now may this man be likely never to fall in the peril of breaking that appointment, sith[9] of some ten thousand that so shall examine themself, never one shall fall in the peril. And yet to have that good purpose all their life seemeth me no more harm the while than a poor beggar that hath never a penny to think that if he had great substance he would give great alms for God's sake.

But now is all the peril if the man answer himself that he would in such case rather forsake the faith of Christ with his mouth and

3. decision.   4. Matt. 26:33–35, 69–75.   5. intention.
6. perhaps.   7. kind of.   8. happen.   9. since.

keep it still in his heart than for the confessing of it to endure a painful death. For by this mind he falleth in deadly sin, while he never cometh in the case indeed. If he never had put himself the case, he never had fallen in. But in good faith me thinketh that he, which upon that case put unto himself by himself will make himself that answer, hath the habit of faith so faint and so cold that to the better knowledge of himself and of his necessity to pray for more strength of grace he had need to have the question put him either by himself or some other man.

Besides this, to counsel a man never to think on that case is, in my mind, as much reason as the medicine that I have heard taught one for the toothache: to go thrice about a churchyard and never think on a foxtail. For if the counsel be not given them, it cannot serve them, and if it be given them, it must put the point of the matter in their mind, which by and by[1] to reject and think therein neither one thing nor other is a thing that may be sooner bidden than obeyed.

I ween also that very few men can escape it, but that though they would never think thereon by themself, but that yet in one place or other where they shall hap to come in company, they shall have the question by adventure so proponed[2] and put forth that, like as while he heareth one talking to him he may well wink[3] if he will, but he cannot make himself sleep, so shall he, whether he will or no, think one thing or other therein.

Finally when Christ spake so often and so plain of the matter, that every man should upon pain of damnation openly confess his faith,[4] if men took him and by dread of death would drive him to the contrary, it seemeth me in a manner implied therein that we be bounden conditionally to have evermore that mind, actually some-time, and evermore habitually, that if the case so should fall, then with God's help so we would.

And thus much thinketh me necessary for every man and

1. *by and by:* immediately.
2. *adventure so proponed:* chance so proposed.   3. close his eyes.
4. Cf. Matt. 10:32–33; Mark 8:38; and Luke 12:9.

woman to be alway of this mind and often to think thereupon, and where they find in the thinking thereon their hearts agrise[5] and shrink in the remembrance of the pain that their imagination representeth to the mind, then must they call to mind and remember the great pain and torment that Christ suffered for them, and heartily pray for grace that, if the case should so fall, God should give them strength to stand. And thus with exercise of such meditation, though men should never stand full out of fear of falling, yet must they persevere in good hope and in full purpose of standing.

And this seemeth me, cousin, so farforth[6] the mind that every Christian man and woman must needs have that me thinketh every curate should often counsel all his parishens,[7] and every man and woman, their servants and their children, even beginning in their tender youth, to know this point and think thereon, and little and little fro their very childhood to accustom them dulcely[8] and pleasantly in the meditation thereof, whereby the goodness of God shall not fail so to aspire[9] the grace of his Holy Spirit into their hearts, in reward of that virtuous diligence, that through such actual meditation he shall conserve them in such a sure habit of spiritual, faithful strength that all the devils in hell, with all the wrestling that they can make, shall never be able to wrest it out of their heart.

Vincent

By my troth, uncle, me thinketh that you say very well.

Antony

I say surely, cousin, as I think. And yet all this have I said concerning them that dwell in such places as they be never like in their lives to come in the danger to be put to the proof. Howbeit many a man may ween[1] himself far therefro, that yet may fortune by some one chance or other to fall in the case[2] that either for the

5. shudder with terror.   6. *so farforth:* to such an extent.
7. parishioners.   8. sweetly.   9. breathe.   1. think.
2. condition, situation.

truth of faith, or for the truth of justice, which go almost all alike, he may fall in the case. But now be you and I, cousin, and all our friends here far in another point. For we be so likely to fall in the experience thereof so soon that it had been more[3] time for us, all other things set aside, to have devised[4] upon this matter and firmly to have settled ourself upon a fast point[5] long ago than to begin to comen[6] and counsel upon it now.

Vincent

In good faith, uncle, you say therein very truth, and would God it had come sooner in my mind. But better is it yet late than never. And I trust God shall yet give us respite and time. Whereof, uncle, that we leese[7] no part, I pray you proceed now with your good counsel therein.

Antony

Very gladly, cousin, shall I now go forth in the fourth temptation, which only remaineth to be treated of, and properly pertaineth whole[8] unto this present purpose.

The Second Chapter

Of the fourth temptation, which is persecution for the faith, touched in these words of the prophet, *Ab incursu et demonio meridiano*.[9]

The fourth temptation, cousin, that the prophet speaketh of in the foreremembered psalm, *Qui habitat in adjutorio altissimi etc,* is plain, open persecution, which is touched in these words, *ab incursu*

---

3. rather.   4. meditated.   5. *fast point:* firm resolution.
6. discuss.   7. lose.   8. completely.
9. Ps. 90:6: "From the assault of the noonday devil."

et demonio meridiano. And of all his temptations this is the most perilous, the most bitter sharp, and the most rigorous. For whereas in other temptations he useth either pleasant allectives[1] unto sin, or either secret sleights and trains,[2] and cometh in the night, and stealeth on in the dark unware, or in some other part of the day flieth and passeth by like an arrow, so shaping himself sometime in one fashion, sometime in another, and so dissimuling himself and his high, mortal malice that a man is thereby so blinded and beguiled that he may not sometime perceive well what he is. In this temptation, this plain open persecution for the faith, he cometh even in the very midday, that is to wit, even upon them that have an high light of faith shining in their heart, and openly suffereth himself so plainly be perceived by his fierce, malicious persecution against the faithful Christians for hatred of Christ's true Catholic faith that no man having faith can doubt what he is. For in this temptation he showeth himself such as the prophet nameth him, *demonium meridianum:* the midday devil, he may be so lightsomely[3] seen with the eye of a faithful soul by his fierce, furious assault and incursion. For therefore saith the prophet that the truth of God shall compass that man round about, that dwelleth in the faithful hope of his help, with a pavis,[4] *ab incursu et demonio meridiano:* from the incursion and the devil of the midday, because this kind of persecution is not a wily temptation, but a furious force and a terrible incursion. In other of his temptations he stealeth on like a fox, but in this Turk's persecution for the faith, he runneth on roaring with assault like a ramping[5] lion.

This temptation is of all temptations also the most perilous; for whereas in temptations of prosperity, he useth only delectable allectives to move a man to sin, and in other kinds of tribulation and adversity, he useth only grief and pain to pull a man into murmur, impatience and blasphemy, in this kind of persecution for the faith of Christ, he useth both twain, that is to wit both his allective of quiet and rest by deliverance from death and pain, with other

1. attractions.   2. *sleights and trains:* stratagems and schemes.
3. clearly.   4. large shield.   5. raging.

pleasures also of this present life, and beside that the terror and infliction of intolerable pain and torment.

In other tribulation, as loss, or sickness, or death of our friends, though the pain be peradventure as great, and sometime greater too, yet is not the peril nowhere nigh half so much. For in other tribulations, as I said before, that necessity that the man must of fine force[6] abide and endure the pain, wax[7] he never so wroth and impatient therewith, is a great reason to move him to keep his patience therein, and be content therewith, and thank God thereof, and of necessity to make a virtue that he may be rewarded for. But in this temptation, this persecution for the faith, I mean not by fight in the field by which the faithful man standeth at his defense and putteth the faithless in half the fear and half the harm too, but where he is taken and in hold,[8] and may for the forswearing or the denying of his faith be delivered and suffered to live in rest and some in great worldly wealth also. In this case, I say, this thing that he needeth not to suffer, this trouble and pain, but he will,[9] is a marvelous great occasion for him to fall into the sin that the devil would drive him to, that is to wit, the forsaking of the faith. And therefore, as I say, of all the devil's temptations is this temptation, this persecution for the faith, the most perilous.

Vincent

The more perilous, uncle, that this temptation is, as indeed of all temptations the most perilous it is, the more need have they that stand in peril thereof to be before, with substantial advice and good counsel, well armed against it, that we may with the comfort and consolation thereof the better bear that tribulation when it cometh and the better withstand the temptation.

Antony

You say, Cousin Vincent, therein very truth, and I am content to fall therefore in hand[1] with it. But for as much, cousin, as me

6. *of fine force:* by absolute necessity.   7. become.   8. captivity.
9. *but he will:* unless he wishes.   1. *fall . . . hand:* concern myself.

thinketh that of this tribulation somewhat you be more feared than I, and of truth somewhat more excusable it is in you than it were in me, mine age considered and the sorrow that I have suffered already, with some other considerations upon my part beside, rehearse[2] you therefore the griefs and the pains that you think in this tribulation possible to fall unto you, and I shall against each of them give you counsel, and rehearse you such occasion of comfort and consolation as my poor wit[3] and learning can call unto my mind.

Vincent

In good faith, uncle, I am not all thing afeard in this case only for myself, but well you wot[4] I have cause to care also for many mo, and that folk of sundry sorts, men and women both, and that not all of one age.

Antony

All that you have cause to fear for, cousin, for all them have I cause to fear with you too, sith[5] all your kinsfolk and allies within a little[6] be likewise unto me. Howbeit, to say the truth, every man hath cause in this case of fear both for himself, and also for every other. For sith as the scripture saith, *Unicuique dedit deus curam de proximo suo:* God hath given every man cure[7] and charge of his neighbor,[8] there is no man that hath any spark of Christian love and charity in his breast, but that in a matter of such peril as this is, wherein the soul of man standeth in so great danger to be lost, he must needs care and take thought not for his friends only, but also for his very foes. We shall therefore, cousin, not rehearse your harms or mine that may befall in this persecution, but all the great harms in general, as near as we can call to mind, that may hap[9] unto any man.

2. relate.   3. intellect.   4. know.   5. since.
6. *allies . . . little:* close relatives.   7. care.   8. Ecclus. 17:12.
9. happen.

The Third Chapter

Sith a man is made of the body and the soul, all the harm that any man may take, it must needs be in one of these two, either immediately, or by the mean of some such thing as serveth for the pleasure, weal,[1] or commodity[2] of the tone[3] of these two. As for the soul, first, we shall need no rehearsal of any harm that by this kind of tribulation may attain thereto but if[4] that by some inordinate love and affection that the soul bear to the body, she consent to slide fro the faith and thereby doth her harm herself.

Now remain there the body and these outward things of fortune which serve for the maintenance of the body and minister matter of pleasure to the soul also through the delight that she hath in the body for the while that she is matched therewith.

Consider then first the loss of those outward things as somewhat the less in weight than is the body itself. In them what may a man lose, and thereby what pain may he suffer?

Vincent

He may lose, uncle, of which I should somewhat lose myself, money, plate, and other moveable substance, then offices, authority, and finally all the lands of his inheritance forever that himself and his heirs perpetually might else enjoy. And of all these things, uncle, you wot well that myself have some—little in respect of that that some other have here, but somewhat more yet than he that hath most here would be well content to lose.

Upon the loss of these things follow neediness and poverty, the pain of lacking, the shame of begging, of which twain I wot not well which is the most wretched necessity, beside the grief of heart and heaviness in beholding good men and faithful and his dear friends bewrapped in like misery, and ungracious[5] wretches and infidels and his mortal enemies enjoy the commodities that himself and his friends have lost.

Now for the body. Very few words shall serve us, for therein I see

1. well-being.   2. benefit.   3. one.   4. *but if:* unless.
5. wicked.

none other harm but loss of liberty, labor, imprisonment, painful and shameful death.

Antony

There needeth not much more, cousin, as the world is now. For I fear me that less than a fourth part of this will make a man sore[6] stagger in his faith and some fall quite therefro that yet at this day, before he come to the proof, weeneth himself that he would stand very fast. And I beseech our Lord that all they that so think and would yet when they were brought unto the point swerve therefro for fear or for pain may get of God the grace to ween[7] still as they do, and not to be brought to the assay[8] where pain or fear should show them, as it showed Saint Peter, how far they be deceived now.

But now, cousin, against these terrible things, what way shall we take in giving men counsel of comfort? If the faith were in our days as fervent as it hath been ere this in time before passed, little counsel and little comfort would suffice. We should not much need with words and reasoning to extenuate and minish[9] the vigor and asperity of the pains, but the greater, the more bitter that the passion[1] were, the more ready was of old time the fervor of faith to suffer it.

And surely, cousin, I doubt it little in my mind but that if a man had in his heart so deep a desire and love, longing to be with God in heaven, to have the fruition of his glorious face as had those holy men that were martyrs in old time, he would no more now stick at the pain that he must pass between than at that time those old holy martyrs did. But alas our faint and feeble faith, with our love to God less than lukewarm by the fiery affection that we bear to our own filthy flesh, make us so dull in the desire of heaven that the sudden dread of every bodily pain woundeth us to the heart and striketh our devotion dead. And therefore hath there every man, cousin, as I said before, much the more need to think upon this thing many time and oft aforehand ere any such peril fall, and by much devising[2] thereupon before they see cause to fear it, while

6. severely.   7. think.   8. test.   9. lessen.   1. suffering.
2. meditation.

the thing shall not appear so terrible unto them, reason shall better enter and through grace working with their diligence engender and set sure, not a sudden, slight affection of sufferance[3] for God's sake, but by a long continuance a strong, deep-rooted habit, not like a reed ready to wave with every wind, nor like a rootless tree scant up an end[4] in a loose heap of light sand that will with a blast or two be blown down.

The Fourth Chapter

For if we now consider, cousin, these causes of terror and dread that you have recited, which in this persecution for the faith this midday devil may by these Turks rear against us to make his incursion with, we shall well perceive, weighing them well with reason, that albeit somewhat they be indeed, yet every part of the matter pondered, they shall well appear in conclusion things nothing so much to be dread and fled fro as to folk at the first sight they do suddenly seem.

The Fifth Chapter

Of the loss of the goods of fortune.

For first to begin at the outward goods that neither are the proper goods of the soul nor of the body, but are called the goods of fortune, that serve for the substance[5] and commodity of man for the short season of this present life, as worldly substance, offices, honor, and authority—what great good is there in these things of themself for which they were worthy so much as to bear the name by which the world of a worldly favor[6] customably[7] calleth them?

---

3. *affection of sufferance:* disposition toward endurance.
4. *scant . . . end:* hardly up on end.   5. maintenance.
6. preference.   7. customarily.

For if the having of strength make a man strong, and the having of heat make a man hot, and the having of virtue make a man virtuous, how can those things be verily and truly good which he that hath them may by the having of them, as well be the worse as the better, and as experience proveth more oft is the worse than the better? What[8] should a good man greatly rejoice in that, that he daily seeth most abound in the hands of many that be nought?[9] Do not now the great Turk and his bashaws[1] in all these advancements of fortune surmount very far above any Christian estate[2] and any lords living under him? And was there not yet hence upon twenty years the great Soldan of Syria, which many a year together bare as great a port as the great Turk, and after in one summer unto the great Turk the whole empire was lost?[3] And so may all his empire now, and shall hereafter by God's grace, be lost into Christian men's hands likewise, when Christian people shall be mended and grow in God's favor again.

But when that whole kingdoms and mighty, great empires are of so little surety to stand, but be so soon translated[4] from one man unto another, what great thing can you or I, yea, or any lord, the greatest in this land, reckon himself to have by the possession of an heap of silver or gold, white and yellow metal, not so profitable of their own nature, save for a little glistering,[5] as the rude, rusty metal of iron?

The Sixth Chapter

Of the unsurety of lands and possessions

Lands and possessions many men yet much more esteem than money, because the lands seem not so casual[6] as money is or plate,

---

8. For what reason.   9. wicked.
1. pashas, high-ranking officers in the Turkish army.   2. nobleman.
3. The Mameluke Empire of Syria and Egypt fell to the Ottoman Turks in the summer of 1516.
4. transferred.   5. glittering.   6. subject to chance.

for that[7] though their other substance may be stolen and taken away, yet evermore they think that their land will lie still where it lay. But what are we the better that our land cannot be stirred but will lie still where it lay, while ourself may be removed and not suffered to come near it? What great difference is there to us whether our substance be moveable or unmoveable, sith we be so moveable ourselves that we may be removed from them both and lose them both twain, saving that sometime in the money is the surety somewhat more? For when we be fain[8] ourself to flee, we may make shift to carry some of our money with us, whereof our land we cannot carry one inch.

If our land be of more surety than our money, how happeth it then that in this persecution we be more feared to lose it? For if it be a thing of more surety, then can it not so soon be lost. In the translation of these two great empires, Greece first, sith myself was born, and after Syria, since you were born too,[9] the land was lost before the money was found.

Oh, Cousin Vincent, if the whole world were animated with a reasonable soul, as Plato had went[1] it were,[2] and that it had wit and understanding to mark and perceive all thing, Lord God, how the ground on which a prince buildeth his palace would loud laugh his lord to scorn, when he saw him proud of his possession and heard him boast himself that he and his blood are forever the very lords and owners of that land! For then would the ground think the while in himself, "Ah, thou seely,[3] poor soul that weenest thou were half a god and art, amid thy glory, but a man in a gay gown. I that am the ground here, over whom thou art so proud, have had an hundred such owners of me, as thou callest thyself, mo than ever thou hast heard the names of. And some of them that proudly went over my head lie now low in my belly, and my side lieth over them. And many one shall, as thou dost now, call himself mine owner after thee, that neither shall be sib[4] to thy blood, nor any word hear of thy name." Who ought[5] your castle, cousin, three thousand years ago?

7. *for that:* because.   8. obliged.
9. Greece fell in 1453, Syria in 1516.   1. thought.
2. *Timaeus,* 34A–37C.   3. pitiable.   4. akin.   5. owned.

Vincent

Three thousand, uncle? Nay, nay, in any king, Christian or heathen, you may strike off a third part of that well enough, and as far as I ween, half of the remnant too. In far fewer years than three thousand it may well fortune that a poor ploughman's blood may come up to a kingdom, and a king's right royal kin on the tother[6] side fall down to the plough and cart, and neither that the king know that ever he came fro the cart, nor the carter know that ever he came fro the crown.

Antony

We find, Cousin Vincent, in full antique[7] stories many strange changes as marvelous as that come about in the compass of very few years in effect. And be such things then in reason so greatly to be set by,[8] that we should esteem the loss at so great, when we see that in the keeping our surety is so little?

Vincent

Marry, uncle, but the less surety that we have to keep it, sith[9] it is a great commodity to have it, the further by so much and the more loath we be to forego it.

Antony

That reason shall I, cousin, turn against yourself. For if it be so as you say, that sith the things be commodious, the less surety that you see you have of the keeping, the more cause you have to be afeard of the losing, then on the tother side, the more that a thing is of his nature such that the commodity thereof bringeth a man little surety and much fear, that thing of reason the less have we cause to love. And then the less cause that we have to love a thing, the less cause have we to care therefor, or fear the loss thereof, or be loath to go therefrom.

6. other.   7. *full antique:* very ancient.   8. *set by:* valued.
9. since.

The Seventh Chapter

These outward goods or gifts of fortune are by two manner wise[1] to be considered.

We shall yet, cousin, consider in these outward goods of fortune, as riches, good name, honest estimation, honorable fame, and authority—in all these things we shall, I say, consider that either we love them and set by them as things commodious[2] unto us for the state and condition of this present life, or else as things that we purpose, by the good use thereof, to make them matter of our merit with God's help in the life after to come. Let us then first consider them as things set by and beloved for the pleasure and commodity of them for this present life.

The Eighth Chapter

The little commodity of richesse,[3] being set by but for this present life.

Now riches loved and set by for such, if we consider it well, the commodity that we take there thereof, is not so great as our own fond[4] affection and fantasy maketh us imagine it. It maketh us (I say not nay) go much more gay and glorious in sight, garnished[5] in silk (but cloth[6] is within a little[7] as warm). It maketh us have great plenty of many kind of delicate and delicious victual, and thereby to make more excess. But less exquisite and less superfluous fare, with fewer surfeits and fewer fevers growing thereon too, were within a little as wholesome. Then the labor in the getting, the fear in the keeping, and the pain in the parting fro do more than counterpoise a great part of all the pleasure and commodity that

1. *manner wise:* kinds of ways.   2. beneficial.   3. wealth.
4. foolish.   5. embellished.   6. woolen fabric.
7. *within a little:* almost.

they bring; beside this, that riches is the thing that taketh many times from his master all his pleasures and his life too, for many a man is for his richesse slain. And some that keep their richesse as a thing pleasant and commodious for their life, take none other pleasure in a manner[8] thereof in all their life than as though they bare the key to another man's coffer, and rather are content to live in neediness miserably all their days than they could find in their heart to minish their hoard, they have such fantasy[9] to look thereon. Yea, and some men, for fear lest thieves should steal it fro them, be their own thieves and steal it fro themself, while they dare not so much as let it lie where themself may look thereon, but put it in a pot and hide it in the ground, and there let it lie safe till they die, and sometime seven year after; from which place if the pot had been stolen away five year before his death, all the same five year that he lived after, weening[1] alway that his pot lay safe still, what had he been the poorer while he never occupied[2] it after?

Vincent

By my troth, uncle, not one penny for aught that I perceive.

The Ninth Chapter

The little commodity of fame, being desired but for worldly pleasure.

Antony

Let us now consider good name, honest estimation, and honorable fame. For these three things are of their own nature one and take their difference in effect but of the manner of the common speech in diversity of degrees.[3] For a good name may a man have,

---

8. *in a manner:* so to speak.   9. desire.   1. thinking.
2. had possession of.
3. *in . . . degrees:* i.e., in referring to men of different social ranks.

be he never so poor; honest estimation, in the common taking[4] of the people, belongeth not unto any man, but him that is taken for one of some countenance and havior,[5] and among his neighbors had in some reputation. In the word of honorable fame, folk conceive the renown of great estates,[6] much and far spoken of by reason of their laudable acts.

Now all this gear,[7] used as a thing pleasant and commodious for this present life, pleasant it may seem to him that fasteneth his fantasy therein, but of the nature of the thing itself, I perceive no great commodity that it hath. I say "of the nature of the thing itself," because it may be by chance some occasion of commodity, as if it hap[8] that for the good name the poor man hath, or for the honest estimation that a man of some havior and substance standeth in among his neighbors, or for the honorable fame wherewith the great estate is renowned—if it hap, I say, that any man bearing them the better will[9] therefor, do them therefor any good. And yet as for that, like as it may sometime so hap, and sometime so happeth indeed, so may it hap sometime on the tother side, and on the tother side so it sometime happeth indeed, that such folk are of some other envied and hated, and as readily by them that envy them and hate them take harm, as they take by them that love them good.

But now to speak of the thing itself in his own proper nature: what is it but a blast of another man's mouth, as soon passed as spoken, whereupon he that setteth his delight, feedeth himself but with wind, whereof be he never so full, he hath little substance therein?

And many times shall he much deceive himself, for he shall ween that many praise him that never speak word of him, and they that do, say it much less than he weeneth and far more seldom too. For they spend not all the day, he may be sure, in talking of him alone. And whoso commend him most will yet, I ween, in every four and

4. opinion.   5. *countenance and havior:* standing and wealth.
6. *great estates:* men in high positions.   7. business.   8. happen.
9. *bearing . . . will:* holding them (men of good reputation) in higher regard.

twenty hours wink[1] and forget him once; besides this, that while one talketh well of him in one place, another sitteth and saith as shrewdly[2] of him in another. And finally some that most praise him in his presence, behind his back mock him as fast,[3] and loud laugh him to scorn, and sometime slyly to his own face too. And yet are there some fools so fed with this fond fantasy of fame that they rejoice and glory to think how they be continually praised all about, as though all the world did nothing else day nor night but ever sit and sing *sanctus, sanctus, sanctus*[4] upon them.

The Tenth Chapter
Of flattery.

And into this pleasant frenzy of much foolish vainglory be there some men brought sometime by such as themself do, in a manner, hire to flatter them, and would not be content if a man should do otherwise, but would be right angry not only if a man told them truth when they do nought indeed, but also if they praise it but slenderly.

Vincent

Forsooth, uncle, this is very truth. I have been ere this, and not very long ago, where I saw so proper experience of this point that I must stop your tale for so long while I tell you mine.

Antony

I pray you, cousin, tell on.

1. close his eyes.   2. maliciously.   3. readily.
4. holy, holy, holy. I.e., as though they were God. Cf. Isa. 6:1–3, where God is described on his throne surrounded by seraphim, who sing, "Holy, holy, holy, Lord God of hosts." The phrase is also used at the beginning of the consecration in the mass.

Vincent

When I was first in Almaine,[5] uncle, it happed[6] me to be somewhat favored with a great man of the church and a great state,[7] one of the greatest in all that country there. And indeed whosoever might spend as much as he might in one thing and other were a right great estate in any country of Christendom. But glorious[8] was he very far above all measure, and that was great pity, for it did harm and made him abuse many great gifts that God had given him. Never was he satiate of hearing his own praise.[9]

So happed it one day that he had in a great audience made an oration in a certain manner, wherein he liked himself so well that at his dinner he sat, him thought, on thorns till he might hear how they that sat with him at his board[1] would commend it. And when he had sit musing awhile, devising,[2] as I thought after, upon some pretty, proper way to bring it in withal, at the last for lack of a better, lest he should have letted[3] the matter too long, he brought it even blunt forth and asked us all that sat at his board's end (for at his own mess[4] in the mids[5] there sat but himself alone), how well we liked his oration that he had made that day.

But in faith, uncle, when that problem was once proponed,[6] till it was full answered no man, I ween, ate one morsel of meat more, every man was fallen in so deep a study for the finding of some exquisite praise. For he that should have brought out but a vulgar and a common commendation would have thought himself shamed forever.

Then said we our sentences by row as we sat, from the lowest

---

5. Germany.   6. happened to.   7. wealth, estate.
8. haughty.
9. Harpsfield (pp. 34–35) identifies this "great man of the church" as Cardinal Wolsey.
1. table.   2. meditating.   3. postponed.
4. serving of food, course of dishes. More is being ironic. The word "mess" was often used to indicate a small group of people at a banquet who were served from the same dishes, but here the great man sits alone in the middle of the table with his guests crowded together at the end.
5. middle.   6. proposed.

unto the highest in good order, as it had been a great matter of the commonweal in a right solemn council. When it came to my part (I will not say it, uncle, for no boast) me thought, by our Lady, for my part I quit[7] myself meetly[8] well, and I liked myself the better because me thought my words, being but a stranger,[9] went yet with some grace in the Almaine tongue, wherein, letting my Latin alone, me listed to show my cunning.[10] And I hoped to be liked the better because I saw that he that sat next me and should say his sentence after me was an unlearned priest; for he could speak no Latin at all. But when he came forth for his part with my lord's commendation, the wily fox had be[1] so well accustomed in court with the craft of flattery that he went beyond me too too far. And then might I see by him what excellence a right mean wit may come to in one craft, that in all his whole life studieth and busieth his wit about no mo but that one. But I made after a solemn vow to myself that if ever he and I were matched together at that board again, when we should fall to our flattery, I would flatter in Latin, that he should not contend with me no more. For though I could be content to be outrun of an horse, yet would I no more abide it to be outrun of an ass.

But, uncle, here began now the game. He that sat highest and was to speak last was a great beneficed[2] man and not a doctor only, but also somewhat learned indeed in the laws of the church.[3] A world it was to see how he marked every man's word that spake before him. And it seemed that every word, the more proper that it was, the worse he liked, for the cumbrance[4] that he had to study out a better to pass it. The man even sweat with the labor, so that he was fain in the while[5] now and then to wipe his face. Howbeit in conclusion when it came to his course,[6] we that had spoken before him had so taken up all among us before that we had not left him one wise word to speak after.

7. acquitted.   8. reasonably.   9. foreigner.
10. *me listed . . . cunning:* it pleased me . . . knowledge.   1. been.
2. one holding important benefices or ecclesiastical livings.
3. i.e., not only a theologian, but also learned in canon law.
4. encumbrance.   5. *fain . . . while:* obliged meanwhile.   6. turn.

Antony

Alas, good man, among so many of you, some good fellow should have lent him one.

Vincent

It needed not as hap was, uncle. For he found out such a shift that in his flattering he passed[7] us all the many.

Antony

Why, what said he, cousin?

Vincent

By our Lady, uncle, not one word. But like as, I trow,[8] Plinius telleth, that when Apelles the painter, in the table[9] that he painted of the sacrifice and the death of Iphigenia,[1] had in the making of the sorrowful countenances of the other noble men of Greece that beheld it spent out so much his craft and his cunning that when he came to make the countenance of King Agamemnon, her father, which he reserved for the last, lest if he had made his visage before, he must in some of the other after either have made the visage less dolorous than he could and thereby have forborne[2] some part of his praise, or doing the uttermost of his craft, might have happed to make some other look more heavily for the pity of her pain than her own father, which had been yet a far greater fault in his painting. When he came, I say, to the making of his face therefor last of all, he could devise no manner[3] of new heavy cheer[4] or countenance for her father, but that he had made there already in some of the tother a much more heavy before. And therefore to the intent that no man should see what manner countenance it was that

7. surpassed.   8. believe.   9. picture.
1. The daughter of Agamemnon, who was sacrificed by her father at Aulis to appease the wrath of Artemis and allow the Greek fleet to sail for Troy.
2. gone without.   3. kind of.   4. expression of the face.

her father had, the painter was fain to paint him holding his face in his handkerchief.[5]

The like pageant in a manner played us there this good, ancient, honorable flatterer. For when he saw that he could find no words of praise that would pass all that had been spoken before already, the wily fox would speak never a word, but as he that were ravished unto heavenward with the wonder of the wisdom and eloquence that my lord's grace had uttered in that oration, he fet[6] a long sigh, with an "Oh!" fro the bottom of his breast, and held up both his hands, and lift up his head, and cast up his eyes into the welkin,[7] and wept.

Antony

Forsooth, cousin, he played his part very properly. But was that great prelate's oration, cousin, anything praiseworthy, for you can tell I see well? For you would not, I ween, play as Juvenal[8] merrily describeth the blind senator, one of the flatterers of Tiberius the Emperor, that among the remnant so magnified the great fish that the emperor had sent for them to show them, which this blind senator, Montanus, I trow they called him, marveled of as much as any that marveled most, and many things he spake thereof, with some of his words directed thereunto, looking himself toward his left side, while the fish lay on his right side. You would not, I trow, cousin, have taken upon you to praise it so but if[9] you had heard it?

Vincent

I heard it, uncle, indeed, and to say the truth, it was not to dispraise; howbeit, surely somewhat less praise might have served it by more a great deal than the half. But this am I sure, had it been the worst that ever was made, the praise had not been the less of

5. *Nat. Hist.*, XXXV, xxxvi, 73–74. The painter was not Apelles, but Timanthes, who lived in Cythnus and later in Sicyon in the late fifth century B.C. The Iphigenia was his most famous work. Apelles of Cos (*fl.* 332–329 B.C.) was the most renowned painter of antiquity.
6. brought forth.   7. sky.   8. *Sat. IV,* 119–21.   9. *but if:* unless.

one hair. For they that used to praise him to his face never considered how much the thing deserved, but how great a laud and praise themself could give his good grace.

Antony

Surely, cousin, as Terence saith, such folk make men of fools even stark mad,[1] and much cause have their lords to be right angry with them.

Vincent

God hath indeed and is, I ween. But as for their lords, uncle, if they would after wax[2] angry with them therefor, they should in my mind do them very great wrong, when it is one of the things that they specially keep them for. For those that are of such vainglorious mind, be they lords or be they meaner men, can be much better contented to have their devices commended than amended and require they their servants and their friend never so specially to tell them the very truth, yet shall they better please them if he speak them fair than if he telleth them truth. For they be in the case that Martialis speaketh of in an epigram unto a friend of his, that required[3] his judgment how he liked his verses. But he prayed him in any wise[4] to tell him even the very truth. To whom Martial made answer in this wise:

> The very truth of me thou dost require.
> The very truth is this, my friend dear:
> The very truth thou wouldst not gladly hear.[5]

And in good faith, uncle, the selfsame prelate that I told you my tale of, I dare be bold to swear it, I know it so surely, had on a time made of his own drawing a certain treatise,[6] that should serve for a league between that country and a great prince. In which treatise

---

1. i.e., such folk turn fools into madmen. Cf. *Eunuchus*, II, 254.
2. become.   3. asked.   4. way.   5. *Epig.*, VIII, lxxvi.
6. treaty.

himself thought that he had devised his articles so wisely and indited them so well that all the world would allow them. Whereupon, longing sore[7] to be praised, he called unto him a friend of his, a man well learned and of good worship,[8] and very well expert in those matters, as he that had be divers times ambassador for that country and had made many such treatises himself. When he took him the treatise, and that he had read it, he asked him how he liked it and said, "but I pray you heartily tell me the very truth," and that he spake so heartily that the tother[9] had went[1] he would fain[2] have heard the truth. And in trust thereof he told him a fault therein. At the hearing whereof, he sware in great anger, "By the mass, thou art a very fool." The tother afterward told me that he would never tell him truth again.[3]

Antony

Without question, cousin, I cannot greatly blame him. And thus themself make every man mock them, flatter them, and deceive them—those, I say, that are of such vainglorious mind. For if they be content to hear the truth, let them then make much of them that tell them the truth and withdraw their ear from them that falsely flatter them. And they shall be more truly served than with twenty requests praying men to tell them true.

King Ladislaus, our Lord assoil[4] his soul, used much this manner[5] among his servants. When one of them praised any deed of his or any condition in him, if he perceived that they said but the truth, he would let it pass by uncontrolled.[6] But when he saw that they set a gloss[7] upon it for his praise of their own making beside, then would he shortly say unto them, "I pray thee, good fellow, when thou say grace at my board, never bring in *gloria patri* without

7. extremely.   8. honor, distinction.   9. other.   1. thought.
2. gladly.
3. Chambers suggests that this also is a personal anecdote (*Thomas More,* pp. 161–62). Stapleton (pp. 136–37) tells of a similar occasion in which Wolsey called More a fool.
4. absolve.   5. custom.   6. undisputed.
7. flattering interpretation.

a *sicut erat*.[8] Any act that ever I did, if thou report it again to mine honor with a *gloria patri,* never report it but with a *sicut erat*, that is to wit, even as it was and none otherwise. And lift me not up with no lies, for I love it not."

If men would use this way with them that this noble king used, it would minish[9] much of their false flattery. I can well allow that men should commend, keeping them within the bonds of truth, such things as they see praiseworthy in other men, to give them the greater courage to the increase thereof. For men keep still in that point one condition of children: that praise must prick[1] them forth. But better it were to do well and look for none. Howbeit, they that cannot find in their heart to commend another man's good deed show themself either envious or else of nature very cold and dull.

But out of question, he that putteth his pleasure in the praise of the people hath but a fond fantasy.[2] For if his finger do but ache of an hot blain,[3] a great many men's mouths, blowing out his praise, will scantly[4] do him among them all half so much ease as to have one boy blow upon his finger.

The Eleventh Chapter

The little commodity[5] that men have of rooms,[6] offices, and authority, if they desire them but for their worldly commodity.

Let us now consider in likewise[7] what great worldly wealth ariseth unto men by great offices, rooms, and authority, to those

---

8. *gloria . . . erat:* the first words of the lesser doxology, "Glory be to the Father, and to the Son, and to the Holy Spirit," usually followed by: "as it was (*sicut erat*) in the beginning, is now, and ever shall be, world without end, amen."
9. reduce.   1. urge, incite.   2. *fond fantasy:* foolish delusion.
3. inflammation.   4. hardly.   5. advantage.   6. offices.
7. *in likewise:* in the same manner.

worldly disposed people, I say, that desire them for no better purpose. For of them that desire them for better we shall speak after anon.[8]

The great thing that they chief like all therein is that they may bear a rule, command, and control other men, and live uncommanded and uncontrolled themself. And yet this commodity took I so little heed of that I never was ware it was so great, till a good friend of ours merrily told me once that his wife once in a great anger taught it him. For when her husband had no list[9] to grow greatly upward in the world, nor neither would labor for office of authority, and over that forsook a right worshipful room when it was offered him, she fell in hand with[1] him, he told me, and all to rated him,[2] and asked him, "What will you do, that you list not to put forth yourself as other folk do? Will you sit still by the fire and make goslings[3] in the ashes with a stick as children do? Would God I were a man, and look what I would do."

"Why, wife," quoth her husband, "what would you do?"

"What! By God, go forward with the best. For as my mother was wont to say, God have mercy on her soul, it is ever more better to rule than to be ruled. And therefore, by God, I would not, I warrant you, be so foolish to be ruled where I might rule."

"By my troth, wife," quoth her husband, "in this I dare say you say truth, for I never found you willing to be ruled yet."

Vincent

Well, uncle, I wot where you be now well enough. She is indeed a stout master woman.[4] And in good faith, for ought that I can see, even that same womanish mind of hers is the greatest commodity that men reckon upon in rooms and offices of authority.

---

8. *after anon:* immediately after.   9. desire.
1. *fell in hand with:* went to work on.
2. *all . . . him:* reproved him vehemently.
3. figures of goslings or young geese.
4. Harpsfield (pp. 94–95) again identifies this as a personal anecdote involving More and Dame Alice.

Antony

By my troth, and me thinketh very few there are of them that
attain any great commodity therein. For first there is in every
kingdom but one that can have an office of such authority that no
man may command him or control him. None officer can there
stand in that case but the king himself, which only uncontrolled or
uncommanded may control and command all. Now of all the
remnant, each is under him. And yet beside him, almost everyone
is under mo commanders and controllers too than one. And some
man that is in a great office commandeth fewer things and less
labor to many men that are under him than someone that is over
him commandeth him alone.

Vincent

Yet it doth them good, uncle, that men must make courtesy to
them, and salute them with reverence, and stand barehead
before them, or unto some of them kneel peradventure[5] too.

Antony

Well, cousin, in some part they do but play at gleke,[6] receive
reverence, and to their cost pay honor again therefor. For except,
as I said, only a king, the greatest in authority under him receiveth
not so much reverence of no man as according to reason himself
doth honor to him, nor twenty men's courtesies do him not so
much pleasure as his once kneeling doth him pain, if his knee hap[7]
to be sore.

And I wist[8] once a great officer of the king's say, and in good
faith I ween[9] he said but as he thought, that twenty men standing
barehead before him kept not his head half so warm as to keep on
his own cap. Nor he took never so much ease with their being
barehead before him as he caught once grief with a cough that
came upon him by standing barehead long before the king.

But let it be that these commodities be somewhat such as they be.

5. perhaps.   6. a card game.   7. happen.   8. knew.
9. think.

Yet then consider whether that any incommodities be so joined therewith that a man were almost as good lack both as have both.

Goeth all thing evermore as everyone of them would have it? That were as hard as to please all the people at once with one weather. While in one house the husband would have fair weather for his corn, and his wife would have rain for her leeks. So while they that are in authority be not all evermore of one mind, but sometime[1] variance among them either for the respect[2] of profit, or for contention of rule, or for maintenance of matters,[3] sundry parties[4] for their sundry friends, it cannot be that both the parties can have their own mind. Nor often are they content which see their conclusion quail,[5] but ten times they take the missing of their mind[6] more displeasantly than other poor men do. And this goeth not only to men of mean authority, but unto the very greatest. The princes themself cannot have, you wot[7] well, all their will. For how were it possible while each of them almost would, if he might, be lord over all the remnant? Then many men under their princes in authority are in that case that privy malice and envy many bear them in heart,[8] falsely speak them full fair and praise them with their mouth, which, when there happeth[9] any great fall unto them, bawl and bark and bite upon them like dogs.

Finally, the cost and charge, the danger and peril of war, wherein their part is more than a poor man's is, sith[1] the matter more dependeth upon them. And many a poor ploughman may sit still by the fire while they must arise and walk. And sometime their authority falleth by change of their master's mind. And of that see we daily in one place or other ensamples such and so many that the parable of the philosopher can lack no testimony, which likened the servants of great princes unto the counters[2] with which men do cast account. For like as that counter, that standeth sometime for a

1. i.e., sometimes are at.   2. consideration.   3. the state of affairs.
4. factors.   5. *conclusion quail:* argument give way.
6. intention, desire.   7. know.
8. *that . . . heart:* who bear secret malice and envy against them in their hearts.
9. happens.   1. since.
2. beads on an abacus or computing device.

farthing, is suddenly set up and standeth for a thousand pound, and after as soon set down eftsoon[3] beneath to stand for a farthing again, so fareth it, lo, sometime with those that seek the way to rise and grow up in authority by the favor of great princes, that as they rise up high, so fall they down again as low.[4]

Howbeit, though a man escape all such adventures and abide in great authority till he die, yet then at the leastwise every man must leave it at the last. And that which we call "at last" hath no very long time to it. Let a man reckon his years that are passed of his age ere ever he can get up aloft, and let him, when he have it first in his fist, reckon how long he shall be like to live after, and I ween that then the most part shall have little cause to rejoice, they shall see the time likely to be so short that their honor and authority by nature shall endure, beside the manifold chances whereby they may lose it more soon. And then when they see that they must needs leave it, the thing which they did much more set their heart upon than ever they had reasonable cause, what sorrow they take therefor, that shall I not need to tell you.

And thus it seemeth unto me, cousin, in good faith, that sith in the having the profit is not great, and the displeasures neither small nor few, and of the losing so many sundry chances, and that by no mean a man can keep it long, and that to part therefrom is such a painful grief, I can see no very great cause for which as an high worldly commodity men should greatly desire it.

The Twelfth Chapter

That these outward goods, desired but for worldly wealth, be not only little good for the body, but are also much harm for the soul.

And thus far have we considered hitherto in these outward goods, that are called the gifts of fortune, no further but the

3. again, soon afterwards.
4. For the story, see Polybius, *Hist.*, *V*, xxvi, 12–13.

slender commodity that worldly-minded men have by them. But
now if we consider further what harm to the soul they take by them
that desire them but only for the wretched wealth of this world,
then shall we well perceive how far more happy is he that well
loseth them than he that evil[5] findeth them.

These things, though they be such as are of their own nature
indifferent, that is to wit, of themself things neither good nor bad,
but are matter that may serve to the tone or the tother,[6] after as
men will use them, yet need we little to doubt it but that they that
desire them but for their worldly pleasure and for no further godly
purpose, the devil shall soon turn them from things indifferent
unto them and make them things very nought.[7] For though that
they be indifferent of their nature, yet cannot the use of them
lightly stand indifferent, but determinately[8] must either be good or
bad.[9] And therefore he that desireth them but for worldly pleasure
desireth them not for any good. And for better purpose than he
desireth them, to better use is he not likely to put them, and
therefore not unto good, but consequently to nought.

As for ensample, first consider it in riches. He that longeth for
them as for thing of temporal commodity and not for any godly
purpose—what good they shall do him Saint Paul declareth where
he writeth unto Timothy, *Qui volunt divites fieri, incidunt in tentationem, et in laqueum diaboli, et desideria multa inutilia et noxia, quae
mergunt homines in interitum et perditionem:* They that long to be rich
fall into temptation, and into the grin[1] of the devil, and into many
desires unprofitable and noyous,[2] which drown men into death
and into perdition.[3] And the holy scripture saith also in the twen-
tieth chapter of the proverbs, *Qui congregat thesauros impingetur ad
laqueos mortis:* He that gathereth treasures shall be shoved into the

5. wickedly.   6. *tone . . . tother:* one . . . other.   7. bad.
8. definitely.
9. More's discussion of the categories of good, bad, and indifferent and the
proper use (as opposed to the enjoyment) of worldly things is fundamen-
tally Augustinian. Cf. *De Sermone Domini in Monte,* II, 18 (*PL 34,* 1297) and
De Doctrina Christiana, I, iv (*PL 34,* 20).
1. snare.   2. annoying, vexatious.   3. 1 Tim. 6:9.

grin of death.[4] So that whereas by the mouth of Saint Paul, God saith that they shall fall into the devil's grin, he saith in the tother place that they shall be pushed and shoved in by violence. And of truth while a man desireth richesse[5] not for any good godly purpose, but for only worldy wealth, it must needs be that he shall have little conscience in the getting, but by all evil ways that he can invent shall labor to get them, and then shall he either niggardly heap them up together, which is, you wot well, damnable, or wastefully misspend them about worldly pomp, pride and gluttony, with occasion of many sins mo. And that is yet much more damnable.

As for fame and glory, desired but for worldly pleasure, doth[6] unto the soul inestimable harm, for that setteth men's hearts upon high devices and desires of such things as are immoderate and outrageous, and by help of false flatterers puff up a man in pride and make a brotel[7] man, lately made of earth, and that shall again shortly be laid full low in earth, and there lie and rot and turn again into earth, take himself in the meantime for a god here upon earth and ween to win himself to be lord of all the earth.

This maketh battles between these great princes, and with much trouble to much people and great effusion of blood, one king to look to reign in five realms, that cannot well rule one. For how many hath now this great Turk and yet aspireth to mo? And those that he hath he ordereth evil and yet himself worse.

Then offices and rooms[8] of authority, if men desire them only for their worldly fantasies, who can look[9] that ever they shall occupy them well, but abuse their authority and do thereby great hurt? For then shall they fall from indifferency and maintain false matters of their friends, bear up their servants and such as depend upon them with bearing down of other innocent folk and not so able to do hurt as easy to take harm. Then the laws that are made against malefactors shall they make, as an old philosopher said, to be much like unto cobwebs, in which the little nits and flies stick still and hang fast, but the great humble bees[1] break them and fly quite

4. Prov. 21:6. More's reference to Prov. 20 is a mistake.
5. wealth.   6. *doth:* i.e., that doth.   7. brittle, mortal.
8. positions.   9. expect.   1. *humble bees:* bumblebees.

through.[2] And then the laws that are made as a buckler in the defense of innocents, those shall they make serve for a sword to cut and sore[3] wound them with, and therewith wound they their own souls sorer.

And thus you see, cousin, that of all this outward goods, which men call the goods of fortune, there is never one that unto them which long therefor, not for any godly purpose, but only for their worldly wealth, hath any great commodity[4] to the body, and yet are they all, in such case besides that, very deadly destruction unto the soul.

The Thirteenth Chapter

Whether men desire these outward goods for their own worldly wealth, or for any good, virtuous purpose, this persecution of the Turk against the faith will declare, and the comfort[5] that both twain may take in the losing them thus.

Vincent

Verily, good uncle, this thing is so plainly true that no man may by any good reason deny it. But I ween,[6] uncle, also that there will no man say nay. For I see no man that will for very shame confess that he desireth riches, honor, and renown, offices, and rooms of authority for his own worldly pleasure. For every man would fain[7] seem as holy as an horse, and therefore will every man say, and would it were believed too, that he desireth these things, though for his own worldly wealth a little so, yet principally to merit thereby through doing some good therewith.

---

2. Attributed to Anacharsis by Plutarch in his *Life of Solon,* v, and to Solon by Diogenes Laertius (I, ii, 59). In the Renaissance it was sometimes attributed to Anacharsis but more generally taken to be a common proverb.
3. severely.   4. benefit.   5. consolation.   6. believe.
7. gladly, willingly.

Antony

This is, cousin, very sure so, that so doth every[8] say. But first he that in the desire thereof hath his respect[9] therein unto his worldly wealth, as you say, but a little so; so much as himself weeneth[1] were but a little may soon prove a great deal too much. And many men will say so too, that have indeed their principal respect therein unto their worldly commodity, and unto Godward therein little or nothing at all. And yet they pretend the contrary, and that unto their own harm, *quia deus non irridetur:* God cannot be mocked.[2]

And some peradventure[3] know not well their own affection themself, but there lieth more imperfection secret in their affection than themself are well ware of, which only God beholdeth. And therefore saith the prophet unto God, *Imperfectum meum viderunt oculi tui:* Mine imperfection have thine eyes beholden;[4] for which the prophet prayeth, *Ab occultis meis munda me domine:* Fro mine hid sins cleanse thou me, good Lord.[5]

But now, cousin, this tribulation of the Turk, if he so persecute us for the faith that those that will forsake their faith shall keep their goods, and those shall lose their goods that will not leave their faith—this manner of persecution, lo, shall like a touchstone try them, and show the feigned fro the true-minded, and teach also them, that ween they mean better than they do indeed, better to discern themself. For some there are that ween they mean well while they frame[6] themself a conscience, and ever keep still a great heap of superfluous substance by them, thinking ever still[7] that they will bethink themself upon some good deed, whereon they will well bestow it once,[8] or that else their executors shall. But now if they lie not unto themself, but keep their good for any good purpose, to the pleasure of God indeed, then shall they in this persecution, for the pleasure of God in keeping of his faith, be glad to depart fro them.

And therefore as for all these things, the loss I mean of all these

8. everyone.   9. consideration.   1. thinks.   2. Gal. 6:7.
3. perhaps.   4. Ps. 138:16.   5. Ps. 18:13.   6. shape, devise.
7. *ever still:* always.   8. all at once.

outward things that men call the gift of fortune, this is, me thinketh, in this Turk's persecution for the faith, consolation great and
sufficient, that sith every man that hath them either setteth by[9]
them for the world or for God, he that setteth by them for the
world hath, as I have showed you, little profit by them to the body
and great harm unto the soul, and therefore may well, if he be wise,
reckon that he winneth by the loss, although he lost them but by
some common chance, and much more happy then, while he loseth
them by such a meritorious mean. And on the tother side, he that
keepeth them for some good purpose, intending to bestow them
for the pleasure of God, the loss of them in this Turk's persecution
for keeping of the faith can be no manner[1] grief unto him, sith that
by his so parting fro them he bestoweth them in such wise[2] unto
God's pleasure that, at the time when he loseth them, by no way
could he bestow them unto his high pleasure better. For though it
had be[3] peradventure better to have bestowed them well before,
yet sith he kept them for some good purpose, he would not have
left them unbestowed if he had foreknown the chance, but being
now prevented so by persecution that he cannot bestow them in
that other good way that he would, yet while he parteth fro them
because he will not part fro the faith, though the devil's escheator[4]
violently take them from him, yet willingly giveth he them to God.

The Fourteenth Chapter

Another cause for which any man should be content to forego his goods in the Turk's said persecution.

Vincent

I cannot in good faith, good uncle, say nay to none of this. And
indeed unto them that by the Turk's overrunning of the country

---

9. *setteth by:* values.   1. kind of.   2. a way.   3. been.
4. confiscator.

were happed[5] to be spoiled and robbed, and all their substance
moveable and unmoveable bereft and lost already, their persons
only fled and safe, I think that these considerations (considered
therewith[6] that, as you lately said, their sorrow could not amend
their chance) might unto them be good occasion of comfort and
cause them, as you said, make a virtue of necessity. But in the case,
uncle, that we now speak of, that is to wit, where they have yet their
substance untouched in their own hands, and that the keeping or
the losing shall hang both in their own hands, by the Turk's offer,
upon the retaining or the renouncing of the Christian faith: here,
uncle, I find it as you said, that this temptation is most sore and
most perilous. For I fear me that we shall find few of such as have
much to lose that shall find in their hearts so suddenly to forsake
their goods, with all those other things aforerehearsed, whereupon
their worldly wealth dependeth.

Antony

That fear I much, cousin, too. But thereby shall it well, as I said,
appear that, seemed they never so good and virtuous before, and
flattered they themself with never so gay a gloss[7] of good and
gracious purpose that they keep their goods for, yet were their
hearts inwardly in the deep sight of God not sound and sure, such
as they should be, and as peradventure some had themself went
they had be, but like a puff ring of paris,[8] hollow, light, and
counterfeit indeed.

And yet they being even such, this would I fain ask one of
them—and I pray you, cousin, take you his person upon you and in
this case answer for him—what letteth[9] you, would I ask (for we will
take no small man for a sample in this part, nor him that had little to
lose; for such one were, me think, so far from all frame,[1] that would

5. *were happed:* happened.
6. *considered therewith:* if it is also considered.
7. flattering interpretation.
8. *puff . . . paris:* counterfeit ring, the stone made of plaster of paris (?).
9. hinders.   1. natural, normal state of mind.

cast away God for a little, that he were not worthy to talk with), what letteth, I say, therefore, your lordship, that you be not gladly content without any deliberation at all in this kind of persecution, rather than to leave your faith, to let go all that ever you have at once?

Vincent

Sith you put it, uncle, unto me, to make the matter the more plain, that I should play that great man's part that is so wealthy and have so much to lose, albeit I cannot be very sure of another man's mind, nor what another man would say, yet as far as mine own mind can conjecture I shall answer in his person what I ween would be his let.[2]

And therefore to your question I answer that there letteth me the thing that yourself may lightly[3] guess, the losing of the manifold commodities which I now have: richesse and substance, lands and great possessions of inheritance, with great rule and authority here in my country; all which things the great Turk granteth me to keep still in peace and have them enhanced too, so that[4] I will forsake the faith of Christ. Yea, I may say to you, I have a motion[5] secretly made me further to keep all this yet better cheap,[6] that is to wit, not be compelled utterly to forsake Christ, nor all the whole Christian faith, but only some such parts thereof as may not stand[7] with Mahomet's law, and only granting Mahomet for a true prophet and serving the Turk truly in his wars against all Christian kings. I shall not be letted to praise Christ also, and to call him a good man, and worship him and serve him too.

Antony

Nay, nay, my lord, Christ hath not so great need of your lordship as rather than to lose your service, he would fall at such covenants with you, to take your service at halves to serve him and his enemy

2. obstacle.   3. easily.   4. *so that:* provided that.   5. proposal.
6. *better cheap:* more cheaply.   7. be compatible.

both. He hath given you plain warning already by Saint Paul that he will have in your service no parting fellow,[8] *Quae societas lucis ad tenebras Christi ad Belial:* What fellowship is there between light and darkness, between Christ and Belial?[9] And he hath also plainly showed you himself by his own mouth, *Nemo potest duobus dominis servire:* No man may serve two lords at once.[1] He will have you believe all that he telleth you, and do all that he biddeth you, and forbear[2] all that he forbiddeth you, without any manner exception. Break one of his commandments and break all; forsake one point of his faith and forsake all, as for any thank you get of him for the remnant.

And therefore if you devise as it were indentures[3] between God and you, what thing you will do for him and what thing you will not do, as though he should hold him content with such service of yours as yourself list to appoint[4] him—if you make, I say, such indentures, you shall seal both the parts yourself, and you get thereto none agreement of him.

And this I say, though the Turk would make such an appointment[5] with you as you speak of, and would when he had made it keep it, whereas he would not, I warrant you, leave you so, when he had once brought you so farforth, but would little and little after, ere he left you, make you deny Christ altogether and take Mahomet in his stead. And so doth he in the beginning, when he will not have you believe him to be God. For surely if he were not God, he were not good man neither while he plainly said he was God.

But though he would never go so farforth[6] with you, yet Christ will, as I said, not take your service to halves, but will[7] that you shall love him with all your whole heart. And because that while he was living here fifteen hundred year ago, he foresaw this mind[8] of yours that you have now, with which you would fain serve him in

8. *parting fellow:* partner.   9. 2 Cor. 6:14–15.   1. Matt. 6:24.
2. do without.
3. a contract or covenant, especially one binding a servant to his master.
4. *as . . . appoint:* as it pleases you to grant him.   5. covenant.
6. far.   7. desires.   8. intention.

some such fashion as you might keep your worldly substance still, but rather forsake his service than put all your substance from you, he telleth you plain fifteen hundred year ago his[9] own mouth that he will no such service of you, saying, *Non potestis servire Deo et mammone:* You cannot serve both God and your riches together.[1]

And therefore this thing stablished for a plain conclusion, which you must needs grant if you have faith, and if you be gone from that ground of faith already, then is all our disputation, you wot well, at an end. For whereto[2] should you then rather lose your goods than forsake your faith, if you have lost your faith and let it go already?

This point, I say, therefore put first for a ground between us both twain agreed, that you have yet the faith still and intend to keep it alway still in your heart, and are but in doubt whether you will lose all your worldly substance rather than forsake your faith in your only word.[3] Now shall I reply to the point of your answer wherein you tell me the loathness of your loss and the comfort of the keeping letteth you to forego them and moveth you rather to forsake your faith.

I let pass all that I have spoken of the small commodity[4] of them unto your body and of the great harm that the having of them do to your soul. And sith the promise of the Turk made unto you for the keeping of them is the thing that moveth you and maketh you thus to doubt, I ask you first whereby you wot that, when you have done all that he will have you do against Christ to the harm of your soul, whereby wot you, I say, that he will keep you his promise in these things that he promiseth you, concerning the retaining of your well-beloved worldly wealth for the pleasure of your body?

Vincent

What surety can a man have of such a great prince but his promise, which for his own honor it cannot become him to break?

9. i.e., by means of his.   1. Matt. 6:24.   2. to what end.
3. *only word:* word alone.   4. benefit.

Antony

I have known him and his father afore him to break mo promises than five as great as this is that he should make with you. Who shall come and cast in his teeth[5] and tell him it is a shame for him to be so fickle and so false of his promise? And then what careth he for those words, that he woteth well he shall never hear? Not very much, although they were told him too. If you might come after and complain your grief unto his own person yourself, you should find him as shamefaced as a friend of mine, a merchant, found once the Soldan[6] of Syria, to whom, being certain years about his merchandise in that country, he gave a great sum of money for a certain office, meet[7] for him there for the while, which he scant[8] had him granted and put in his hand but that, ere ever it was aught worth unto him, the Soldan suddenly sold it to another of his own sect and put our Hungarian out. Then came he to him and humbly put him in remembrance of his grant, passed[9] his own mouth and signed with his own hand. Whereunto the Soldan answered him with a grim countenance, "I will thou wit it, losel,[1] that neither my mouth nor my hand shall be master over me, to bind all my body at their pleasure, but I will so be lord and master over them both that whatsoever the tone say or the tother[2] write, I will be at mine own liberty to do what my list[3] myself and ask them both no leave. And therefore go get thee hence out of my country, knave.

Ween you now, my lord, that Soldan and this Turk, being both of one false sect, you may not find them both like false of their promise?

Vincent

That must I needs jeopard,[4] for other surety can there none be had.

---

5. *cast . . . teeth:* reproach or upbraid him.   6. Sultan.
7. suitable, i.e., the sum of money was sufficient for a while.
8. hardly.   9. approved by.
1. *I . . . losel:* I want you to know it, scoundrel.
2. *tone . . . tother:* one . . . other.   3. *my list:* pleases me.
4. risk.

Antony

An unwise jeoparding to put your soul in peril of damnation for the keeping of your bodily pleasures, and yet without surety thereof must jeopard them too.

But yet go a little further, lo. Suppose me[5] that you might be very sure that the Turk would break no promise with you. Are you then sure enough to retain all your substance still?

Vincent

Yea, then.

Antony

What if a man should ask you how long?

Vincent

How long? As long as I live.

Antony

Well, let it be so then. But yet as far as I can see, though the great Turk favor you never so much and let you keep your goods as long as ever you live, yet if it hap[6] that you be this day fifty year old, all the favor he can show you cannot make you one day younger tomorrow. But every day shall you wax[7] elder than other, and then within a while must you, for all his favor, lose all.

Vincent

Well, a man would be glad for all that to be sure not to lack while he liveth.

Antony

Well then, if the great Turk give you your good, can there then in all your life none other take them from you again?

5. *Suppose me:* Imagine.   6. chance.   7. become.

Vincent

Verily, I suppose no.

Antony

May he not lose this country again unto Christian men, and you with the taking of this way,[8] fall in the same peril then, that you would now eschew?

Vincent

Forsooth, I think that if he get it once, he will never lose it again in our days.

Antony

Yes, by God's grace. But yet if he lose it after your days, there goeth your children's inheritance away again. But be it now that he could never lose it, could none take your substance from you then?

Vincent

No, in good faith, none.

Antony

No? None at all? Not God?

Vincent

God? What yes, pardie.[9] Who doubteth of that?

Antony

Who? Marry, he that doubteth whether there be any God or no. And that there lacketh not some such, the prophet testifieth where he saith, *Dixit insipiens in corde suo non est Deus:* The fool hath said in

---

8. *taking . . . way:* i.e., choice you made.   9. an oath: "by God."

his heart, there is no God.[1] With the mouth the most foolish will forbear to say[2] it unto other folk, but in the heart they let[3] not to say it softly to themself. And I fear me there be many mo such fools than every man would ween[4] there were, and would not let to say it openly too, if they forbare it not more for dread or shame of men than for any fear of God. But now those that are so frantic foolish as to ween there were no God and yet in their words confess him, though that, as Saint Paul saith, in their deeds they deny him,[5] we shall let them pass till it please God show himself unto them, either inwardly by time[6] by his merciful grace, or else outwardly, but overlate for them, by his terrible judgment.

But unto you, my lord, sith[7] you believe and confess, like as a wise man should, that though the Turk keep you promise in letting you keep your substance because you do him pleasure in the forsaking of your faith, yet God, whose faith you forsake and therein do him displeasure, may so take them from you that the great Turk with all the power he hath is not able to keep you them, why will you be so unwise with the loss of your soul to please the great Turk for your goods, while you wot well that God, whom you displease therewith, may take them from you too?

Besides this, sith you believe there is a God, you cannot but believe therewith that the great Turk cannot take your good from you without his will or sufferance,[8] no more than the devil could from Job.[9] And think you then that, if he will suffer the Turk take away your good, albeit that by the keeping and confessing of his faith you please him, he will, when you displease him by forsaking his faith, suffer[1] you of those goods that you get or keep thereby to rejoice or enjoy any benefit in?

Vincent

God is gracious. And though that men offend him, yet he suffereth them many times to live in prosperity long after.

---

1. Ps. 13:1 and Ps. 52:1.   2. *forbear to say:* refrain from saying.
3. hesitate.   4. think.   5. Titus 1:16.
6. *by time:* before it is too late.   7. since.   8. permission.
9. Cf. Job 1:12.   1. permit.

Antony

Long after? Nay, by my troth, my lord, that doth he no man. For how can that be that he should suffer you live in prosperity long after, when your whole life is but short in altogether,[2] and either almost half thereof or more than half, you think yourself I dare say, spent out already before? Can you burn out half a short candle and then have a long one left of the remnant? There cannot be in this world a worse mind[3] than that a man to[4] delight and take comfort in any commodity that he taketh by sinful mean. For it is the very straight way toward the taking of boldness and courage in sin, and finally to fall into infidelity[5] and think that God careth not nor regardeth not what things men do here, nor what mind we be of. But unto such minded folk speaketh holy scripture in this wise: *Noli dicere peccavi, et nihil mihi accidit triste, patiens enim redditor est dominus:* Say not I have sinned, and yet there hath happed[6] me no harm, for God suffereth[7] before he strike.[8] But, as Saint Austin saith, the longer that he tarrieth or[9] he strike, the sorer[1] is the stroke when he striketh.[2]

And therefore if ye will well do, reckon yourself very sure that, when you deadly displease God for the getting or the keeping of your goods, God shall not suffer those goods to do you good, but either shall he take them shortly from you, or suffer you to keep them for a little while to your more harm. And after shall he, when you least look therefor, take you away from them. And then what a heap of heaviness will there enter into your heart, when you shall see that you shall so suddenly go from your goods, and leave them here in the earth in one place, and that your body shall be put in the earth in another place, and, which then shall be most heaviness of all, when you shall fear, and not without great cause, that your soul

2. *in altogether:* considered as a whole.   3. attitude.
4. i.e., should.   5. loss of faith.
6. happened.   7. is patient.
8. Ecclus. 5:4.   9. before.   1. more severe.
2. *Epistola* CXXXVIII, ii, 14 (*PL 33*, 531).

shall first forthwith,[3] and after that at the final judgment your body too, be driven down deep toward the center of the earth into the very pit and dungeon of the devil of hell, there to tarry in torment world without end. What goods of the world can any man imagine whereof the pleasure and commodity could be such in a thousand year as were able to recompense that intolerable pain that there is to be suffered in one year, yea, or one day, or one hour either? And then what a madness is it, for the poor pleasure of your worldly goods of so few years, to cast yourself both body and soul into the everlasting fire of hell, whereof there is not minished the mountenance[4] of a moment by the lying there the space of an hundred thousand years. And therefore our Savior in few words concluded and confuted all those follies of them that, for the short use of this worldly substance, forsake him and his faith and sell their souls unto the devil forever where he saith, *Quid prodest homini si universum mundum lucretur, animae vero suae detrimentum patiatur:* What availeth it a man if he won all the whole world and lost his soul?[5] This were, me thinketh, cause and occasion enough to him, that had never so much part of this world in his hand, to be content rather to lose it all than, for the retaining or increasing of his worldly goods, to lose and destroy his soul.

Vincent

This is, good uncle, in good faith very true. And what other thing any of them that would not for this be content have for to allege in reason for the defense of their folly, that can I not imagine nor list[6] in this matter to play their part no longer. But I pray God give me the grace to play the contrary part indeed, and that I never for any goods or substance of this wretched world forsake my faith toward God neither in heart nor tongue, as I trust in his great goodness I never shall.

3. at once.   4. *minished the mountenance:* lessened the amount.
5. Matt. 16:26.   6. desire.

The Fifteenth Chapter

This kind of tribulation trieth what mind men have to their goods, which they that are wise will at the fame[7] thereof see well and wisely laid up safe before.

Antony

Me thinketh, cousin, that this persecution shall not only, as I said before, try men's hearts when it cometh and make them know their own affections, whether they have a corrupt, greedy, covetous mind or not, but also the very fame and expectation thereof may teach them this lesson ere ever the thing fall upon them itself, to their no little fruit, if they have the wit[8] and the grace to take it in time while they may. For now may they find sure places to lay their treasure in, so that all the Turk's army shall never find it out.

Vincent

Marry, uncle, that way they will, I warrant you, not forget, as near as their wits will serve them. But yet have I known some, that have ere this thought that they had hid their money safe and sure enough, digging it full deep in the ground, and have missed it yet when they came again, and have found it digged out and carried away to their hands.[9]

Antony

Nay, fro their hands, I ween you would say. And it was no marvel, for some such have I known too, but they have hid their goods foolishly in such place as they were well warned before that they should not. And that were they warned by him that they well knew for such one as wist[1] well enough what would come thereon.

---

7. rumor.   8. intelligence.
9. *to their hands:* without exertion on their part.   1. knew.

Vincent

Then were they more than mad. But did he tell them too where they should have hid it to have it sure?

Antony

Yea, by Saint Mary, did he, for else had he told them but half a tale. But he told them an whole tale, bidding them that they should in no wise[2] hide their treasure in the ground. And he showed them a good cause, for there thieves use[3] to dig it out and steal it away.

Vincent

Why, where should they hide it then, said he? For thieves may hap to find it out in any place.

Antony

Forsooth, he counselled them to hide their treasure in heaven and there lay it up, for there it shall lie safe. For thither, he said, there can no thief come till he have left his theft and be waxen[4] a true man first. And he that gave this counsel wist what he said well enough, for it was our Savior himself, which in the sixth chapter of St. Matthew saith, *Nolite thesaurizare vobis thesauros in terra, ubi aerugo et tinea demolitur, et ubi fures effodiunt et furantur. Thesaurizate vobis thesauros in caelo ubi neque aerugo neque tinea demolitur et ubi fures non effodiunt nec furantur. Ubi enim est thesaurus tuus, ibi est et cor tuum:* Hoard not up your treasures in earth where the rust and the moth fret it out,[5] and where thieves dig it out and steal it away. But hoard up your treasures in heaven, where neither the rust and the moth fret them out, and where thieves dig them not out and steal them away. For whereas[6] is thy treasure, there is thine heart too.[7]

If we would well consider these words of our Savior, Christ, we

2. way.   3. are accustomed.   4. grown.
5. *fret it out:* gnaw it away.   6. where.   7. Matt. 6:19–21.

should, as me think, need no more counsel at all, nor no more comfort neither concerning the loss of our temporal substance in this Turk's persecution for the faith. For here our Lord in these words teacheth us where we may lay up our substance safe before the persecution come: if we put it into the poor men's bosoms, there shall it lie safe. For who would go search a beggar's bag for money? If we deliver it to the poor for Christ's sake, we deliver it unto Christ himself. And then what persecutor can there be so strong as to take it out of his hand?

Vincent

These things are, uncle, undoubtedly so true that no man may with words wrestle therewith. But yet ever there hangeth in a man's heart a loathness[8] to lack a living.

Antony

There doth indeed in theirs that either never or but seldom hear any good counsel thereagainst, and when they hear it, hearken it but as though they would an idle tale, rather for a pastime or for the manner sake[9] than for any substantial intent and purpose to follow good advertisement[1] and take any fruit thereby. But verily, if we would not only lay our ear, but also our heart thereto, and consider that the saying of our Savior, Christ, is not a poet's fable nor an harper's song, but the very holy word of almighty God himself, we would, and well we might, be full sore ashamed in ourself and full sorry too when we felt in our affection those words to have in our hearts no more strength and weight but that we remain still of the same dull mind as we did before we heard them.

This manner of ours, in whose breasts the great, good counsel of God no better settleth nor taketh no better root, may well declare us that the thorns and the breres[2] and the brambles of our worldly substance grow so thick and spring up so high in the ground of our

---

8. unwillingness.   9. *the manner sake:* the sake of appearances.
1. advice.   2. briars.

hearts that they strangle, as the gospel saith, the word of God that was sown therein.[3] And therefore is God very good Lord unto us when he causeth like a good husbandman his folk come[4] on field; for the persecutors be his folk to this purpose, and with their hooks and their stoking irons[5] grub up this wicked weeds and bushes of our earthly substance and carry them quite away from us, that the word of God sown in our hearts may have room therein and a glad[6] roundabout for the warm sun of grace to come to it and make it grow. For surely those words of our Savior shall we find full true, *Ubi thesaurus tuus, ibi est et cor tuum:* Whereas thy treasure is, there is also thine heart. If we lay up our treasures in earth, in earth shall be our hearts; if we send our treasure into heaven, in heaven shall we have our hearts. And surely the greatest comfort that any man may have in his tribulation is to have his heart in heaven.

If thine heart were indeed out of this world and in heaven, all the kinds of torment that all the world could devise could put thee to no pain here. Let us then send our hearts hence thither, in such manner[7] as we may, by sending thither our worldly substance hence. And let us never doubt it but we shall, that once done, find our hearts so conversant in heaven, with the glad consideration of[8] our following the gracious counsel of Christ, that the comfort of his Holy Spirit, inspired us[9] therefor, shall mitigate, minish,[1] assuage, and in manner[2] quench the great, furious fervor of the pain that we shall happen to have by his loving sufferance[3] for our further merit in our tribulation.

And therefore, like as if we saw that we should be within a while driven out of this land and fain[4] to fly into another, we would ween[5]

3. Matt. 13:3–9, the parable of the sower and the seed. But More refers specifically to Jesus' explanation of the parable in Matt. 13:22.
4. i.e., to come.
5. *stoking irons:* agricultural implements used for uprooting.
6. glade, clearing.   7. a way.
8. *with . . . of:* due to the happy fact of.   9. i.e., in us.
1. lessen.   2. *in a manner:* so to speak.
3. permission; i.e., God will allow us to suffer pain here to increase our merit in heaven.
4. obliged.   5. think.

that man were mad which would not be content to forbear[6] his goods here for the while and send them into that land before him, where he saw he should live all the remnant of his life, so may we verily think ourself much more mad, seeing that we be sure it cannot be long ere we shall be sent spite of our teeth[7] out of this world, if the fear of a little lack or the love to see our goods here about us, and the loathness to part from them for this little while which we may keep them here, shall be able to let[8] us fro the sure sending them before us into the tother[9] world, in which we may be sure to live wealthily with them if we send them thither, or else[1] shortly leave them here behind us and then stand in great jeopardy[2] there to live wretches forever.

Vincent

In good faith, good uncle, me thinketh that concerning the loss of these outward things these considerations are so sufficient comforts that for mine own part, save only grace well to remember them, I would, me think, desire no more.

The Sixteenth Chapter

Another comfort and courage against the loss of worldly substance.

Antony

Much less than this may serve, cousin, with calling and trusting upon God's help, without which much more than this cannot serve. But the fervor of the Christian faith so sore[3] fainteth nowadays and decayeth, coming from hot unto lukewarm and fro lukewarm almost to key-cold, that men must now be fain, as at a fire that is

6. do without.   7. *spite . . . teeth:* despite our utmost efforts.
8. prevent.   9. other.
1. otherwise; i.e., we will leave our possessions behind us in a short while anyway, even if we try to hang on to them.
2. danger.   3. severely.

almost out, to lay many dry sticks thereto and use much blowing thereat. But else would I ween, by my troth, that unto a warm, faithful man one thing alone, whereof we spake yet no word, were comfort enough in this kind of persecution against the loss of all his goods.

Vincent

What thing may that be, uncle?

Antony

In good faith, cousin, even the bare remembrance of the poverty that our Savior willingly suffered for us. For I verily suppose that if there were a great king, that had so tender a love to a servant of his that he had, to help him out of danger, forsaken and left off all his worldly wealth and royalty, and become poor and needy for his sake, that servant could scant[4] be founden, that were of such an unkind, villain courage,[5] that if himself came after to some substance would not with better will lose it all again than shamefully to forsake such a master.

And therefore, as I say, I do surely suppose that if we would well remember and inwardly consider the great goodness of our Savior toward us, not yet being his poor, sinful servants, but rather his adversaries and his enemies, and what wealth of this world that he willingly forsook for our sake, being indeed universal king thereof and so having the power in his own hand to have used it if he had would,[6] instead whereof to make us rich in heaven he lived here in neediness and poverty all his life and neither would have authority nor keep neither lands nor goods: the deep consideration and earnest advisement[7] of this one point alone were able to make any kind[8] Christian man or woman well content rather for his sake again to give up all that ever God hath lent them, and lent them hath he all that ever they have, than unkindly and unfaithfully to forsake him. And him they forsake if that for fear they forsake the confessing of his Christian faith.

4. hardly.   5. *unkind . . . courage:* unnatural, base spirit.
6. desired.   7. pondering.   8. natural.

And therefore, to finish this piece withal, concerning the dread of losing our outward, worldly goods, let us consider the slender commodity[9] that they bring, with what labor they be bought, how little while they abide with whomsoever they abide longest, what pain their pleasure is mingled withal, what harm the love of them doth unto the soul, what loss is in the keeping, Christ's faith refused for them, what winning in the loss, if we lose them for God's sake, how much more profitable they be well given than evil kept, and finally, what unkindness it were if we would not rather forsake them for Christ's sake than unfaithfully forsake Christ for them, which while he lived for our sake forsook all the world, beside the suffering of shameful and painful death, whereof we shall speak after. If we these things, I say, will consider well and will pray God with his holy hand to print them in our hearts, and will abide and dwell still in the hope of his help, his truth shall, as the prophet saith, so compass us about with a pavis[1] that we shall not need to be afeard *ab incursu et demonio meridiano:* of this incursion of this midday devil, this open, plain persecution of the Turk, for any loss that we can take by the bereaving from us of our wretched, worldly goods, for whose short and small pleasure in this life forborne,[2] we shall be with heavenly substance everlastingly recompensed of God in joyful bliss and glory.

The Seventeenth Chapter

Of bodily pain, and that a man hath no cause to take discomfort in persecution, though he feel himself in an horror at the thinking upon bodily pain.

Vincent

Forsooth, uncle, as for these outward goods, you have so far-forth[3] said that albeit no man can be sure what strength he shall

9. advantage.   1. large shield.   2. gone without.   3. far.

have or how faint and how feeble he may hap[4] to find himself when
he shall come to the point, and therefore I can make no warrantise[5]
of myself, seeing that St. Peter so suddenly fainted[6] at a woman's
word and so cowardly forsook his master for whom he had so
boldly fought within so few hours before,[7] and by that fall in
forsaking, well perceived that he had been too rash in his promise[8]
and was well worthy to take a fall for putting so full trust in himself.
Yet, in good faith, me thinketh now (and God shall, I trust, help me
to keep this thought still) that if the Turk should take all that I have
unto my very shirt except[9] I would forsake my faith and offer it me
all again with five times as much thereto to fall into his sect, I would
not once stick thereat[1] rather to forsake it every whit than of
Christ's holy faith to forsake any point. But surely, good uncle,
when I bethink me further on the grief and the pain that may turn
unto my flesh, here find I the fear that forceth mine heart to
tremble.

Antony

Neither have I cause thereof to marvel nor you, cousin, cause to
be dismayed therefore. The great horror and the fear that our
Savior had in his own flesh against[2] his painful passion[3] maketh me
little to marvel, and I may well make you take that comfort too that
for no such manner of grudging[4] felt in our sentiall[5] parts, the flesh
shrinking at the meditation of pain and death, your reason shall
give over, but resist it and manly master it, and though you would
fain[6] flee from the painful death and be loath to come thereto, yet
may the meditation of his great, grievous agony move you, and
himself shall, if you so desire him, not fail to work with you therein
and get and give you the grace that you shall submit and conform
your will therein unto his, as he did his unto his Father, and shall

4. happen.   5. assurance.   6. turned fainthearted.
7. John (18:10, 26) is the only gospel that identifies Peter as the man who
fought and cut off Malchus' ear when Jesus was betrayed by Judas.
8. Luke 22:33.   9. unless.   1. *stick thereat:* hesitate.
2. in anticipation of.   3. Luke 22:39–46.
4. *manner of grudging:* kind of protest.   5. sensual.   6. gladly.

thereupon be so comforted with the secret, inward inspiration of his Holy Spirit, as he was with the personal presence of that angel, that after his agony came and comforted him,[7] that you shall as his true disciple follow him, and with good will without grudge do as he did, and take your cross of pain and passion[8] upon your back, and die for the truth with him, and thereby reign with him crowned in eternal glory.[9] And this I say to give you warning of the thing that is truth, to the intent when a man feeleth such an horror of death in his heart, he should not thereby stand in outrageous fear that he were falling, for many such man standeth for all that fear full fast[1] and finally better abide the brunt, when God is so good unto him as to bring him thereto and encourage him therein, than doth some other that in the beginning feeleth no fear at all. And yet may it be, and most often so it is. For God, having many mansions and all wonderful wealthful[2] in his Father's house, exalteth not every good man up to the glory of a martyr, but foreseeing their infirmity, that, though they be of good will before and peradventure[3] of right good courage too, would yet play Saint Peter if they were brought to the point and thereby bring their souls into the peril of eternal damnation, he provideth otherwise for them before they come thereat, and either findeth a way that men shall not have the mind[4] to lay any hands upon them, as he found for his disciples when himself was willingly taken,[5] or that if they set hand upon them, they shall have no power to hold them, as he found for St. John the Evangelist, which let his sheet fall fro him, whereupon they caught hold and so fled himself naked away and escaped fro them;[6] or though they hold him and bring him to prison too, yet God sometime delivereth them thence, as he did Saint Peter.[7] And

7. Luke 22:43.   8. suffering.   9. Luke 9:23.   1. firmly.
2. *wonderful wealthful:* flourishing in a wonderful way; the allusion is to John 14:2.
3. perhaps.   4. intention.   5. John 18:8–9.
6. Mark 14:51–52. The young man is not named in the gospel. Ambrose, Chrysostom, Gregory, and a number of the early fathers identify him as St. John; others thought he was St. James or simply an unknown servant in the house where the last supper was held.
7. Acts 12:6–11.

sometime he taketh them to him out of the prison into heaven and suffereth them not to come to their torment at all, as he hath done by many a good, holy man. And some he suffereth to be brought into the torments and yet suffereth them not to die therein, but live many years after and die their natural death, as he did by Romanus that should have been beheaded as Eusebius telleth,[8] *Blandina et apud Divum Ciprianum quidam et relictus pro mortuo*,[9] Saint John the Evangelist,[1] and by many another mo, as we may well see both by sundry stories and in the epistles of St. Cyprian also.[2]

And therefore, which way God will take with us, we can not tell. But surely if we be true Christian men, this can we well tell, that without any bold warrantise of ourself or foolish trust in our own strength, we be bound upon pain of damnation that we be not of the contrary mind, but that we will with his help, how loath soever we feel our flesh thereto, rather yet than forsake him or his faith afore the world, which if we do he hath promised to forsake us afore his Father and all his holy company of heaven[3]—rather, I say, than we would so do, we would with his help endure and sustain for his sake all the tormentry that the devil with all his faithless tormentors in this world would devise. And then, when we be of this mind and submit our will unto his, and call and pray for his grace, we

---

8. *De Martyribus Palaestinae*, II (*PG* 22, 1463–70). More's memory has failed him, however. Romanus of Caesarea (*d.* A.D. 303) did not die a natural death; he was strangled in prison after enduring incredible torments.

9. "Blandina and in St. Cyprian a certain one also left for dead." Blandina was tortured until her torturers became exhausted. She was eventually executed by having her throat cut in imitation of a sacrificial victim. See Eusebius, *Historiae Ecclesiastica*, V, i (*PG* 20, 407–34). In *Epistola* XXXV, Cyprian mentions a certain Numidicus, who was left for dead after being burned and stoned. He was later found by his daughter and revived (*PL 4*, 333–34).

1. During the persecutions of Domitian, St. John is said to have been thrown into boiling oil but to have emerged unharmed (Tertullian, *De Praescriptionibus*, xxxvi [*PL* 2, 48–50]). He died years later, full of age, at Ephesus (Eusebius, *Historiae Ecclesiastica*, III, xxxi [*PG* 20, 279]).

2. Cf. *Epistola* VIII, as well as the accounts of Celerinus and Aurelius in *Epistola* XXXIV and XXXIII (*PL 4*, 255, 329–33, 325–29).

3. A combination of the phrasing in Matt. 10:33 and Luke 12:9.

can tell well enough that he will never suffer them to put more upon us than his grace will make us able to bear, but will also with their temptation provide for us a sure way. For *Fidelis est deus,* saith Saint Paul, *qui non patitur vos temptare, supra id quod potestis sed dat etiam cum tentatione proventum ut possitis ferre:* God is, saith the apostle, faithful, which suffereth you not to be tempted above that you may bear, but giveth also with the temptation a way out.[4] For either, as I said, he will keep us out of their hands, though he before suffered us to be feared with[5] them to prove our faith withal, that we may have by the examination of our own mind some comfort[6] in hope of his grace and some fear of our own frailty to drive us to call for grace, or else if we fall in their hands, so that we fall not fro the trust of him nor cease to call for his help, his truth shall, as the prophet saith, so compass us about with a pavis[7] that we shall not need to fear this incursion of this midday devil. For either shall these Turks, his tormentors that shall enter this land and persecute us, either they shall, I say, not have the power to touch our bodies at all, or else the short pain that they shall put unto our bodies shall turn us to eternal profit, both in our souls and in our bodies too. And therefore, cousin, to begin with, let us be of good comfort. For sith[8] we be by our faith very sure that holy scripture is the very[9] word of God, and that the word of God cannot be but true, and that we see that, both by the mouth of his holy prophet and by the mouth of his blessed apostle also, God hath made us so faithful promises, both that he will not suffer us to be tempted above our power, but will both provide a way out for us, and that he will also roundabout so compass us with his pavis and defend us that we shall have no cause to fear this midday devil with all his persecution, we cannot now but be very sure, except we be very shamefully cowardous of heart, and toward God in faith out of measure[1] faint, and in love less than lukewarm or waxen[2] even key-cold, we may be very sure, I say, that either God shall not suffer

---

4. 1 Cor. 10:13.   5. *feared with:* afraid of.   6. consolation.
7. large shield.   8. since.   9. true.
1. *out of measure:* extremely.   2. become.

the Turks to invade this land, or if they do, God shall provide such resistance that they shall not prevail. Or if they prevail, yet if we take the way that I have told you, we shall by their persecution take little harm, or rather none harm at all, but that that shall seem harm shall indeed be to us none harm at all but good. For if God make us and keep us good men, as he hath promised to do, if we pray well therefor, then, saith holy scripture, *Bonis omnia cooperantur in bonum:* Unto good folk, all things turn them to good.[3]

And therefore, cousin, sith that God knoweth what shall happen and not we, let us in the meanwhile, with a good hope in the help of God's grace, have a good purpose with us of sure standing by his holy faith against all persecutions, from which if we should, which our Lord forbid, hereafter either for fear or pain, for lack of his grace lost in our own default,[4] mishap to decline,[5] yet had we both won the well-spent time in this good purpose before to the minishment[6] of our pain and were also much the more likely that God should lift us up after our fall and give us his grace again. Howbeit, if this persecution come, we be, by this meditation and well continued intent and purpose before, the better strengthened and confirmed, and the much more likely for to stand indeed. And if it so fortune, as with God's grace at men's good prayers and amendment of our evil lives, it may fortune full well that the Turks shall either be well withstanden and vanquished, or peradventure not invade us at all, then shall we, pardie,[7] by this good purpose get ourself of God a very good, cheap thank.

And on the tother[8] side, while we now think thereon (as not to think thereon in so great likelihood thereof, I ween,[9] no wise man can), if we should for the fear of worldly loss or bodily pain framed[1] in our own minds, think that we would give over and to save our goods and our lives forsake our Savior by denial of his faith, then whether the Turks come or come not, we be gone from God the while. And then if they come not indeed or come and be driven to

3. Rom. 8:28.   4. neglect, failure.
5. *mishap to decline:* have the ill fortune to turn away.   6. lessening.
7. an oath: "by God."   8. other.   9. think.   1. formed.

flight, what a shame should this be to us before the face of God, in so shameful, cowardous wise to forsake him for fear of that pain that we never felt nor never was falling[2] toward us.

Vincent

By my troth, uncle, I thank you. Me thinketh that though you never said more in the matter, yet have you even with this, that you have of the fear of bodily pain in this persecution spoken here already, marvelously comforted mine heart.

Antony

I am glad, cousin, if your heart have taken comfort thereby. But and if you so have, give God the thank and not me, for that work is his and not mine. For neither am I able any good thing to say but by him, nor all the good works in the world—no, not the holy words of God himself and spoken also with his own holy mouth—can be able to profit the man with the sound entering at his ear but if[3] the Spirit of God therewith inwardly work in his soul. But that is his goodness ever ready to do, except the let[4] be through the untowardness[5] of our own froward[6] will.

The Eighteenth Chapter

Of comfort against bodily pain and first against captivity.

And therefore, now being somewhat in comfort and courage before, whereby we may the more quietly consider everything, which is somewhat more hard and difficile[7] to do when the heart is

---

2. coming.   3. *but if:* unless.
4. *except the let:* unless the obstacle.   5. perversity.   6. unruly.
7. difficult.

before taken up and oppressed with the troublous affection of
heavy, sorrowful fear, let us examine the weight and the substance
of those bodily pains as the sorest part of this persecution which
you rehearsed[8] before, which were, if I remember you right,
thralldom, imprisonment, painful and shameful death. And first
let us, as reason is, begin with the thralldom, for that was, as I
remember, the first.

Vincent

I pray you, good uncle, say then somewhat thereof, for me
thinketh, uncle, that captivity is a marvelous heavy thing, namely[9]
when they shall, as they most commonly do, carry us far from
home into a strange, uncouth[1] land.

Antony

I cannot say nay, but that grief it is, cousin, indeed, but yet as
unto me[2] not half so much as it would be if they could carry me out
into any such unknown country that God could not wit[3] where, nor
find the mean to come at me. But in good faith, cousin, now, if my
transmigration[4] into a strange country should be any great grief
unto me, the fault should be much in myself. For sith I am very sure
that whithersoever men convey me God is no more verily here than
he shall be there, if I get, as I may if I will, the grace to set my whole
heart upon him and long for nothing but him, it can then make me
no great matter to my mind whether they carry me hence or leave
me here. And then if I find my mind much offended therewith that
I am not still in mine own country, I must consider that the cause of
my grief is mine own wrong imagination whereby I beguile myself
with an untrue persuasion, weening[5] that this were mine own
country, whereas of truth it is not so. For as Saint Paul saith, *Non
habemus hic civitatem manentem sed futurum inquerimus:* We have here

---

8. related.   9. especially.   1. unfamiliar.
2. *as unto me:* as far as I'm concerned.   3. know.   4. removal.
5. thinking.

no city nor dwelling country at all, but we seek for one that we shall come to.[6] And in what country soever we walk in this world, we be but as pilgrims and wayfaring men. And if I should take any country for mine own, it must be the country to which I come and not the country from which I came.

That country that shall be to me then for a while so strange shall yet, pardie, be no more strange to me, nor longer strange to me neither, than was mine own native country when I came first into it. And therefore, if that point of my being far from hence be very grievous to me and that I find it a great pain that I am not where I would be, that grief shall great part grow for lack of sure setting and settling my mind in God where it should be, which fault of mine when I mend I shall soon ease my grief.

Now as for all other griefs and pains that are in captivity, thralldom, and bondage, I cannot deny but many there are and great. Howbeit they seem yet somewhat—what say I somewhat? I may say a great deal—the more because we take our former liberty for more a great deal than indeed it was. Let us therefore consider the matter thus: captivity, bondage, or thralldom, what is it but the violent restraint of a man, being so subdued under the dominion, rule, and power of another that he must do what the tother list[7] to command him and may not do at his liberty such things as he list himself? Now when we shall be carried away with a Turk and be fain[8] to be occupied about such things as he list to set us, here shall we lament the loss of our liberty and think we bear an heavy burden of our servile condition, and so to do we shall have, I grant well, many times great occasion. But yet should we, I suppose, set thereby somewhat the less if we would remember well what liberty that was that we lost and take it for no larger than it was indeed. For we reckon as though we might before do what we would, but therein we deceive ourself. For what free man is there so free that can be suffered to do what him list? In many things God hath restrained us by his high commandment, so many that, of those things which else we would do, I ween it be more than the half.

6. Heb. 13:14.   7. wishes.   8. obliged.

Howbeit because (God forgive us) we let[9] so little therefor, but do what we list as though we heard him not, we reckon our liberty never the less[1] for that.

But then is our liberty much restrained by the laws made by men for the quiet and politic governance of the people, and these would, I ween, let[2] our liberty but a little neither, were it not for fear of the pains that fall thereupon.

Look then whether other men that have authority over us command us never no business which we dare not but do, and therefore, do it full oft full sore[3] against our wills, of which things some service is sometime so painful and so perilous too that no lord can lightly[4] command his bondman worse, nor seldom doth command him half so sore.

Let every free man that reckoneth his liberty to stand in doing what he list consider well these points, and I ween he shall then find his liberty much less than he took it before.

And yet have I left untouched the bondage that almost every man is in that boasteth himself for free; the bondage, I mean, of sin, which to be a very bondage I shall have our Savior himself to bear me good record. For he saith, *Qui facit peccatum, servus est peccati:* He that committeth sin is the thrall or bondman of sin.[5] And then if this be thus, as it must needs be so sith God saith it is so, who is there then that may make so much boast of his liberty that he should take it for so sore a thing and so strange to become through chance of war bond[6] unto a man, while he is already through sin become willingly thrall and bond unto the devil?

Let us look well how many things and of what vile, wretched sort the devil driveth us to do daily through the rash braids[7] of our blind affections,[8] which we be for our faultful lack of grace fain to follow and are too feeble to refrain,[9] and then shall we find in our natural freedom our bond service such that never was there any man lord of any so vile a villain, that ever would for very shame

9. hesitate.   1. *never the less:* not at all diminished.   2. hinder.
3. *full . . . sore:* most often most grievously.   4. easily.
5. John 8:34.   6. slave.   7. outbursts.   8. passions.
9. control.

command him so shameful service. And let us in the doing of our service to the man that we be slave unto remember what we were wont to do about the same time of the day while we were at our free liberty before and were well likely if we were at liberty to do the like again, and we shall peradventure[1] perceive that it were better for us to do this business than that.

Now shall we have great occasion of comfort[2] if we consider that our servitude, though in the count[3] of the world it seem to come by chance of war, cometh yet in very deed unto us by the provident sand[4] of God and that for our great good, if we will take it well, both in remission of sins and also matter of our merit.

The greatest grief that is in bondage or captivity is this, as I trow:[5] that we be forced to do such labor as with our good will we would not. But then against that grief Seneca teacheth us a good remedy, *Semper da operam, ne quid invitus facias:* Endeavor thyself evermore that thou do nothing against thy will.[6] But that thing that we see we shall needs do, let us use alway to put our good will thereto.

Vincent

That is, uncle, soon said, but it is hard to do.

Antony

Our froward[7] mind maketh every good thing hard and that to our own more hurt and harm. But in this case if we will be good Christian men, we shall have great cause gladly to be content for the great comfort that we may take thereby, while we remember that in the patient and glad doing of our service unto that man for God's sake, according to his high commandment by the mouth of Saint Paul, *Servi obedite dominis,*[8] we shall have our thank and our reward of God.

1. perhaps.   2. spiritual consolation.   3. estimation.
4. dispensation or ordinance.   5. believe.
6. *Epistolae Morales,* LXI, 2.   7. unruly.
8. Eph. 6:5–8: "Slaves, obey your masters."

Finally, if we remember the great, humble meekness of our Savior, Christ himself, that he, being very[9] almighty God, *Humiliavit semet ipsum formam servi accipiens:* Humbled himself and took the form of a bondman or slave[1] rather than his Father should forsake us, we may think ourself very unkind caitiffs[2] and very frantic fools too, if, rather than to endure this worldly bondage for a while, we would forsake him that hath by his own death delivered us out of everlasting bondage of the devil, and will for our short bondage give us everlasting liberty.

Vincent

Well fare you,[3] good uncle, this is very well said. Albeit that bondage is a condition that every man of any courage[4] would be glad to eschew and very loath to fall in, yet have you well made it open[5] that it is a thing neither so strange nor so sore as it before seemed unto me and specially far from such as any man that any wit[6] hath should for fear thereof shrink from the confession of his faith. And now, therefore, I pray you, somewhat speak of your prisonment.[7]

The Nineteenth Chapter
Of imprisonment and comfort thereagainst.

Antony

That shall I, cousin, with good will. And first if we would consider what thing imprisonment is of his own nature, we should not, me thinketh, have so great horror thereof. For of itself it is, pardie, but a restraint of liberty which letteth a man from going whither he would.

9. truly.   1. Phil. 2:7–8.   2. *unkind caitiffs:* unnatural wretches.
3. *Well fare you:* May you fare well.   4. spirit.   5. evident.
6. intelligence.   7. *your prisonment:* your idea of imprisonment.

Vincent

Yes, by Saint Mary, uncle, me thinketh it is much more sorrow
than so, for beside the let and restraint of liberty, it hath many mo
displeasures and very sore[8] griefs, knit and joined thereto.

Antony

That is, cousin, very true indeed, and those pains, among many
sorer than those, thought I not after to forget. Howbeit I purpose
now to consider first imprisonment, but as imprisonment only
without any other incommodity beside. For a man may be, pardie,[9]
imprisoned and yet not set in the stocks nor collared fast by the
neck, and a man may be let walk at large where he will and yet a pair
of fetters fast riveted on his legs, for in this country, ye wot[1] well,
and in Seville and Portugal too, so go all the slaves.[2]

Howbeit, because that for such things men's hearts hath such
horror thereof, albeit that I am not so mad as to go about to prove
that bodily pain were no pain, yet sith[3] that because of these
manner[4] of pains we so specially abhor the state and condition of
prisoners, we should, me thinketh, well perceive that a great part of
our horror groweth of our own fantasy, if we would call to mind
and consider the state and condition of many other folk in whose
state and condition we would wish ourself to stand, taking them for
no prisoners at all that stand yet for all that in much part of the
self-same points that we abhor imprisonment for. Let us therefore
consider these things in order.

And first, as I thought to begin, because those other kinds of
griefs that come with imprisonment are but accidents[5] thereunto,
and yet neither such kinds of accidents as either be proper thereunto, but that they may almost all fall unto a man without it, nor are
not such accidents thereunto as are unseparable therefro, but that

8. severe.   9. an oath: "by God."   1. know.
2. Personal slavery persisted throughout the Renaissance in those areas of
Europe that bordered on the Moslem Empire.
3. since.   4. kinds.   5. non-essential qualities.

imprisonment may fall to a man and none of all them therewith, we will, I say, therefore begin with the considering what manner pain or incommodity we should reckon imprisonment to be of himself and of his own nature alone. And then in the course of our communication, you shall as you list increase and aggrieve[6] the cause of your horror with the terror of those painful accidents.

Vincent

I am sorry that I did interrupt your tale. For you were about, I see well, to take an orderly way therein. And as yourself have devised,[7] so, I beseech you, proceed. For though I reckon imprisonment much the sorer thing by sore and hard handling therein, yet reckon I not the prisonment of itself any less than a thing very tedious,[8] all were it[9] used in the most favorable manner that it possibly might. For, uncle, if it were a great prince that were taken prisoner upon the field and in the hand of a Christian king, which use[1] in such case, for the consideration of their former estate and mutable chance of the war, to show much humanity to them and in very favorable wise entreat them[2]—for these infidel emperors handle ofttimes the princes that they take more villainously than they do the poorest men, as the great Tamburlaine kept the great Turk, when he had taken him, to tread on his back alway while he leapt on horseback[3]—but as I began to say by the sample of a prince taken prisoner, were the imprisonment never so favorable, yet were it in my mind no little grief in itself for a man to be penned up though not in a narrow chamber, but although his walk were right large and right fair gardens too therein, it could not but grieve his heart to be restrained by another man within certain limits and bounds and lose the liberty to be where him list.

6. aggravate.   7. planned.   8. disagreeable.
9. *all were it:* even if it were.   1. are accustomed.
2. *in . . . them:* treat them in a very favorable way.
3. After defeating Bajazeth I in a battle near Ankara on July 20, 1402, Tamburlaine is said to have kept him in a cage for almost a year, feeding him with scraps from his table and occasionally using him as a mounting block. Cf. Marlowe's *Tamburlaine,* IV, ii, 1–30.

Antony

This is, cousin, well considered of you. For in this you perceive well that imprisonment is of himself and his own very nature alone nothing else but the retaining of a man's person, within the circuit of a certain space, narrower or larger as shall be limited unto him, restraining his liberty fro the further going into any other place.

Vincent

Verily well said, as me thinketh.

Antony

Yet forgot I, cousin, to ask you one question.

Vincent

What is that, uncle?

Antony

This, lo: if there be two men kept in two several[4] chambers of one great castle, of which two chambers the tone is much more larger than the tother,[5] whether be they prisoners both or but the tone that hath the less room to walk in?

Vincent

What question is it, uncle, but that they be prisoners both, as I said myself before, although the tone lay fast locked in the stocks and the tother had all the whole castle to walk in?

Antony

Me thinketh verily, cousin, that you say the truth. And then if imprisonment be such a thing as yourself here agree it is, that is to

---

4. separate.   5. *tone . . . tother:* one . . . other.

wit, but a lack of liberty to go if we list, now would I fain wit[6] of you what any one man you know that is at this day out of prison?

Vincent

What one man, uncle? Marry, I know almost none other, for surely prisoner am I none acquainted with that I remember.

Antony

Then I see well you visit poor prisoners seld.[7]

Vincent

No, by troth, uncle, I cry God mercy. I send them sometime mine almoise,[8] but by my troth, I love not to come myself where I should see such misery.

Antony

In good faith, Cousin Vincent, though I say it before you, you have many good conditions,[9] but surely, though I say it before you too, that condition is none of them, which condition if you would amend, then should you have yet the mo good conditions by one, and peradventure the mo by three or four, for I assure you it is hard to tell how much good to a man's soul the personal visiting to poor prisoners doth.

But now sith you can name me none of them that are in prison, I pray you name some one of all them that you be, as you say, better acquainted with—men I mean that are out of prison, for I know, me thinketh, as few of them as you know of the tother.

Vincent

That were, uncle, a strange case, for every man is, uncle, out of prison that may go where he will, though he be the poorest beggar

6. know.   7. seldom.   8. alms.   9. personal qualities.

in the town. And in good faith, uncle, because you reckon imprisonment so small a matter of itself, the poor beggar that is at his
liberty and may walk where he will is, as me seemeth, in better case
than is a king kept in prison that cannot go but where men give him
leave.

Antony

Well, cousin, whether every way-walking[1] beggar be by this
reason out of prison or no, we shall consider further when ye will.[2]
But in the meanwhile I can by this reason see no prince that
seemeth to be out of prison, for if the lack of liberty to go where a
man will be imprisonment, as yourself say it is, then is the great
Turk, by whom we so fear to be put in prison, in prison already
himself, for he may not go where he will, for and[3] he might, he
would into Portugal, Italy, Spain, France, Almain[4] and England,
and as far on another quarter[5] too, both Prester John's land[6] and
the Grand Cam's[7] too.

Now the beggar that you speak of, if he be, as you say he is, by
reason of his liberty to go where he will in much better case than a
king kept in prison, because he cannot go but where men give him
leave, then is that beggar in better case not only than a prince in
prison, but also than many a prince out of prison too. For I am sure
there is many a beggar that may without let[8] walk farther upon
other men's ground than many a prince at his best liberty may walk
upon his own. And as for walking out abroad upon other men's,
that prince might hap[9] to be said nay and holden fast, where that
beggar with his bag and his staff should be suffered to go forth and
hold on his way.

1. vagrant.   2. wish.   3. if.   4. Germany.
5. *on . . . quarter:* in another region.
6. Prester John was the ruler of a legendary Christian kingdom beyond
Persia and Armenia, in India or Ethiopia.
7. "The Great Khan" (of which *Cam* is an obsolete form) was a title used
variously for the Emperor of China or the rulers of the Tartars and
Mongols.
8. hindrance.   9. happen.

But for as much, cousin, as neither the beggar nor the prince is at free liberty to walk where they will, but that if[1] they would walk in some place[2] neither of them both should be suffered, but men would withstand them and say them nay, therefore if imprisonment be, as you grant it is, a lack of liberty to go where we list,[3] I cannot see but, as I say, the beggar and the prince, whom you reckon both at liberty, be by your own reason restrained in prison both.

Vincent

Yea, but, uncle, both the tone and the tother have way enough to walk, the tone in his own ground, the tother in other men's or in the common highway, where they may walk till they be both weary of walking ere any man say them nay.

Antony

So may, cousin, that king that had, as yourself put the case, all the whole castle to walk in, and yet you say not nay but that he is prisoner for all that, though not so straitly kept, yet as verily prisoner as he that lieth in the stocks.

Vincent

But they may go at the leastwise to every place that they need or that is commodious[4] for them, and therefore they do not will to go but where they may go. And therefore be they at liberty to go where they will.

Antony

Me needeth not, cousin, to spend the time about the impugning every part of this answer. For letting pass by that though a prisoner were with his keeper brought into every place where need re-

---

1. *but that if:* unless.   2. i.e., place where.   3. please.
4. advantageous.

quired, yet sith he might not when he would go where he would for
his only pleasure, he were, ye wot well, a prisoner still. And letting
pass over also this, that it were to this beggar need and to this king
commodious to go into divers places where neither of them both
may come, and letting pass also that neither of them both is lightly[5]
so temperately determined,[6] but that they both fain[7] so would do
indeed, if this reason of yours put them out of prison and set them
at liberty and make them free, as I will well grant it doth if they so
do indeed, that is to wit, if they have no will to go but where they
may go indeed, then let us look on our other prisoners enclosed
within a castle, and we shall find that the straitest kept of them both,
if he get the wisdom and the grace to quiet his own mind and hold
himself content with that place and long not, like a woman with
child for her lusts,[8] to be gadding out anywhere else, is by the same
reason of yours, while his will is not longing to be anywhere else, he
is, I say, at his free liberty to be where he will and so is out of prison
too.

And on the tother side, if though his will be not longing to be
anywhere else, yet because that, if his will so were, he should not so
be suffered,[9] he is therefore not at his free liberty but a prisoner
still. So sith your free beggar, that you speak of, and the prince, that
you call out of prison too, though they be, which I ween[1] very few
be, by some special wisdom so temperately disposed that they have
not the will to be but where they see they may be suffered to be, yet
sith that if they would have that will they could not then be where
they would, they lack the effect of free liberty and be both twain in
prison too.

Vincent

Well, uncle, if every man universally be by this reason in prison
already, after the very propriety[2] of imprisonment, yet to be imprisoned in this special manner, which manner is only commonly

---

5. in all probability.   6. *temperately determined:* moderately disposed.
7. gladly.   8. desires.   9. permitted.   1. think.   2. nature

called imprisonment, is a thing of great horror and fear both for the straitness of the keeping and the hard handling that many men have therein, of all which griefs and pains and displeasures in this other general imprisonment that you speak of we feel nothing at all. And therefore, every man abhorreth the tone and would be loath to come into it, and no man abhorreth the tother, for they feel none harm nor find no fault therein. Wherefore, uncle, in good faith, though I cannot find answers convenient[3] wherewith to avoid[4] your arguments, yet to be plain with you and tell you the very truth, my mind findeth not itself satisfied in this point, but that ever me thinketh that these things wherewith you rather convince and conclude[5] me than induce a credence and persuade me, that every man is in prison already, be but sophistical fantasies and that, except those that are commonly called prisoners, other men are not in any prison at all.

Antony

Well fare thine heart,[6] good Cousin Vincent. There was in good faith no word that you spake since we talked of these matters that half so well liked[7] me as this that you speak now. For if you had assented in words and in your mind departed unpersuaded, then if the thing be true that I say, yet had you lost the fruit, and if it be peradventure[8] false and myself deceived therein, then while I should ween that it liked you too, you should have confirmed me in my folly. For in good faith, cousin, such an old fool am I that this thing, in the persuading whereof unto you I had went[9] I had quit me well, and when I have all done appeareth to your mind but a trifle and a sophistical fantasy, myself have so many years taken for so very substantial truth that as yet my mind cannot give[1] me to think it any other. Wherefore, lest I play as the French priest played, that had so long used to say *Dominus* with the second

3. appropriate.   4. refute.
5. *convince and conclude:* overcome and refute.
6. *Well . . . heart:* May your heart fare well.
7. pleased.   8. perhaps.   9. thought.   1. tell, suggest to.

syllable long that at last he thought it must needs be so and was ashamed to say it short,[2] to the intent you may the better perceive[3] me, or I the better myself, we shall here between us a little more consider the thing. And heartily spit well on your hands and take good hold and give it not over against your own mind, for then were we never the near.[4]

Vincent

Nay, by my troth, uncle, that I intend not nor nothing did yet since we began, and that may you well perceive by some things which without any great cause, save for the further satisfaction of mine own mind, I repeated and debated again.

Antony

That guise,[5] cousin, hold on heartily still, for in this matter I purpose to give over my part except I make yourself perceive both that every man universally is a very[6] prisoner in very prison plainly without any sophistication at all, and that there is also no prince living upon earth but he is in worse case prisoner by this general imprisonment that I speak of than is many a lewd,[7] simple wretch by that special imprisonment that you speak of. And over this that in this general imprisonment that I speak of, men are for the time that they be therein so sore[8] handled and so hardly and in such painful wise[9] that men's hearts have with reason great cause as sore to abhor this hard handling that is in this imprisonment as the tother that is in that.

2. More seems to have combined here two anecdotes that follow one another on the same page of Richard Pace's *De Fructu qui ex Doctrina Percipitur,* ed. and trans. F. Manley and R. S. Sylvester (New York, 1967), p. 102. The earliest analogue, however, is an anecdote of Erasmus; see *Erasmi Epistolae,* ed. P. S. Allen et al. (Oxford, 1906–58), II, 323; III, 40.
3. understand.   4. nearer.   5. practice.   6. true.
7. ignorant.   8. harshly.   9. *such . . . wise:* so painful a way.

Vincent

By my troth, uncle, these things would I fain see well proved.

Antony

Tell me, cousin, first by your troth, if there were a man attainted[1] of treason or felony, and after judgment given of his death, and that it were determined that he should die, only the time of his execution delayed till the king's further pleasure known, and he thereupon delivered to certain keepers and put up in a sure place out of which he could not scape: were this man a prisoner or no?

Vincent

This man, quoth he? Yea, marry, that he were in very deed if ever any man were.

Antony

But now what if for the time that were mean[2] between his attainder[3] and his execution he were so favorably handled that he were suffered to do what he would, as he was while he was abroad, and to have the use of his lands and his goods, and his wife and his children license to be with him, and his friends leave at liberty to resort unto him and his servants not forboden to bide[4] about him, and add yet thereunto that the place were a great castle royal with parks and other pleasures therein a very great circuit about, yea, add yet and ye will that he were suffered to go and ride also both when he would and whither he would; only this one point alway provided and foreseen, that he should ever be surely seen to and safely kept fro scaping, so that took[5] he never so much of his own mind in the meanwhile all other ways save scaping, yet he well knew that scape he could not, and that when he were called for, to death

1. convicted.   2. *time . . . mean:* the time between, the meantime.
3. condemnation.   4. remain.   5. considered.

and execution he should.[6] Now, Cousin Vincent, what would you call this man? A prisoner because he is kept for execution, or no prisoner because he is in the meanwhile so favorably handled and suffered to do all that he would save scape? And I bid you not here be hasty in your answer but advise[7] it well, that you grant no such thing in haste as you would after mislike by leisure and think yourself deceived.

Vincent

Nay, by my troth, uncle, this thing needeth no study at all in my mind, but that for all this favor showed him and all this liberty lent him, yet being condemned to death and being kept therefor, and kept with such sure watch laid upon him that he cannot escape, he is all that while a very plain prisoner still.

Antony

In good faith, cousin, me thinketh you say very true. But then one thing must I yet desire you, cousin, to tell me a little further. If there were another laid in prison for a fray[8] and through the jailer's displeasure were bolted and fettered and laid in a low dungeon in the stocks, where he might hap to lie peradventure for awhile and abide[9] in the mean season some pain but no danger of death at all, but that out again he should come well enough: whether of these two prisoners stood in worse case, he that hath all this favor or he that is thus hardly handled?

Vincent

By our Lady, uncle, I ween the most part of men if they should needs choose had lever[1] be such prisoners in every point as he that so sorely lieth in the stocks than in every point such as he that at such liberty walketh about the park.

---

6. i.e., should go.   7. consider.   8. brawl.   9. put up with.
1. rather.

Antony

Consider then, cousin, whether this thing seem any sophistry to you that I shall show you now, for it shall be such as seemeth, in good faith, substantial true to me. And if it so happen that you think otherwise, I will be very glad to perceive which of us both is beguiled. For it seemeth to me, cousin, first, that every man coming into this world here upon earth, as he is created by God, so cometh he hither by the providence of God. Is this any sophistry, first, or not?

Vincent

Nay, verily, this is very substantial truth.

Antony

Now take I this also for very truth in my mind, that there cometh no man nor woman hither into the earth but that ere ever they come quick[2] into the world out of the mother's womb, God condemneth them unto death by his own sentence and judgment for the original sin that they bring with them, contracted in the corrupted stock of our forefather Adam. Is this, cousin, think you, verily thus or not?

Vincent

This is, uncle, very true indeed.

Antony

Then seemeth this true further unto me, that God hath put every man here upon earth under so sure and under so safe keeping that of all the whole people living in this wide world, there is neither man, woman nor child, would they never so fain wander about and seek it, that possibly can find any way whereby they may

2. alive.

scape fro death. Is this, cousin, a fond,[3] imagined fantasy, or is it very truth indeed?

Vincent

Nay, this is none imagination, uncle, but a thing so clearly proved true that no man is so mad to say nay.

Antony

Then need I no more, cousin, for then is all the matter plain and open, evident truth, which I said I took for truth, which is yet more a little now than I told you before when you took my proof yet but for a sophistical fantasy and said that for all my reasoning that every man is a prisoner, yet you thought that except these whom the common people call prisoners, there is else no man a very prisoner indeed. And now you grant yourself again for very substantial, open truth that every man is here, though he be the greatest king upon earth, set here by the ordinance of God in a place, be it never so large—a place, I say, yet (and you say the same) out of which no man can escape, but that therein is every man put under sure and safe keeping to be readily fet[4] forth when God calleth for him, and that then he shall surely die. And is not then, cousin, by your own granting before, every man a very prisoner when he is put in a place to be kept to be brought forth when he would not and himself wot not whither?

Vincent

Yes, in good faith, uncle, I cannot but well perceive this to be so.

Antony

This were, you wot well, true, although a man should be but taken by the arm and in fair manner led out of this world unto his judgment. But now while we well know that there is no king so

3. foolish.   4. fetched.

great but that all the while he walketh here, walk he never so loose,[5] ride he with never so strong an army for his defense, yet himself is very sure, though he seek in the mean season some other pastime to put it out of his mind, yet is he very sure, I say, that escape he cannot, and very well he knoweth that he hath already sentence given upon him to die, and that verily die he shall, and that himself, though he hope upon long respite of his execution, yet can he not tell how soon, and therefore, but if[6] he be a fool, he can never be without fear that either on the morrow or on the self same day the grizzly, cruel hangman death, which from his first coming in hath ever hoved aloft[7] and looked toward him and ever lyen[8] in a wait on him, shall amid among all his rialty[9] and all his main strength neither kneel before him, nor make him any reverence, nor with any good manner[1] desire him to come forth, but rigorously and fiercely grip him by the very breast and make all his bones rattle, and so by long and diverse sore torments strike him stark dead in this prison, and then cause his body to be cast into the ground in a foul pit within some corner of the same, there to rot and be eaten with wretched worms of the earth, sending yet his soul out further unto a more fearful judgment whereof at his temporal death his success is uncertain, and therefore, though by God's grace not out of good hope, yet for all that in the meanwhile in very sore dread and fear and peradventure in peril inevitable of eternal fire.

Me thinketh therefore, cousin, that, as I told you, this keeping of every man in this wretched world for execution of death, it is a very plain imprisonment indeed, and that, as I say, such that the greatest king is in this prison in much worse case in all his wealth than many a man is by the tother[2] imprisonment, that is therein sore and hardly handled; for where some of those lie not there attainted nor condemned to death, the greatest man of this world and the most wealthy in this universal prison is laid in to be kept undoubtedly for death.

5. freely.   6. *but if:* unless.   7. *hoved aloft:* waited above.
8. lain.   9. royalty.   1. custom.   2. other.

Vincent

But yet, uncle, in that case is the tother prisoner too, for he is as sure that he shall die too, pardie.

Antony

This is very true, cousin, indeed, and well objected to. But then you must consider that he is not in danger of death by reason of that prison into which he is put, peradventure but for a light fray, but his danger of death is by the tother imprisonment by which he is prisoner in the great prison of this whole earth, in which prison all the princes thereof be prisoners as well as he. If a man, condemned to death, were put up in a large prison, and while his execution were respited,[3] he were for fighting with his fellows put up in a strait place part of the same, he is in danger of death in that strait prison, but not by the being in that, for therein he is but for the fray. But his deadly imprisonment was the tother, the larger I say, into which he was put for death.

So the prisoner that you speak of is, beside that narrow prison, a prisoner of the broad world, and all the princes thereof therein prisoners with him, and by that imprisonment both they and he in like danger of death not by that strait imprisonment that is commonly called imprisonment, but by that imprisonment which, because of the large walk, men call it liberty, and which prison you therefore thought but a fantasy sophistical to prove it any prison at all. But now may you, me thinketh, very plainly perceive that this whole earth is not only for all the whole kind[4] of man a very plain prison indeed, but also that every man without exception, even those that are most at their liberty therein and reckon themselves great lords and possessioners[5] of a very great parcel thereof, and thereby wax[6] with wantonness so forgetful of their own state that they ween[7] they stand in great wealth, do stand for all that indeed, by the reason of that imprisonment in this large prison of the whole earth, in the selfsame condition that other do stand, which in the

3. postponed.   4. race.   5. possessors.   6. grow.
7. believe.

narrow prisons, which only be called prisons and which only be reputed prisons in the opinion of the common people, stand in the most fearful and in the most odious case, that is to wit, condemned already to death.

And now, cousin, if this thing that I tell you seem but a sophistical fantasy to your mind, I would be glad to know what moveth you so to think. For, in good faith, as I have told you twice, I am no wiser but that I verily ween that the thing is thus of very plain truth in very deed.

The Twentieth Chapter

Vincent

In good faith, uncle, as for this farforth,[8] I not only can make with any reason no resistance thereagainst, but also see very clearly proved that it can be none otherwise but that every man is in this world a very prisoner, sith[9] we be all put here into a sure hold to be kept till we be put to execution as folk already condemned all unto death. But yet, uncle, that strait keeping, collaring, bolting, and stocking, with lying in straw or on the cold ground, which manner[1] of hard handling is used in these special prisonments, that only be called commonly by that name, must needs make that imprisonment, which only beareth among the people that name, much more odious and dreadful than the general imprisoning wherewith we be every man universally prisoned at large, walking where we will roundabout the wide world, in which broad prison out of those narrow prisons there is with the prisoners no such hard handling used.

Antony

I said, I trow,[2] cousin, that I purposed to prove you further yet that in this general prison, the large prison I mean of this whole

8. far.   9. since.   1. kind of.   2. believe.

world, folk be for the time that they be therein as sore[3] handled and as hardly, and wrenched and wronged and braked[4] in such painful wise[5] that our hearts, save that we consider it not, have with reason good and great cause to grudge[6] against and, as farforth as pertaineth only to the respect[7] of pain, as much horror to conceive against the hard handling that is in this prison as the tother that is in that.

Vincent

Indeed, uncle, truth it is that this you said you would prove.

Antony

Nay, so much said I not, cousin, but I said I would if I could, and if I could not, then would I therein give over my part. But that trust I, cousin, I shall not need to do, the thing seemeth me so plain. For, cousin, not only the prince and king, but also, though he hath both angels and devils that are jailers under him, yet the chief jailer over this whole, broad prison, the world, is, as I take it, God. And that I suppose ye will grant me too.

Vincent

That will I not, uncle, deny.

Antony

If a man be, cousin, committed to prison for no cause but to be kept, though there be never so great charge[8] upon him, yet his keeper, if he be good and honest, is neither so cruel that would pain the man of malice nor so covetous that would put him to pain to make him seek his friends to pay for a pennyworth of ease. Else if the place be such that he be sure to keep him safe otherwise, or that he can get surety for the recompense of more harm than he seeth

3. harshly.   4. broken.   5. way.   6. murmur.
7. consideration.   8. *so great charge:* serious charges.

he should have if he scaped,[9] he will never handle him in any such hard fashion as we most abhor imprisonment for. But, marry, if the place be such as the keeper cannot otherwise be sure, then is he compelled to keep him after the rate the straiter.[1] And also if the prisoner be unruly and fall to fighting with his fellows, or do some other manner of shrewd turns,[2] then useth[3] the keeper to punish him sundry wise[4] in some of such fashions as yourself have spoken of.

So is it now, cousin, that God, the chief jailer, as I say, of this broad prison, the world, is neither cruel nor covetous. And this prison is also so sure and so subtly builded that albeit that it lieth open on every side without any wall in the world, yet wander we never so far about therein, the way to get out at shall we never find, so that he needeth not to collar us nor to stock us for any fear of scaping away. And therefore, except[5] he see some other cause than our only keeping for death, he letteth us in the meanwhile, for as long as he list[6] to respite[7] us, walk about in the prison and do therein what we will, using ourself in such wise as he hath by reason and revelation fro time to time told us his pleasure.

And hereof it commeth, lo, that by reason of this favor for a time we wax, as I said, so wanton[8] that we forget where we be, weening that we were lords at large, whereas we be indeed, if we would consider it, even seely,[9] poor wretches in prison. For of very truth our very[1] prison this earth is. And yet thereof we cant[2] us[3] out, part by covenants that we make among us and part by fraud and part by violence too, diverse parts diversely to ourself, and change the

9. *Else . . . scaped:* i.e., besides, if the prison is such that the jailer can be sure that his prisoner is securely kept, or that he can get a bond or assurance to be more than compensated for any harm that might come to him should the prisoner actually escape.
1. *But . . . straiter:* i.e., if the prison is not so secure, the jailer must take more rigorous precautions insofar as the situation demands it.
2. *manner . . . turns:* kinds of injuries.   3. is accustomed.
4. *sundry wise:* in different ways.   5. unless.   6. pleases.
7. reprieve.   8. undisciplined, rebellious.   9. pitiful.
1. true.   2. parcel.   3. ourselves.

name thereof fro the odious name of prison and call it our own land and our livelihood.

Upon our prison we build our prison: we garnish it with gold and make it glorious. In this prison they buy and sell; in this prison they brawl and chide; in this they run together and fight; in this they dice; in this they card; in this they pipe and revel; in this they sing and dance. And in this prison many a man reputed right honest letteth[4] not for his pleasure in the dark privily to play the knave.

And thus while God, our king and our chief jailer too, suffereth us and letteth us alone, we ween ourself at liberty, and we abhor the state of those whom we call prisoners, taking ourself for no prisoners at all. In which false persuasion of wealth and forgetfulness of our own wretched state (which is but a wandering about for a while in this prison of this world till we be brought unto the execution of death) where we forget with our folly both ourself and our jail, and our underjailers, angels and devils both, and our chief jailer, God, too—God that forgetteth not us but seeth us all the while well enough, and being sore[5] discontent to see so shrewd rule[6] kept in the jail, beside that he sendeth the hangman death to put to execution here and there sometime by the thousands at once, he handleth many of the remnant, whose execution he forbeareth[7] yet unto a further time, even as hardly and punisheth them as sore in this common prison of the world as there are any handled in those special prisons, which for the hard handling used, you say, therein, your heart hath in such horror and so sore abhorreth.

Vincent

The remnant will I not again-say,[8] for me thinketh I see it so indeed. But that God, our chief jailer in this world, useth any such prisonly fashion of punishment, that point must I needs deny; for I neither see him lay any man in the stocks, or strike[9] fetters on his legs, or so much as shut him up in a chamber either.

---

4. hesitates.   5. extremely.
6. *so shrewd rule:* such wicked behavior.   7. puts off.   8. deny.
9. fasten.

Antony

Is he no minstrel, cousin, that playeth not on an harp? Maketh no man melody but he that playeth on a lute? He may be a minstrel and make melody, you wot well, with some other instrument, some strange fashioned, peradventure,[1] that never was seen before. God, our chief jailer, as himself is invisible, so useth he in his punishments invisible instruments and therefore not of like[2] fashion as the tother[3] jailers do, but yet of like effect and as painful in feeling as those. For he layeth[4] one of his prisoners with an hot fever as evil[5] at his ease in a warm bed as the tother jailer layeth his in the cold ground. He wringeth[6] them by the brows with a megrim;[7] he collareth them by the neck with a quinsy;[8] he bolteth them by the arms with a palsy that they cannot lift their hands to their head; he manacleth their hands with the gout in their fingers; he wringeth them by the legs with the cramp in their shins; he bindeth them to the bedboard with the crick in the back; and layeth one there a long[9] and as unable to rise as though he lay by the feet fast in the stocks.

Some prisoner of another jail singeth and danceth in his two fetters and feareth not his feet for stumbling[1] at a stone, while God's prisoner that hath his one foot fettered with the gout lieth groaning on a couch and quaketh and crieth out if he fear there would fall on his foot no more but a cushion. And therefore, cousin, as I said, if we consider it well we shall find this general prison of this whole earth a place in which the prisoners be as sore handled as they be in the tother. And even in the tother some make as merry too as there do some in this that are very merry at large out of that.

And surely, like as we ween ourself out of prison now, so if there were some folk born and brought up in a prison, that never came on the wall, nor looked out at the door, nor never heard of other

1. perhaps.   2. the same.   3. other.   4. lays low, prostrates.
5. ill.   6. squeezes.   7. migraine.
8. inflammation of the throat.   9. *a long:* at full length.
1. *for stumbling:* that they may stumble.

world abroad, but saw some for their shrewd turns[2] done among themself locked up in some strait room, and heard them only called prisoners that were so served and themself ever called free folk at large, the like opinion would they have there of themself then that we have here of ourself now. And when we take ourself for other than prisoners now, as verily be we now deceived as those prisoners should there be then.

Vincent

I cannot, uncle, in good faith, say nay but that you have performed all that you have promised. But yet sith that for all this there appeareth no more but that as they be prisoners so be we too, and that as some of them be sore handled so be some of us too, sith we wot well for all this that when we come to those prisons we shall not fail to be in a straiter prison than we be now and to have a door shut upon us where we have none shut on us now—this shall we be sure of at the leastwise, if there come no worse. And then may there come worse, ye wot well, it cometh there so commonly. Wherefore, for all this, it is yet little marvel though men's hearts grudge much thereagainst.

Antony

Surely, cousin, in this you say very well. Howbeit, somewhat had your words touched me the nearer if I had said that imprisonment were no displeasure at all. But the thing that I say, cousin, for our comfort therein, is that our fantasy frameth[3] us a false opinion by which we deceive ourself and take it for sorer[4] than it is. And that do we by the reason that we take ourself before for more free than we be and prisonment for a stranger thing to us than it is indeed. And thus farforth, as I said, have I proved very truth indeed. But now the incommodities that you repeat again, those I say that are proper to the imprisonment of their own nature, that is to wit, to have less room to walk in and to have the door shut upon us, these

2. *shrewd turns:* injuries.   3. forms.   4. something much worse.

are, me thinketh, so very slender and slight that in so great a cause as to suffer for God's sake we might be sore ashamed so much as once to think upon them.

Many a good man there is, you wot well, which without any force at all or any necessity wherefore he should so do, suffereth these two things willingly of his own choice with much other hardness more: holy monks, I mean, of the Charterhouse order,[5] such as never pass their cells but only to the church, set fast[6] by their cells, and thence to their cells again; and Saint Bridget's order and St. Clare's[7] much like, and in a manner[8] all close[9] religious houses; and yet anchors and anchoresses[1] most especially, all whose whole room is less than a meetly[2] large chamber. And yet are they there as well content many long years together as are other men, and better too, that walk about the world. And therefore you may see that the loathness of less room and the door shut upon us, while so many folk are so well content therewith and will for God's love live so to choose, is but an horror enhanced of[3] our own fantasy.

And indeed I wist[4] a woman once that came into a prison to visit of her charity a poor prisoner there, whom she found in a chamber, to say the truth, meetly fair, and at the leastwise it was strong enough. But with mats of straw the prisoner had made it so warm both under the foot and round about the walls that in these things for keeping of his health she was on his behalf glad and very well comforted. But among many other displeasures that for his sake she was sorry for, one she lamented much in her mind: that he should have the chamber door upon him by night made fast by the

5. The Carthusians, a contemplative order founded by St. Bruno in 1084. The members of the order lead a life of isolation in individual cells, coming together only occasionally for prayers.

6. near.

7. *Saint . . . Clare's:* The Brigettines or Order of the Most Holy Savior was founded by St. Bridget of Sweden in 1370. The order follows a semi-cloistered Augustinian rule. The Poor Ladies or Poor Clares was founded in 1212 by St. Clare of Assisi, friend of St. Francis.

8. *in a manner:* so to speak.   9. cloistered.

1. *anchors and anchoresses:* male and female religious hermits.

2. fairly.   3. *enhanced of:* increased by.   4. knew.

jailer, that should shut him in. "For by my troth," quod she, "if the
door should be shut upon me, I would ween[5] it would stop up my
breath." At that word of hers the prisoner laughed in his mind, but
he durst not laugh aloud nor say nothing to her. For somewhat
indeed he stood in awe of her and had his finding[6] there much part
of[7] her charity for almoise.[8] But he could not but laugh inwardly
while he wist well enough that she used on the inside to shut every
night full surely her own chamber to her, both door and windows
too, and used not to open them of all the long night. And what
difference then as to the stopping of the breath, whether they were
shut up within or without?[9]

And so surely, cousin, these two things that you speak of are
neither nother[1] of so great weight that in Christ's cause ought to
move a Christian man, and the tone[2] of the twain is so very a
childish fantasy that in a matter almost of three chips,[3] but if[4] it
were in chance of fire, never should move any man.

As for those other accidents[5] of hard handling[6] therein, so mad
am I not to say they be no grief, but I say that our fear may imagine
them much greater grief than they be. And I say that such as they
be, many a man endureth them, yea, and many a woman too that
after fare full well.[7]

And then would I wit[8] what determination[9] we take, whether for
our Savior's sake to suffer some pain in our bodies, sith[1] he suffered in his blessed body so great pain for us, or else to give him

5. think.
6. maintenance. Prisoners were required to pay for their own meals and all
other incidental expenses.
7. by means of.   8. alms.
9. Harpsfield (pp. 98–99) identifies this as a personal anecdote and links it
with Roper's famous account of Dame Alice's visit to More in the Tower
(pp. 83–84). If so, it is the only description we have of the interior of More's
cell and the actual circumstances of his confinement.
1. *neither nother:* neither the one nor the other.   2. one.
3. *in . . . chips:* i.e., in such a trivial matter—hardly worth three chips.
4. *but if:* unless.   5. non-essential qualities.   6. treatment.
7. *fare full well:* gets along very well.   8. know.   9. decision.
1. since.

warning to be[2] at a point rather utterly to forsake him than suffer any pain at all. He that cometh in his mind unto this latter point, from which kind of unkindness[3] God keep every man, comfort he none needeth; for he will fly the need, and counsel, I fear, availeth him little and if[4] grace be so far gone from him. But on the tother[5] side, if rather than forsake our Savior we determine ourself to suffer any pain at all, I cannot then see that the fear of hard handling should anything stick with us[6] and make us so to shrink as we rather would forsake his faith than to suffer for his sake so much as imprisonment, sith the handling is neither such in prison but that many men many years, and many women too, live therewith and sustain it, and afterward yet fare full well, and yet that[7] it may well fortune that beside the very bare imprisonment there shall hap[8] us no hard handling at all, nor that same haply[9] but for a short while neither, and yet beside all this, peradventure not at all. And specially sith which of all these ways shall be taken with us lieth all in his will, for whom we be content to take it and which, for that mind[1] of ours, favoreth us and will suffer[2] no man to put more pain unto us than he well woteth we shall be well able to bear. For he will give us the strength thereto himself, as you have heard his promise already by the mouth of St. Paul, *Fidelis deus qui non patitur vos tentari supra id quod potestis ferre sed dat etiam cum tentatione proventum:* God is faithful, which suffereth you not to be tempted above that you may bear but giveth also with the temptation a way out.[3]

But now, if we have not lost our faith already before we come to forsake it for fear, we know very well by our faith that by the forsaking of our faith we fall into the state to be cast into the prison of hell and that can we not tell how soon. But as it may be that God will suffer us to live a while here upon earth, so may it be that he will throw us in that dungeon beneath before the time that the Turk shall once ask us the question. And therefore if we fear imprison-

2. *to be:* i.e., that we are.   3. unnaturalness.   4. *and if:* if.
5. other.   6. *stick with us:* cause us to hesitate.
7. *yet that:* in addition.   8. happen to.   9. perhaps.
1. intention.   2. permit.   3. 1 Cor. 10:13.

ment so sore, we be much more than mad that we fear not most for the more sore; for out of that prison shall no man never get, and in this other shall no man abide[4] but a while.

In prison was Joseph while his brethren were at large, and yet afterward were his brethren fain[5] to seek upon him for bread.[6]

In prison was Daniel and the wild lions about him, and yet even here God kept him harmless and brought him safe out again.[7] If we think that he will not do the likewise for us, let us not doubt but he will do for us either the like or better, for better may he do for us if he suffer us there to die.

St. John the Baptist was, you wot well, in prison, while Herod and Herodias sat full merry at the feast. And the daughter of Herodias delighted them with her dancing till with her dancing she danced off St. John's head.[8] And now sitteth he with great feast in heaven at God's board,[9] while Herod and Herodias full heavily sit in hell burning both twain, and to make them sport withal, the devil with the damsel dance in the fire afore them.

Finally, cousin, to finish this piece with—our Savior was himself taken prisoner for our sake, and prisoner was he carried, and prisoner was he kept, and prisoner was he brought forth before Annas, and prisoner from Annas carried unto Caiphas, then prisoner was he carried from Caiphas unto Pilate, and prisoner was he sent from Pilate to King Herod, prisoner from Herod unto Pilate again, and so kept as prisoner to the end of his passion.[1]

The time of his imprisonment, I grant well, was not long, but as for hard handling, which our hearts most abhor, he had as much in that short while as many men among them all in much longer time. And surely then if we consider of what estate[2] he was, and therewith that he was prisoner in such wise[3] for our sake, we shall, I trow,[4] but if[5] we be worse than wretched beasts, never so shamefully play the unkind cowards as for fear of imprisonment sinfully

4. remain.   5. obliged.   6. Gen. 39–45.   7. Dan. 5–6.
8. Matt. 14:1–2; Mark 6:17–29.   9. table.
1. A combination of the gospels. Most of the sequence is taken from John 18:13–14, 24, 28. Luke 23:1–16 adds the detail that Christ was taken from Pilate to Herod and back again to Pilate.
2. rank in society.   3. a way.   4. believe.   5. *but if:* unless.

to forsake him, nor so foolish neither as by forsaking of him to give him the occasion again to forsake us, and with the avoiding of an easier prison fall into a worse, and instead of a prison that cannot keep us long, fall into that prison out of which we can never come, where the short prisonment would win us everlasting liberty.

The Twenty-first Chapter
The fear of shameful and painful death.

Vincent

Forsooth, uncle, our Lord reward you therefor, if we feared not further beside imprisonment the terrible dart of shameful and painful death. As for imprisonment I would verily trust that, remembering these things which I have here heard of you, rather than I should forsake the faith of our Savior, I would with help of grace never shrink thereat.

But now are we comen, uncle, with much work at the last unto the last and uttermost point of the dread that maketh *incursum et demonium meridianum:* this incursion of this midday devil. This open invasion of the Turk and his persecution against the faith seem so terrible to men's minds that, although the respect of God vanquish all the remnant of the troubles that we have hitherto perused, as loss of goods, lands, and liberty, yet when we remember the terror of shameful and painful death, that point so suddenly putteth us in oblivion of all that should be our comfort that we feel (all men, I fear me, for the most part) the fervor of our faith wax[6] so cold and our hearts so faint that we feel ourself at the point to fall even therefro for fear.

Antony

To this I say not nay, cousin, but that indeed in this point is the sore[7] pinch. And yet you see for all this that even this point too

6. grow.   7. severe.

taketh increase and minishment[8] of dread, after[9] the difference of the affections that are before fixed and rooted in the mind, so farforth[1] that you see some man set so much by his worldly substance that he less feareth the loss of his life than the loss of lands. Yea, some man shall you see that abideth[2] deadly torment, and such as some other had liefer[3] die than endure, rather than he would bring forth the money that he hath hid.

And I doubt not but you have heard of many by right antique[4] stories, that, some for one cause, some for other, have not letted[5] willingly to suffer death, divers in divers kinds[6] and some both with despiteful rebuke[7] and painful torment too. And therefore, as I say, we may see that the affections of men's minds toward[8] the increase or decrease of dread maketh much of the matter.

Now are the affections of men's minds imprinted by divers means, one way by the mean of the bodily senses, moved by such things pleasant or displeasant as are outwardly through sensible, worldly things offered and objected[9] unto them. And this manner of receiving of impression of affection is common unto men and beasts. Another manner of receiving affections is by the mean of reason, which both ordinately[1] tempereth those affections that the bodily five wits imprint, and also disposeth a man many times to some spiritual virtues very contrary to those affections that are fleshly and sensual. And those reasonable dispositions been the affections spiritual, and proper to the nature of man, and above the nature of beast.[2]

Now as our ghostly[3] enemy, the devil, enforceth[4] himself to

8. diminishment.   9. according to.   1. far.   2. puts up with.
3. rather.   4. *right antique:* very ancient.   5. hesitated.
6. *diverse . . . kinds:* i.e., different ones in different ways.
7. *despiteful rebuke:* insulting shame.
8. in reference to.   9. presented.   1. in an orderly manner.
2. In scholastic psychology the sensible soul (common to both beasts and man) receives the impressions from the various senses and combines them by means of the phantasy into an image of the thing perceived. The rational soul, on the other hand, belongs to man alone. It is immortal and therefore not entirely dependent on the body.
3. spiritual.   4. exerts.

make us lean unto the sensual affections and beastly, so doth almighty God of his goodness by his Holy Spirit inspire us good motions[5] with aid and help of his grace toward the tother affections spiritual, and by sundry means instructeth our reason to lean unto them, and not only to receive them as engendered and planted in our soul, but also in such wise water them with the wise advertisement[6] of godly counsel and continual prayer, that they may be habitually radicate[7] and surely take deep root therein. And after as[8] the tone kind of affection or the tother beareth the strength in our heart, so be we stronger or feebler against the terror of death in this cause.

And therefore will we, cousin, assay[9] to consider what things there are for which we have cause in reason to master that affection fearful and sensual; and, though we cannot clean avoid it and put it away, yet in such wise to bridle it at the least that it run not out so far like an headstrong horse that spite of our teeth[1] it carry us out unto the devil.

Let us therefore now consider and well weigh this thing that we dread so sore, that is to wit, shameful and painful death.

The Twenty-second Chapter

Of death considered by himself alone, as a bare leaving of this life only.

And first I perceive well by these two things that you join unto death, that is to wit, shameful and painful, you would esteem death so much the less if he shall come alone without either shame or pain.

5. inclinations, promptings.   6. advice.
7. rooted, firmly established.   8. *after as:* depending on whether.
9. attempt.   1. *spite . . . teeth:* despite our utmost efforts.

Vincent

Without doubt, uncle, a great deal the less. But yet, though he should come without them both by himself, whatsoever I would, I wot[2] well many a man would be for all that very loath to die.

Antony

That I believe well, cousin, and the more pity it is, for that affection happeth in very few but that either the cause is lack of faith, lack of hope, or finally, lack of wit. They that believe not the life to come after this and ween[3] themself here in wealth are loath to leave this, for then they think they lose all. And therefor cometh the manifold, foolish, unfaithful words which are so rife in over[4] many mouths: "This world we know, and the tother we know not." And that some say in sport and think in earnest, "The devil is not so black as he is painted, and let him be as black as he will, he is no blacker than a crow," with many such other foolish fantasies of the same sort.

Some that believe well enough, yet through the lewdness[5] of living fall out of good hope of salvation, and then though they be loath to die, I very little marvel. Howbeit, some that purpose to mend and would fain[6] have some time left them longer to bestow somewhat better may, peradventure, be loath to die also by and by.[7] And that manner[8] loathness, albeit a very good will gladly to die and to be with God, were in my mind so thankful[9] that it were well able to purchase as full remission both of sin and pain as peradventure he were like, if he lived, to purchase in many years' penance. Yet will I not say but that such kind of loathness to die may be before God allowable. Some are there also that are loath to die, that are yet very glad to die and long for to be dead.

Vincent

That were, uncle, a very strange case.

2. know.   3. suppose.   4. too.   5. wickedness.   6. gladly.
7. *by and by:* immediately.   8. kind of.   9. beneficial.

Antony

The case I fear me, cousin, falleth not very often, but yet sometime it doth, as where there is any man of that good mind that St. Paul was, which for the longing that he had to be with God would fain have been dead, but for the profit of other folk was content to live here in pain and defer and forbear[1] for the while his inestimable bliss in heaven. *Cupio dissolvi et esse cum Christo: bonum autem mihi manere propter vos.*[2]

But of all these kinds, cousin, of folks that are loath to die, except the first kind only that lacketh faith, there is, I suppose, none but that, except the fear of shame or sharp pain joined unto death should be the let,[3] would else for the bare respect[4] of death alone let[5] to depart hence with good will in this case of the faith, well witting by his faith that his death taken for the faith should cleanse him clean of all his sins and send him straight to heaven. And some of these (namely[6] the last kind) are such that shame and pain both joined unto death were unlikely to make them loathe death or fear death so sore but that they would suffer death in this case with good will, sith[7] they know well that the refusing of the faith for any cause in this world, were the cause never so good in sight, should yet sever them fro God with whom, save for other folks' profit, they so fain would be. And charity can it not be for the profit of the whole world deadly to displease him that made it.[8]

Some are there, I say also, that are loath to die for lack of wit,[9] which albeit that they believe the world that is to come and hope also to come thither, yet they love so much the wealth of this world and such things as delight them therein that they would fain keep them as long as ever they might, even with tooth and nail. And when they may be suffered[1] in no wise to keep it no longer, but that death taketh them therefro, then if it may be no better, they will

---

1. put off.
2. Phil. 1:23–24: "I want to die and be with Christ, but it is good for me to stay because of you."
3. obstacle.   4. consideration.   5. hesitate.   6. especially.
7. since.   8. Luke 9:25.   9. intelligence.   1. permitted.

agree to be, as soon as they be hence, hawsed[2] up in heaven and be with God by and by.

These folks are as very nidiot[3] fools as he that had kept from his childhood a bagful of cherry stones, and cast such a fantasy thereto[4] that he would not go from it for a bigger bag filled full of gold.

These folk fare, cousin, as Aesop telleth a fable that the snail did. For when Jupiter, whom the poets feign for[5] the great god, invited all poor worms of the earth to a great solemn feast that it pleased him (I have forgot upon what occasion) upon a time to prepare for them, the snail kept her at home and would not come thereat. And when Jupiter asked her after wherefore she came not at his feast, where he said she should have been welcome and have faren well, and should have seen a goodly palace and been delighted with many goodly pleasures, she answered him that she loved no place so well as her own house. With which answer Jupiter waxed so angry that he said, sith she loved her house so well, she should never after go from home, but should alway bear her house upon her back wheresoever she went. And so hath she done ever since, as they say, and at the leastwise, I wot well, she doth so now and hath done as long time as I can remember.[6]

Vincent

Forsooth, uncle, I would ween[7] the tale were not all feigned. For I think verily that so much of your tale is true.

Antony

Aesop meant by that feigned fable to touch the folly of such folk as so set their fantasy upon some small, simple pleasure that they

2. raised.   3. idiotic.
4. *cast . . . thereto:* had such false ideas about it.   5. *feign for:* pretend is.
6. *Aesopi Phrygis, et Aliorum Fabulae,* ed. Laurentius Valla, Erasmus, Angelus Politianus, *et al.* (Lugduni, 1540), pp. 84–85. The occasion which More forgot was a wedding feast, and it was the turtle who was punished, not the snail.
7. think.

cannot find in their heart to forbear[8] it, neither for the pleasure of a better man, nor for the gaining of a better thing, by which their fond,[9] froward[1] fashion, they sometime fall in great indignation[2] and take thereby no little harm.

And surely such Christian folk as by their foolish affection, which they have set like the snail upon their own house here in this earth, cannot for the loathness of leaving that house find in their heart with their good will to go to the great feast that God prepareth in heaven, and of his goodness so gently calleth them to, be like, I fear me, but if[3] they mend that mind[4] in time, to be served as the snail was and yet much worse too. For they be like to have their house here, the earth, bound fast upon their backs forever and not walk therewith where they will, as the snail creepeth about with hers, but lie fast bound in the mids[5] with the foul fire of hell about them. For into this folly they bring themself by their own fault, as the drunken man bringeth himself into drunkenness, whereby the evil that he doth in his drunkenness is not forgiven him for his folly, but to his pain imputed to his fault.

Vincent

Surely, uncle, this seemeth not unlikely, and by their fault they fall in such folly indeed. And yet if this be folly indeed, there are then some folk fools that ween themself right wise.

Antony

That ween themself wise? Marry, I never saw fool yet that thought himself other than wise. For as it is one spark of soberness left in a drunken head, when he perceive himself drunk and getteth him fair[6] to bed, so if a fool perceive himself a fool, that point is no folly, but a little spark of wit.

But now, cousin, as for these kind of fools, sith they be loath to die for the love that they bear to their worldly fantasies,[7] which they

---

8. do without.   9. foolish.   1. perverse.
2. angry or contemptuous treatment.   3. *but if:* unless.
4. attitude.   5. middle.   6. straight.   7. desires.

should by their death leave behind them and forsake, they that would for that cause rather forsake the faith than die would rather forsake it than lose their worldly goods, though there were offered them no peril of death at all. And then as touching those that are of that mind, we have, you wot well, said as much as yourself thought sufficient this afternoon here before.

Vincent

Verily, uncle, that is very true, and now have you rehearsed,[8] as far as I can remember, all the other kinds of them that would be loath to die for any other respect[9] than the grievous qualities of shame and pain joined unto death. And of all these kinds, except the kind of infidelity,[1] whom no comfort[2] can help but counsel only to the attaining of faith, which faith must be to the receiving of comfort presupposed and had ready before, as you showed in the beginning of our communication,[3] the first day that we talked of the matter—but else,[4] I say, except that one kind, there is none of the remnant of those that were before untouched which were likely to forsake their faith in the persecution for the fear and dread of death, save for those grievous qualities: pain, I mean, and shame, that they see well would come therewith.

And therefore, uncle, I pray you give us some comfort against those twain. For in good faith, if death should come without them in such case as this is, wherein by the losing of this life we should find a far better, mine own reason giveth[5] me that save for the tother[6] griefs going before the change, there would no man, that wit hath, anything stick at all.[7]

Antony

Yes, peradventure suddenly, before they gather their wits unto them and therewith well weigh the matter. But they, cousin, that

---

8. related.   9. consideration.   1. lack of faith.
2. spiritual consolation.   3. conversation.   4. otherwise.
5. tells.   6. other.   7. *anything ... all:* hesitate to any extent at all.

will consider the matter well, reason, grounded upon the foundation of faith, shall show them very great, substantial causes for which the dread of those grievous qualities, that they see shall come with death—shame, I mean, and pain also—shall not so sore abash[8] them as sinfully to drive them therefro. For the proof whereof let us first begin at the consideration of the shame.

The Twenty-third Chapter

Of shame that is joined with the death in the persecution for the faith.

How can any faithful, wise man dread the death so sore for any respect of shame, when his reason and his faith together may shortly make him perceive that there is therein no piece of very[9] shame at all? For how can that death be shameful that is glorious, or how can that be but glorious to die for the faith of Christ, if we die both for the faith and in the faith, joined with hope and charity, while the scripture so plainly saith, *Preciosa in conspectu domini mors sanctorum ejus:* Precious is in the sight of God the death of his saints?[1] Now if the death of his saints be glorious in the sight of God, it can never be shameful in very deed, how shameful soever it seem here in the sight of men. For here we may see and be sure that not at the death of Saint Stephen only, to whom it liked him to show himself with the heaven open over his head, but at the death also of every man that so dieth for the faith, God with his heavenly company beholdeth his whole passion[2] and verily looketh on.[3]

Now if it were so, cousin, that ye should be brought through the broad, high street of a great, long city, and that all along the way that ye were going, there were on the tone[4] side of the way a rabble

8. *sore abash:* severely confound.   9. true.   1. Ps. 115:15.
2. suffering, but with an allusion also to Christ's passion.
3. Acts 7:55–58.   4. one.

of ragged beggars and madmen that would despise you and dispraise[5] you with all the shameful names that they could call you and all the railing words that they could say to you, and that there were then all along the tother side of the same street where you should come by, a goodly company standing in a fair range,[6] a row of wise and worshipful folk allowing[7] and commending you, mo than fifteen times as many as that rabble of ragged beggars and railing madmen are, would you let your way[8] by your will[9] weening that you went unto your shame for the shameful jesting and railing of those mad, foolish wretches, or hold on your way with a good cheer[1] and a glad heart, thinking yourself much honored by the laud[2] and approbation of that other honorable sort?

Vincent

Nay, by my troth, uncle, there is no doubt but I would much regard the commendation of those commendable folk and not regard a rush[3] the railing of all those ribalds.[4]

Antony

Then, cousin, can there no man that hath faith account himself shamed here by any manner[5] death that he suffereth for the faith of Christ, while, how vile and how shameful soever it seem in the sight here of a few worldly wretches, it is allowed and approved for very precious and honorable in the sight of God and of all the glorious company of heaven, which as perfectly[6] stand and behold it as those peevish[7] people do, and are in number mo than an hundred to one. And of that hundred every one an hundred times more to be regarded and esteemed than of the tother an hundred such whole rabbles.

And now if a man would be mad as for fear of the rebuke that he

---

5. censure.   6. line.   7. praising.
8. *let your way:* stop your journey.   9. *by your will:* voluntarily.
1. expression on the face.   2. praise.
3. *not . . . rush:* take no account of.   4. knaves.   5. kind of.
6. surely.   7. foolish.

should have of such rebukeful[8] beasts he would be ashamed to confess the faith of Christ, then with fleeing from a shadow of shame, he should fall into a very shame and a deadly, painful shame indeed. For then hath our Savior made a sure promise that he will show himself ashamed of that man before the Father of Heaven and all his holy angels, saying in the ninth chapter of St. Luke, *Qui me erubuerit et meos sermones, hunc filius hominis erubescet quum venerit in majestate sua et patris et sanctorum angelorum:* He that is ashamed of me and of my words, of him shall the Son of Man be ashamed, when he shall come in majesty of himself and of his Father and of his holy angels.[9] And what manner a shameful shame shall that be then? If a man's cheeks glow sometime for shame in this world, they will fall on fire for shame when Christ shall show himself ashamed of them there.

To suffer the thing for Christ's faith that we worldly, wretched fools ween were villainy and shame, the blessed apostles reckoned for great glory. For they, when they were with despite[1] and shame scourged, and thereupon commanded to speak no more of the name of Christ, went their way fro the council joyful and glad that God had vouchsafed to do them the worship[2] to suffer shameful despite for the name of Jesu. And so proud were they of that shame and villainous pain put unto them that, for all the forbidding of that great council assembled, they ceased not every day to preach out the name of Jesu still, not in the temple only, out of which they were fet[3] and whipped for the same before, but also, to double it with, went preaching that name about from house to house too.[4]

I would, sith we regard so greatly the estimation of worldly folk, we would, among many naughty[5] things that they use,[6] regard also some such as are good. For it is a manner[7] among them in many places that some by handicraft, some by merchandise, some by other kind of living arise and come forward in the world. And commonly folk are in youth set forth to convenient[8] masters under

8. deserving of rebuke.   9. Luke 9:26.   1. scorn.   2. honor.
3. brought forth.   4. Acts 5:17–42.   5. wicked.   6. do.
7. custom.   8. suitable.

whom they are brought up and grow. But now whensoever they find a servant such as he disdaineth to do such things as he that is his master did while he was servant himself, that servant every man accounteth for a proud unthrift,[9] never like to come to good proof.[1]

Let us, lo, mark and consider this and weigh well therewithal that our master, Christ, not the master only, but the maker too of all this whole world, was not so proud to disdain for our sakes the most villainous and most shameful death, after the worldly count,[2] that then was used in the world, and the most despiteful mocking therewith joined to most grievous pain, as crowning him with sharp thorn that the blood ran down about his face. Then they gave him a reed in his hand for a scepter, and kneeled down to him and saluted him like a king in scorn, and beat then the reed upon the sharp thorns about his holy head.[3]

Now saith our Savior that the disciple or servant is not above his master.[4] And therefore sith[5] our master endured so many kinds of painful shame, very proud beasts may we well think ourself if we disdain to do as our master did. And whereas he through shame ascended into glory, we would be so mad that we rather will fall into everlasting shame both before heaven and hell than for fear of a short worldly shame to follow him into everlasting glory.

The Twenty-fourth Chapter
Of painful death to be suffered in the Turk's persecution for the faith.

Vincent

In good faith, uncle, as for the shame, ye shall need to take no more pain, for I suppose surely that any man that hath reason in

9. shiftless person.   1. *come . . . proof:* become successful.
2. *after . . . count:* according to the reckoning of the world.
3. Matt. 27:27–31 and Mark 15:16–20.   4. Matt. 10:24–25.
5. since.

his head shall hold himself satisfied with this. But of truth, uncle, all the pinch is in the pain. For as for shame, I perceive well enough a man may with wisdom so master it that it shall nothing move[6] him at all, so farforth[7] that it is almost in every country become a common proverb that shame is as it is taken.[8] But, by God, uncle, all the wisdom in this world can never so master pain but that pain will be painful, spite of all the wit[9] in this world.

Antony

Truth it is, cousin, that no man can with all the reason he hath in such wise[1] change the nature of pain that in the having of pain he feel it not, for but if[2] it be felt it is, pardie,[3] no pain. And that is the natural cause, cousin, for which a man may have his leg stricken off by the knee and grieve him not, if his head be off but half an hour before.

But reason may make a reasonable man, though he would not be so foolish as causeless[4] to fall therein, yet upon good causes either of gaining some kind of great profit, or avoiding of some great loss, or eschewing thereby the suffering of far greater pain, not to shrink therefro and refuse it to his more hurt and harm, but for his far greater advantage and commodity,[5] content and glad to sustain it.

And this doth reason alone in many cases where it hath much less help to take hold of than it hath in this matter of faith. For well you wot[6] to take a sour and bitter potion is great grief and displeasure, and to be lanced and have the flesh cut is no little pain. Now when such things shall be ministered unto a child, or to some childish man either, they will by their own wills rather let their sickness or their sore grow unto their more grief till it be become incurable

6. incite.   7. far.
8. M. P. Tilley, *The Proverbs in England in the Sixteenth and Seventeenth Centuries* (Ann Arbor, 1950), S 274. See also Erasmus, *Adagia*, "Ubi timor, ibi et pudor," sig. G₁ (I. II. lxiv) and "Lucrum pudori praestat," sig. Kkk₂v (III. VII. xiv).
9. reason.   1. a way.   2. *but if:* unless.   3. an oath: "by God."
4. without reason.   5. benefit.   6. know.

than abide the pain of the curing in time, and that for faint heart joined with lack of discretion. But a man that hath more wisdom, though he would without cause no more abide the pain willingly than would the tother, yet sith reason showeth him what good he shall have by the suffering and what harm by the refusing, this maketh him well content and glad also for to take it.

Now then, if reason alone be sufficient to move a man to take pain for the gaining of some worldly rest or pleasure, and for the avoiding of another pain through peradventure more,[7] yet endurable but for a short season, why should not reason, grounded upon the sure foundation of faith and holpen[8] also forward with aid of God's grace, as it ever is undoubtedly when folk for a good mind[9] in God's name comen together thereon, our Savior saying himself, *Ubi sunt duo vel tres congregati in nomine meo ibi et ego sum in medio eorum:* Where there are two or three gathered together in my name, there am I also even in the very mids[1] of them[2]—why should not then reason, I say, thus furthered with faith and grace, be much more able first to engender in us such an affection, and after by long and deep meditation thereof so to continue that affection that it shall turn into an habitual, fast,[3] and deep-rooted purpose of patient suffering the painful death of this body here in earth for the gaining of everlasting, wealthy life in heaven and avoiding of everlasting, painful death in hell?

Vincent

By my troth, uncle, words can I none find that should have any reason with them (faith alway presupposed, as you protested[4] in the beginning, for a ground)—words, I say, can I none find wherewith I might reasonably counterplead this that you have said here already.

But yet I remember the fable that Aesop telleth of a great, old hart that had fled from a little bitch, which had made suit[5] after him

---

7. *through . . . more:* perhaps by means of more.   8. helped.
9. purpose.   1. midst.   2. Matt. 18:20.   3. steadfast.
4. declared.   5. pursuit.

and chased him so long that she had lost him, and, as he hoped, more than half given him over. By occasion whereof, having then some time to talk and meeting with another of his fellows, he fell in deliberation with him what were best for him to do: whether to run on still and fly farther from her, or turn again and fight with her.

Whereunto the tother[6] hart advised him to fly no farther, lest the bitch might happen to find him again at such time as he should with the labor of further flying be fallen out of breath, and thereby all out of strength too, and so should he be killed, lying where he could not stir him. Whereas, if he would turn and fight, he were in no peril at all. "For the man with whom she hunteth is more than a mile behind her, and she is but a little body, scant[7] half so much as thou, and thy horns may thrust her through before she can touch thy flesh by more than ten times her tooth length."

"By my troth," quoth the tother hart, "I like your counsel well, and me thinketh that the thing is even soothly[8] such as you say. But I fear me when I hear once that urchin[9] bitch bark, I shall fall to my feet and forget altogether. But yet and[1] you will go back with me, then me think we shall be strong enough against that one bitch between us both." Whereunto the tother hart agreed, and so they both appointed them[2] thereon.

But even as they were about to busk them[3] forward to it, the bitch had found the foot again,[4] and on she came yearning[5] toward the place; whom as soon as the harts heard, they too go both twain apace.[6]

And, in good faith, uncle, even so I fear it would fare by[7] myself and many other too, which, though we think it reason that you say and in our minds agree that we should do as you say, yea, and do peradventure[8] think also that we would indeed do as ye say, yet as

6. other.   7. scarcely.   8. truly.   9. ill-tempered.   1. if.
2. *appointed them:* resolved, made up their minds.   3. *busk them:* hasten.
4. *found . . . again:* recovered the scent.   5. baying, giving tongue.
6. *they . . . apace:* they quickly ran away. The fable is not by Aesop and does not appear in any of the standard collections of fables, Renaissance or modern. The story may well be More's own invention.
7. *fare by:* happen to.   8. perhaps.

soon as we should once hear these hell hounds, these Turks come yelping and bawling upon us, our hearts should soon fall as clean[9] from us as those other harts fly from the hounds.

(Here it must be known of some man that can skill[1] of hunting whether that we mistake not our terms, for then are we utterly shamed, ye wot well. And I am so cunning[2] that I cannot tell whether among them a bitch be a bitch or no. But as I remember she is no bitch, but a brach.[3] This is a high point in a low house.[4] Beware of barking, for there lacketh another hunting term. At a fox[5] it is called crying. I wot not what they call it at a hart, but it shall make no matter of a fart.[6])

Antony

Cousin, in those days that Aesop speaketh of, though those harts and other brute beasts mo had, if he saith sooth,[7] the power to speak and talk, and in their talking, power to talk reason too, yet to follow reason and rule themself thereby, thereto had they never given them the power. And in good faith, cousin, as for such things as pertain toward the conducting of reasonable men to salvation, I think without help of grace, men's reasoning shall do little more.

But then are we sure, as I said before, that as for grace, if we desire it, God is at such reasoning alway present and very ready to give it, and but if that men will afterward willingly cast it away, he is ever still as ready to keep[8] it and fro time to time glad to increase it. And therefore biddeth us our Lord by the mouth of the prophet that we should not be like such brutish and unreasonable beasts as were those harts, and as are our horses and mules: *Nolite fieri sicut*

9. completely.   1. *can skill:* has knowledge.   2. knowledgeable.
3. a hound that hunts by scent.
4. Like most of the humanists, More had a low opinion of hunting. Cf. *Utopia, CW 4*, 170/11–12.
5. *At a fox:* i.e., At the hunting of a fox.
6. This paragraph is evidently a note of More's to his secretary (or possibly himself) reminding him (humorously) to check the hunting terms. It was copied into the MS by mistake.
7. truth.   8. continue granting.

equus et mulus in quibus non est intellectus: Be not you like an horse and a mule that hath none understanding.[9]

And therefore, cousin, let us never dread but that if we will apply our minds to the gathering of comfort[1] and courage against such persecutions, and hear reason, and let it sink into our heart, and cast it not out again, vomit it not up, nor even there choke it up and stifle it with pampering in[2] and stuffing up our stomachs[3] with a surfeit of worldly vanities, God shall so well work therewith that we shall feel strength therein, and not in such wise have all such shameful, cowardous hearts as to forsake our Savior, and thereby lose our own salvation, and run into eternal fire for fear of death joined therewith, though bitter and sharp, yet short for all that and, in a manner,[4] a momentary pain.

Vincent

Every man, uncle, naturally grudgeth[5] at pain and is very loath to come at it.

Antony

That is very truth, nor no man holdeth[6] any man to go run into it, but that if he be taken and may not fly, then we say that reason plainly telleth us that we should rather suffer and endure the less and shorter here than in hell the sorer[7] and so far the longer too.

Vincent

I heard, uncle, of late where such a reason was made as you make me now, which reason seemeth undoubted and unevitable[8] unto me. Yet heard I late, as I say, a man answer it thus. He said that if a man in this persecution should stand still in the confession of his faith and thereby fall into painful tormentry,[9] he might, peradventure, hap for the sharpness and bitterness of the pain to forsake

---

9. Ps. 31:9.   1. strength.   2. *pampering in:* overfeeding.
3. i.e., spirits.   4. *in a manner:* so to speak.   5. complains.
6. requires.   7. more severe.   8. inevitable.   9. torture.

our Savior even in the mids,[1] and die there with his sin, and so be damned forever. Whereas by the forsaking of the faith in the beginning betime,[2] and for the time,[3] and yet not but in word[4] neither, keeping it still nevertheless in his heart, a man may save himself from that painful death, and after ask mercy and have it, and live long and do many good deeds, and be saved as St. Peter was.

Antony

That man's reason, cousin, is like a three-footed stool, so tottering on every side that whoso sit thereon may soon take a foul fall. For these are the three feet of this tottering stool: fantastical[5] fear, false faith, false flattering hope.

First, it is a fantastical fear that the man conceiveth that it should be perilous to stand in the confession of the faith at the beginning, lest he might afterward through the bitterness of pain fall to the forsaking, and so die there in the pain therewith out of hand,[6] and thereby be utterly damned, as though that if a man with pain were overcome and so forsook his faith, God could not or would not as well give him grace to repent again, and thereupon give him forgiveness as him that forsook his faith in the beginning and did set so little by[7] him that he would rather forsake him than suffer for his sake any manner[8] pain at all, as though the more pain that a man taketh for God's sake, the worse would God be to him.

If this reason were not unreasonable, then should our Savior not have said, as he did, *Ne terreamini ab his qui occidunt corpus et post haec non habent amplius quid faciant:* Be not afeard of them that kill the body and after that have nothing that they can do further.[9] For he should by this reason have said: Dread and fear them that may slay the body, for they may by the torment of painful death, but if[1] thou forsake me betimes in the beginning and so save thy life, and get of

---

1. middle.   2. before it is too late.   3. occasion.
4. *but in word:* only in word.   5. irrational.   6. *out of hand:* at once.
7. *set . . . by:* value.   8. kind of.
9. Luke 12:4. The quotation, which appears only partially here, emerges fully at the beginning of the next chapter.
1. *but if:* unless.

me thy pardon and forgiveness after, make thee, peradventure, forsake me too late and so to be damned forever.

The second foot of this tottering stool is a false faith. For it is but a feigned faith for a man to say to God secretly that he believeth him, trusteth him, and loveth him, and then openly, where he should to God's honor tell the same tale and thereby prove that he doth so, there to God's dishonor, as much as in him is, flatter God's enemies and do them pleasure and worldly worship[2] with the forsaking of God's faith before the world, and is either faithless in his heart too, or else woteth well that he doth God this despite[3] even before his own face. For except[4] he lack faith he cannot but know that our Lord is everywhere present and, while he so shamefully forsaketh him, full angrily looketh on.

The third foot of this tottering stool is false, flattering hope. For sith[5] the thing that he doth when he forsaketh his faith for fear is by the mouth of God, upon the pain of eternal death, forboden,[6] though the goodness of God forgiveth many folk the fault, yet to be the bolder in offending for the hope of forgiving is a very false, pestilent[7] hope, wherewith a man flattereth himself toward his own destruction.

He that in a sudden braid[8] for fear or other affection unadvisedly[9] falleth, and after in laboring to rise again comforteth[1] himself with hope of God's gracious forgiveness, walketh in the ready way toward his salvation. But he that with the hope of God's mercy to follow doth encourage himself to sin and therewith offendeth God first—I have no power to shet[2] the hand of God fro giving out his pardon where he list,[3] nor would if I could, but rather help to pray therefor; but yet I very sore[4] fear that such a man may miss the grace to require[5] it in such effectual wise[6] as to have it granted. Nor I can not suddenly now remember any sample or promise expressed in holy scripture that the offender in such a

2. honor.   3. scorn.   4. unless.   5. since.
6. forbidden. Cf. Matt. 10:32–33; Luke 12:8–9.   7. pernicious.
8. attack.   9. unexpectedly.   1. consoles.   2. restrain.
3. pleases.   4. strongly.   5. *miss . . . require:* lack . . . request.
6. way.

kind[7] shall have the grace offered after in such wise to seek for pardon, that God hath by his other promises of remission promised to penitents bounden himself to grant it.

But this kind of presumption under the pretext of hope seemeth rather to draw near on the tone side, as despair doth on the tother[8] side, toward the abominable sin of blasphemy against the Holy Ghost, against which sin, concerning either the impossibility or at the least the great difficulty of forgiveness our Savior hath showed himself in the twelfth chapter of Saint Matthew and in the third chapter of St. Mark, where he saith that blasphemy against the Holy Ghost shall never be forgiven, neither in this world, nor in the world to come.[9] And where the man that you speak of took in his reason a sample[1] of St. Peter, which forsook our Savior and got forgiveness after, let him consider again on the tother side that he forsook him not upon the boldness of any such sinful trust, but was overcome and vanquished upon a sudden fear. And yet by the forsaking St. Peter won but little, for he did but delay his trouble but a little while, you wot well. For beside that he repented forthwith[2] very sore that he had so done and wept therefor by and by full bitterly,[3] he came forth at the Whitsuntide ensuing and confessed his master again,[4] and soon after that he was imprisoned therefor, and not ceasing so, was thereupon sore scourged for the confession of his faith,[5] and yet after that imprisoned again afresh, and being from thence delivered stinted[6] not to preach on still[7] until that after manifold labors, travails, and troubles, he was at Rome crucified and with cruel torment slain.[8]

---

7. *the offender . . . kind:* i.e., he who offends in such a way.

8. *tone . . . tother:* one . . . other.

9. Matt. 12:31–32; Mark 3:28–29; Luke 12:10. More refers in this passage to the traditional definition of the sin against the Holy Spirit as both presumption and despair. See Aquinas, *Summa Theologica,* II–II, Q. 14, a. 2.

1. *a sample:* an example.

2. *beside . . . forthwith:* in addition to the fact that he repented immediately.

3. Matt. 26:75.   4. Acts 2:1–38.   5. Acts 4:1–22.

6. ceased.   7. Acts 5:12–42.

8. The tradition that Peter was crucified upside down at Rome was first recorded by Tertullian in his *Adversus Gnosticos Scorpice,* 15 (*PL* 2, 151).

And in like wise I ween[9] I might in a manner[1] well warrant that
there should no man, which denieth our Savior once, and after
attaineth remission, escape through that denying one penny the
better cheap,[2] but that he shall ere he come in heaven full surely
pay therefor.

Vincent

He shall, peradventure, uncle, afterward work it out in the
fruitful works of penance, prayer, and almsdeed done in true faith
and due charity and attain in such wise forgiveness well enough.

Antony

All his forgiveness goeth, cousin, you see well, but by "perhaps."
But as it may be perhaps yea, so may it be perhaps nay. And where
is he then? And yet you wot[3] well by no manner hap[4] he shall never
hap finally to scape fro death, for fear of which he forsook his faith.

Vincent

No, but he may die his natural death and escape that violent
death, and then he saveth himself fro much pain and so winneth
therewith much ease. For evermore a violent death is painful.

Antony

Peradventure he shall not avoid a violent death thereby, for God
is without doubt displeased and can bring him shortly to a death as
violent by some other way.

Howbeit, I see well that you reckon that whoso dieth a natural
death dieth like a wanton even at his ease. You make me remember
a man that was once in a galley subtile[5] with us on the sea, which

---

9. think.   1. *in a manner:* so to speak.
2. *the better cheap:* more cheaply.   3. know.
4. *by no . . . hap:* by no kind of chance occurrence.
5. *galley subtile:* narrow, flat ship propelled by sails and oars. Such a ship
would have a terrible roll.

while the sea was sore wrought[6] and the waves rose very high, and
he came never on the sea before and lay tossed hither and thither,
the poor soul groaned sore, and for pain he thought he would very
fain[7] be dead, and ever[8] he wished, "Would God I were on land
that I might die in rest." The waves so troubled him there with
tossing him up and down, to and fro, that he thought that trouble
letted[9] him to die because the waves would not let him rest. But if
he might get once to land, he thought, he should then die there
even at his ease.

Vincent

Nay, uncle, this is no doubt but that death is to every man
painful, but yet is not the natural death so painful as is the violent.

Antony

By my troth, cousin, me thinketh that the death which men call
commonly natural is a violent death to every man whom it fetcheth
hence by force against his will, and that is every man which when he
dieth is loath to die and fain would yet live longer if he might.

Howbeit, how small the pain is in the natural death, cousin, fain
would I wit[1] who hath told you. As far as I can perceive, those folk
that commonly depart of[2] their natural death have ever one disease
and sickness or other, whereof if the pain of that whole week or
twain in which they lie pining[3] in their bed were gathered together
into so short a time as a man hath his pain that dieth a violent death,
it would, I ween, make double the pain that that is. So that he that
naturally dieth ofter[4] suffereth more pain than less, though he
suffereth it in a longer time. And then would many a man be more
loath to suffer so long lingering in pain than with a sharper to be
sooner rid.

And yet lieth many a man mo days than one in well near as great

6. agitated.   7. gladly.   8. always.   9. did not allow.
1. know.   2. by means of.   3. suffering.   4. more often.

pain continually as is the pain that with the violent death riddeth[5] the man in less than half an hour. Except a man would ween that whereas the pain is great to have a knife to cut his flesh on the outside fro the skin inward, the pain would be much less if the knife might begin on the inside and cut fro the mids[6] outward. Some we hear in their deathbed complain that they think they feel sharp knives cut atwo[7] their heart strings. Some cry out and think they feel within the brainpan their head pricked even full of pins. And they that lie in a pleurisy think that every time they cough they feel a sharp sword swap[8] them to the heart.

The Twenty-fifth Chapter

The consideration of the pains of hell in which we fall if we forsake our Savior may make us set all the painful death of this world at right nought.

Howbeit, what should we need to make any such comparison between the natural death and the violent for the matter that we be in hand with here? We may put it out of doubt that he which for the fear of the violent death forsaketh the faith of Christ putteth himself in the peril to find his natural death more painful a thousand times, for his natural death hath his everlasting pain so suddenly knit unto it that there is not one moment of an hour between, but the end of the tone is the beginning of the tother, that after never shall have end. And therefore was it not without great cause that Christ gave us so good warning before when he said, as St. Luke in the twelfth chapter rehearseth,[9] *Dico autem vobis amicis meis, ne terreamini ab his qui occidunt corpus, et post haec non habent amplius quid faciant. Ostendam autem vobis quem timeatis. Timete eum qui postquam occiderit, habet potestatem mittere in gehennam: ita dico vobis hunc timete:* I say to you that are my friends, be not afeard of them that kill the body and which, when that is done, are able to do no

5. dispatches.   6. middle.   7. in two.   8. strike.   9. relates.

more. But I shall show you whom you should fear. Fear him which, when he hath killed, hath in his power further to cast him whom he killeth into everlasting fire. So I say to you, be afeard of him.[1]

God meaneth not here that we should nothing dread at all any man that can but kill the body, but he meaneth that we should not in such wise dread any such that we should for dread of them displease him, that can everlastingly kill both body and soul with a death ever dying and that yet never die. And therefore he addeth and repeateth in the end again the fear that we should have of him and saith, *Ita dico vobis hunc timete:* So I say to you, fear him.

Oh, good God, cousin, if a man would well weigh those words and let them sink as they should do down deep into his heart, and often bethink himself thereon, it would, I doubt not, be able enough to make us set at nought all the great Turk's threats and esteem him not at a straw, but well content to endure all the pain that all the world would put upon us for so short while as all they were able to make us dwell therein, rather than by the shrinking fro those pains, though never so sharp, yet but short, to cast ourself into the pain of hell, an hundred thousand times more intolerable and whereof there shall never come an end. A woeful death is that death in which folk shall evermore be dying and never can once be dead, whereof the scripture saith, *Vocabunt mortem et mors fugiet ab eis:* They shall call and cry for death, and death shall fly from them.[2]

Oh, good Lord, if one of them were now put in choice of the both, they would rather suffer the whole year together the most terrible death that all the Turks in Turkey could devise than the death that they lie in for the space of an half an hour. In how wretched folly fall then those faithless or feeble faithed folk, that, to avoid the pain so far the less and so short, fall in the stead thereof into pain a thousand thousand times more horrible and of which terrible torment they be sure they shall never have end.

This matter, cousin, lacketh, as I believe, but either full faith or sufficient minding. For I think, on my faith, if we have the grace

1. Luke 12:4–5.   2. Rev. 9:6.

verily to believe it and often to think well thereon, the fear of all the Turk's persecution, with all this midday devil were able to make them do in the forcing us to forsake our faith, should never be able to turn us.

Vincent

By my troth, uncle, I think it be as you say, for surely if we would as often think on these pains of hell, as we be very loath to do, and seek ús peevish[3] pastimes of purpose to put such heavy things out of our thought, this one point alone were able enough to make, I think, many a martyr.

The Twenty-sixth Chapter

The consideration of the joys of heaven should make us for Christ's sake abide and endure any painful death.

Antony

Forsooth, cousin, if we were such as we should be, I would scant[4] for very shame in exhortation to the keeping of Christ's faith speak of the pains of hell. I would rather put us in mind of the joys of heaven, the pleasure whereof we should be more glad to get than we should be to fly and escape all the pains in hell. But surely God in that thing wherein he may seem most rigorous is very merciful to us, and that is—which many men would little ween—in that he provided hell. For I suppose very surely, cousin, that many a man and woman too, of whom there now sit some, and more shall hereafter sit, full gloriously crowned in heaven, had they not first been afraid of hell would toward heaven never have set foot forward.

3. foolish.   4. hardly.

But yet, undoubtedly, were it so that we could as well conceive in our hearts the marvelous joys of heaven as we conceive the fearful pains of hell—howbeit, sufficiently we can conceive neither nother[5] but if[6] we would in our imagination draw as much toward the perceiving of the tone as we may toward the consideration of the tother—we should not fail to be far more moved and stirred to the suffering for Christ's sake in this world for the winning of the heavenly joys than for the eschewing of all those infernal pains. But forasmuch as the fleshly pleasures be far less pleasant than the fleshly pains be painful, therefore, we fleshly folk, that are so drowned in these fleshly pleasures and in the desire thereof that we can almost have no manner[7] savor or taste in any pleasure spiritual, have no cause to marvel that our fleshly affections be more abated and refrained[8] by the dread and terror of hell than affections spiritual imprinted in us and pricked[9] forward with desire and joyful hope of heaven.

Howbeit, if we would somewhat set less by the filthy, voluptuous appetites of the flesh, and would by withdrawing from them with help of prayer through the grace of God draw near to the secret, inward pleasure of the spirit, we should by the little sipping that our hearts should have here now, and that sudden taste thereof, have such an estimation of the incomparable and uncogitable joy that we shall have, if we will, in heaven by the very full draught thereof, whereof it is written, *Satiabor quum apparuerit gloria tua:* I shall be satiate, satisfied, and fulfilled when thy glory, good Lord, shall appear[1] (that is to wit, the fruition of the sight of God's glorious majesty face to face), that the desire, expectation, and heavenly hope thereof shall more encourage us and make us strong to suffer and sustain for the love of God and salvation of our soul than ever we could be moved to suffer here worldly pain by the terrible dread of all the horrible pains that damned wretches have in hell.

Wherefore, in the meantime for lack of such experimental[2] taste

5. *neither nother:* neither the one nor the other.   6. *but if:* unless.
7. kind of.   8. restrained.   9. urged.   1. Ps. 16:15.
2. i.e., based on actual experience.

as God giveth here sometime to some of his special servants, to the intent we may draw toward spiritual exercise too, for which spiritual exercise God with that gift, as with an earnest penny[3] of their whole reward after in heaven, comforteth them here in earth, let us not so much with looking to have described what manner of joys they shall be as with hearing what our Lord telleth us in holy scripture how marvelous great they shall be, labor by prayer to conceive in our hearts such a fervent longing for them that we may for attaining to them utterly set at nought all fleshly delight, all worldly pleasures, all earthly losses, all bodily torment and pain.

Howbeit some things are there in scripture expressed of the manner of the pleasures and joys that we shall have in heaven as where, *Fulgebunt justi sicut sol, et qui erudiunt ad justitiam tanquam scintillae in arundineto discurrent:* Righteous men shall shine as the sun and shall run about like sparks of fire among reeds.[4]

Now tell some carnal-minded man of this manner pleasure, and he shall take little pleasure therein, and say he careth not to have his flesh shine he, nor like a spark of fire to skip about in the sky. Tell him that his body shall be impassible[5] and never feel harm, yet if he think then therewith that he shall never be anhungered[6] nor athirst and shall thereby forbear all his pleasure of eating and drinking, and that he shall never have lust[7] to sleep and thereby lose the pleasure that he was wont to take in slugging,[8] and that men and women shall there live together as angels without any manner mind[9] or motion unto the carnal act of generation and that he shall thereby not use there his old filthy, voluptuous fashion, he will say he is better at ease already and would not give this world for that. For as Saint Paul saith: *Animalis homo non percipit ea quae sunt spiritus dei. Stultitia est enim ei.*[1]

3. *earnest penny:* pledge, foretaste.
4. Sap. 3:7. *Sicut sol* is taken from Matt. 13:43, which echoes Sap. 3:7. More also adds the phrase *qui erudiunt ad justitiam* from Dan. 12:3 but does not translate it.
5. not subject to suffering.   6. hungry.   7. desire.
8. lying about idly.   9. intention.
1. 1 Cor. 2:14: "A carnal man does not perceive the things that pertain to the spirit of God, for they are folly to him."

But when the time shall come that these foul, filthy pleasures shall be so taken from him that it shall abhor[2] his heart once to think on them, whereof every man hath among[3] a certain shadow of experience in a fervent grief of a sore,[4] painful sickness, while the stomach can scant abide to look upon any meat, and, as for acts of the tother[5] foul, filthy lust, is ready to vomit if it hap[6] him to think thereon; when men shall, I say, after this life feel that horrible abomination in their heart at the remembrance of those voluptuous pleasures, of which abomination sickness hath here a shadow, for which voluptuous pleasures he would here be loath to change with the joys of heaven; when he shall, I say, after this life have[7] his fleshly pleasures in abomination and shall of those heavenly joys, which he set here so little by, have there a glimmering, though far from a perfect sight—oh, good God, how fain[8] will he then be, with how good will and how glad will he then give this whole world if it were his, to have the feeling of some little part of those joys. And therefore let us all, that cannot now conceive such delight in the consideration of them as we should, have often in our eyen[9] by reading, often in our ears by hearing, often in our mouths by rehearsing, often in our hearts by meditation and thinking, those joyful words of holy scripture by which we learn how wonderful, huge and great those spiritual, heavenly joys are of which our carnal hearts hath so feeble and so faint a feeling, and our dull, worldly wits[1] so little able to conceive so much as a shadow of the right imagination.[2] A shadow I say, for as for the thing as it is, that can not only no fleshly, carnal fantasy conceive, but over that, no spiritual, ghostly[3] person peradventure[4] neither that here is here living still in this world. For sith[5] the very[6] substance essential of all the celestial joy standeth in[7] blessed beholding of the glorious Godhead face to face, there may no man presume or look to attain it in this life; for God hath so said himself, *Non videbit me homo et vivet:* There shall no man here living behold me.[8] And, therefore,

2. disgust.   3. occasionally.   4. severe.   5. other.
6. happen.   7. hold.   8. willing.   9. eyes.
1. mental faculties.   2. Cf. 1 Cor. 2:9–10.   3. spiritual.
4. perhaps.   5. since.   6. true.   7. *standeth in:* consists of.
8. Exod. 33:20.

we may well know that for the state of this life we be not only shut from the fruition of the bliss of heaven, but also that the very best man living here upon earth (the best man, I mean, being no more but a man) cannot, I ween,[9] attain the right imagination thereof. But those that are very virtuous are yet in a manner[1] as far therefro as the born blind man fro the right imagination of colors.

The words that St. Paul rehearseth[2] of the prophet Isaias, prophesying of Christ's incarnation, may properly be verified of the joys of heaven: *Nec oculus vidit, nec auris audivit, nec in cor hominis ascendit, quae preparavit deus diligentibus se.*[3] For surely, for this state of this world, the joys of heaven are by man's mouth unspeakable, to man's ears not audible, to men's hearts uncogitable, so farforth[4] excel they all that ever men have heard of, all that ever men can speak of, and all that ever any man can by natural possibility think on. And yet where the joys of heaven be such prepared for every saved soul, our Lord saith yet by the mouth of St. John that he will give his holy martyrs that suffer for his sake many a special kind of joy. For he saith, *Vincenti dabo edere de ligno vitae:* To him that overcometh, I shall give him to eat of the tree of life.[5] And also, he that overcometh shall be clothed in white clothes, and I shall confess his name before my Father and before his angels.[6] And also he saith: Fear none of those things that thou shalt suffer etc., but be faithful unto the death, and I shall give thee the crown of life; he that overcometh shall not be hurt of the second death.[7] He saith also, *Vincenti dabo manna absconditum, et dabo illi calculum candidum. Et in calculo nomen novum scriptum quod nemo scit nisi qui accipit:* To him that overcometh will I give manna secret and hid, and I will give him a white suffrage[8] and in his suffrage a new name written, which no man knoweth but he that receiveth it.[9]

They used of old in Greece, where Saint John did write, to elect

9. think.   1. *in a manner:* so to speak.   2. relates.

3. 1 Cor. 2:9: "The eye has not seen, nor has the ear heard, nor has it risen in the heart of man what God has prepared for those who love him."

4. far.   5. Rev. 2:7.   6. Rev. 3:4–5.   7. Rev. 2:10–11.

8. vote; specifically, an object, such as a small pebble, used to indicate a vote.

9. Rev. 2:17.

and choose men unto honorable rooms,[1] and every man's assent
was called his suffrages, which in some place was by the voices, in
some place by hands, and one kind of those suffrages was by
certain things that are in Latin called *calculi,* because that in some
places they used thereto round stones.[2] Now saith our Lord that
unto him which overcometh he will give a white suffrage; for those
that were white signified approving, as the black signifieth reprov-
ing, and in those suffrages did they use to write the name of him to
whom they gave their voice. And now saith our Lord that unto him
that overcometh he will in the suffrage give him a new name, which
no man knoweth but he that receiveth it. He saith also, he that
overcometh, I will make him a pillar in the temple of my God, and
he shall go no more out thereof, and I shall write upon him the
name of my God and the name of the city of my God, the new
Jerusalem, which descendeth from heaven fro my God, and I shall
write on him also my new name.[3]

If we should dilate[4] and were able to declare these special gifts,
with yet other mo specified in the second and the third chapter of
the Apocalypse, there would it appear how far those heavenly joys
shall surmount above[5] all the comfort that ever came in the mind of
any man living here upon earth.

The blessed apostle, St. Paul, that suffered so many perils and so
many passions,[6] he that saith of himself that he hath been *In
laboribus pluribus, in carceribus abundantius, in plagis supra modum etc.:*
In many labors, in prisons ofter than other,[7] in stripes[8] above
measure, at point of death oftentimes, of the Jews had I five times
forty stripes save one. Thrice have I been beaten with rods; once
was I stoned; thrice have I been in shipwreck; a day and a night was
I in the depth of the sea; in my journeys oft have I been in peril of
floods, in peril of thieves, in perils by the Jews, in perils by the
paynims,[9] in perils in the city, in perils in desert,[1] in perils in the

---

1. offices.   2. The word *calculi* means small stones or pebbles.
3. Rev. 3:12.   4. discourse at length.
5. *surmount above:* surpass.   6. pains.
7. *ofter than other:* more often than others.
8. wounds from whipping.   9. pagans.   1. i.e., the desert.

sea, perils by false brethren, in labor and misery, in many nights'
watch, in hunger and thirst, in many fastings, in cold and naked-
ness; beside those things that are outward, my daily, instant[2] labor,
I mean my care and solicitude about all the churches.[3] And yet
saith he more of his tribulations, which for[4] the length I let pass;
this blessed apostle I say for all the tribulations that himself suffered in the continuance of so many years, and calleth yet all the
tribulations of this world but light[5] and as short as a moment in
respect of[6] the weighty glory that it after this world winneth us, *Id
enim quod in presenti est momentaneum et leve tribulationis nostrae supra
modum, in sublimitate eternum gloriae pondus operatur in nobis non
contemplantibus nobis quae videntur sed quae non videntur; quae enim
videntur temporalia sunt, quae autem non videntur aeterna sunt:* This
same short and momentary tribulation of ours, that is in this
present time, worketh within us the weight of glory above measure
in sublimitate, on high; we beholding not those things that we see,
but those things that we see not. For those things that we see be but
temporal things, but those things that are not seen are eternal.[7]

Now to this great glory can there no man come headless. Our
head is Christ,[8] and therefore to him must we be joined, and as
members of his must we follow him, if we will come thither. He is
our guide to guide us thither and is entered in before us, and he
therefore that will enter in after, *Debet sicut ille ambulavit et ipse
ambulare:* The same way that Christ walked, the same way must he
walk.[9] And what was the way by which he walked into heaven?
Himself showeth what way it was that his Father had provided for
him, where he said unto the two disciples going toward the castle[1]
of Emmaus, *Nesciebatis quia oportebat Christum pati, et sic introire in
regnum suum?* Knew you not that Christ must suffer passion, and by
that way enter into his kingdom?[2] Who can for very shame desire to

2. urgent.
3. 2 Cor. 11:23–28. More quotes only a portion of the passage and trans-
lates the remainder.
4. because of.   5. easy.   6. *in respect of:* in comparison with.
7. 2 Cor. 4:17–18.   8. Col. 1:18. See also Eph. 1:22–23; 4:15–16.
9. 1 John 2:6.   1. walled town.   2. Luke 24:26.

enter into the kingdom of Christ with ease, when himself entered not into his own without pain?

The Twenty-seventh Chapter

The consideration of the painful death of Christ is sufficient to make us content to suffer painful death for his sake.

Surely, cousin, as I said before, in bearing the loss of worldly goods, in suffering of captivity, thralldom, and imprisonment, and in the glad sustaining of worldly shame, that if we would in all those points deeply ponder the sample of our Savior himself, it were of itself alone sufficient to encourage every kind[3] Christian man and woman to refuse none of all those calamities for his sake. So say I now for painful death also, that if we could and would with due compassion conceive in our minds a right imagination and remembrance of Christ's bitter, painful passion, of the many sore, bloodly strokes that the cruel tormentors with rods and whips gave him upon every part of his holy, tender body, the scornful crown of sharp thorns beaten down upon his holy head, so straight and so deep that on every part his blessed blood issued out and streamed down, his lovely limbs drawn and stretched out upon the cross to the intolerable pain of his forbeaten[4] and sore beaten veins and sinews, new feeling with the cruel stretching and straining pain, far passing[5] any cramp, in every part of his blessed body at once. Then the great, long nails cruelly driven with hammers through his holy hands and feet, and in this horrible pain lift up and let hang with the payce[6] of all his body bearing down upon the painful, wounded places so grievously pierced with nails, and in such torment without

3. natural; i.e., grateful.
4. The word probably means "beaten previously," though it may possibly be a usage of "forbeat," "to beat severely."
5. surpassing.   6. weight.

pity, but not without many despites,[7] suffered to be pinned and pained the space of more than three long hours, till himself willingly gave up unto his Father his holy soul. After which, yet to show the mightiness of their malice after his holy soul departed, pierced his holy heart with a sharp spear, at which issued out the holy blood and water whereof his holy sacraments have inestimable, secret strength. If we would, I say, remember these things in such wise,[8] as would God we would, I verily suppose that the consideration of his incomparable kindness could not fail in such wise to inflame our key-cold hearts and set them on fire in his love, that we should find ourself not only content, but also glad and desirous to suffer death for his sake, that so marvelously lovingly letted[9] not to sustain so far passing painful death for ours.

Would God we would here, to the shame of our cold affection, again toward[1] God, for such fervent love and inestimable kindness of God toward us, would God we would, I say, but consider what hot affection many of these fleshly lovers have borne and daily do to those upon whom they dote. How many of them have not letted to jeopard[2] their lives, and how many have willingly lost their lives indeed without either great kindness showed them before? And afterward, you wot[3] well, they could nothing win, but even that yet contented and satisfied their mind that by their death their lover should clearly see how faithfully they loved; the delight whereof, imprinted in their fantasy, not assuaged only, but counterpoised also, they thought, all their pain. Of these affections, with the wonderful dolorous effects following thereon, not only old written stories, but over that, I think, in every country, Christian and heathen both, experience giveth us proof enough. And is it not then a wonderful shame for us for[4] the dread of temporal death to forsake our Savior, that willingly suffered so painful death rather than he would forsake us, considering that beside that he shall for our suffering so highly reward us with everlasting wealth?

7. contemptuous or scornful actions.   8. a way.   9. hesitated.
1. *again toward:* in return to.   2. endanger.   3. know.
4. because of.

Oh, if he that is content to die for his love, of whom he looketh after for no reward,[5] and yet by his death goeth from her, might by his death be sure to come to her and ever after in delight and pleasure to dwell with her, such a lover would not let here to die for her twice. And how cold lovers be we then unto God if, rather than die for him once, we will refuse him and forsake him forever, that both died for us before and hath also provided that if we die here for him, we shall in heaven everlastingly both live and also reign with him. For as Saint Paul saith, *Si compatimur et conregnabimus:* If we suffer with him we shall reign with him.[6]

How many Romans, how many noble courages[7] of other sundry countries have willingly given their own lives and suffer great deadly pains and very painful deaths for their countries, and the respect[8] of winning by their deaths the only reward of worldly renown and fame? And should we then shrink to suffer as much for eternal honor in heaven and everlasting glory? The devil hath also some so obstinate heretics, that endure willingly painful death for vainglory, and is it not then more than shame that Christ shall see his Catholics forsake his faith rather than suffer the same for heaven and very[9] glory?

Would God, as I many times have said, that the remembrance of Christ's kindness in suffering his passion for us, the consideration of hell, that we should fall in by forsaking of him, the joyful meditation of eternal life in heaven, that we shall win with this short, temporal death patiently taken for him, had so deep a place in our breast as reason would they should and as, if we would do our devoir[1] toward it, and labor for it, and pray therefor, I verily think they should. For then should they so take up our mind and ravish it all another way that, as a man hurt in a fray[2] feeleth not sometime his wound nor yet is not ware thereof till his mind fall more thereon, so farforth[3] that sometime another man showeth him that he hath lost an hand before that he perceiveth it himself,

5. *of whom . . . reward:* from whom he expects no reward.
6. Rom. 8:17.   7. spirits.   8. consideration.   9. true.
1. utmost and best endeavor.   2. fight.   3. *so farforth:* so much so.

so the mind ravished in the thinking deeply of those other things, Christ's death, hell and heaven, were likely to minish[4] and put away of our painful death four parts of the feeling either of the fear or the pain. For of this am I very sure: if we had the fifteenth part of the love to Christ that he both had and hath to us, all the pain of this Turk's persecution could not keep us from him, but that there would be at this day as many martyrs here in Hungary as have been afore in other countries of old.

And of this point put I nothing doubt[5] but that if the Turk stood even here with all his whole army about him, and everyone of them all were ready[6] at our hand with all the terrible torments that they could imagine, and but if[7] we would forsake the faith were setting their torments to us, and to the increase of our terror fell all at once in a shout with trumpets, taborets, and timbrels[8] all blown up at once, and all their guns let go therewith to make us a fearful noise; if you should suddenly then on the tother[9] side the ground quake and rive atwain,[1] and the devils rise out of hell and show themself in such ugly shape as damned wretches shall see them, and with that hideous howling that those hell hounds should shriche,[2] lay hell open on every side roundabout our feet, that as we stood we should look down into that pestilent pit and see the swarm of seely[3] souls in the terrible torments there, we would wax[4] so feared of that sight that as for the Turk's host, we should scantly[5] remember we saw them.

And, in good faith, for all that, yet think I further this: that if there might then appear the glory of God, the Trinity in his high marvelous majesty, our Savior in his glorious manhood sitting on his throne with his immaculate mother and all that glorious company calling us there unto them, and that yet our way should lie through marvelous painful death before we could come at them—upon the sight, I say, of that glory, there would, I ween,[6] be

4. lessen.   5. *put . . . doubt:* I have no doubt.   6. already.
7. *but if:* unless.
8. *taborets, and timbrels:* small drums and tambourines.   9. other.
1. *rive atwain:* split in two.   2. shriek.   3. pitiable.   4. become.
5. hardly.   6. think.

no man that once would shrink thereat, but every man would run on toward them in all that ever he might though there lay for malice to kill us by the way both all the Turk's tormentors and all the devils too.

And therefore, cousin, let us well consider these things, and let us have sure hope in the help of God, and then I doubt not but that we shall be sure that, as the prophet saith, the truth of his promise shall so compass us with a pavis[7] that of this incursion of this midday devil, this Turk's persecution, we shall never need to fear. For either if we trust in God well and prepare us therefore, the Turk shall never meddle with us, or else if he do, harm shall he none do us, but instead of harm inestimable good. Of whose gracious help wherefore should we so sore[8] now despair (except we were so mad men as to ween that either his power or his mercy were worn out already), when we see so many a thousand holy martyrs by his holy help suffered as much before as any man shall be put to now? Or what excuse can we have by the tenderness of our flesh when we can be no more tender than were many of them, among whom were not only men of strength, but also weak women and children?

And sith[9] the strength of them all stood in the help of God, and that the very strongest of them all was never able of themself, and with God's help the feeblest of them all was strong enough to stand against all the world, let us prepare ourself with prayer, with our whole trust in his help, without any trust in our own strength. Let us think thereon and prepare us in our mind thereto long before. Let us therein conform our will unto his, not desiring to be brought unto the peril of persecution—for it seemeth a proud, high mind to desire martyrdom—but desiring help and strength of God if he suffer[1] us to come to the stress, either being sought, founden, and brought out against our wills, or else being by his commandment, for the comfort of our cure,[2] bounden to abide.[3]

7. large shield.   8. greatly.   9. since.   1. permit.
2. *for the . . . cure:* for the strengthening of those for whom we are spiritually responsible.
3. *bounden to abide:* obligated to remain.

Let us fall to fasting, to prayer, to almsdeed in time, and give that unto God that may be taken from us. If the devil put in our mind the saving of our land and our goods, let us remember that we cannot save them long. If he fear[4] us with exile and flying[5] from our country, let us remember that we be born in the broad world, and not like a tree to stick still in one place, and that whithersoever we go God shall go with us.

If he threaten us with captivity, let us tell him again,[6] better is to be thrall unto man awhile for the pleasure of God than by displeasing God be perpetual thrall unto the devil. If he threat us with imprisonment, let us tell him we will rather be man's prisoners awhile here in earth than by forsaking the faith be his prisoners ever in hell.

If he put in our minds the terror of the Turks, let us consider his false sleight[7] therein. For this tale he telleth us to make us forget him. But let us remember well that in respect of[8] himself, the Turk is but a shadow, nor all that they all can do can be but a fly biting in comparison of the mischief that he goeth about. The Turks are but his tormentors, for himself doth the deed. Our Lord saith in the Apocalypse, *Diabolus mittet aliquos vestrum in carcerem ut tentemini:* The devil shall send some of you to prison to tempt you.[9] He saith not that men shall, but that the devil shall himself, for without question the devil's own deed it is to bring us by his temptation with fear and force thereof into eternal damnation. And therefore saith Saint Paul, *Non est nobis colluctatio adversus carnem et sanguinem sed etc.:* Our wrestling is not against flesh and blood *etc.*[1] Thus may we see that in such persecutions it is the midday devil himself that maketh such incursion upon us by the men that are his ministers, to make us fall for fear. For till we fall, he can never hurt us. And therefore saith St. Peter, *Resistite diabolo et fugiet a vobis:* Stand

4. frighten.   5. fleeing.   6. in return.   7. deceit.
8. *in respect of:* in comparison with.   9. Rev. 2:10.
1. Eph. 6:12–13: "Our struggle is not against flesh and blood, but against princes and powers, against the rulers of this world of shadows, against spiritual wickedness in high places. Take therefore the armor of God so you can resist on the evil day and, perfect in all things, stand."

against the devil, and he shall fly fro you.[2] For he never runneth upon a man to season[3] him with his claws till he see him down on the ground, willingly fallen himself. For his fashion is to set his servants against us and by them to make us for fear or for impatience to fall. And himself in the meanwhile compasseth[4] us, running and roaring like a ramping[5] lion about us, looking who will fall that he then may devour him. *Adversarius vester diabolus,* saith St. Peter, *sicut leo rugiens circuit quaerens quem devoret:* Your adversary, the devil, like a roaring lion runneth about in circuit, seeking whom he may devour.[6] The devil it is therefore that, if we for fear of men will fall, is ready to run upon us and devour us. And is it wisdom then so much to think upon the Turks that we forget the devil? What madman is he that when a lion were about to devour him would vouchsafe to regard the biting of a little fisting[7] cur? Therefore, when he roareth out upon us by the threats of mortal men, let us tell him that with our inward eye we see him well enough and intend to stand and fight with him even hand to hand. If he threaten us that we be too weak, let us tell him that our captain Christ is with us and that we shall fight with his strength that hath vanquished him already.

And let us fence us with faith, and comfort us with hope, and smite the devil in the face with a firebrand of charity. For surely if we be of that tender, loving mind[8] that our master was, and not hate them that kill us but pity them and pray for them with sorrow for the peril that they work unto themself, that fire of charity thrown in his face striketh the devil suddenly so blind that he cannot see where to fasten a stroke on us.

When we feel us too bold, remember our own feebleness; when we feel us too faint, remember Christ's strength. In our fear let us remember Christ's painful agony, that himself would for our comfort suffer before his passion to the intent that no fear should make us despair, and ever call for his help, such as himself list[9] to send us,

---

2. James 4:7. The reference to Peter is incorrect.   3. seize upon.
4. circles.   5. raging.   6. 1 Pet. 5:8.   7. farting.
8. attitude.   9. wishes.

and then need we never to doubt but that either he shall keep us from the painful death, or shall not fail so to strength us in it that he shall joyously bring us to heaven by it, and then doth he much more for us than if he kept us fro it. For as God did more for poor Lazarus in helping him patiently to die for hunger at the rich man's door than if he had brought him to the door all the rich glutton's dinner,[1] so though he be gracious to a man whom he delivereth out of painful trouble, yet doth he much more for a man if through right[2] painful death he deliver him from this wretched world into eternal bliss. From which whosoever shrink away with forsaking his faith and falleth in the peril of everlasting fire, he shall be very sure to repent it ere it be long after. For I ween that whensoever he falleth sick next, he will wish that he had be[3] killed for Christ's sake before. What folly is it then for fear to fly fro that death which thou seest thou shalt shortly after wish thou hadst died? Yea, I ween almost every good Christian man would very fain this day that he had been for Christ's faith cruelly killed yesterday, even for the desire of heaven though there were none hell, but to fear while the pain is coming, there is all our let.[4] But then if we would remember hell-pain on the tother side into which we fall while we fly fro this, then should this short pain be no let at all. And yet should we be more pricked[5] forward if we were faithful by deep considering of the joys of heaven, of which the apostle saith, *Non sunt condignae passiones hujus temporis ad futuram gloriam quae revelabitur in nobis:* The passions of this time be not worthy to the glory that is to come, which shall be showed in us.[6] We should not, I ween, cousin, need much more in all this whole matter than that one text of Saint Paul, if we would consider it well. For surely, mine own good cousin, remember that if it were possible for me and you alone to suffer as much trouble as the whole world doth together, all that were not worthy of itself to bring us to the joy which we hope to have everlastingly. And therefore I pray you let the consideration of that joy put out all worldly trouble out of your heart, and also pray

1. Luke 16:19–25.   2. very.   3. been.   4. hindrance.
5. urged.   6. Rom. 8:18.

that it may do the same in me. And even thus will I, good cousin, with these words make a sudden end of mine whole tale and bid you farewell. For now begin I to feel myself somewhat weary.

Vincent

Forsooth, good uncle, this is a good end, and it is no marvel though you be waxen[7] weary. For I have this day put you to so much labor that, saving for the comfort that yourself may take of your time so well bestowed and for the comfort that I have myself taken, and mo shall, I trust, of your good counsel given, or else would I be very sorry to have put you to so much pain. But now shall our Lord reward and recompense you therefor, and many shall I trust pray for you. For, to the intent that the mo may take profit by you, I purpose, uncle, as my poor wit[8] and learning will serve me, to put your good counsel in remembrance, not in our own language only, but in the Almain[9] tongue too. And thus, praying God to give me and all other that shall read it the grace to follow your good counsel therein, I shall commit you to God.

Antony

Sith you be minded, cousin, to bestow so much labor thereon, I would it had happed you[1] to fetch the counsel at some wiser man, that could have given you better. But better men may set mo things and better also thereto. And in the meantime I beseech our Lord to breathe of his Holy Spirit into the reader's breast, which inwardly may teach him in heart, without whom little availeth all that all the mouths of the world were able to teach in men's ears. And thus, good cousin, farewell till God bring us together again, either here or in heaven. Amen.

Finis.

7. grown.   8. intelligence.   9. German.
1. *I would . . . you:* I wish you had happened.

INDEX